THE MACINTOSH READER

DOUG CLAPP

Douglas Adams   Stewart Alsop   Rick Barron   Tony Bove   David Bunnell   Denise Caruso   Don Crabb
Chris Crawford   John C. Dvorak   Mary Eisenhart   Michael Fraase   James Horswill   Daniel Ichbiah   Susan Kare
Guy Kawasaki   Dan Kottke   Bob LeVitus   Mary Jane Mara   Randy Nelson   Carl Philabaum
Andrew Pollack   Cheryl Rhodes   Jock Root   Dennis Runkle   Pat Ryall   Neil Shapiro   Burrell Smith   Karen Thomas
Bruce Tognazzini   Trici Venola   C.J. Weigand   Jeffrey S. Young

RANDOM HOUSE
ELECTRONIC PUBLISHING

New York

The Macintosh Reader

Random House Electronic Publishing is a division of Random House, Inc., 201 E. 50th St., NY, NY 10022.

Manufactured in the United States of America

98765432 24689753 23456789

First Edition

Library of Congress Cataloging-in-Publication Data
Clapp, Doug, 1950-
      The Macintosh reader / written by Doug Clapp.
          p.   cm.
      Includes index.
      ISBN 0-679-74242-5 : $25.00
      1. Macintosh (Computer)   I. Title.
QA76.8.M3C58   1992
338.7'61004165--dc20   92-23856
                                            CIP

Dedication

This one, dear reader, is for you.

Copyright Summary

INTRODUCTION

Welcome to the most fun I've ever had—working.

If you can call it working.

Let me explain.

It started in November 1991. I was chatting with Dr. Michael Mellin, the top guy at Random House's Electronic Publishing Division. A few months before the chat, I had retired. And, a few months later, un-retired. I was bored and casting around for a book to write. So there I was, on the phone, bouncing book ideas off Mike Mellin.

Bounce, thud, bounce, thud. Like that. I had a few ideas, but none aroused more than a flicker of interest from Mellin.

Then I heard "Doug, why don't you do a Mac book?"

And I had absolutely nothing to say. Nothing. I was wrapped in silence. Finally, I said something profound like "Well…"

Because it was a problem. And I didn't have the answer.

This was the problem: *What* Mac book? A beginner's book? Some kind of encyclopedic overview book? A System 7 book? A tip book? An application-specific book? A niche book like…networking? Multimedia? Desktop publishing?

Those books had already been done—and done well. They line my shelves. A Mac book? Jeez, there were a ton of Mac books already! A ton!

I hung up the phone and despaired. For the next two days, I agonized like a Zen novice struggling with his first koan. Mac book? Mac book? Mac book? What makes the grass grow? What was your face before…

But I think I got it, at last. The result, the "it," is in your hands: *The Macintosh Reader*.

So what is it? What is this "Macintosh Reader" thing?

The selfish (and immodest) truth is that this book, above all, is the book that *I'd* like to find at a bookstore, take home, and read and read and read.

But you deserve a better—or at least another—answer.

So here goes. *The Macintosh Reader* is an anthology, sort of. It's a collection of previously published (though often in obscure locations) and original material by some of the best writers in the Macintosh field: John C. Dvorak, Guy Kawasaki, Jeff Young, Doug Adams, and many, many more. And a few people who aren't writers, don't claim to be writers, and had to be muscled into putting fingers to keyboards. Because they had something to say that I wanted you to hear.

There are many voices in this book. Some are polished; some aren't. Life's like that.

So it's anthology. Sort of. And it's also a history. Sort of. Not a complete history, not an unbiased history, not even a sequential history. Just a few flashes, here and there. Most, but not all, about Macintosh. Not necessarily "the truth" (whatever that is), but often dead-on.

See if you agree.

And it's a book of opinions. There are plenty of pundits in these pages. The opinions range from quaint and wistful to take-no-prisoners. The breadth of thought is the result of being blessed with a broad-minded constituency—you—and an editor who will glee-fully include anything good, regardless: me.

It's also a book of tips. And a book of secrets. And there's good advice for the young and old, the novice and the jaded. And information you need to know: "How to Build a World," "How to Make a Million in Software," and "Something to Try When You Crash."

And a few bad jokes—and some that are pretty good. And some amazing Macintosh art. And...

You get the idea. In your hands is a bunch of "stuff." Good stuff, fun stuff, neat stuff, provocative stuff, old stuff, new stuff, great stuff.

Macintosh stuff.

Making this book was the most fun I've ever had—working. If you can call it working.

Work? Nah, it's a party. And you, dear reader, are the reason and purpose for the festivities. So com'on in; pull up a mouse. It's a good crowd. Enjoy. Have fun.

Be happy.

Doug Clapp
Edina, Minnesota
May 4, 1992

Acknowledgments

My first thanks go to my agent, Matt Wagner of Waterside Productions, who made the deal. Thank you, Matt.

To Random House, in general, and Michael Mellin and Julie Ann O'Leary, in particular, thank you. Michael asked the question that led to this book. Julie O'Leary, my editor, was a dream: sharp, smart, and always available. Writer's hells are staffed with bad editors. Julie is one of the good ones. Her deft touch and insightful comments greatly improved this book. And, having worked with many publishers, I'm happy to report that Random House provided me with all a writer can hope for and more: a class act.

To Stella Townsend and David Lien, who typed much of the manuscript and transcribed tape-recorded interviews full of static and hum, thank you.

To those authors whose work wasn't included, because of size considerations or deadline pressures (both yours and mine), thank you. You're first on the list when we do this again.

To the publishers, agents, and organizations who graciously granted me reprint permission—Addison-Wesley, Ed Victor, Ltd., Prentice-Hall Computer Publishing, Prima Publishing, BAM Publications, New Media, Verbum, The New York Times, and American Online—thank you.

To Jill Larson, for the printer and so much paper, thank you.

To Steve Jobs, who flew me out to Apple and kept me in business all these years, thank you.

Most of all, thanks to the people whose art and thought and words fill these pages. Thank you, Douglas Adams. Thank you, Stewart Alsop. Thank you, Rick Barron. Thank you, David Bunnell. Thank you, Denise Caruso. Thank you, Don Crabb. Thank you, Chris Crawford. Thank you, John C. Dvorak. Thank you, Mary Eisenhart. Thank you, Mike Frasse. Thank you, James Horswill. Thank you, Daniel Ichbiah. Thank you, Dennis James. Thank you, Susan Kare. Thank you, Guy Kawasaki. Thank you, Michel Kripalani. Thank you, Dan Kottke. Thank you, Bob LeVitus. Thank you, Mary Jane Mara. Thank you, Alex Narvey. Thank you, Randy Nelson. Thank you, Carl Philabaum. Thank you, Tony Bove and Cheryl Rhodes. Thank you, Jock Root. Thank you, Dennis Runkle. Thank you, Neil Shapiro. Thank you, Burrell Smith. Thank you, Karen Thomas. Thank you, Bruce Toganzinni. Thank you, Trici Venola. Thank you, C.J. Weigand. Thank you, Jeffrey S. Young.

Contents

THE MACINTOSH READER

by Doug Clapp and friends

PART

I

IN THE BEGINNING

3

A SHORT HISTORY OF APPLE AND MAC'S CREATION

DOUG CLAPP

W*e begin with a story of modes, Macintosh, and the two Steves, Jobs and Wozniak. It's a tale told before that will, no doubt, be told a few more times. Other accounts are more journalistic and less gushy—Jeff Young's piece, which follows, is a good case in point—but your author was in a state of high gushiness at the time (early 1984) and is utterly unapologetic for any sugar-stained prose below. And I like the part where Bill Atkinson slams into the semi.*

Please remember that this was written a long, long time ago…

❧

To understand Macintosh, we must begin at the beginning. In the beginning (this beginning, anyway), there were computers. Big computers. Big, *expensive* computers.

As technology advanced, computer parts became smaller. Oddly enough, though, the big computer manufacturers didn't think small computers were a big idea. The large corporations thought small computers were a silly idea—if they thought about small computers at all! So they didn't make any small computers.

Hobbyists, however, thought differently. In the basements of America, they were busy soldering circuit boards, inserting chips, stringing wires, and trying to make their contraptions "listen" to keyboards and "talk" to television screens.

In those days, hobby computers had rows of toggle switches on the front panel. The switches were used to program the computer by entering a precise series of ones and zeros.

Only a true hobbyist could withstand such a grueling task.

Apple's Beginnings

About this time, the mists of history recede a bit. Enter Steve Jobs and Steve Wozniak, one a hobbyist/visionary, and one a hobbyist/engineer. Jobs, at the time, was one of the first ten programmers hired by Atari to program video arcade machines. Wozniak was a technician employed by Hewlett-Packard, a large computer manufacturer. Wozniak helped design calculators for HP, but found calculator design boring, at least in comparison to designing computers. He asked for a transfer to HP's Research and Development division, but was turned down. After all, he was only a degree-less technician, not a Computer Engineer.

Scorned, Wozniak designed a computer anyway, putting in four months of almost non-stop after-hours work. The result was a motherboard: the complete circuitry of a computer, less display, drives, and keyboard.

Wozniak brought the computer to his supervisors. Did Hewlett-Packard want to sell it? No. They did, however, grant Wozniak a legal release for his design.

Wozniak proudly showed his creation to fellow members of the now legendary Stanford Homebrew Computer Club, many of whose members went on in the early seventies to create Silicon Valley's high-flying, hi-tech companies.

Another of the club's members was Steve Jobs, who convinced Wozniak to form a business and market a computer based on Wozniak's design.

Wozniak and Jobs next met with Paul Terrell, who had started a chain of hobbyist computer stores. Terrell agreed to buy 50 of the circuit boards for $549 each, provided they could deliver the boards in a month.

Making computer boards meant spending money for parts. Jobs happened to own a VW minibus (fittingly). Wozniak owned a scientific desktop calculator (appropriately). The bus and the calculator were sold and pawned (respectively).

Jobs and Wozniak next paid a visit to a large computer parts distributor. They presented their list of required parts and were told that the terms were "net 30 days."

Jobs and Wozniak didn't know what "net 30 days" meant, but they did know it meant they didn't have to pay immediately. So they took the parts.

"Net 30 days" means, of course, that the entire balance is due in 30 days. It was a hefty balance.

Few computers were ever assembled as quickly as those that next flowed from Jobs's garage. By month's end, twenty boards were completed and delivered. And they worked.

Jobs, from the beginning, saw beyond the small-scale hobbyist operation. With help from Wozniak's father, himself an engineer, he persuaded Wozniak to integrate the computer into an case, complete with keyboard (a unique idea, in those days), for sale as a consumer item (another unique thought).

Sales boomed, talented people and investment capital both arrived at the proper times, and Apple Computer was born and prospered.

A happy ending.

A happy middle, actually. Because Jobs and Wozniak weren't the only would-be small computer manufacturers in the late 1970s. Others tried, but most failed. Some, but not many, of the others are still around today.

Explaining Success

Apple's success can be explained in many ways, timing being not the least of them. But the crucial ingredient was probably this: as Jobs envisioned from the start, Apples have always been created for use by ordinary people.

Not dull, simple-minded, or illiterate people, but reasonably intelligent adults (and children) who aren't necessarily fascinated by Computer Science. People who want computers for what they can do, not merely for what they are.

People who aren't thrilled by toggle switches. Which almost brings us to the Apple Macintosh Computer.

From Whence Mac Sprang

The Xerox Alto and Xerox Star were Mac's ancestors, but the story begins somewhat earlier. A good place to begin is with Alan Kay, a man who was, and still is, a brilliant computer scientist.

In the early 1970s, Kay founded the Learning Research Group at the Xerox Palo Alto Research Center. The LRG at Xerox PARC, as it was called, conducted research in a number of areas aimed at making computers more powerful and easier to use. Much of the group's work was fueled by Alan Kay's vision of personal computing: the Dynabook.

The Dynabook was a simple but stunning idea: a computer with the power of a mainframe contained in a portable unit the size of a notebook. The Dynabook would have a flat screen, video and audio communications capabilities, and be able to tap into computing and information networks.

In one form or another, scientists have been trying to realize the Dynabook ever since.

The Demise of Modes

One piece of the Dynabook puzzle was the Preemption Dilemma. This dilemma is familiar to everyone who works with computers, although most people don't know that the condition has an academic-sounding title. It means simply that computers "trap" you into doing things "their" way, and heaven help you if you're not sure what that way is.

The traps are called modes. With most computers, you're always in one mode or another; some things can be done in one place, other things can't. To get from, say, Edit mode to System mode, you need to know the right commands. If you forget what those commands are, or use them incorrectly, you won't get where you want to go. Instead, you may get somewhere you greatly don't want to go.

Much of the misery inflicted on computer users over the years comes from these omnipresent modes. The dilemma of the Preemption Dilemma is that choices you might desire are denied, or preempted, by the computer. "Do it my way, or else!" seems to be the message.

About this time, most people have a few messages of their own for the computer.

So the LRG of the PARC set about the task of eliminating modes. It wasn't easy. When you eliminate modes, you have to change quite a few other things as well.

The standard user interface was the next target for demolition.

The user is you. The Interface is everything between you and whatever you want the computer to do. Generally, it means how information is displayed on the screen, and how information is entered from the keyboard or other devices.

If modes are bad, most user interfaces are worse. It's still possible, this very day, to visit your local computer store, plunk down four or five thousand dollars, and take home a computer that, when turned on, greets you with the marvelously expressive symbol

    A:

on an otherwise blank screen. Not, you'll agree, a swell user interface.

The solution to all this was the concept of windowing, a solution that made what was in the computer visible to users outside the computer.

The hammer-stroke of inspiration was that windows shouldn't just appear on the screen; they should overlap, like sheets of paper. If you can shuffle papers, you should be able to shuffle windows; and each window could contain information entirely different from information in other windows. Each window could hold a different document, and a different tool to work with each document. If you don't like where you are, leave.

No traps.

That's a pretty good basic definition of Macintosh.

Implementing the ideas was difficult. It's easier to merely want something than it is to actually do it. Often, some of the best ideas are impractical—the technology isn't perfected or affordable, or possibly not even invented yet. A: isn't friendly, but it is a cheap and simple way to design a user interface.

Bill Atkinson and QuickDraw

The most difficult part of the "Macintosh story" is determining which story to tell. There are many.

But here's one you might like. It's the story of QuickDraw, the amazing software that underlies everything you see on the Macintosh screen. Because it's the story of QuickDraw, it's also the story of Bill Atkinson, QuickDraw's inventor.

And, of course, Steve Jobs enters the tale, as does that fateful visit to Xerox.

Before The Visit

The famous visit to Xerox wasn't Jobs's idea, and Jobs wasn't even convinced that the trip was necessary. Jef Raskin and Bill Atkinson talked him into it.

Jef Raskin, if credit is given fairly, conceived of the machine that would become the Macintosh. Raskin's vision is hard to see in the final machine, but it was the original impetus behind the Macintosh project. Not surprisingly, the original idea sounds quite a bit like "Dynabook."

Macintosh may have happened without Raskin, but Macintosh would *never* have happened without Steve Jobs.

Of Atkinson, there is much to say. A bona fide genius, Atkinson is a driven man who admits to having little in his life outside of computer programming. He's also a man who doesn't consider himself a programmer. He considers himself an artist, a sculptor, a man who takes the concepts of programming and treats them like modeling clay, shaping and reshaping over and over and over again; powered by will, unwilling to stop until the last limit of invention and speed and compaction has been reached—the hardware limit of the machine. Beyond here, no man can go: when that limit is reached, the software is as utterly fast as it can ever be for the particular computer it runs on.

There is no conceit in Atkinson's characterization of himself. No vanity. He speaks quietly of how computers "should be." He uses no jargon, no techno-speak. He becomes angry only when explaining how computers, even now, often make users think, "Oh, stupid me."

Atkinson knows that computers are the stupid ones. He's using his life to change that.

Bill Atkinson began in chemistry, gulped down the field, then moved into neural chemistry, the chemistry of the brain. He began using computers in his studies and became entranced with the power and wonder of computer graphics, an amazingly complex field of computer science littered with arcane and difficult mathematical concepts.

A fellow researcher was slicing human brains in an attempt to gain understanding into basic physical structures. Atkinson took the brain slices, photographed them, converted the photographs into three-dimensional computer graphics, then mapped in structures: "what" is "where" in the human brain.

It had never been done before. The results were stunning, an achievement in both the field of medicine and the field of computer graphics. Atkinson's work can be seen on the October 1978 cover of *Scientific American.* The film he produced is now used in over 600 medical schools across the country.

Bill Atkinson is not your ordinary guy.

With success in both fields, the decision had to be made: chemistry or computers. Atkinson choose computers, and founded a company to develop medical computer interfaces for hospitals: Synaptic Systems Corporation. The company rapidly became a success.

And so it was that the life of Bill Atkinson was perfectly in order when, in March 1978, a friend who worked for a company called Apple telephoned. A few days later, plane tickets arrived in the mail. Atkinson journeyed to Cupertino to find a company that employed 30 people and was already a force in the then small, small computer field. After all, Apple had actually shipped over 900 machines!

Apple also had Jobs, Wozniak, and something more important: a dream about how computers should be. Seduced by the dream, Atkinson became Apple employee 31. Not the first, or last, of the seductions of dreams, Jobs, Wozniak, or Apple: a company which seemed have everything going their way. What Apple didn't have was a "software development problem." Or so they thought.

Atkinson thought otherwise. Not believing that BASIC was powerful enough to fuel Apple's growth, he set out to investigate USCD Pascal, a new computer language then under development.

He became a believer, and battled for the inclusion of Pascal into Apple's marketing plans. He argued with Steve Jobs, who could see no use for Pascal. He was rebuffed. Jobs, admittedly, is a tough person to argue with. "Jobs knows when somebody's bullshitting him," Atkinson remembers, "and he also knows when someone isn't."

The final argument ended with Jobs saying, "Okay, you've got two months to convince me." Atkinson did, then convinced Apple's President Mike Markkula.

History records that Apple Pascal was an hit. Like VisiCalc®, it legitimized Apple as a real computer, capable of serious computing tasks.

The Visit

Atkinson had heard about the research at Xerox. Along with Jef Raskin, he convinced Steve to take the 30-minute trip from Cupertino to the Xerox PARC labs.

The visit lasted about an hour. All were amazed. Windows! Bit-mapped graphics! Smalltalk! Sure that he had seen the future of computing, Jobs was determined to incorporate the Xerox discoveries into Apple products.

For his part, Atkinson was sure that he could duplicate the Xerox programming efforts, spectacular as they were. The list was long. At the top of the list was something called "'arbitrary clipping."

"Clipping" is a computer graphics term. It is something that can be done fast or done in great detail, but not both at once. The math necessary hadn't been discovered that would permit both graphic speed and graphic detail. Atkinson, having gotten only a glimpse of the Xerox computers, thought that Xerox had, indeed, discovered the philosopher's stone of graphic computing.

If they could do it, he reasoned, he could do it.

But they hadn't. The solution had eluded the scientists at Xerox. How to overlap windows, move them around, yet quickly display the contents of windows underneath the second they came into view? Quickly make a window smaller, and see what's underneath? What's showing? An edge, a sliver of another window? How many windows can there be, how large is the stack, how can the display show them all, quickly, in different sizes and positions?

In reality, a window on a computer display isn't a window, but a region. A window is a "region," but anything can be a region. Graphics are regions. Regular shapes such as squares and circles are regions, but so are irregular shapes. Polygons, freehand drawings, even squiggles are regions. But how is it done?

Atkinson set about duplicating the secret that hadn't been discovered. Six months later, six long agonizing months of pushing at the limits of mathematics, he was closer to discovery, but still the secret eluded his grasp.

Fortunately, Atkinson doesn't sleep. At least, not sleep as most of us know it. For months, he had kept a dream-log of his mind's activities during sleep. Now, when he slept, it was a mix of consciousness and unconsciousness: half dreams and half wakefulness. Much like an advanced yogi, Atkinson flowed downward without ever completely losing awareness of self, dreamed, and surfaced again, remembering what had occurred. Even during the night, the intellect persisted, the problems were gnawed on and probed.

The answer came in that twilight between dreams and reality. Atkinson woke, fully aware that he had solved the problem at last, and wrote down the secret.

Atkinson named the secret QuickDraw.

The secret of QuickDraw was his alone on the morning he got into his car, headed for Apple, and woke up in a hospital bed.

He remembers nothing after entering the car. His best guess is that he was thinking, his mind lost somewhere, wrestling with a problem. Or it might have been a dog in the street, or a small child that ran between two cars.

No one knows. What is known is this: his sports car was traveling at high speed when it hit the rear of the parked semi-trailer. The car slammed into the semi and kept on going, completely shearing off the top of the car. Miraculously, Atkinson survived. When Jobs was notified of the accident, he raced to the hospital. He remained at the bedside until Atkinson regained consciousness.

When Atkinson finally regained consciousness, he looked at Jobs and said "Don't worry, Steve, I still remember how to do regions."

Atkinson went on to regain his health, with no lasting effects from the accident. The Lisa would be born, and the Macintosh would follow. Both machines would incorporate the revolutionary QuickDraw software.

As a reward, Atkinson was named an "Apple Fellow," a rare honor. Apple Fellows also receive an envelope from Steve Jobs. Apple Fellows don't talk about what's inside.

No Apple Fellow, however, has ever returned the envelope.

To Come

To casual users, QuickDraw receives a showcase in MacPaint, a program that Atkinson created on the condition that the MacPaint functions and appearance would be his, and his alone. Once again, Bill Atkinson got his way. The resulting program is clearly the creation of one man, and shows a consistency that is impossible in software "team efforts." True to his tenacious nature, Atkinson labored over MacPaint through revision after revision, adding new features and refining present features, always seeking a maximum of speed and function and smallness.

What's next? Again, it's a secret. But guesses can be made, especially in light of this Atkinson comment: "If I don't do it, some other corporation will. It they do it, they'll screw it up. If I do it, it'll be done right."

But there's no vanity in the statement. Atkinson says the words quietly, simply, and sincerely. It just happens to be true, and might as well be admitted.

When you look into his eyes, you believe him.

— Copyright 1984 © Doug Clapp; from the book *Macintosh! Complete.* Condensed and revised somewhat from the original material.

What was it that Atkinson believed he could do "right"? HyperCard? That's my guess, but it's only a guess. I really don't know…

STEVE ON THE LOOSE

JEFFREY S. YOUNG

L et's back up. To understand Macintosh, we need to understand Lisa—
the machine that came before Macintosh. And we need to take a closer
look at Apple itself in those heady, early days.

Which brings us, of course, to Steven P. Jobs, Boy Wonder and Captain
of Industry.

Steve, for years, has fascinated Apple users, writers, and corporate-
watchers of all stripes. The late 1980s saw a rash of "Apple books," each
with a different take on Apple in general, and Steve in particular. Most
of the books had, if not precisely an axe to grind, a definite "attitude."

The best of the bunch was a book that took Steve head-on. A straightforward biography that never never lapsed into enlightened second-
guessing or envious back-biting. A good book by a good writer blessed
with a marvelous subject.

So back we go, to the days before Macintosh. Journalist Jeffrey S.
Young picks up the story in an excerpt from his biography Steve Jobs:
The Journey is the Reward.

Building another computer based on the same microprocessor as
the Apple II held about as much fascination for Steve as taking a
vacation. He was determined that Apple would change the world
with computers, but it couldn't be done with the Apple II. The
company had to pioneer the next generation of personal computing.

The Apple III was not it, and was never meant to be. He had to find a new technology to supersede the Apple II and III. Part of that motivation was his desire to build the most incredible machine ever made, as well as his love for the cresting edge of new technology, the latest in "whizzy" gear. He also wanted to prove that he was a responsible and serious person who could run a complicated project.

Steve was on the loose, searching for the way to make a totally new kind of computer. The best example he knew was that of his garage predecessors, Bill Hewlett and David Packard.

"A lot of Steve's product design instincts came from working on H-P products, and looking at them," says Trip Hawkins, an early Apple employee. "The two of us went to the H-P offices one day and practically got kicked out, because he was so obnoxious and started climbing around looking underneath their latest model, the H-P 150. It was pretty obvious we weren't there for a sales call."

The Conception of Lisa

Steve hired two seasoned engineering managers from Hewlett-Packard, John Couch and Ken Rothmueller, to design a brand new computer. He named the project Lisa.

Steve's all-consuming passion was always the new product, the next generation of machines. "I wrote the original Lisa plan with Steve," says Trip Hawkins. "It called for a $2000 system that would be based around a 16-bit architecture, rather than the 8-bit Apple II architecture—exactly what the Macintosh turned out to be. We were real excited about it. We were convinced we could change the world."

The basic machine was supposed to have two floppy drives and be targeted at the office market. Ken Rothmueller, a former H-P manager, was to be head of engineering. John Couch, the other H-P defector, was to head up the software divisions. From the second half of 1979 on through 1980, a design war was on. Couch stayed out of the Lisa project at first because he had never been a big fan of Rothmueller. It was part of Steve's thinking that if the two guys heading the project were at loggerheads, they would compete better and bring a further drive for excellence. It quickly developed "...that to a lot of us, with the exception of Rothmueller, we weren't happy with the direction in which it was going," says Hawkins.

By late 1979, Rothmueller had designed a bit-mapped, green phosphor monitor machine with a built-in keyboard. It was not very attractive or inspiring, and it looked like the kind of machine that H-P would have built, not the innovative kind of design that Steve specialized in. This early Lisa was large and clunky, but it was based around an expensive and powerful new microprocessor from Motorola, the 68000. The microprocessor, so new it wasn't available yet, was the hottest thing in the business, and Steve loved it. Rothmueller didn't seem to be able to do anything very stimulating with all its power. The prototype was slow in both processing speed and screen refresh. Steve started to grow antsy.

The Lisa software group was doing some interesting tricks with screen graphics, however. Atkinson was experimenting with various-sized letters and proportional spacing by controlling every dot on the screen. The rudiments of on-screen computer painting—bit-mapped graphics—in higher resolution than the Apple II or III could support, were also possible, and it seemed that if only the 68000 could be pushed to near its limits, they might have a machine that would really excite the public.

As 1979 drew to a close, the vice president of research and development, and vice chairman of the board, Steve Jobs, wanted a few more things in the works. He wanted something more compelling to a consumer than the box Rothmueller was designing. Steve wanted something sexy, as sexy as the latest in home stereos. He started with a detachable keyboard. Steve believed that a movable keyboard would offer users a much more comfortable relationship with the computer. It was not a brand new idea—IBM had used them in the 1960s with some mainframes—but it was fresh to the brave new world of personal computing.

Beyond that, he was having a hard time conceptualizing or articulating the look of the on-screen environment that the user would use to operate the machine. All he knew was that it had to

be new and radically different from anything yet seen. Steve needed something to stimulate him; he wasn't an original thinker. He
was great at taking the ideas of others and massaging them, spinning them into something better and more accessible. He needed
inspiration, and he needed it soon. He was obsessed by speed, and
had convinced everyone on the Lisa project that they had to have
the machine ready to ship in 1981.

Apple and Xerox

The Lisa, like the Apple III, was aimed at the nebulous office market. The Apple heads of state convinced themselves that the Lisa
would be an office solution, while the Apple III would be aimed at
small businesses, and the Apple II would keep its focus on homes,
kids, and schools. This was how they segmented the market for
personal computers.

To develop the right product for the office market, Steve
became convinced that Apple should consider a strategic alliance
with one of the giants who already had a firm foothold in that territory. He was smart enough to know then that he knew nothing
about offices and those kinds of businesses. So he hired people
from H-P, who he was convinced did know that market. But as he
saw what Rothmueller and his colleagues were coming up with, he
also knew enough not to put all of Apple's eggs in their basket.

Steve went in search of a partner. There were only two choices,
and one, IBM, was anathema to all the countercultural blithe spirits and make-the-world-a-better-place types who populated Apple.
IBM was the enemy; Apple couldn't get into bed with them. The
other choice was Xerox, whose name was synonymous with office
automation and copying systems, and whose reputation was
unbesmirched by the long shadows of mainframes.

In the company's second private investment placement, con-
cluded in 1979, among the Arthur Rocks, venture capital firms,
and investors, was Xerox. Early in the year, Steve had approached
the Xerox Development Corporation, the venture capital arm of
the copier-based empire, and told them, "I will let you invest a
million dollars in Apple if you will sort of open the kimono at

Xerox PARC." The Xerox Palo Alto Research Center was rumored to be a Land of Oz of computer knowledge and advanced research, and was whispered to be on the verge of an enormous adventure in personal computers. With his remarkable salesmanship, Steve succeeded in getting exactly what he wanted. Xerox signed an agreement never to purchase more than five percent of Apple's shares and invested $1 million by buying 100,000 shares at $10. Steve got the chance to see what a real revolution in computing could be.

Steve had been encouraged to pursue Xerox by a collection of Apple's characters, with Jef Raskin and Bill Atkinson at the forefront. By that time Raskin, concerned that all the company's new machines were ever more expensive, was heading a small R&D project of his own at Apple to build an inexpensive home computer, one that would cost less than $1000. This machine would come as a self-contained unit, software included. He had three engineers working on it, and they were casually focusing on this proposed "desktop appliance." But Raskin had worked with the fellows at PARC a few years earlier through some work he did at the Stanford Artificial Intelligence Lab, and he knew that Apple should find out what they were up to.

Atkinson's interest lay in the world of graphics—how to make a computer draw rectangles, spheres, or half-moons smoothly, quickly, and simply. As soon as the Lisa project was launched in early 1979, he joined up, and began to work on a series of programming routines that would define the way every Apple computer after the Apple III looked and worked. His procedures, which he first called LisaGraf primitives, would give the Lisa complete control over the screen display.

The Apple II had been a bit-map machine—but it was crude. What the Lisa team, and Atkinson, had in mind was something more sophisticated. There would be many more dots, or "pixels," resulting in much more detailed graphics. They would actually control each pixel individually. What they gave up with all this manipulation was color—adding color to every dot was prohibitive in cost—but they gained elegant graphics and an appealing visual look. By late 1979, Atkinson had a sketchy collection of his LisaGraf primitives running, but he was faced with a few problems. While they were providing new graphics capabilities for their inchoate system, they still didn't have any idea about what their on-screen environment should look like.

Tessler and the Alto

At Xerox PARC, Larry Tessler was working with the Smalltalk programming environment that his group had created for the Alto computer, an office computer systems project. Xerox was having trouble figuring out how to manufacture computers cheaply enough, and was looking at Apple to possibly build cheap versions of Xerox machines, which is why they had invested in the first place. In many ways, the Alto was what the Lisa was aiming for. It reflected a number of the ideas of seminal computer thinker Alan Kay. Kay was a firm believer in simplicity, smaller is better, and the mouse, but he also had a classic academician's problem: he was working toward a holy grail of computing that was still at least a dozen years away in 1979.

"Up to then I had believed in the Alan Kay vision," says Tessler, "that computers would not really happen until they had the power of a VAX [a type of computer], could be held in your hand, and cost $1000 or less apiece. He called that computer the Dynabook."

Tessler was the designated Xerox personal computer expert. He was the only person in the Smalltalk group who believed that personal computers—the ones on the market, not the ones Xerox was developing—were serious. He had purchased several computers by the time Apple came around in December of 1979 to look at what Xerox was doing. Tessler had dealt with Commodore over a personal computer at his daughter's school, and was not impressed. When the group from Apple came by, he figured, "These were a bunch of hackers and they didn't really understand computer science. They wouldn't really understand what we were doing, and just see pretty dancing things on the screen." It was part of the superiority of formally-trained computer scientists, an attitude that was just beginning to infiltrate the original corps of self-taught hackers at Apple as more and more "trained" people, especially H-P engineers and MBA marketers, were hired.

Unveiling the working Xerox system at PARC had been preceded by several meetings where the ground rules were laid out. Finally Steve, Couch, Mike Scott, Rothmueller, Hawkins, Atkinson, Richard Page (a Lisa systems software architect) and Tom Whitney (Apple's head of engineering and another H-P alumnus) were taken into a demo room. Tessler unveiled the machine and operating environment Xerox had developed. It was instant pandemonium.

What they witnessed was like nothing they had ever seen on a computer before. The revolutionary element of the Xerox Smalltalk environment was that the user could interact easily with the computer through icons, windows, and menus without ever typing a single letter or command. Xerox's concept was a computer-style "desktop." The environment of the screen was graphically based, with icons instead of typed names to represent files and programs; used a mouse for pointing and moving things on the screen; had individual windows open containing different documents; and demonstrated rudimentary, on-screen, pull-down menus. It was thoroughly intuitive, and clearly the right way to interact with a computer.

The keyboard was nearly superfluous. Up until then, all computer operations—such as those on both the Apple II and Apple III—had been invoked by typing at least one, and usually several, lines of programming code or instructions. You might eventually get to a game that used a joystick, or a spreadsheet that employed cursor keys, but lines of characters were always essential to start you off.

The mouse, a three-button plastic deck-of-cards-shaped box that fit into the palm and rolled across a desk or table, moved the on-screen cursor or insertion point, which could be centered over an icon or menu title. Clicking one of the three buttons performed different operations on the file or program represented by that icon. Furthermore, across the top of the screen were a series of menu titles, each of which could hold a number of choices such as Save, Close, and Quit. These were also reached by using the mouse and buttons. It was an absolute revelation to the visitors from Apple.

"Atkinson was peering very closely at the screen, with his nose about two inches away from it, looking at everything very carefully," remembers Tessler. "And Jobs was pacing around the room acting up the whole time. He was very excited. Then, when he began seeing the things I could do on-screen, he watched for about a minute and started jumping around the room, shouting, 'Why aren't you doing anything with this?? This is the greatest thing! This is revolutionary!'"

The Xerox machine demonstrated the fundamental idea behind the bit-mapped screen concept, and though they had grasped it intellectually, the Apple contingent had never before seen it in operation on such a sophisticated level. It was all done with layers of dots. You could look at a drawing, and then zoom in to look deeper and find more dots. For Steve and the other Apple acidheads, the PARC experience was like dropping acid for the first time and getting the big insight—Satori. This was the Tao of high technology, the right way to build a computer.

The high-resolution, bit-mapped screen, with all the dots arrayed before their eyes, allowed them to voyage inside the digital world and swim around among the pixels. Like opening the doors of perception, this was crossing the boundary. It was the electronic acid test. If you got the idea, you were on the bus. If you didn't, you were left on the curb.

Atkinson and the others were asking Tessler questions, one after the other. "What impressed me was that their questions were better than any I had heard in the seven years I had been at Xerox—from anybody, Xerox employee, visitor, university professor, or student. Their questions showed that they understood all the implications and the subtleties. They understood that it was important that things looked good, that the font was attractive, that the icons were cute. That everything worked together smoothly."

By the end of the demo, Tessler was convinced that he was going to leave Xerox and go to Apple, which he did a few months later. These guys understood what personal computing could be, and they could make a mass market product. They had the right stuff, as far as Tessler was concerned.

What the Xerox group had shown them was a revolution, but it wasn't an earth-shaking revelation, according to Atkinson. "I was aware of most of what they were doing from the trade press. But here it was working. It looked nearly complete. They had actually done it, and that reinforced our direction, which was along the same path. If they could do it, we could do it. It energized us. It gave us something to strive for."

Steve immediately wanted to create a computer like the one at Xerox, but much better. On the drive back to Cupertino, he turned to Atkinson, who was equally inspired, and asked how long he thought it would take to get a system like that up and running on a 68000 machine like his Lisa. Atkinson, a gifted programmer, but with little experience writing operating system languages and interfaces, said, "About six months." That was all Steve needed. He was off and running.

Redesigning Lisa

At Apple, the most advanced programming to date had been done with the new Apple III operating system utilities, where menu commands could be stepped through from the keyboard. But this system, called SOS (for System Operating Software), was still a command-oriented environment, with none of the finesse and ease of use of the mouse-and-icon world they had just seen at Xerox. For Steve, it was obvious: throw the old-fashioned work on the Lisa out the window and start over again on a new operating environment. According to Steve, the mouse was obviously a superior way to operate a computer, and when the co-founder and resident evangelist went on a crusade, he usually won.

Steve wanted Rothmueller to redesign the Lisa to make it work with a mouse and support a new graphics-oriented interface with icons and windows. The former H-P engineer objected, and resented having to make the whole machine over again. It started a seesaw battle through the corridors of engineering at Cupertino. Steve, with his band of cohorts—including Atkinson, Page, Hawkins, and Couch—started proselytizing and building demonstration programs. Rothmueller, with Raskin, fought them. Steve ordered Rothmueller to do it. He refused.

"Steve has a power of vision that is almost frightening," says Hawkins, who is a believer in that vision. "When Steve believes in something, the power of that vision can literally sweep aside any objections or problems. They just cease to exist."

Steve, Hawkins, Atkinson, and Couch began to map out a new vision of an office computer. In the wake of the Xerox visit, Steve and Hawkins wrote up a new specification for the machine. At one point they typed "THINK DOTS" in the middle of a section about what the screen should be based on. They showed it to the head of engineering, Whitney, along with a few demonstration tricks that Atkinson and Page had put together.

"There were no mice for computers in those days," recalls Hawkins, "so to prove how great the mouse was, we found the only guy who made them, in Berkeley, by hand, out of a single block of wood. We gave one to Atkinson, and he wrote some kind of driver for it so we could show a simple little drawing program that he called MouseSketch.

"We called it the 'clandestine mouse,' and when we started to demonstrate it around the engineering labs, we won about half the crew over to it."

It was by no means an instant sale. For those who had been formally trained on mainframes, the mouse was an entirely heretical way of interacting with a computer. For the self-taught Steve Jobs and his corps of supporters, the guys who had no tie to the past, who saw computing as an exciting quest based in giving as much power as possible to the user—the people who were not comfortable typing letters and commands like the BASIC commands that a programmer had to work with daily—it made perfect sense.

For the Apple II marketplace of 1981, that machine had reached critical mass. Enough Apple IIs were out in the world so that it made some business sense to write a program for them—you could make money doing it. This was a watershed. By late 1979, Apple had sold about 50,000 computers. With the success of VisiCalc the next year, that number more than doubled, to 125,000.

Apple was also changing direction in its software development for the Lisa. The decision had been made to offer a complete set of application programs that would be created within the company. This was partly to control the profits, and partly to ensure that there were quality programs in the key software areas. There was no guidebook on how to write programs for personal computers, with their extremely limited memories and erratic operating environments, and there were few people competent enough to write them. Instead of depending on the Apple II hackers, who had proved their worth, Steve believed his advisors from H-P, who told him that the Lisa needed classically-trained programmers with experience. It was the best of choices—but also the worst of choices.

Hackers and Teenagers

The company employed teenagers and self-taught hackers—Wigginton, Espinosa, Bruener, Kottke, Tognazzini, Scott, Atkinson, and Markkula, all of whom loved to cut code. Their attitude toward traditional programming values was typified by something Wigginton once said about someone's program. "You've got too many comments," he complained. When the programmer explained that you had to have comments to tell other people what you were doing, the teenager replied, "Comments are for sissies."

For the original Apple hackers, the brilliant overall design and haphazard writing of a program counted much more than methodical planning. They were the maestros of software. Child prodigies and idiot savants, passionate plodders and inspired amateurs, they pursued programming like Mozart wrote symphonies: they never outlined and never looked back—it was all intuition.

A machisimo developed among the early hackers that had to do with how fast you could get something up and running. A program riddled with bugs that took a day was worth much more than a clean, neat program that took a month. After only one day, a decision could be made about whether to continue with it by actually seeing the working model, not by discussing theoretical issues ad infinitum. As the company grew, it would become a bone of increasingly cantankerous contention between the classically-trained engineers of Lisaland and the self-taught hackers from the company's founding.

As the Lisa project gelled and more programmers and engineers with formal degrees were hired to work on it, the software-by-trial-and-error teenagers were left out. The new, pedigreed program-mers built programs after long discussions, carefully debugging on paper before ever beginning a prototype. This was programming as a profession. Steve and the hackers saw themselves as artists, and artists lived by the seats of their pants, not some cast-in-bronze rules. The dichotomy created dissent and tension at the heart of the team building Apple's new computer.

Steve was at the center of this controversy. He knew little about designing computers in the professional world on which the Lisa group was focusing, but he desperately wanted to know more. He wanted to learn how to build a real computer system, and he believed the software team models that the H-P guys were telling him about were the way to proceed. He abandoned the teenagers and adopted the "professional model" with the same gusto he brought to all his enthusiasms.

By 1980, serious frictions were developing among various fac-tions of the company. The first and oldest faction, the Apple II camp, was populated by "the straights," the plodding thinkers and organized folks who handled the day-to-day details of running a mature product line. These people were working at noncreative functions, as Steve saw it. They had an exploding bureaucracy of software and hardware managers, tech support, and engineering support folks who were far removed from the creative flow of building new machines. These people had come in after the fun part was finished.

Then there was the team of incremental thinkers who were deep into creating the interim step, the marginally-improved Apple III. They were primarily advanced hobbyists, hackers who had learned enough to try to follow Woz (Steve Wozniak). The group was peo-pled with the early joiners, the first engineers and technicians the company had hired. It was a true group effort. All the key people in the company were part of the planning stages.

Finally, there was the Lisa group, which was searching for the breakthrough computer product to take Apple into the eighties. The Lisa was meant to be a professional computer, not a hobbyist's hacked up machine. To do it right, the company had to bring in serious professional engineers. A large part of this was Steve's doing. He was determined that if the company was going to strike out in a bold new direction, if it was going to finally leave the legacy of Woz behind and create a machine without his indelible stamp on it, they had to start fresh with new people who weren't tied to the ghosts of the past.

He was tired of seeing the Apple II referred to as Woz's machine. While he could use Woz to stimulate the hackers who were all in awe of the legendary designer and wanted to emulate him, he was also increasingly determined to exorcise Woz's overwhelming spirit throughout the company. He wanted to have a machine that was his alone, and he knew that the Lisa, with its mouse and icons, was his answer to the Apple II. By late summer 1980, they had a crude working prototype of the Lisa hardware, and were predicting, in all their naiveté, product shipment in 1981.

Internal Chaos

By late summer 1980, the Apple III was falling into disrepute internally. It still didn't work right, no software was available for it, but since they had already announced it, they would have to ship no matter what, or lose market credibility. Like Pontius Pilate, Steve washed his hands of the entire project. He would stay out of their rat's nest and not help them solve their problems, and they were going to stay out of his baby, the Lisa.

He and Couch devised a management theory that isolated and separated the new team from the rest of Apple. The Lisa group had an elitism that was quickly apparent to the rest of the company. You couldn't even enter their quarters, a new building along Bandley Drive, unless you were wearing a special orange badge. For an avowedly democratic, humanistic company, it was a startling contradiction in terms. They weren't going to do it like the hackers of the Apple II world, and they weren't going to make the mistakes of the Apple III. Lisa would do it right.

Steve had seen Apple go from nothing more than a few dreams and a computer designed by Woz, to a serious business enterprise that was making him a rich man. The acid-dropping, India-tripping, Zen Buddhist meditator had, in the space of three years, surrounded himself with layers of management and bureaucracy that were enough to stifle anyone. Success bred management, and while he knew that the cash cow of the Apple II had to run smoothly to ensure the company's future growth, he also knew that he wanted to work on a more spontaneous level. There had to be a way to mix corporate structure with humanistic values. Steve was determined to find it, and somehow he thought that the Zen monk's off-the-wall craziness might be the ticket. He became all the more impossible.

When the company was small and Steve could be reined in by Scotty, Markkula, or Woz, it was good to have a house loony whose reactions were sure to be crazed and emotional. Calmer voices could intercede. In the early days, there was a "no-gloves" attitude at the company, a give-and-take that allowed anyone to make a comment on any other aspect of the company. That atmosphere, which Steve fostered and supported both consciously and subconsciously, grew less prevalent as the company burgeoned to 200, then 600, then more than 1000 employees. By 1980, Apple had become a place that looked good on a résumé. Working there was no longer powered by passion; it was powered by the career ladder.

As the company grew, corporate culture changed. Apple actively worked at having an enlightened management style. This was partly a result of Steve's espousal of the currents and winds of the time, and partly a matter of prevailing Silicon Valley culture. H-P had built a company on a foundation of enlightened management, and in Steve's mind, Apple was going to emulate and surpass H-P. Furthermore, the Valley, with the explosion of consumer electronics and computers, had dozens of start-up companies and an (almost) unwritten rule that they had to provide the most advanced working environments in the world.

Creating a clan of Esalen types was not compatible with the bang-'em-up abrasive management style of Steve Jobs. He hated long meetings, with their interminable discussions of petty details. He wanted to be able to look at an approach to some problem, make an instinctive decision, and then move on to another decision without looking back. If you could be passionate about your opposing point of view, about the reasons he was wrong, you could push Steve back onto the right track. But you had to use aggression and force in your counter-attack.

Because Steve's off-the-wall attacks could come at any time, Apple's people learned to marshal all their arguments, to think through every angle, and to be prepared to defend a point of view with eloquence. It created an environment of excellence, so that even when he did not question your decision, when he surprised you by agreeing without argument, you had already done the requisite thinking.

Apple Culture

By threatening irrational, emotional responses, the company co-founder produced remarkably well-informed employees. Fuzzy, unclear decision-making was unacceptable. So was democracy, when Steve was involved. The constant exchange of ideas, the building to a consensus as it had developed in Apple's no-confrontation, modern-management style, never worked for him. He might have been deeply influenced by aspects of the self-realization movement, but he was not of that world. Steve never had any trouble saying exactly what was on his mind, and letting the chips fall where they might.

What happened, as the company went through its paces and tried to deal with its explosive growth, was that the only person who continued to operate under the aggressive, say-what-you-will, tell-the-truth-if-it-hurts attitude was Steve. He became even more combative, abrupt, and, yes, obnoxious.

"Apple was very much like a club," says Phil Roybal. "We would have management retreats at spectacular resorts, like the Pajaro Dunes, south of Monterey and right on the ocean. There would be a couple of days of meetings, and at night we would open the bar and dance until we dropped. Apple was asking an incredible amount of us. We were working around the clock. At the very least, we had to give everyone a sense of mission and purpose. We decided to try and quantify what we all believed in. It was called the Apple Values project."

In 1979 and 1980 "Apple Culture," and the definitions of it, were a focus of attention in the company. Up to then it had been an unwritten set of rules that only Apple could ever have tried to write, or to quantify. They did it as part of the Apple Quality of Life Project. They created memos that included lines such as the following, most of which were quotations from Chairman Steve:

> One person, one computer.
>
> We are going for it, and we will set aggressive goals.
>
> We are all on the adventure together.
>
> We build products we believe in.
>
> We are here to make a positive difference in society as well as make a profit.
>
> Each person is important; each has the opportunity and the obligation to make a difference.
>
> We are all in it together, win or lose.
>
> We are enthusiastic!
>
> We are creative; we set the pace.
>
> We want everyone to enjoy the adventure we are on together.
>
> We care about what we do.
>
> We want to create an environment in which Apple values flourish.

As the company developed an extraordinarily relaxed corporate culture—a culture with health club memberships, lots of parties, T-shirts, and personal computers at cost for every employee—Steve was becoming more of a monster. He was approaching his twenty-fifth birthday as 1980 began, with money, success, unrelenting drive, ambition, and no social graces—or an interest in

developing them—to soften the
blows that his Zen-trained, reac-
tive mind dealt out. He seemed
to have taken half the message of
Zen. He took the mental clarity
and the emphasis on intuition,
but he didn't weld it to the con-

> Q. What's the difference between Apple
> Computer and the Boy Scouts of America?
>
> A. The Boy Scouts have adult supervision.
>
> —From John Sculley's "Odyssey"

templative and thoughtful personality that could never make a cutting or dismissive remark to another human. Zen Buddhism was
founded on the Japanese belief in respect for elders and the time-
lessness of the universe. Steve was a brash American who had the
counterculture's disdain for previous generations, and an obsession
with cramming as much as possible into every day. He was creating
a new kind of "Zen business," and Apple was his testing ground.

Steve's meddling in the Lisa group finally got to Rothmueller,
who made it clear that he wasn't getting on Steve's bus. He depart-
ed about halfway through 1980. John Couch took over the project. It became apparent that this scheme of Steve's was a real alternative to the way computing was done in the rest of the world,
and through the year, more and more of the company's key engineers hopped onto the bandwagon. The company started to
believe that this was indeed the proper direction for the Lisa project, and Steve's preaching the gospel didn't hurt.

With the hardware and software teams charting a new course
for personal computing, some of the excitement and enthusiasm
was transformed into extreme cost overruns. "We just went crazy,"
says Hawkins, "everybody, Steve included. Lisa became a kind of
kitchen sink where we were trying to do everything that could possibly be done with a computer, and suddenly the cost factor, which
in the original plan was set at $2000, went out the window.

"We made two radical underestimations: how much things were
going to cost, and how long it would take to do them. Steve was
such a biddler, always changing things, that many things were
done again and again, because he would get bored with it being a
certain way and want to change it, which just produced interminable delays."

As 1980 proceeded, and the Lisa design and engineering teams went through paroxysms of change created by Steve's whims, other people in the company looked on in horror. John Couch was a friendly, low-key person with an unfailingly optimistic mindset, and no desire to buck the vice chairman's unrealistic schedules. He didn't have the personality to stand up to Steve, and as the Lisa's design issues looked like they were about resolved, he and the co-founder started to snipe at each other.

Steve decided he had no time for Couch, who had been his prime supporter in shifting the direction of the Lisa project, and started to dismiss him. He thought that his product vision had now been vindicated, and in his inexperience thought that the top management of the company, the executive staff, was ready to hand over the actual implementation of the product line to him. Couch, who was in his late thirties and very good at the politics of a corporation, cultivated another ally, Mike Scott.

It was quickly apparent at the top of the company that the Apple III was not going to be the kind of success that the Apple II had been. The circuit board was too complex, and the trace lines of solder—the rivers of electric current that make a circuit do its magic—were far too close. The connectors for components didn't seat correctly. Mysterious, nonrepeating bugs terrorized operators. The press and public smelled the problems almost immediately, and the machine was fatally tainted.

If the Lisa were to be the company's savior, they had to do something radical about turning the project into a serious and substantial product group, not just a whim of Steve's. The haphazard, friendly way that the III had been designed was not the way to do it.

Couch plumped for the H-P model of work groups, secrecy, and insularity, a close-knit group that could make all the decisions democratically. Steve was flying off the handle, having wild and amazing ideas, working in secrecy with Atkinson and Page, and making preemptive strikes and unilateral decisions. In 1980, the company's revenues approached $117 million, every penny of it earned through sales of the Apple II and the burgeoning library of software that Apple was publishing. There was urgency in the corridors of Apple. The company was defining the world of personal computers on every front, and everyone was on the firing line. However, behind the bulging coffers, concern was building on many levels.

On his side, Couch wanted to create a semblance of equality in the Lisa group, and that was the last kind of arrangement in which Steve was interested in working. Up until then, Apple had always been driven by the edicts of the few, especially Steve's. Something had to give.

"Steve had an incredible ability to rally people towards some common cause," says Howkins, "by painting an incredibly glorious cosmic objective. One of his favorite statements about the Lisa was, 'Let's make a dent in the universe. We'll make it so important that it will make a dent in the universe.'

"On its face, that is a completely ridiculous idea. But people would rally around stuff like that, especially engineers who had spent their lives bottled up in a lab somewhere, missing out on all the fun. He had a very charismatic style of communicating, and it works because deep inside, he really wants to make a massive contribution. You have to admire that. A lot of capable people are just looking for their own security, the trappings of wealth."

Steve and the Media

As Couch tried to make sense of the ever-changing demands for an entirely new generation of computers, and the sudden elevation of the Lisa from just another project to the company's "great white hope," he and Steve found themselves increasingly at odds. Then another set of events occurred that made the young founder even more difficult to control, and which swelled his youthful head. In the summer of 1980, the publicity engine of Regis McKenna's agency was introducing a new ad campaign that would thrust Steve into the public's eye as the boy wonder. It would also position him as the creator of personal computing, the new field that was sweeping the country as the bad news from Iran continued to come in. It was a new field that was all-American, homegrown, and almost magical.

The success of the firm was starting to create rumblings about a public stock offering. It seemed like the right time to develop an "institutional" advertising campaign aimed at influencing professional investors. This would be the initial step in going public.

"It was the *Wall Street Journal* campaign that really put us in the public eye," recalls Fred Hoar, Apple's first director of corporate communications, who was hired in 1980. "The most famous headline was 'When We Created the Personal Computer, We Created a Twenty-First-Century Bicycle.' The first one featured Steve, with an extensive quote about computers."

Here, in part, is what the ad said:

> What is a personal computer? Let me answer with the analogy of the bicycle and the condor.
>
> A few years ago, I read a study, I believe, in *Scientific American*, about efficiency of locomotion in various species on the earth, including man. The study determined which species was the most efficient in terms of getting from point A to point B with the least amount of energy exerted. The condor won. Man made a rather unimpressive showing, about one-third of the way down the list. But someone there had the insight to test man riding the bicycle. Man was twice as efficient as the condor.
>
> This illustrated man's ability as a tool maker. When man created the bicycle, he created a tool that amplified an inherent ability. That's why I like to compare the personal computer to the bicycle.
>
> The Apple computer is the twenty-first-century bicycle, if you will, because it's a tool that can amplify a certain part of our inherent intelligence. There's a special relationship that develops between one person and one computer that ultimately improves productivity on a personal level.

It went on in that vein, filling a full page in the *Wall Street Journal.* Following that series, the company was suddenly in the public eye, and Steve was high-tech's poet laureate. In the photo of him that accompanied the ad, he had a beard and looked very much like a modern-day John the Baptist. The campaign made some outrageous claims, such as "Steve Wozniak and I invented the personal computer."

The ads were written by Arlene Jaffe, a copywriter at the McKenna agency. (She, ironically, would later write the Charlie Chaplin ads for IBM.) The ads were filled with the extravagant, yet compelling, claims that Steve was used to making in the company, but they were now directed to the business public. It was a perfectly timed, deftly designed campaign, and Steve captured the imagination of a number of editors.

The second ad, which also featured Steve, was headlined, "When we created the personal computer, we created a new generation of entrepreneurs," which was guaranteed to hook everyone who hadn't read the first one. It was this brilliant series of advertising moves that lifted Apple out of the obscurity of electronics, from the hobbyist world of Apple IIs into the consciousness of America's mainstream of business. It also gave Steve a swollen sense of self-importance, especially since it was only at the last minute that they had changed the copy from "I" to "we." The original idea had been to make the campaign personal to him. Woz was furious. Even though he had slipped out of the mainstream of Apple life with the completion of the disk drive in 1978, he was still around enough to be consulted. Hurriedly, the agency people added Woz into the prose, but it was plain that in his heart Steve Jobs believed that it was indeed he alone who had taken Apple over the top as a company. And he was probably right. Regis McKenna remarked once that "Woz designed a great machine. But it would have sat on the shelf had he not discovered an evangelist."

In 1980, benchmark market testing showed less than a 10 percent name recognition for the company with the public at large, but Apple was just beginning to come out of its cocoon. The first enormous "event," which was to become an ongoing part of the emerging marketing strategy of the company, had been held for the Apple III's introduction at Disneyland. It would be a year of firsts for Apple: the first event marketing extravaganza, the first ads in the *Wall Street Journal.* It was also the first for something else. Just as Steve was riding high, featured in a smashing series of ads,

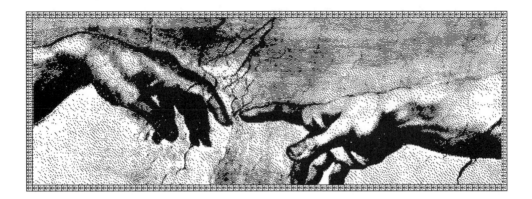

at the helm of a new line of computers, and with the company that he had founded making oodles of money, his wings were clipped. The only person at Apple who could cut him down to size did just that.

Steve's Descent

Mike Scott watched Steve's ego inflation with growing distaste. Scotty was a complex person who prided himself on cutting through the bull. He had no time for the childish concerns that Steve and his cronies espoused. He was a pragmatist, concerned with getting computers out the door, and the airy-fairy intellectual ideas and pretensions of the company co-founder left him cold.

Apple had also grown too large, and was unwieldy in its present haphazard, unstructured form. In anticipation of taking the company public, Scotty, in concert with Markkula, decided to reorganize the firm, a decision that had been made at the August 1980 Board of Directors meeting. Over the following weeks, in secret, with only a couple of key managers involved, the two plotted a new structure for Apple. The business would be divisionalized. The first division was the Personal Computer Systems, which comprised the Apple II and Apple III product lines. The new Lisa computer was to be the flagship in a new Professional Office Systems division. But instead of putting Steve at the helm of it, Scotty put John Couch in charge. Finally, a third division, the Accessories Division, handled all other items—printers, add-on circuit boards, and especially the new disk drive that Apple was developing at Steve's insistence. None of these divisions were to be run by Steve Jobs.

The plan to reorganize and go public was first revealed to the company at an executive management retreat in September, held at a golf course in Carmel Valley. Steve was shocked. "After setting up the framework for the concepts and finding the key people and sort of setting the technical directions, Scotty decided I didn't have the experience to run the thing," recalled Steve. "It hurt a lot. There's no getting around it."

At that point, Lisa was Steve's baby. He had more personal involvement in it than anyone else, and handing it over to Couch was a slap in the face. This unforeseen reorganization removed him from any day-to-day operating role doing what he loved to do: building new machines. Scotty and Markkula made Steve chairman of the board, knowing that having a 25-year-old at the head of a $100 million company—especially a young guy with such a seductive manner—could only be good for the stock offering. Scotty tried to soften the blow by telling Steve that it was done to free him for the publicity that the public offering would generate.

Steve felt abandoned. It was products that he loved, that made him feel loved, and he had been hit right where it hurt the most. Even worse, John Couch, feeling his new corporate oats and determined to make the Lisa team in his image, not Steve's, made it clear to Steve that he didn't want him meddling in the affairs of his division any longer.

"Steve was real unhappy about all of that," says Hawkins. "He was unhappy about the way that Scotty had pulled this stunt without informing or consulting him—it was his company, after all!—and he was upset about losing direct involvement with Lisa. And he didn't particularly like the choice of John Couch to head it. He was really bent out of shape."

Steve accepted the role of chairman to marshal the company through the most successful public stock offering in history. He told himself that it was good for the company, but all the while his bitterness smoldered. Within six months he would get back at

Mike Scott, and then, using the power that he had consolidated, his actions would in turn destroy the Lisa, the computer that he had created and named after his child.

But he couldn't live on vindictiveness alone. Steve needed a project, a new crusade to make him whole, to pour his energy into. Apple was a chaotic place, with projects always starting and being canceled. A great idea, and enough enthusiasm, could convince one of the leaders to offer three months of development time to work something out. If a usable concept came of it, great. If not, as was nearly always the case, there was so much money rolling in the door that it made no difference to the bottom line. In the fall of 1980, cut loose from the Lisa, Steve started to look around for a new computer to pour all his passion into, a new machine he could make the world love. Luckily, he didn't have to look far.

NOTES ON *MY* JOURNEY

JEFFREY S. YOUNG

O kay. My picks are Wilfred Brimley as Andy Hertzfeld; Robert Redford and "The Emperor" in Star Wars as John Sculley (alternating). William Hurt as Bill Atkinson (remember "Altered States"?). Jeffrey S. Young? It's coming…Ed Begley, Jr. Steve Jobs? Easy: Madonna.

What a long strange journey it has been! I first saw a Mac in the summer of 1983, sitting at a kitchen table in Marin County. The first editor-in-chief of *Macworld*, Andrew Fluegelmann, had made me sign a long non-disclosure form before he turned me loose on the unmarked box of gear at my feet. When I unwrapped it, I was astonished. Remember, this was six months before the little beige (it was beige back then, remember ?) box burst into the world, and I had never seen anything like it. This was a computer for the rest of us, for someone like me who was a writer, not an engineer. Within minutes I became a partisan, and was hooked for life.

That day I got to take the machine back to my house in order to write about MacPaint, which was my assignment, and the pirates in Bandley 3. It was all I could do not to enthuse and effuse about the machine to everyone I knew, but I tried to keep my mouth shut. It was particularly hard one day when a tall and enthusiastic guy knocked on my door and asked me where the Mac was. I'd never met Marc Canter before, but somehow he had heard that I had the only Mac in Marin County, maybe the only one outside the Apple community. He was determined to find it, and only the fact that I had stashed it in a downstairs closet saved the secret that day as he marched through my house in heavy pursuit.

At that point my affection for the machine was waning. I was in the midst of a long love/hate relationship with the Twiggy disk drive. Apple had not yet totally committed to the Sony 3.5" mechanism, and my machine still sported the wide grin of the ill-fated Lisa drives. The big problem with the drives, and the operating system as it stood in those days, was that unless you shut down the system in one particular sequence of keystrokes—and a thoroughly counter-intuitive sequence it was, I might add—the disk would freeze and be unusable. The result was that I would go down to Cupertino at least once a week to pick up a new collection of Twiggy floppies from the Mac group's software librarian.

As it turned out, this wasn't such a bad thing, because it forced me to spend a lot of time down in Bandley 3 with the Mac team. It was on one of these trips that I first met Steve Jobs. One evening, as I stood inside the Bandley 3 fishbowl where the Mac programmers lived, Steve appeared. He stopped dead in his tracks, looked me up and down, and yelled, "Who the hell are you?" Mine was a new face in the heart of his empire, and he was as protective as a mother hen. I happened to have a few of my published articles with me—I had given them to a programmer as credentials—and by showing them I was able to mollify him. Since I didn't back down, I gained a certain respect from the project leader. In the months to come, with Steve's tacit approval, I became a silent member of the team and was welcome in meetings, discussions, parties, and the group's endless informal pizza and falafel feasts. I had a unique ringside seat to the last six months of frenetic activity as the Macintosh was prepared and released. I wrote about the machine, and the people who created it, for *Macworld*, until early 1986, when our paths diverged.

Over the next few years I ran into Steve on numerous occasions—the lobby of Bandley 3, Friday afternoon beer "busts" in the Mac building, big events at Apple and elsewhere, private dinner parties, industry forums and seminars, annual meetings—and we would discuss whatever was on his mind. After the release of the Macintosh he grew much more guarded and calculating, and as a member of the press it became hard to get through the charming mask he wore in public to reach the off-the-cuff and unpredictable personality that made him so interesting. From mid-1983 through 1985 I witnessed close-up his ascent to enormous fame and worldwide celebrity, and then his swift fall from grace. And on Black Friday—September 13, 1985—the day he left the company to found NeXT, I happened to be in Cupertino interviewing original Mac team members for a story about the history of the making of Macintosh.

Steve was given a number of chances to comment on the contents of my book. I last saw him in person at a small Christmas party in December 1986 given by one of the key Macintosh creators, Bill Atkinson. Surrounded by Woz and many of his former employees, he was nervous and skittish. I told him about this project and asked for an interview. He agreed. Several letters were sent to him both at his home and his office, with no reply. Phone messages were left on his answering machine, with no reply. I left notes in his mailbox, and with his housekeeper. Finally I reached him one Saturday morning. I'd been told that Steve always meditated on Saturday mornings, and that if I could reach him then he would be at his most receptive.

He initially turned me down, but it was a couple of days after the millionth Macintosh had come off the factory assembly line. Steve was angry and a little bitter that the machine had been given to Jef Raskin, not to him, and he wanted to talk. He warmed to the idea, and agreed to be interviewed later in the week. In the meantime, he derided Sculley's recent management moves at Apple, and made sure that I had the story of the genesis of desktop publishing—Bob Bellville's influence—right.

A week later, an employee of NeXT called and cancelled the interview. I called Steve back directly, and he agreed to an interview once more. This time the NeXT employee who called was irate, and I was told to stop calling him directly. It was the last time I tried.

Journey was published in hardcover by Scott-Foresman in 1988, then in paperback by Lynx Books. Unfortunately, it is no longer in print, but the film rights are under option and there is the possibility of a film version one day. Who do you think should play Steve and the cast of characters who make up the Mac team? Send me your dream casting, care of this book's publisher.

And may *your* journey be rewarding...

— Copyright © 1992 Jeffrey S. Young.

JEFFREY S. YOUNG is the author of four books, as well as numerous articles for international, national, and regional magazines. He is currently completing an autobiography with Philippe Kahn, *Barbarian!,* to be published by Bantam Books in late 1992. In addition, he has also directed a number of *CLIO* award-winning television commercials, and is the screenwriter of several film and television productions.

As one of the founders of *Macworld* Magazine he was involved with the Macintosh computer six months before its introduction, has known Steve Jobs personally since then, and is a well-known commentator on the computer's fortunes. His book, *Steve Jobs: The Journey is the Reward,* is a biography of the co-founder of Apple Computer, Inc., published in hardcover by Scott, Foresman and Company in 1988. His previous books include *Improper Access,* the story of the largest single-handed computer-assisted bank robbery to date, based upon his article originally published in *Esquire;* and *Inside MacPaint—Sailing through the Sea of Fatbits on a Single Pixel Raft,* an irreverent paean to discovering art with a computer.

He was raised in northern California and London, where he attended St. Paul's School. He received his B.A. from Amherst, and M.F.A. from the UCLA Film School. He is married, has two small children, and lives near San Francisco in Redwood City, California.

HOW *MACWORLD* MAGAZINE
MADE THE MACINTOSH

DAVID BUNNELL

T wo days before this book's deadline, a Federal Express package arrived.
In it was this article.

*Why so late? Because I hadn't gotten up the nerve to ask David
Bunnell to contribute until I already had a bunch of great pieces from
a bunch of great people. Some people are intimidated by Steve Jobs.
I'm intimidated by David Bunnell, a man who's had vast—and
deserved—success as a publisher.*

*Four days after a brief, happy chat with David Bunnell, the article
arrives.*

And it's just great. See for yourself.

Borland founder Philippe Kahn was half right in January 1985,
when he called the early Macintosh "a piece of shit." It was under-
powered, had very little software, no hard drive, no compelling
application like desktop publishing, and it was marketed by a
company that seemed to be near death.

Thinking back on this time, I can't help but be amused by all
the pumped-up bravado I hear and read about the people who created the Macintosh. To hold up the Macintosh experience as an
example of how to create a great product, launch an industry, or
spark a revolution, is a cruel joke. Anyone who models their business startup on the Macintosh startup is doomed to failure.
Miracles, like the Macintosh, can only happen once.

I took my first Macintosh home in October 1983, nearly four months before the machine was introduced at the 1984 Apple Annual Meeting. As founder of *Macworld* magazine, I had a rare inside view of the Macintosh development effort. I had access to Steve Jobs and Mike Murray. I could drive down to Apple and stroll into the Macintosh building and just hang out if I wanted to.

My viewpoint may be iconoclastic, self-serving, and argumentative, but it is my truth and it comes from personal experience. The facts, as I choose to remember them, back me up.

I first heard about the Macintosh from Bill Gates in December, 1982, when I interviewed him for an article in *PC World* magazine. He said, "Apple's got this great new machine which is going to change everything." (Then, as now, most large companies leak from the top.)

I knew something about Apple's Lisa computer, so I asked Bill if that was what he was referring to. "Oh no," he replied, "this is a low cost machine. It is a machine anyone can afford. This is the first machine," Gates continued, "that is so easy to use that my mother could use it."

The most compelling feature of the Macintosh, according to Bill Gates, was that it had a "bit-mapped screen." For one thing, this meant was you could easily mix graphics with text. Unlike character-based IBM PCs, you could have different fonts and type styles. Bill also told me about the Mac's mouse and about its icons.

I remember saying to Bill, "It sounds like a Xerox Star word-processor."

"Oh yeah," he replied, "Steve hired away a bunch of people from the Xerox research park."

A few years later I met a bright fellow named Jef Raskin, who claimed the Macintosh was his idea. Apparently he was muscled out of Apple when Steve Jobs was looking for something to do because no one wanted him around the Lisa project or the Apple II division. Steve saw the Macintosh as something he could sink his teeth in.

There's an old saying that applies to many high-tech situations, which is, "Success has a thousand fathers, but failure is an orphan."

Soon after the Gates interview, I called Apple's VP of Communications, Fred Hoar, and told him I wanted to start a magazine called "AppleWorld." Fred was very interested in this idea and invited me to a meeting in Cupertino with some "key" Apple executives, none of whom I remember.

My concept was to publish a magazine that would cover all Apple computers. After starting *PC Magazine* and *PC World,* I was painfully bored with the spreadsheet-driven IBM DOS universe. I wanted to start a radically new computer magazine with sparkle and guts—something that didn't need to be so stuffy, so corporate. Apple users were creative and relaxed. They wore blue jeans and sneakers. IBM users wore suits with starched shirts, and ties so tightly knotted that their necks bulged out.

The key to my AppleWorld scheme was to build circulation by getting mailing rights to the Apple II warranty card list. Unfortunately, Apple had, just two weeks, earlier given exclusive mailing rights to the Apple II warranty card list to Ziff-Davis for use in the launch of an Apple II-specific magazine called "A+".

Upon hearing about the Ziff deal, I felt pretty bummed out. "Why exclusive?" I asked.

"Well," Fred said, "we didn't know about your plans, and the people from Ziff insisted upon exclusivity for nine months."

"Nine months in personal computing," I exclaimed, "is fucking eternity!"

On that sour note, everyone in the conference room fell silent. We hung our heads, fidgeted with pens and notebooks, and tapped our feet. It was the end of a dream. Think of the computer world as a monopoly game, except when you get adventuresome and land on the wrong square, you don't go to jail. Worse, you go back to DOS.

I can only describe what followed as a moment of divine intervention. A little voice inside my head whispered, "Take a chance, tell them you know about the Macintosh and you'd really like to publish *Macworld.*"

"How about we publish *Macworld?*" I said.

"*Macworld*, about the Macintosh, that's a great idea." Fred answered, "But how did you know about the Macintosh?"

"Bill Gates told me."

"Well, we're glad he did." The whole room lit up, and thus *Macworld* was conceived.

Macworld's gestation and birth was tortuously tricky. Events were not always in my control.

Jumbo roadblock number one was to convince Pat McGovern, the chairman of our parent company, that it was worthwhile for us to even pursue the Macintosh. My editor-in-chief, Andrew Fluegelman, and myself (I was publisher) were very "Mac" eager, but McGovern was pushing us to publish a magazine for IBM's new home computer, the PCjr.

After much bickering, he agreed we could investigate the opportunity further, but if we wanted to publish *Macworld* we would have to get Apple to pay for it. If Apple agreed to underwrite the startup, he would give us the OK. If not, then we would publish *PCjr World* instead (again, back to DOS).

To me, it seemed painstakingly ridiculous that we could convince Apple to pay us to start a magazine which IDG would own. But, after racking my brain during a few sleepless nights, I came up with a potential resolution. Perhaps we could get Apple to pay for trial subscriptions if we offered them to Macintosh buyers in exchange for filling out their warranty cards.

I knew from my conversation with Fred Hoar that Apple was disappointed that more Apple computer buyers didn't send in their warranty cards. It occurred to me that if we could offer Macintosh purchasers a free trial subscription to *Macworld* for sending in these cards, Apple was bound to capture a much higher percentage of names and addresses of Macintosh buyers. This they would pay for.

Out of the pressure from McGovern, an idea was born which later proved to drive the success of *Macworld*, and become the envy of many a magazine publisher, namely, the Apple-*Macworld* warranty card subscription program.

Jumbo roadblock number two was getting Steve Jobs to like us. Steve had to approve any magazine project about his Macintosh. Fred set up a meeting for Andrew and me with Steve and Mike Murray at the Mac building on Bandley Drive in Cupertino. For me, just seeing Steve Jobs from a distance was a big thrill, so the mere concept of actually talking to him was totally nerve-racking. I was so excited that Andrew insisted on driving when we went down to Cupertino.

Andrew, who invented shareware—only he called it "freeware"—was an extraordinary writer and unusually gifted ex-lawyer who had worked with Stewart Brand on the *Whole Earth Quarterly*. He was totally cool about meeting Jobs. We drove up to the Mac building on Bandley Drive, which in earlier days had been Apple headquarters.

Other than having a pirate flag fluttering over it, the Mac headquarters was an ordinary one-story, boring Silicon Valley office building that affected a quasi-Spanish style. We could tell that Steve was in, because his blue Mercedes was parked in the handicap zone in front. As I was to learn, Steve always parked there. He parked there because when he parked to the side, or to the back of the building, disgruntled Apple employees from the Lisa or Apple II divisions would come by and scratch his Mercedes with their keys.

Once inside, the receptionist asked us to wait in a small conference room just to the side of the reception area. "You can't go inside the main area until Steve says you're safe," she said.

We waited and waited. I was still very excited. Steve Jobs was then easily the most famous person in personal computing. Gates was a distant second, or was it Wozniak, or Mitch Kapor?

Steve Jobs was the enigma, the magnet that drew me to the Macintosh. I sat there wondering, not for the first time, what kind of fellow was this guy who walked barefoot through India, this vegetarian, ex-long-haired hippy who happened to be richer than God. What special human qualities did he have, what drive, to make him the folk hero of Silicon Valley?

When at last Steve arrived, I wasn't disappointed, but I was definitely startled by his informality, his bouncy step, and his dark, penetrating, glittering eyes. He had deep, deep pupils that burned into me like lasers. During the next few weeks I found that Steve wasn't afraid to look anyone in the eye. He could make me uncomfortable by staring intently, directly, at me for long periods of time. From the first time I met him, it was clear, Steve was someone who knew what he wanted.

"Hi guys," said Macintosh product manager Mike Murray, who seemed invisible next to Steve. "This is Steve Jobs. Steve, this is David and Andrew."

Though he was later forced out of the company by a vindictive John Sculley, Mike Murray was one of the finest facilitators I have ever met. He had to be. A tiny but mighty fellow, Mike was obliged to be the interface between Steve Jobs and the real world.

We chatted about computers and about magazines. Steve and Mike had been looking at *PC World,* and Steve could see from an aesthetic point of view it was the best looking magazine in the computer field. Compared to *Byte* magazine and *PC* magazine, he liked us best, or at least he *said* he did.

"We like you guys, too," Steve added. "You seem to be our kind of people."

"Yeah," chimed in Mike, "there were some other guys in here with a whole slick presentation. They wore suits. We didn't like them very much."

"So I guess you pass the test," Steve said as he jumped up from his seat. "Follow me," He bounded off. We hastily followed. We had just met, and Steve had us in his spell. He was the alchemist and we were being put into the soup.

We walked past the receptionist through the sacred passageway into the main Mac development area. The first thing I saw was an open area with three rather unexpected objects: a baby grand piano, a BMW motorcycle, and a ping-pong table.

"What the hell kind of business is this," I remember thinking at the time.

Steve led us into another conference room. As we sat down he picked up a beige oversized box-shaped case by its handle and plopped it on the table in front of us. "Here's a Macintosh," he said, "why don't you take it out of the case and see if you like it."

"Blow this and we're dead," I thought. I turned to Andrew and said, "You're the editor, Andrew, why don't you try it?"

So Andrew opened the case, and for the first time I saw a Macintosh. With very little coaxing from Steve or Mike, Andrew was able to figure out how to plug in the keyboard and the mouse. He stuck a disk into the machine and powered it up.

At this point, Mike took over the controls for a moment to show us how to boot up the first application, which was a buggy version of MacPaint. He showed us how you could draw images on the screen, and do all sorts of things to them like rotating them, moving them, filling them in, etc. I must say that coming from the world of the famous DOS "A:" prompt, MacPaint was like dying and going to heaven.

"Holy shit," exclaimed Andrew, "this is going to knock the world out of orbit, that's all."

"Wow, this is just too cool," I added.

So they were impressed with us and we were certainly impressed with the machine. "The Macintosh," Mike Murray said, was being built to be the machine "...we all want. We're building it for ourselves."

Convinced we had a tiger by the tail, Andrew and I charged back to San Francisco to rally our staff and to work on the agreement. We wanted Apple to grant us access to the Macintosh's development team, and to loan us a few early machines. With their help, we could do something that had never been done before: we could publish the first issue of *Macworld* on the very day Apple introduced the Macintosh—which was targeted to be January 24, 1984.

All systems were go, except for one little snag. I hadn't yet screwed up the courage to tell Jobs we wanted Apple to buy enough trial subscriptions (at $3 each) to give every Macintosh owner who bought the machine during the first year a chance to read *Macworld*.

Steve had told us he expected Apple to sell 600,000 Macs during the first twelve months after its introduction. That meant that the deal could be worth $1.8 million.

Soon Andrew and I were back in Cupertino, meeting again with Jobs and Murray. I told Steve what we wanted, and, to put it mildly, he was momentarily speechless.

Making matters worse, Steve had just heard a rumor that Pat McGovern had paid $6 million for a group of rather schlocky-looking computer magazines published by Wayne Green in Peterborough, New Hampshire. "You mean McGovern paid six million dollars for Wayne Green's magazines, and now he wants us to pay you $1.8 million to start *Macworld*?" he hollered.

"He didn't pay $6 million for Wayne Green's magazines," I protested. "You should ask him if you don't believe me."

Steve took me up on this on the spot. He picked up the phone and called Pat McGovern's main office in Framingham, Massachusetts. As luck would have it, Chairman Pat was at his desk.

Events were getting out of hand. Staring at me, Steve, spoke into the phone, "Wayne Green's magazines look like yesterday's leftover oatmeal, and you want me to pay you to have David and Andrew start *Macworld*? You must be a terrible businessman if you paid Wayne Green six million dollars. You should belly up to the bar, if you want to own *Macworld*."

Steve Jobs was telling my boss, whom he had never met, that he was a crummy business man, and here I was wondering if I'd ever be able to publish *Macworld*. I felt the dream slipping away.

Kicking me under the table, Andrew smiled and winked at me. Andrew sensed something I didn't pick up. This was just Steve's style of negotiation. He simply humiliated his opponent before going in for the kill. Sometimes Steve gets what he wants, sometimes he only takes a few bites. So if you want to play, this is just something you put up with.

I could hear McGovern's excited voice coming through the headphone. And though I couldn't tell exactly what he was saying, I sensed from the tone and from Steve's subsequent statements that Pat was explaining how Wayne Green didn't get that much money. As a matter of fact, the magazines they bought were in such bad shape they would have to invest heavily in them. Because of this, they just didn't have the money to invest in *Macworld*.

IDG didn't have any money for *Macworld* but they apparently had plenty of money for *Micro 80*, which was a magazine for the Radio Shack computer, Steve countered. I had to admit, Steve had a point.

Mystically, we somehow still convinced Steve that the increase in people sending in the warranty card was worth $3 per subscription. By October 1983, we had the draft of an agreement that seemed acceptable to both sides.

So we set about creating *Macworld*. First, we commandeered the conference room at PC World Communications, covered the windows with butcher paper and installed a new lock in the door. This would be the Mac war room. Here, still secret pre-released Macintoshes would be reviewed and used to produce *Macworld* copy. Only Andrew Fluegelman, Dan Farber, and people working directly for them could enter this room.

Our magazine designer, Margery Spiegelman, is the daughter of a very brilliant physicist, and it seemed for some reason she just totally understood the Macintosh. At her suggestion, we designed *Macworld* to be an oversized magazine that was slightly wider than standard magazines. On one hand, the design incorporated graphic elements that reflected the icons and bit-mapped graphics of the Macintosh, and on the other hand we splashed color across the pages in a dramatic fashion to counterbalance the fact that the early Mac only came with a black-and-white monitor.

Almost as neatly as it came together, the Apple-*Macworld* agreement was falling apart. McGovern was delighted that Apple was willing to pay us 1.8 million dollars to deliver three issues of

Macworld to the first 600,000 buyers to mail in their warranty cards, but he didn't believe they could ship 600,000 machines. "Look at the Apple III," he said. "What makes you think Apple can ever do anything right?"

McGovern's solution was to demand that Apple agree to a guaranteed payment plan. They would pay X amount on such and such a date regardless of how many Macintoshes they had delivered. McGovern wanted to make sure he didn't waste any money on the Macintosh. He was pretty much convinced it would fail.

Compounding matters, an article in the *San Francisco Examiner* appeared, reporting that we were working on a magazine called *Macworld* and Apple expected to sell 600,000 Macintoshes the first year.

Steve suspected that I had tipped the reporter about the 600,000 figure. I hadn't, but perception is reality, and he was pissed. "If you ever want to work with us again, you need to explain to my colleagues why you preannounced the details of our plans to the stupid *San Francisco Examiner*," he said.

I wrote a letter to apologize for any misunderstandings. I printed out several copies of the letter, drove down to Cupertino to hand deliver them to Steve and Mike, and to anyone on the Macintosh team who cared to listen. I didn't know what else to do.

My letter led to another meeting between Steve and Mike, myself and Jim Riding, whom I had hired recently to be the executive vice president of PC World Communications. Jim, who is a fussy, old-boy *Time* magazine guy, was so out of his element at Apple that they found him very charming and likable.

Jim's style was to tell you very nicely exactly what was on his mind. "Listen, Steve," Jim said, "*Macworld* magazine is going to help you sell more Macintoshes, so let's work this thing out. We're on your side. David and I want you to help you. Andrew and his editors are at this very moment creating a great magazine."

Steve's strategy for this meeting was to beat us up until were so tattered and weak we would do anything. McGovern was the enemy and we were the pawns. He would browbeat us over to his side and then he would force McGovern to be more reasonable.

"What if Andrew or David dies," Steve said to Jim Riding, "if they die are you going to bring Wayne Green in to run *Macworld*?"

Steve wanted a death clause in the Apple *Macworld* contract. If Andrew or I died, he wanted the right to veto IDG's choice for a replacement. "If Andrew dies," he said, "who knows what kind of editor would replace him?"

This meeting marked a low point for the *Macworld* negotiations, but it wasn't as dangerous as the reality Andrew and I were beginning to uncover at the Mac development building.

The Macintosh project was in complete disarray. Due to the unavailability of 65K memory chips, and in order to meet the introduction deadline of January 24, 1984, the initial Macintosh could only have 128K of memory. Considering the demands of the operating system and the bit-mapped screen, this was not nearly enough memory to make the Macintosh functionality anywhere near competitive to the IBM PC.

After discussing the situation with me, Andrew wrote an open memo to the Macintosh development team, urging them to postpone the Macintosh announcement. This memo pointed out all the obvious shortcomings: the glaring lack of a hard drive, the amazing number of bugs in the operating software, the lack of application software. To my surprise, Andrew's memo was posted on bulletin board, throughout the Mac development building.

I was terrified that Steve would be pissed off about Andrew's memo and kick us out of the project, but he didn't. To their credit, Steve and his crew appreciated the thought that went into it. They expressed deep concern about the issues Andrew raised. In the end, though, they did nothing about them. They were determined to have their fun at the annual meeting, and nothing like a lame computer was going to get in their way.

The original Macintosh didn't have a hard drive or the facility to add one, because that would require a fan, and fans are noisy. Steve didn't like noisy fans. With noisy fans in your computer you can't sit at night in the dark, meditate, and then keyboard your great thoughts into the computer. Noisy fans spoil your concentration.

The original Macintosh didn't have slots so you could add memory or extra peripherals, because it was such a beautifully designed masterpiece that no one should want to alter it. Jobs claimed this would be a "great advantage" to software developers, because unlike the Neanderthal DOS machines, which were configured in thousands of individual, sometimes quirky ways, all Macintoshes would be the same. If you were a programmer, you would know what you were writing for.

My first major complaint about the Macintosh was based on my insight that the developers of the Macintosh had never worked in a real office. Just look at the ImageWriter and think about addressing an envelope. Unless you are a flaming masochist, it is impossible to address an envelope and print it out on an ImageWriter.

Because the Macintosh was so poorly designed for office use, people who used Macintoshes in the office had to keep their typewriters, so they could address envelopes.

Sensing our growing dispair, Steve and Michael asked us down to Cupertino to boost our spirits and to share some of their promotional plans.

We shouldn't worry about the under-powered initial model. Soon they would have the new memory chips, and customers could upgrade for free or at a nominal price. "People can't wait for the Macintosh," Steve claimed.

Post-pep-talk, as we were about to leave, Mike pulled us aside and said, "Hey, you want to see our first TV commercial for the Macintosh?"

There's no way I can describe all the mixed emotions I experienced while watching this so-called commercial. It was weirdly, outlandishly, bizarre. It was so balls-out, it gave me goose bumps. A chesty blond babe runs down the aisle of a movie theater populated by dusty looking zombies. She hurls a hammer into the screen and shatters it. This is followed by the message: "On January 24, 1984, Apple will introduce the Macintosh and you will see why 1984 won't be 1984."

"We're only going to show it twice," Mike said. "First we're going to run it early in the morning on a station in Montana so it will qualify for this year's advertising awards. Then we're going to show it for real during the halftime of the Super Bowl on January 20."

"No kidding," I said, "How much is this going to cost?"

"A million dollars for air time," Mike answered, "and we already spent a few hundred thousand to produce it. What do you think of it?"

"I think if you show this commercial you'll get a lot of attention. But I wonder if it will help you sell computers," I said.

"Apple doesn't have any future plans to work with IBM, does it?" Andrew quipped. We all laughed.

Around this time, it was becoming clear to me that there would indeed be a *Macworld* magazine. Andrew, Jim Riding, and I were totally committed to it, and Steve Jobs and Mike Murray were counting on us. Somehow, *Macworld* would become a reality.

Reconciling McGovern's demands for a payment schedule with Steve Jobs's paranoia about IDG seemed totally impossible. Andrew, Jim, and I met with Mike and his right-hand, Steve Schier, for lunch at the Whole Earth Restaurant in Cupertino. At this meeting, which took place sometime in November 1983, we decided that *Macworld* magazine would be published on January 24, 1984, regardless of whether or not our respective chairmen saw eye-to-eye and signed the contract.

Macworld magazine had ceased to be a business proposition. *Macworld* magazine had become a missionary quest. It would be published no matter what.

Articles were written. Illustrations were commissioned. Advertising was sold. With or without the contract, *Macworld* was approaching the day of reckoning, which was the day we sent film to the printer.

I called Steve Jobs to ask him if he would pose for the cover of the magazine. He said he would do it if I hired a really great photographer, and even then he could only give us a few minutes of his precious time.

So we hired Will Mosgrove and crossed our fingers. Will was top notch. His work had appeared in many notable publications.

Will carefully set up the shot. Three Macintoshes on a tabletop, each showing a different screen image. Steve would stand behind the table, his hands outstretched, leaning on the two outside machines.

A standing model was hired to take Steve's position until the lighting was just right.

Steve was called in only when everything was perfect. All we needed was to have Steve stand in position for five minutes, and then he could go. It was just as he requested.

Steve walked into the room. He didn't like the images on the three Macintosh monitors.

We worked feverishly to fix them.

Meanwhile, Steve glared at the photographer and said, "Are you one of those type of photographers who takes dozens of photos and hopes one turns out okay?"

"Take a picture of this," Steve said, holding up his middle finger. We stared at him in disbelief.

We got our Steve Jobs photograph and it is a classic, but if I wasn't a nimble thinker it would never have appeared. A couple weeks after the photo shoot Steve called me and said, "Gee, I've changed my mind, I don't want to be on the cover of *Macworld*."

"Too late, Steve," I lied, "the cover is already at the printer and we can't change it."

Our reality was that some pages were being shipped to the printer, yet we didn't have a signed agreement. *Macworld* was in danger of being stillborn. I called McGovern and said, "Listen, Pat, you've got to help me. Unless you come to Apple and settle on the terms of this agreement we are going to end up wasting all the money we invested in *Macworld* so far."

I had learned that the secret to working with McGovern was to tell him how much money we would lose if he didn't do the things I wanted him to do.

Luckily, Steve Jobs withdrew from the negotiation process. He was too busy arguing with Sculley over the introductory price of the Macintosh to be bothered with us. Steve turned his part over to Apple lawyer David Kopf. "If you can work it out with the lawyers, I'll sign the agreement," he said.

In the end, McGovern got his guaranteed payment schedule, only it added up to $600,000 instead of $1.8 million. Pat still figured the whole thing would flop, and at least the $600,000 would pay for the initial launch. We would break even, and David and Andrew would learn their lesson. We would go back to DOS and be good boys once again.

January 24, 1984, turned out to be a crisp, bright blue Northern California day—a good day to change the world of computing forever. I grew up dreading 1984. 1984 was supposed to herald in an era of digital oppression. Humankind forever enslaved, cruelly manipulated, and alienated by impersonal computers.

5,000 copies of the premiere issue of *Macworld* had been air freighted to Cupertino from our printer in Minnesota. Copies of *Macworld* were waiting at the doors to the auditorium at DeAnza College to be passed out to the devoted, right after the introduction. Steve didn't want us to pass them out before, because he feared people would be looking through the pages instead of paying attention to his presentation.

I felt like a proud father. *Macworld* was gorgeous.

What a triumph! Created in the conference room that had become our secret lab, its 148 pages included reviews of Multiplan, MacPaint, MacWrite, and the ImageWriter. We had an indepth interview with Bill Gates where he claimed that the Mac's paltry 128K memory was more than adequate for any personal computer. There were articles about how the Macintosh was pioneered, and there were interviews from key members of the Macintosh development team. "Hardware Wizard" Burrell Smith explained how he came from a "lowly background as a service technician" to being promoted to a very top technical position. MacPaint author Bill Atkinson said his "central job has been to make sure that the Lisa and the Macintosh are compatible," while Steve Jobs explained that to his employees, the Macintosh "is more important than their personal lives."

At the Mac intro there was a sign-up table in the parking lot. I walked up to it and said, "Hi, I'm David Bunnell from *Macworld.*"

"We know who you are," responded the healthy, well-groomed young woman behind the table. Apple PR flack. I bet she knows every editor by sight.

It was a huge thrill to just be at the Mac product introduction. Officially, this was Apple's annual stockholders meeting. In reality, it was a high-tech religious revival for those hip computer freaks who had been knocked out of orbit by the IBM PC, and who had prayed for a major Apple comeback. It was Woodstock for nerds. Big Blue was identified too much with the forces of evil. Don't trust them. They'll network everyone and seize back the power.

Wayne Green, the balding wizard of ham radio who had unknowingly rankled Steve Jobs, was standing bowlegged with a cup of tea. He had two Radio Shack laptop computers, one slung from each shoulder. Wayne was chatting with Maggie Cannon, the brilliant, vivacious editor of *A+.* The irony was that if it wasn't for *A+,* there wouldn't have been a *Macworld.* I couldn't help but chuckle, thinking of *A+* as a magazine for users of Apple's faltering Apple II. Has-beens. I felt smug. It was definitely my turn in the sun.

"Hi, Wayne, I haven't seen you in a long time. You still publishing that laptop magazine?" I asked.

Wayne smiled at me all too knowingly and replied, "Yeah, there's a big future in laptops."

"How come you got two computers, Wayne?"

"Well, each of these babies holds 32K of ram, so I carry two of them. When one runs out of memory I go to the backup."

"Think they'll ever have laptops with floppies?" I asked.

"Sure, laptops are really the wave of the future. I hear this machine of Steve's is a real loser."

"Be nice, Wayne," I warned. "The computer world needs Apple. Otherwise, we'll be stuck with DOS for all eternity."

I detected a flash of anger in Wayne's eyes. He said, "Why should I be nice? Steve Jobs has never been nice to anyone. Why should I be nice to him?"

Peripherally, I could see the other Steve—Steve Wozniak, nerd co-founder of Apple, creator of the first floppy disk drive for personal computers—standing on the edge of the sidewalk. Head down, he was mumbling something to John Sculley.

Woz, as everyone who was anyone in computerdom called him, was kicking up pieces of dirt with his scruffy slip-on shoes. From his body language I could see that he felt unappreciated. As it turned out, Apple division employees, with the exception of Woz, had been shut out of the hall, while front and center seats were reserved for Macintosh division employees.

Even though the highly profitable Apple II had afforded Steve Jobs the opportunity to lavishly tend to the needs and whims of his Mac team—had fueled the incredible growth of Apple—had made both him and Woz at tender age very rich and even more famous—Jobs thumbed his nose at it.

Sculley was the reluctant diplomat. He knew that Apple needed Woz, and he tried to soothe the wounds. Sculley was trying to cure cancer with a Band-Aid.

Moving inside the theater-style auditorium I could hear loudspeakers blaring out rock music—the lyrics, "It's so exciting," years later still ring in my consciousness. Several thousand people milling about, waiting for the great event. Propeller heads in blue jeans mixing it up with stockholders in suits. On the stage you could see a small table upon which an object about the size of a watermelon turned on its end was draped with a black cloth. It was the Mac—ready (my fingers were crossed) for its first public unveiling.

You have to marvel at the sheer chutzpah that went into the planning of this day. The PR and advertising buildup had been tremendous. Hundreds of reporters, dozens of TV cameras, thousands of devoted employees and fanatical followers anxiously awaiting for the world's fifth largest computer company to unveil a new product. They called it "event marketing," and Apple Computer, with chairman Jobs in the cockpit, was the all-time master of this technique.

I got the sense that if Steve had any real talent he would have much preferred to be a rock star to a computer entrepreneur. So once fate put him into a position where he could do whatever he wanted, he tried to turn Apple into a rock-and-roll computer company. He saw himself as John Lennon. Sculley was Brian Epstein —the head bean counter. And Woz was the kind-hearted but lesser-talented Paul McCartney.

Steve was the one. Everyone else played backed up. Steve had allowed Woz to sing a few songs, but deep down he found them too sentimental—they were interesting, but not revolutionary.

The music stopped. The auditorium lights were dimmed and the announcer said, "Ladies and gentlemen, the chairman of Apple Computer, Steven P. Jobs."

Beaming, the glitter in his eyes visible throughout the hall, Steve briskly bounded across the stage to the podium. His jet black hair hung over his forehead. His hawk-like chin thrust forward; he smiled his evil genius smile.

Steve was in his bow tie phase. He wore double-breasted suits and bow ties. This made him look like a young Howard Hughes. He strutted around the stage a lot like I imagined a young Howard Hughes would do. He bounced. He nearly skipped. He acted a little crazy. This was his moment of triumph. Today, Steve Jobs could rub dirt in the faces of his enemies and they would like it.

All he had to say was "Hello, I'm Steve Jobs," and the crowd went bananas.

Steve didn't waste any time. He hopped over to the object under the black cloth; with a deft movement he unveiled it. "Ohhhhh," they moaned. He turned the Macintosh on and the little smiley Mac icon was projected onto a gigantic screen behind his head. The cute little computer-that-could mimicked its master. It said,

```
"Hello, I'm Macintosh."
```

The audience at a live performance never sees all the chaos that can goes on behind the stage. They don't necessarily know that everything is held together with rubberbands; all they see is the show itself. Apple technicians had been up all night kludging together the demo that was to follow. This day, the Macintosh was to perform feats never seen before. It was going to wow the chip heads and completely snow the journalists. It was going to do amazing things NOW, which in fact it couldn't actually do for another four or five years, if ever, but who's counting?

The Macintosh sang to us. It performed mathematical calculations with the blinding speed of a desktop Cray. It drew beautiful pictures. It communicated with a mainframe and with other Macintoshes. It bounced rays off satellites and it sent subversive messages to the Soviet Union. At this moment, the Mac seemed capable of doing anything Steve willed it to do. At the same time, is was apparently easy as pie to use, and as friendly as your kindergarten teacher. It was the first teddy bear computer.

The press gobbled this all up, and for awhile it seemed that Steve and his crew had pulled it off, in spite of Andrew Fluegelman's warning. People lined up at computer stores across the nation to look at the Macintosh. The 1984 commercial was so jarring to the Super Bowl audience that it was replayed on CBS Evening News.

Once the hoopla receded, first the computer press and then the business press began to zero in on the Macintosh's obvious shortcomings. Under-powered and inflexible, but really cute, the Macintosh was called a "yuppie machine." People complained about the lack of software. At the Mac introduction, Mitch Kapor from Lotus, Fred Gibbons from Software Publishing, and Bill Gates from Microsoft had all stood on the stage with Steve Jobs and proclaimed they would support the Macintosh with application software. Of the three, only Gates came through.

The first issue of *Macworld* sold out on the newsstands and by the fourth issue we were profitable. Profitable but plenty worried. After an initial surge, sales of the Macintosh were dropping. Even when the 512K "fat" Mac came out a few months later the market was very shaky. People wanted a hard disk. They wanted slots. And they wanted solid, productivity software. In spite Steve Job's better judgment, customers wanted a real computer.

Surveys we took at the time showed that 90 percent of Macintosh owners read *Macworld* before they bought their machine. Furthermore, the owners of the Macintosh were not new to computing. "The computer for the rest of us" was selling to people who already had two or three computers. Early Macintosh owners, like the early owners of other computers, were early adopters. They were technologists who simply had to have latest, hippest new machine.

Macworld was able to capture a much larger percentage of Macintosh owners than we had imagined, and this helped make up for the lack of shipments. The magazine was wildly successful. The computer was not.

Because so many Macintosh owners and potential buyers read *Macworld* it was a very effective way for third-party developers to sell their products. One ad virtually reached the whole market. This fact helped developers achieve enough success to keep the market going.

John Sculley told me later that Steve had worked his Macintosh development team so hard for so long that as soon as the introduction was over they became totally lethargic. "A whole year was wasted," he said. The necessary improvements required to make the Macintosh sing were put on hold. Steve Jobs was asleep at the wheel.

Years later, I can look back on this with a great deal of amusement and satisfaction. I have launched four more magazines since *Macworld* but none of them have captured the magic that that magazine seemed to have from Day One. And I'm very proud to say that much of the magic is still there in the pages of what has to be the best computer magazine of all time.

I'm satisfied, but very aware that we were lucky to have pulled it off, and lucky that Apple survived. Apple was lucky that Jobs self-destructed, so they could fix the Macintosh before the company went belly-up. They made the Macintosh into the machine it should have been in the first place.

I went down the San Francisco Peninsula to see Steve Jobs when he was starting his NeXT Computer company. He had traded in his Mercedes for a black Porsche convertible. Along with Dan'l Lewin, Steve drove me to the Stanford campus to have lunch in the student cafeteria. Upon arriving at the campus, Steve couldn't find a parking space. He complained about the number of parking spaces for handicapped people, which always seem to be empty, but he didn't park in one of them. I guess he'd grown up a little.

About this time, Steve was considering running for the U.S. Senate. The fact that he hadn't bothered to vote for his entire life didn't deter him from entertaining the fantasy that he was just so popular he could overcome anything.

During lunch, Steve told me he had sold all his Apple stock except one share, so he could continue to get stockholder reports. "Apple will fail," he said.

Steve also told me that NeXT would deliver at least 40,000 machines the first year, because there were at least that many people who would buy any computer he made, regardless. He didn't seem concerned that the NeXT Computer had no floppy drive, or that its UNIX operating system was totally incompatible with all other UNIX-based computers. The black cube was totally radical and that was enough.

It was then that I knew for certain Steve Jobs dwells on some other planet. The Macintosh startup was an elaborate make-believe mind trip. It generated a mythology that will be foolishly held up for years as an example of how to do great things.

All I can say is God help those who follow the Macintosh way.

"HELLO. I AM MACINTOSH."

DOUG CLAPP

O*nce again, it's January 24, 1984. You've read David Bunnell's memories of the Macintosh introduction.*

Here's how I remember it.

On January 24, 1984, Macintosh was officially introduced during Apple's annual stockholders meeting. The setting was Cupertino's Flint Center auditorium, just a few blocks from Apple.

Steve Jobs began the show with lyrics from Bob Dylan's "The Times They Are A-Changin':"

Come writers and critics who prophesize with your pens

And keep your eyes wide, the chance won't come again.

And don't speak too soon for the wheel's still in spin

And there's no telling who that it's naming.

For the loser now will be later to win for the times they are a-changin.

Al Eisenstat then took care of official business. John Sculley then made brief remarks. The stage darkened, and Steve Jobs returned to begin the dramatic unveiling of Macintosh.

"It is 1958," he began. "IBM passes up the chance to buy a young, fledgling company that has just invented a new technology called xerography. Two years later, Xerox is born, and IBM has been kicking itself ever since.

"It is ten years later: the late sixties. Digital Equipment Corporation and others invent the minicomputer. IBM dismisses the minicomputer as too small to do serious computing and, therefore, unimportant to its business. DEC grows to become a multi-hundred-million-dollar corporation before IBM finally enters the minicomputer market.

"It is now ten years later: the late seventies. In 1977, Apple, a young fledgling company on the West Coast"—Steve and the crowd are both enjoying it now—"invents the Apple II, the first personal computer as we know it today. IBM dismisses the personal computer as too small to do serious computer and therefore unimportant to its business.

"The early 1980s...1981. The Apple II has become the world's most popular computer and Apple has grown to a $300-million-dollar corporation, becoming the fastest-growing company in American business history. With over fifty companies vying for a share, IBM enters the personal computer market in November of 1981 with the IBM PC.

"1983. Apple and IBM emerge as the industry's strongest competitors, each selling approximately $1 billion worth of personal computers in 1983.

"The shakeout is now in full swing. The first major firm goes bankrupt, with others teetering on the brink. Total industry losses for 1983 overshadow even the combined profits of Apple and IBM for personal computers."

Jobs pauses, then continues. The air is electric with anticipation.

"It is now 1984. It appears that *IBM wants it all.* Apple is perceived to be the only hope to offer IBM a run for its money. Dealers, initially welcoming IBM with open arms, now fear an

IBM-dominated and -controlled future. They are increasingly turning back to Apple, the only force that can ensure their future freedom."

Scattered cheers come from the audience. Jobs is up there, crowd in hand, living and loving one of the great moments of his young life. He ratchets it up now, voice close to a yell, feeding on the crowd's enthusiasm, laying it on.

"IBM wants it all and is aiming its guns on its last obstacle to industry control: Apple. Will Big Blue dominate the entire computer industry? The entire information age?"

Now he yells.

"*Was George Orwell right?*"

And, as the crowd roars back with a wash of gleeful "No's!," the "1984" commercial, thunderously loud, blazes on a huge screen behind Jobs.

The commercial ends and Jobs speaks about the Macintosh, how the Mac is Lisa technology made affordable; the power of the 68000; the innovative 3.5 inch disk drive.

The theme from *Chariots of Fire* fills the hall.

"Today," Jobs says, unzipping a carrying case and lifting out a Mac, "for the first time ever, I'd like to let Macintosh speak for itself."

And in the cutest computery voice you've ever heard, from the Macintosh comes:

"Hello. I am Macintosh. It sure is great to get out of that bag. Unaccustomed as I am to public speaking, I'd like to share with you a thought that occurred to me the first time I met an IBM mainframe: never trust a computer you can't lift."

The crowd loves it. More whoops are heard.

"Obviously I can talk. But right now I'd like to sit back and listen. So it is with considerable pride that I introduce a man who has been like a father to me: Steve Jobs."

The crowd roars. Macintosh is a product.

In the first hundred days of its availability, Apple would sell 72,000 Macintoshes.

— Doug Clapp

"A VIBRATOR FOR YOUR MIND"

A REVEALING INTERVIEW WITH PROGRAMMERS
BRUCE HORN AND STEVE CAPPS

W*hen Macintosh was released, Regis McKenna, Apple's PR agency, kept tight control of media interviews. The result was a series of carefully coached perfomances by Apple employees.*

This interview finds Bruce Horn and Steve Capps a few weeks after the release of Macintosh, unaccompanied by a censorious "Regette." The result is uncensored great fun, circa 1984.

Ya gotta love these guys ...

Bruce Horn and Steve Capps are programmer's programmers. Together they authored the Macintosh System and Finder, putting in grueling workweeks of ninety hours and more. Their creations are large, complex programs that give Macintosh and Lisa their distinctive, icon-oriented personalities. System governs the appearance of windows, menus, and everything else on the Mac screen, and the Finder serves as a visual way to manage documents and tools.

Mac wouldn't be Mac without the software achievements and innovations of Horn and Capps. Both recently met with writer Doug Clapp for a no-holds-barred interview that covered topics ranging from Mac's design to the experience of being a programmer in the environment that is uniquely Apple Inc. The result was a freewheeling, opinionated, and completely candid conversation.

Media Attention and Taking Credit

DSC: What do you guys think of all the media attention?

Steve Capps: It's fun. There's inequities in it, and sometimes it bothers you and other times it doesn't.

DSC: A lot of Macintosh articles have appeared recently. Were the articles accurate, or did they miss the point of Macintosh?

Steve Capps: Fifty-fifty.

Bruce Horn: I've noticed that Microsoft's taken a lot more credit than they deserve. They're trying to take credit for a couple new designs … in the file system they did have one little idea, but they're trying to take credit for helping to design the Memory Manager and the Finder and all this stuff, and they did none of the above.

Steve Capps: They helped with it. Neil Konzen especially.

Bruce Horn: Neil only, pretty much. He was the only person. But Microsoft didn't have nearly that much to do with the software design.

Steve Capps: It was [Bill] Gates taking credit for Neil's work.

Bruce Horn: And taking credit for our work, too. And that's completely wrong.

User Interface:
"You don't get any manuals with video games."

DSC: A phrase that's omnipresent when discussing Macintosh is user interface. How do you two define user interface?

Bruce Horn: Well, everybody's an expert on "user interface."

Steve Capps: Including us.

Bruce Horn: I think it's just the way that the system is presented, and the way that all the options are presented to the user. You can either type a command to a keyboard, or you can point to a command, or …

Steve Capps: The best quote I've heard about it is "You don't get any manuals with video games." I don't know who said it, but you can certainly walk up to a video game and, three or four quarters later, you've figured it out.

Bruce Horn: That's a definition of a good user interface.

Steve Capps: So that's the idea: How can we make a computer like that? And the neat thing about that is, it could be fun to learn, too!

Bruce Horn: The other way is … how do you encapsulate the complexity of something that's easy and, as you get better and better, "unfolds" instead of presenting you with all the complexity at once?

Steve Capps: To further what Bruce said, that's what they did with Lisa: they designed it for the imbecile. So when you suddenly discover that you do have a brain, you're stuck with this thing that, every two minutes, tells you "Well … I'm about to print. Is that okay?" One thing that would be interesting is a system that once you got a little bit better, would tailor itself to you, that would unfold.

DSC: Like an "expert mode"?

Steve Capps: Well, it wouldn't be a "mode."

Bruce Horn: Levels. Expert levels.

DSC: How do you explain Macintosh to people who don't know anything about computers?

Bruce Horn: You basically say that Macintosh is a computer that you don't have to be a computer whiz to learn how to use, and it's ten times better than an IBM PC at about the same price. And it's going to be one of the next neat things that happen.

Steve Capps: How about this: "A vibrator for the mind"?

DSC: I like that.

Bruce Horn: He's really on to something. But make sure that he said that, not me!

ROM, Def Procs, and Patches

DSC: How about a quick breakdown of what's in ROM, and what the System and Finder are?

Bruce Horn: Okay. What's in ROM? Basically, the whole user interface code: windows, menus, dialog boxes, and things. That's all in ROM. The file system's in ROM, Memory Manager, TextEdit, lots of things.

Steve Capps: But none of the "looks"—none of the ways that things look. The way menus *work* is in ROM, but not the way they look.

Bruce Horn: They way they look is in "definition procedures" that are loaded from the resource file in the system. There's also a thing called System, that has all the fonts and all the definition procedures for windows …

Steve Capps: ROM patches …

Bruce Horn: And ROM patches.

Steve Capps: But we won't talk about those.

Bruce Horn: Right.

DSC: Then what's the Finder?

Bruce Horn: The Finder's this application that "sits on top" and lets you do operating system-like things: copy disks …

DSC: It's the visual shell you see on the screen.

Bruce Horn: That's right.

DSC: The System's about 145-146K?

Bruce Horn: Mostly fonts.

DSC: How do you break that down percentage-wise?

Steve Capps: Three-quarters fonts, maybe a tenth desk accessories.

Bruce Horn: More than that! The Control Panel's 10K!

Steve Capps: Okay, maybe a quarter desk accessories. Then there's def procs.

DSC: What's a "def proc"?

Steve Capps: Those are the things that implement the scroll bars, the buttons, menus, windows, controls … Those are probably another eighth of the size, there. And then there's miscellany. It adds up to seven-eighths.

DSC: So most of it's fonts, some of it is desk accessories, and the rest is def procs?

Steve Capps: That's the order of bigness, yeah.

DSC: And the Finder is about 45K. What's that made up of?

Bruce Horn: It's hard to say.

Steve Capps: About 36K code, and the rest menus and things. There's 3K of text in the Finder.

Bruce Horn: And there's another maybe 1K of text for dialog boxes. All the dialogs and menus are in the resource part of the Finder. Actually, the whole Finder is in the resource part of the Finder!

Steve Capps: There are messages in there that you will probably never see.

DSC: How many messages?

Bruce Horn: Over a hundred.

DSC: What's a really bizarre message?

Steve Capps: My favorite dialog—which I could never put into English, so we left it in Yiddish—is this: Say you've got a folder named "Fred," and its window is open. Now, say you drag a file named "Fred" into that folder. And they're on different disks. Now, obviously, you replaced the thing named "Fred," because that's where you're putting it! Now tell me, in one sentence, what's about to occur? That you can't do that.

DSC: "Name conflict"?

Bruce Horn: No, it's different than a name conflict.

Bruce Horn: I think Steve's first one was "File folder not okay."

Steve Capps: No, I think it was "Destination folder conflicts with source." Yuck!

Bruce Horn: No one will probably ever see that one.

DSC: The System and Finder are entirely on disk?

Bruce Horn: Yeah. The only thing that's not on disk is the ROM. And the Mac is on the table, and …

DSC: The operating system then, in Macish terms, is only doing the hardware stuff: mediating with the disks …

Bruce Horn: That's right. That's the file system: opening and closing files. That's the operating system.

Steve Capps: That's like, say, one-fourth of the ROM. What most people put in ROM is a little piece of their operating system, and usually they get the rest of their operating system off disk. We put the whole thing into ROM, and four times more.

DSC: How much of the System and Finder are moved into RAM when you turn on the machine?

Bruce Horn: All of the Finder. Well … no. Lots of the resources in the Finder are on disk until you need them. The dialog boxes for certain things don't come in until you need them. Those are purgeable. There are some purgeable things, but most of them aren't. So, yeah, about 45K goes into RAM. But when you do a disk copy, Steve purges [deletes from memory] parts of the Finder that aren't used, so you have more buffer space.

Steve Capps: But for a running program to come in, there's X amount of overhead. So, when the program's running, there's maybe 50K of the heap used. Probably more than that, because fonts take up a lot of room. So the working set of memory, less the Finder, is maybe 70K.

DSC: Would it be preferable to have all the System and the Finder in ROM?

Steve Capps: No, because then you couldn't fix the bugs!

Bruce Horn: Yeah, you couldn't change it. It would be preferable to have more memory. Then you could leave part of the Finder.

Then if you were, say, changing applications, the Finder could sit in this little part of memory, then—boom—come right out. That would be nice, but we don't have enough memory. Maybe on the Big Mac.

Steve Capps: It's just too high-level to put into ROM. Because, a year from now, we might not think it's that great. We might want to make it different.

Bruce Horn: That's why disks are so neat: You can give somebody a new disk, then their Mac will actually be different. It'll be better.

Steve Capps: But someday that's going to happen. Somebody's going to write the ultimate word processor, the ultimate drawing program, the ultimate Finder, then stick 'em all into ROM.

The "Twenty-Questions Finder"

DSC: What's the history of the Finder?

Bruce Horn: Well, when I came to Mac, they were experimenting with things like a big picture of a disk on-screen, with little file-names on it. But Tribble invented the term Finder, because the Lisa thing was a "Filer." And Bill Atkinson basically convinced everybody, a few months before I came, that the "pictureFinder," which showed a large disk on-screen, wasn't the way to go. The original Lisa Filer was a standard filer, with lots of dialog boxes and text and things you type.

Steve Capps: In the vernacular, it was the "twenty-questions Finder."

Bruce Horn: No, the "thousand words Filer." So I came in and just started playing around with "classes," and I built a Finder mock-up using little pictures that you could open up and see inside.

Xeroxizing

DSC: Is it fair to say that you "Xeroxized" it?

Bruce Horn: Yeah, pretty much. There were some new ideas.

Steve Capps: That's with a capital "X."

Bruce Horn: Right. "Xerox is a trademark of Xerox Corporation."

DSC: So the Finder as we see it today had its genesis in you, and you had your genesis for those ideas at Xerox?

Bruce Horn: That's basically it. But not the stuff I did at Xerox; the stuff I *saw* at Xerox. Anyway, after I did the Finder I showed it to Bill Atkinson, and he went off with some people and changed the Lisa Finder. Is that about right, Steve?

Steve Capps: Yeah. We were getting close to shipping Lisa. It was the spring of '82 and it was, like, "You better not make any more changes." But they didn't like the twenty-questions Finder.

Bruce Horn: They especially didn't like it once they saw ours. But I didn't Xeroxize any of the original Finder stuff. I actually hadn't even seen the Lisa Finder, and I had only seen one or two of the previous attempts at Mac. I really started from what I thought was right, and what I thought Xerox had done that was right. So I really didn't "take anything else;" I really started from scratch.

DSC: A lot of it had to do with your Smalltalk background?

Bruce Horn: Some of it. Some of it had to do with the [Xerox] Star, and Starware.

Alto and the Star

Steve Capps: The Star is a very similar thing.

DSC: How do you compare the Xerox Alto and the Star to the Mac?

Bruce Horn: The Alto was just a development machine that people used. It did everything; it wasn't specialized for one purpose. It didn't use the mouse like the Star did. The Star is the one that the Mac's more like, because it was more visual.

Steve Capps: The Alto was like your first girl friend.

Bruce Horn: Yeah, the first girl friend that would do anything with you. You could go to the beach …

Steve Capps: And it was terribly slow. There were a lot of things wrong with it, but it was just so neat at the time that it didn't matter.

Bruce Horn: Well, that was 1972. And it wasn't that slow, and you could run the world's best word processor on it, which was Bravo, and you could use different fonts and things. And not much later, the Ethernet [a networking system] was up and people could use that!

"We didn't plan any of it, hardly."

DSC: We'll get back to that later, but I want to ask: How do you go about planning a project as vast as the System and Finder?

Bruce Horn: We didn't plan any of it, hardly. You just do a little bit of thinking ahead and decide what you want it to do. The Finder was somewhat planned.

Steve Capps: That's about the biggest chunk that would ever get planned at Apple. That's not Apple's style, to sit back and plan something like that. Now at Xerox, people will do throwaway systems for a year, then, three or four years later, they'll get it out. But Apple just doesn't have that … patience. It's a wholly different style. One could argue either way: Apple will get out the stuff that makes them rich, while Xerox will get out the stuff that's consistent, but may not be the best.

Bruce Horn: Also, I would say that Xerox will get things out that will be extensible, while Apple might make some shortsighted things and say, "Oh, well, we'll fix that later, but we'll get the thing out now."

Steve Capps: Yes, but that's being too negative. I think both ways are viable.

DSC: At school, they teach you to plan the problem, then plan the inputs, and the outputs, then …

Steve Capps: And those people are cranking COBOL for Blue Cross right now.

Software by Eight

DSC: It's amazing that a company of Apple's size, with almost a billion dollars a year in gross revenues, would put only eight people on the Macintosh software team. Were you understaffed, considering the amount of software that had to be written?

Steve Capps: That depends. If you want to ship and have every program done, and not be up the night before, then there were too few people. If you want to work your behind off, and have loads of fun, it was just fine.

Bruce Horn: That's true. But I also think it would have been nice if we'd had somewhat better tools. Our tools were kind of Dark Ages tools. Capps went and made our tools more useable, but it would have been nice if we had gotten tools from the Lisa group.

DSC: Like what?

Steve Capps: Nice debuggers, for one thing. When I was in Norway, I wrote a debugger that showed you all the registers on-screen all the time. You could say, "Step-step-step," and watch the register changes.

DSC: What a great learning tool.

Bruce Horn: Absolutely.

Steve Capps: What you really want—I was thinking about this last night—is for Instant Pascal [released as Macintosh Pascal] to run Assembler and to make your "Instant Assembler" your debugger.

Bruce Horn: That's just saying, "Write the language and let it debug itself," which is Smalltalk.

DSC: But you're saying that there were and there weren't too few people?

Bruce Horn: Right. But actually I liked it. I like working with a very small group. I like working with Steve, because it's just the two of us. When you get more people involved with something, you start having to communicate too many things.

Steve Capps: It also depends on the people. If you can get people that are self-motivated, you can have an infinite number of them, you don't care. But if you get people that need dependencies, it just starts taking more and more of your time.

DSC: How long did it take to write the Finder?

Bruce Horn: I guess it took about nine person-months.

Steve Capps: Longer than that.

DSC: How many hours a week?

Bruce Horn: Unknown.

Resources

DSC: Let's get the definitive definition of the Resource Manger.

Bruce Horn: Okay, the Resource Manager is a set of routines that let you load and write out objects that have types, and IDs, and, possibly, names. These objects are loaded in dynamically when you need them, by calling the routine. The Memory Manager works with the Resource Manager by purging them out. And that's basically all it does.

DSC: Like overlays?

Steve Capps: It does overlay-like things. The Segment Loader is written to use the Resource Manager, and the Segment Loader does the overlay stuff. But what the Resource Manager does is let you do the same thing with anything you like, not just code segments. But also, it's an interface to the inside of your file, from the outside. It tells people who want to look at it what's in it. So let's say you have a document, and you want to put a picture in it. You put the picture in the resource part of the document, and anyone else can look at that picture and change it. The idea of having applications use resources is that people from the outside can reach in and change all the text, or all the pictures, or completely change the language, without having to redo the entire program.

DSC: And nobody's ever done this before.

Bruce Horn: Well, there are things like Pascal code libraries, but …

Steve Capps: Nobody's ever done it throughout the entire system.

DSC: It's really a programming achievement.

Steve Capps: Really. For instance, there's a list of things in the Finder resource file that gives what should be brought into RAM when you swap disks. Because of the setup, you can sit outside the program and drastically tune up the performance of that program. You could have done this before, in the old days, by having a special file that had these tuning parameters in it, but nobody would ever do that, because it wouldn't be worth the effort. I mean you wouldn't say, "Well, I'll have this special file that will do the tuning parameters, and I'll have this special file that says how to do the fonts, and I'll have this special file for this, and so on." Nobody would ever do that.

What this does, because it becomes a way of life, once you get over the hump of learning it, is make it so you don't ever go: Writeln (Hello, Doug). You go: GetString, then Writeln (String). It's a little different programming than what people are brought up on, but once you overcome that hump, you've got it made.

DSC: How difficult is it going to be for third-party developers to learn all this stuff?

Bruce Horn: It's going to be difficult for some. People that are reasonably smart will pick it up fast.

Steve Capps: Also, we've got to get real good sample programs out there. That's the best way to learn.

DSC: Are there any features you wanted to add, but didn't have time for?

Bruce Horn: It would have been nice to have had a little more time to look at it. There were some things we wanted to speed up—and we're going to work on that stuff.

Steve Capps: In general, anytime you write software you want to throw it all out and write it again. That's a rule of thumb.

Bruce Horn: We did a pretty good job on the Finder. There are some pretty good concepts.

DSC: Will we ever see more entries on the Menu Bar?

Bruce Horn: No.

Steve Capps: There might be a few more entries on the Special menu; that's it. In fact, we might get rid of "Put Back." Put Back is kind of useless. Put Back doesn't make any sense, except on a multiprocessing system. Then you want to put back something, but you need to know what process owns it.

Life in 128K

DSC: How much of a constraint is the 128K limit?

Bruce Horn: It's pretty tight. In our disk-copy stuff it seems to be a problem, because you have to have a certain amount of system stuff around if you want to be in the Finder and do a disk copy, and maintain the visuals. That's what hurts us a little bit.

DSC: So the memory limit is the wall you keep running up against?

Steve Capps: It's hard to say. We've seen Lotus's 1-2-3, and it won't run on a small machine very well. But it's also a huge, huge program that does a ton of stuff. One of the first things I did at Xerox was work on a collection of separate programs that all talked the same language. And we said, "That's not so great." So the next thing we did was write this huge program, and that required you to run it on a machine that had super memory and super disk-swapping—it was a big mainframe. And that didn't turn out to be good. So one might argue that you could have 1-2-3 be separate programs, and, if you had a quick way of jumping between them, you might get away with it on a small machine.

Bruce Horn: It depends on whether you want to do it [jumping between] explicitly or nonexplicitly. Whether you want the program to decide when to swap or whether you want to decide when to swap. Microsoft does that [allows you to decide].

Steve Capps: Right. And I think you can tune the System so you'll get an amazing amount of function out of that small memory. It just requires a little more work—you can't be sloppy.

DSC: Perception is reality. It doesn't matter what the System's really doing, or how much memory it's using, only how the user perceives it.

Bruce Horn: Yeah—only whether you get what you want.

Steve Capps: It's like the way people surprise you daily with the Apple II. They're going to do that with the Mac.

Bruce Horn: Even more.

Programming the 68000: "I'm just not very anal."

DSC: Is the 68000 an easy processor to program on?

Steve Capps: It'd be easier if it had a completely orthogonal [regular] addressing scheme.

DSC: But it's more orthogonal than most processors.

Bruce Horn: Absolutely. It's incredibly good compared to a lot of processors. I used the 8086 for a while, and it had special registers for everything! The 68000 is lots, lots better.

DSC: What were the hardest parts to program?

(Long pause)

Steve Capps: With the Finder, the problem for me was that I'm just not very anal. And I can't do the things where you have to pay attention to a thousand details. I can pay attention to a thousand details as long as they're romantic details.

Bruce Horn: He's specifically talking about disk copy.

Steve Capps: Disk copy I'm not good at.

DSC: It's harder to do things that aren't inherently interesting.

Steve Capps: Well, the scrap [the Scrap Manager] was just as compulsive, and it was probably equally as hard as doing the disk copy stuff, but it was more fun. The neat thing about the ROM is that you're always trying to crunch code, which is fun.

DSC: Crunch code?

Bruce Horn: Making it as small as possible with the most utility. But I'd rather that we used compulsive than anal.

Steve Capps: Larry [Kenyon, author of the Macintosh operating system] is very compulsive. He'd have to be that kind of person to do what he's doing.

Bruce Horn: That's right. We need that, but [what Larry's doing] doesn't require a lot of creativity. Sometimes it does, but …

DSC: It's nuts and bolts stuff.

Bruce Horn: Definitely. You know what you need, you know what you have to hold up, the airplane wing has to be this strong …

Aiming for Saturn

Steve Capps: Well, Bruce, what was your hardest thing?

Bruce Horn: Not programming at all. The hardest thing has been, all along, convincing people that we need something. It was resources at one point, resource grouping at another point. It's been things all along—trying to convince people what's right, what'll make things sensible. Programming was much less difficult than that.

DSC: So the politics were harder than the programming.

Bruce Horn: What I ended up doing was convincing Steve [Capps], and then the two of us would go and talk to people. I used his support for that; it was really useful.

Steve Capps: I want to correct one thing. Politics is such a pregnant term. It's not politics in the usual, backbiting sense; it's more that there's an ingrown conservatism in everybody that says, well, if you've thought something through, then it must be right. Otherwise you wouldn't have come to the conclusion you came to. So, if somebody comes up to you with an idea that's a light year, or at least a half a furlong, better, there's a natural tendency not to think it through right away. And the person that comes in with the idea, of course, has thought it out, so he's way ahead of you. It's just a normal thing. And Bruce really thinks ahead. More so than other people, he's just way out there in space, telling you about something that he understands perfectly. He's too impatient to let us catch up to him. Also, other people have just shot off to Saturn, and they don't want to switch courses.

> "Any sufficiently advanced technology is indistinguishable from magic."
>
> —Arthur C. Clarke, author
>
> "Any sufficiently advanced technology is indistinguishable from a rigged demo."
>
> —Anonymous

Bruce Horn: What they did was this: They had the rocket already built, and the rocket could only make it to the moon, and that's all they thought they really wanted to do. And it wasn't a sensible rocket. And what I was trying to do was to say, "Hey, if you put these little attachments on the end, then you can put another booster on and really get to Saturn." Sometimes they've thought it out and sometimes they haven't. It takes a different way of thinking, rather than saying "Hey, we've got this, why don't we just add something to it?"

DSC: It's easy to be complacent.

Bruce Horn: It's easier to live with what you've got than to try something new.

Bugs and Speed

DSC: Will there be a second software release, and if so, how will it be different?

Bruce Horn: Yes.

Steve Capps: There'll be a couple of releases. One right away, just to fix the embarrassing bugs that we're surprised more people haven't discovered.

Bruce Horn: We have a few bugs to fix; we'd like to speed up some things and finish some things that we thought were finished but weren't. Also, we'd like to make another release to support hard disks, when they come out.

"Are you going to scroll through 500 files?"

DSC: Will the Macintosh support more than two disks? Will it support a hard disk?

Steve Capps: Yes. The operating system will (pause) well … you know the standard file listing in the Finder? Think if you had a hard disk with 500 files. Are you going to scroll through 500 files?

DSC: So you could do it now, but it'd be painful.

Steve Capps: Yeah, but something has to be done.

Bruce Horn: Right. Also, the Finder is optimized for the ejectable disk, so we made some decisions about how that should be done that aren't appropriate for hard disks. Some of that stuff will change.

DSC: But, given a controller card, you could do it right now. It just wouldn't be easy to use.

Bruce Horn: Sure. Larry's operating system is completely geared for anything like that.

Steve Capps: There's a concept built into the ROM of completely external file systems. So while our file system is optimized for these small disks, you can have a whole 'nother way of storing it out on a hard disk.

DSC: A different driver.

Steve Capps: Well, see, a "driver" is something that talks to disks. "File system" is the next layer up that says, "I want filename 'Doug' on this disk." There's a concept that says you can have external file systems, you can make external calls over networks, and stuff like that.

DSC: Some skeptics say that command line-oriented systems, like MS-DOS, offer more flexibility than Mac's icon-oriented system. Well?

Steve Capps: First of all, it's a shell, not an operating system. And anyone who would say that has probably never used ours, and if that's what they want, they can code one!

Bruce Horn: That's right.

Steve Capps: That's the beauty of Mac.

Bruce Horn: You could have a desk accessory that was your command line operating system.

DSC: That's a neat idea. You could have a little box with an "A" prompt inside!

Bruce Horn: Well, we can't do EXEC file [batch files in MS-DOS] that say "Run this program, then this program, then this one." We're not optimized for that; we could have a little routine that does that, or a program that does that, or we could even put something in the Finder. But right now, that's not what most people want to do.

Steve Capps: There's a different head. When you're a programmer, you want something that's different than what the average person off the street wants. And the average person isn't going to figure out how to use EXEC files, much less want them. But they'll be convinced they need them if the salesman gets hot.

Betting the Company?

DSC: Is Mac a "bet the company" machine?

Bruce Horn: I guess. It's the neatest thing that Apple's come out with lately. It's the *only* thing that Apple's come out with lately.

Steve Capps: If Mac failed tomorrow, the company wouldn't die tomorrow, but it definitely wouldn't flourish.

DSC: What's the competition for Macintosh?

Steve Capps: The competition currently is the PC.

Steve Capps: The competition is people's stupidity, I guess.

Bruce Horn: No, not people's stupidity, but their unwillingness to try something new.

Steve Capps: Well, they're ignorant. They'll think that ... well, 1-2-3's going to be on the Mac, so they'll think ...

Bruce Horn: That if it says IBM on it, that's enough for me. That's what we're up against.

Steve Capps: I feel the main job of marketing is to get people in there using the machine. If they can do that, we'll sell all we can make.

1-2-3, 512K and Big Macs

DSC: Will 1-2-3 be out before there are 512K machines?

Steve Capps: Probably not, but about the time that 1-2-3's done, there'll be 512K Macs.

DSC: Which would be when?

Steve Capps: Soon. We have 'em in the lab right now.

DSC: This summer? This year?

Bruce Horn: This year, probably.

Steve Capps: Jobs would promise you by the end of this summer.

DSC: But it's up to the chip manufacturers more than it's up to Apple.

Steve Capps: You got it.

DSC: Who will buy Macs? Apple says knowledge workers. Do you two agree?

Bruce Horn: I don't like the term "knowledge worker," but, yeah, I agree. And I think a lot of college students will buy it, and a lot of people who would've bought PCs will buy it, I hope. I think that more people will buy it than we would ever suspect, or market for.

DSC: Do you want to speculate on the Big Mac?

Bruce Horn: What's a Big Mac? Some people think that Big Mac is already here: the Lisa 2. And some people think that Big Mac is a 512K Mac with a double-sided Sony [disk].

DSC: If you two could decide the changes for the next iteration, what would they be?

Steve Capps: Change the software very, very little, so you'd have complete compatibility, big-screen, and big bits.

Bruce Horn: Big disk and big memory.

DSC: How big?

Steve Capps: As big as you could afford. When we say "big-screen" we don't mean a larger screen, we mean more pixels, more dots. But then we're talking high-tech, because then your video's scanning at ranges up into FM.

DSC: Is 1,024 an achievable goal?

Bruce Horn: Oh, that's pretty big, that's pretty big. Well, the Star's 1,024 by 768, and that's very nice. That's what all the Xerox computers have.

DSC: Is that achievable?

Steve Capps: Yeah, if you want to pay for it.

Bruce Horn: Gray scales are a good one, too.

Steve Capps: It's a tradeoff. You might as well not throw more dots on the screen. You might as well use your memory for visual depth, instead of for width and height.

DSC: More bits per pixel, rather than more pixels on the screen.

Steve Capps: Right.

DSC: Any chance that future Macs will use enhanced processors, like Motorola's 68020 [a full thirty-two-bit processor, running at speeds faster than Macintosh's 8 megahertz]?

Bruce Horn: That would be nice. The 68020 would really make things zip.

Steve Capps: That machine isn't real yet.

DSC: Have they shipped any samples?

Bruce Horn: I don't think so.

DSC: I can't even imagine how fast a twenty-megahertz processor would be in Macintosh.

Steve Capps: But in two years, it'll be too slow.

The Mac in Five Years

DSC: What will be Mac be like in five years?

Steve Capps: They'll be around the same way as Apple IIs.

Bruce Horn: There'll be outrageous software on it. In five years, there'll be a lot of people who know how to program on Macs. It'll be pretty amazing, I think.

Steve Capps: Five years from now, we're going to look back on the Finder and laugh. We'll look back at Alice [a real-time 3-D chess program written by Capps] and say, "But, what a clunky game." We'll look back at MacPaint and say "That was pretty good for its time."

And a Polka-Dot keyboard

DSC: Will we ever see a color Mac?

Steve Capps: Yeah … we'll make the case in teal blue.

Bruce Horn: And a polka-dot red, white, and blue keyboard,

Steve Capps: You know the problem with color, don't you? It's the fuzziness caused by a black matrix; color is too expensive, and you can't stare at it all day. So when those problems get solved …

Bruce Horn: When it's cheap, too. Our tube is incredibly cheap.

Steve Capps: And you've got to get memory that's a lot bigger.

DSC: What kinds of programs would you like to see written for Macintosh? What types of desk accessories?

Bruce Horn: I'd like to see some stuff that Steve would consider boring. I'd like to see some really great engineering stuff. You know, how to design your airplane on Mac. General-purpose design tools would be really exciting. Because I'd use 'em.

Steve Capps: I think that chip design stuff would be great. Right now, to do chip design, you either have to use graph paper or you have to have big machines. And they're getting the silicon foundries down small enough where you could almost afford it on your own.

So having design tools that were on Mac would be real fine. Then your average freshman in college, if he was motivated enough and had a couple of thousand dollars, could get a chip made.

DSC: How about mass-market stuff?

Steve Capps: A checkbook balancing program.

Bruce Horn: Riiight.

(Laughter)

Steve Capps: Seriously, teaching stuff. Education's going to be really big.

Carrying Things Too Far

DSC: And new desk accessories?

Steve Capps: All the business … crap.

Bruce Horn: We're really excited about business stuff.

Steve Capps: That'll be done [original desk accessories] by Lotus's 1-2-3. To give you a great analogy: I was working on a phone dialer today, just a list of names. And somebody came up and said, "Aren't you going to make it look like a Touch-Tone® pad?" There's a reality strangeness there. Why do we need to make a thing look like a Rolodex®, if it doesn't serve a useful purpose. It's neat if it does. You don't want to teach people a new way of looking at a clock, you want a desk accessory clock to look like a clock.

DSC: Objectizing things can get ludicrous if carried too far.

Bruce Horn: If "objectizing" means being the same as in real life. It's as if, in Mac, when you clicked on a pattern, you could paint for a while, and then it would dry up, and you'd have to click on a pattern again.

(Laughter)

DSC: Or the tip of your pencil broke while you were drawing.

Steve Capps: Yeah. Then I suppose you'd have to bring out a sharpener, right? Let's model the real world, right? Well, that's silly.

Bruce Horn: That's why our disks look like disks. Mac doesn't come up with, "Ooh, it's a filing cabinet!" That's a case where the real world is right.

Steve Capps: Then there's the Bic lighter desk accessory, where you click and this flame comes out.

Bruce Horn: And sets your window on fire.

Steve Capps: You've heard about the paperweight ornament [desk accessory]? Well, ornaments are allowed to be—it's not a hard limit—only about 8K. So you have this ornament that's 7,990 bytes and it does nothing. But you're right: I think the world will gravitate toward being all ornaments. You won't have any central application anymore, just these really smart ornaments that know how to talk and interchange information.

Bruce Horn: But each application can have its own ornaments, because each application has its own resource file. So you can have ornaments that talk to each other. We've actually talked about doing some neat stuff that way.

Presaging MultiFinder

Steve Capps: That's going to be a neat way to sneak multiprocessing in.

DSC: When we get 512K, will we have full concurrency?

Bruce Horn: The system's not set up to be concurrent.

DSC: MacBasic is fully concurrent, and events [the way Mac handles inputs from the keyboard or mouse] are set up to make concurrency easy, aren't they?

Steve Capps: I guess the point is that, because of the way the Event Manager is written, you can kind of do concurrency, but you've got to handle all the dispatching of events to processes. Get it? Anyway, you've got to do all the dispatching, whereas in other systems, the dispatching might be handled automatically. But that's very simple to implement. Then we get to storage management. That's another thing about multiprocessing: who owns what storage? Do you just partition up storage, and say "This is your chunk, thou shalt not cross"? That's pretty easy, and we have support for that: you could have multiple heaps. But when you start saying that these guys are sharing all memory, and so this guy wants to purge, should he be allowed to purge another process's stuff? Probably not.

DSC: Those are the traditional problems of multitasking.

Steve Capps: Right. We'll definitely do the … legerdemain, does that sound right? Well, we'll do that, and the average user will think it looks great! But it wasn't designed in from Day One. That's a polite way of saying it.

Becoming a Hot Programmer

DSC: Okay. You guys are hot-shot programmers. Lots of readers want to become hot programmers. What advice would you give them to become good programmers?

Steve Capps: Oh, God! Turn 'em on to Instant Pascal [released as Macintosh Pascal] on Mac, and take a book, or take a class, and just do what you want to do.

DSC: You're in favor of Pascal as a first language?

Steve Capps: Doesn't make any difference.

Bruce Horn: I think Instant Pascal.

Steve Capps: Well, Pascal's great, but Instant Pascal—it's the environment that's the selling feature, I think.

Bruce Horn: I think it's clear—Steve doesn't agree with me—but I think that Basic might teach you bad habits, where Pascal really teaches you about data structures and control structures. So I think Pascal's more preferable.

Steve Capps: I agree with that. But what I'm saying is that it's the environment. You can go get Pascal or Basic for any machine in the world, but you won't have the Instant Pascal environment, which is an incredible aid to learning.

DSC: So get proficient at Pascal, then learn assembly language?

Steve Capps: No. Once you good at programming, you can speak any language.

Bruce Horn: That's right.

Steve Capps: There's only a few classes of languages. If you know Pascal real well, you're not going to pick up APL or Lisp. But if you know Pascal, you're going to pick up Basic and C. And if you know one assembler, you know them all.

Bruce Horn: That's right. And Lisp is in this other class, and Smalltalk's in even another class.

Steve Capps: And APL's in a weird class. SNOBOLS's kind of half in one class, and …

DSC: Are these worthwhile languages to learn? I like Lisp, but I'm not very good in it.

Bruce Horn: I think Lisp is great. I think Smalltalk is incredibly great.

Steve Capps: What was that quote we read? "Never learn a language that doesn't teach you anything." If you know Pascal, there's probably no reason to learn Basic, except for historical purposes.

DSC: So Instant Pascal's the way to go?

Steve Capps: I claim that, if he's smart, your average fourteen-year-old kid with Instant Pascal, no books, and good sample programs can teach himself how to program.

Bruce Horn: That's right. In a week.

DSC: And the reason is that you don't feel like you're programming. You feel like you're editing. But assembly language is hard to learn, right?

Bruce Horn: No, it's not. You just play around with it, you learn the tricks, you learn what you can get around, and you just do it.

Steve Capps: But the point is, if you don't learn it in six months, go to another field. My best friend in high school and I both got excited about computers at the same time but he just didn't get it. So I did all his assignments for him. And now he's running a circus—literally. He just didn't understand it. There's a certain brain that can't.

Whiz Kids

DSC: Now let's do your history. How did you get involved in computers?

Bruce Horn: In the sixth grade, this guy, Nils Nilson, who's at SRI [Science Research Institute, a software thinktank], brought over a terminal to the elementary school. And I got a little involved there. It was fun, I learned Basic …

DSC: You were how old?

Bruce Horn: Eleven or something. After that, when I went to high school, they had HP computers, and I played with them, and programmable calculators.

DSC: Modesty aside, you were a whiz at math, right?

Bruce Horn: Yeah, I love math. But Ted Kaehler came down to the school, and he wanted someone to do some work for him, so I went up to Xerox.

DSC: What kind of work? You were only fourteen, right?

Bruce Horn: I guess. I was supposed to work on Smalltalk, and I did for a while, but then I got into writing assembly code for the Alto.

DSC: Did this knock everybody out at Xerox? That a fourteen-year-old was writing assembly code for the Alto?

Bruce Horn: I don't know. There were lots of smart kids around. I worked at Xerox for a long time. It was neat. The Xerox group was really great. That's where I learned a lot of my stuff.

DSC: What was the Notetaker?

Bruce Horn: I did a lot of the ROM for that. Other people worked on it, but I kind of felt like it was mine. It was a box about the size of an Osborne—this was before Osborne—and it had a screen about …

Steve Capps: Bigger than the Osborne.

Bruce Horn: By a long shot. And a mouse, and a touch-screen, and everything, and it ran Smalltalk. And you carried it around!

DSC: This was when?

Bruce Horn: Nineteen seventy-eight? Seventy-nine?

The Xerox Factor

DSC: How did the Xerox discoveries influence Macintosh?

Bruce Horn: The mouse. Windows. Selecting. Overlapping windows …

Steve Capps: You've heard the "Bill [Atkinson] story." That he went there [to Xerox] and thought they were doing arbitrary updating [of screen images—a tough technical feat], but they weren't.

Bruce Horn: But they are now. I remember being at Xerox when the Apple crowd came in and saw Smalltalk. And they all saw Smalltalk, and I guess what happened is that Steve Jobs said, "I want that!" And at that point the Lisa had function keys along the top, and it was totally different. And I guess Bill brought in all the ideas from Xerox. You know, all that stuff is Xerox!

DSC: So what does QuickDraw [Bill Atkinson's graphic routines, seen on Lisa and Mac] do that Xerox hadn't figured out?

Bruce Horn: QuickDraw is a lot of things. Mostly, it's regions. Arbitrary [graphics] regions as a basic data structure.

DSC: Xerox hadn't figured that out?

Bruce Horn: Xerox hadn't because they didn't really need to. They had stuff like that.

Steve Capps: But they didn't have regions.

Bruce Horn: They had things *like* regions. It depends on what you think regions are. But the point is that regions are unique to Mac and Lisa. That's what Bill did—and along with that, he added all these incredible things you could do. Bill took a lot of things, like ovals, and rectangles, and round-rectangles, and made them real citizens, you know. Ovals are superfast because he optimized for that, and all these other things. And he built that into QuickDraw.

Alto in a Closet

DSC: Steve, there's a story about you finding an Alto in a closet. Apocryphal?

Steve Capps: Well, I was working at Xerox and we had an Alto in the closet. It wasn't a janitor's closet, it was a storeroom. Anyway, you had to go into this hot, stuffy room. And I brought it up, and it was fun. The first thing I discovered [on the Alto] was BitBlt [a graphics routine for high-resolution graphic manipulation]. This was when I was halfway through college, working at Xerox in Rochester, New York. So, instantly I got exposed to all this good stuff, at least what little PARC would let out. We were kind of like the black sheep. They wouldn't give us all the good stuff, but they'd give us a lot.

DSC: Everyone at Xerox is hooked up onto a network of computers. Do you miss that?

Bruce Horn: I miss networking for sure. And I miss the Xerox environment. But I think we [at Apple] can build up something just as good—we just have to do it, and it's going to take a lot of work.

Steve Capps: I think that, for the person who's not exposed to a computer, networking is harder to understand than the mouse. There's this head that says that if they've never used a mouse, they they'll pooh-pooh it. But networking, I think, is even more so than that, because … well, I just happened to be very, very lucky to fall into it at a tender, early age.

DSC: It's quite conceptual.

Steve Capps: If I tell you, "Yeah, you can just sit in your office and send a memo to Bruce in California," you'll say, "Oh, that's neat!" But you don't realize the power of that, and how much fun it really, really is.

Bruce Horn: You can leverage off it. It's not only fun. If you need an answer to a question you can—boom—find out in an hour, from anybody, anywhere. If you want to send mail, you can send mail. If you want to get source code, you can get source code. You can pull anything around.

DSC: It's a quantum leap in brain amplification over using a stand-alone computer.

Bruce Horn: That's right, absolutely.

Pressure and Vitamin C

DSC: The pressure of getting this software out must have been enormous. How did you cope with it?

Bruce Horn: We didn't. We just went crazy. We were sitting in the little cubicles there and we'd pop vitamin C pills all the time. We'd go wacky occasionally and just start babbling around, going crazy.

Steve Capps: Video games.

Bruce Horn: His outlet was video games; I don't know what mine was. Screaming, I guess.

DSC: Were you dreaming about code?

Bruce Horn: Oh yeah, all the time, all the time. Still happens. What's even more interesting is that when you do something different, like when I went skiing—and it was the first time I'd been out of Apple for more than a couple of hours, except for sleeping—it just purges: I had terrible dreams all night, as it purged from me. It was interesting, seeing all that come out. I'd just held it all in until the end, and it had to come out.

Steve Capps: You get used to it. Andy [Hertzfeld, another Mac programmer] used to come up to us and ask how we stood the pressure. And once you've crossed the threshold, there is no more pressure.

Bruce Horn: You're just in a daze from doing it.

DSC: How many hours a week were you working?

Steve Capps: Easily over eighty.

Bruce Horn: The last couple of weeks, we were there all the time.

Steve Capps: The last two days we basically stayed up fifty-eight hours straight. Bruce'd sleep a couple hours …

Bruce Horn: Steve'd play video games. He stayed up the whole time.

DSC: No caffeine?

Bruce Horn: Neptune and Pepsi. And vitamin C.

Steve Capps: Everybody around us was getting sick, and I haven't been sick for I don't know how long. I attribute it to taking thousands of milligrams a day.

Bruce Horn: We'd pop 'em like candy.

Rating the Boss

DSC: Steve Jobs gets a lot of criticism. How was he as a boss?

Steve Capps: He was great. I wouldn't trade him, and all his faults, for any other boss I've ever had.

DSC: Why?

Steve Capps: Just because … this is where the action is. I mean, I could be back at Xerox, with normal blood pressure and a house and 2.1 kids, and I'd die. But out here [at Apple], you can die at thirty.

DSC: And have a lot more fun doing it.

Steve Capps: And have a lot more fun doing it.

— (From *St. Mac* magazine, March 1984. Originally published as "Secrets of the Finder")

A CHAT WITH AN OLD GUY

DOUG CLAPP

W ho to praise? Who to blame? In the flood of publicity after the release of Macintosh, some names were prominent, and other names were seldom mentioned.

What follows is my attempt to put things right. My memories of the making of Macintosh. And a good dose of deserved praise to those overlooked in the hoopla.

But remember: selection isn't reality. That said, here's another take on the pre-release Macintosh, and the team that created it.

It was a nice room. A little beat, sure, but nice. Dark, filled with comfortable old furniture. Lived in. A brick fireplace in the corner held a cheerful fire.

The old man was in a rocking chair before the fire, a blanket covering his lap. He looked up when I entered, took a long pull on his cigarette and smiled impishly. The smoke drifted into the fireplace and quickly disappeared. *It can't kill me now*, the smile said. *Outlasted it.*

"You couldn't smoke anywhere," he began, guessing what the interview would be about. "All this stuff about Apple being a … a new type

98

of corporation. It sure was. Couldn't smoke. Nobody did. You had to go out in the parking lot and sneak 'em. Light up in the programmer's 'cave' and—heh heh—they'd probably string you up.

"Gotta be a clean liver to write assembly language, I guess. They were that. But you don't want to hear about smoking, do you?"

"Well, actually, I wanted to get your impressions about how it was, back then. During development."

"I'll tell you how it was! Boom! Boom! Crashed all the time. You'd breathe on that machine and crash! Boom! Heh.

"MacWrite was the worst. The Worst. Boy that devil was buggy! Whoa!

"You know the idea, don't you, young fella? There was some code called 'CoreEdit.' Like the TextEdit routines in ROM, except CoreEdit let you have different styles and sizes. Hot stuff, back then. CoreEdit was the heart of MacWrite. Early on, Apple thought it'd license CoreEdit to other developers, let 'em use the code in their applications.

"Well let me tell you! Buggy, buggy, buggy. What a mess. You should've read the comments in the source code! Even the guys who wrote it didn't understand it! Imagine that! Boom! No wonder!"

"So what happened?"

"Well, Apple finally decided they weren't going to license it anymore. Probably too embarrassed. And the other thing was that you really couldn't use MacWrite—well you couldn't use it very long! Heh. Had to use an IBM word processor to write about the Macintosh!"

"Well sure," I said. "That was before the machine was released. Everything's buggy when it's in development."

"Yeah, that's true. But there are degrees, you know. Degrees.

"Take the Finder. It had some bugs. Still does, you know! Probably more now then it did then—and isn't that something! But it was always pretty good. Fine piece of work by young Horn. Fine work. That boy just never got the attention he deserved. Imagine: he invented the Finder! He invented resources! Can you imagine a

Macintosh without a Finder? Without resources! Unsung hero, that boy."

"You're always saying that," I said.

"And I'll keep on saying it, too!"

There was a pause. I could tell the old man was trying to remember the train of thought.

"MacPaint, though," he began again, "was just a rock. Always a rock. Even when all the features weren't in. They weren't all there, but what was there worked. Don't think I ever crashed it, not once. Must've had bugs, but I couldn't find 'em.

"You gotta admire that in a programmer. That Atkinson, he just bore down. Wasn't satisfied unless it was perfect. Even then, I don't think he was satisfied.

"Think about QuickDraw. Amazing. I remember … he'd come in some days, big ProFile hard disk under his arm. He'd be excited because he'd just gotten QuickDraw to be faster. Just a little faster. Everything counts. And he'd be tickled. And proud."

"They all loved what they were doing … "

"Oh, yeah. You gotta love it. Can't do nothing if you don't love it. That's the ticket, young fella. The love will pull you along, will pull you when nothing else can. You create something that's never existed before and you're God to that thing. It's a Godlike thing. Can't be God if you don't love, can ya?

"You can cut any of this out if it'll get you in trouble, young man."

"No, it's okay," I said.

The old man chuckled and headed for shallow waters. "Marketing," he said. "Know what they wanted to call The Finder?

"Listen to this: 'The Desktop Organizer'! Ain't that a hoot? The Desktop Organizer!"

"So why was it named The Finder?"

"Because *that's what it was*! It's what the programmers called it. They won that one, too. Good for them."

"Was there much of that? Disagreement between marketing and the programmers?"

"Oh, no. Not that I was aware of. The kids had their hands full as it was. Nobody'd ever done anything like—no, that's not true. There was Lisa, but a bunch—a *big* bunch—of people worked on that one! It showed, too, didn't it? Heh.

"Such a few kids. Burrell Smith did the hardware. Smart little punk, Burrell was. Knew it, too. Atkinson, Hertzfeld. You know all about those guys.

"Horn, of course, the Finder whiz. Steve Capps, big bear of a guy; not one of your effete programmer types. He did a lot of the Finder, lot of the 'unromantic' parts. You know, being able to type a new name under an icon. Not sexy stuff. Not easy, either!

"And Larry Kenyon. You gotta have a guy like Kenyon. He did all the I/O—input, output. Reading and writing disk drives, that type of thing. Not glamorous, but fine work. Fine work.

"And Donn Denman. Nice kid, that Denman. Worked his heart out on MacBasic. But that's another story ..."

"How old were they?" I asked.

"Hell, I don't know how old they were! Think I went around saying 'How old are you, anyway?'! They were kids!"

"Do you think they had an idea were all this would go?"

"Oh, sorta. Programmers are at the mercy of chips, you know. And new chips are around a long time before they show up in a mass-market computer.

"Can't have a four-megabyte computer until you got lots of big, cheap RAM chips! Back then, they were around, but not in the quantities Apple needed. But the programmers and designers knew about 'em. They would've loved to make a 512K machine right off the bat. Simpler for everybody. Just couldn't do it, though. Chips cost too much."

"Uh-huh," I said.

"No, I'll tell you how old they were," the old man said with a cackle. "You look at your Macintosh. See how little everything is?

See how little the scroll arrows are? See how little the Close box is? How about that insertion point! It's just tiny, boy!

"You can tell: young people with good eyes made that machine!"

"Wait a minute," I said, "They also only had a nine-inch screen to work in."

He looked at me, eyes narrowed. *What is this? An interview or an argument?*

Crusty old guy, I thought.

I backpedaled. "I'll be the first to admit it's not perfect … "

"Lemme tell you a story," he said. "Happened just a few days ago.

"I know these folks who own a little printing shop. Mom and pop operation. Well, they had an IBM and just got a Macintosh. SE, I think.

"And I'm over there, a few days back. And, you know, I've been around the block with Macintosh. You run through as many analog boards as I have—heh heh—and you've been around the block!

"So I say: 'How do you like it?'

"And Don says that he loves it. Just loves it.

"So I ask Mary. 'Whaddya think of it?'

"And this is interesting. Mary sorta hems and hahs. She says 'Well…' and gets a sorta grimace on her face.

"Finally, she shakes her head and says, 'I just don't get all this Macintosh stuff,' she says, embarrassed by it all. 'I understood the IBM, but, you know … '

"And that was food for thought, young man. Food for thought.

"But I know how she felt. Look, say she's in the Finder. And she wants to copy a file. So she looks around. Pulls down the menus. She's looking for something that says 'Copy a file … '

"But there isn't anything!"

"It's too simple for her," I say. "She doesn't realize how easy it is!"

"No, no, it's more than that. That's not it," the old man admonishes me. "Here's what it is: the blessing of Macintosh is also the curse of Macintosh."

"How so?"

"Because you don't have modes. Because—with Macintosh—at any given time you can do any number of things. There's no fixed set of choices. It's not 'this or that' or 'choose from 1 through 5.' Nope. It's open-ended. You decide."

"But that's a feature!"

"Sure it is, boy. But it also puts it to ya. When you're not locked in, you've got to decide what you want to do. It's not easy, deciding what you want to do."

"Life's like that," I say.

"So it is. Just like that."

"Well, then … " I begin.

"Yes?"

I blanked. Didn't know where to go with all this.

Again, he chuckled. "I'll get worse, too," he said. "New applications coming up with a mind of their own! You think it's tough deciding what to do? Wait until there's more than one opinion! Won't that be something?"

I remembered a quote of Picasso's: "If a lion could talk, we wouldn't understand what it said."

"The lions will be talking soon, young man. And you'll understand them, all right.

"You just may not agree, that's all.

"Won't that be something?"

He was still cackling as I left the room.

— Doug Clapp, *Macazine*, January 1989

PART

II

EARLY YEARS, EARLY TEARS

HAVE A MAC—FREE

W*e move now to the early years of Macintosh, a time of free Macs, "Fat Macs," and Club Mac. "AppleBus" and laser printers. Jazz and a competitor—sneered at by Jobs—from Seattle. A time of bugs, too. If you were there, you remember. We end, too soon, with sickles, axes, and flaming torches flying in the wind—just the right metaphor for the fine, but frustrating, early years.*

۶؏

To help introduce the Macintosh, a hand-picked group of 50 "luminaries" received a free Macintosh from Apple. Among them were

Andy Warhol, artist

Bob Ciano, *Life* magazine art director

David Rockefeller, financier

Dianne Feinstein, San Francisco mayor

Jim Henson, puppeteer

Kurt Vonnegut, novelist

Lee Iacocca, Captain of Industry

Maya Lin, Vietnam War Memorial designer

Mick Jagger, musician

Milton Glaser, designer

Peter Martins, ballet choreographer

Michael Jackson, musician

Sean Lennon, musician

Stephen Sondheim, composer

Ted Turner, entrepreneur

Eleven of these (in Apple's words) "great imaginations" were featured in an Apple annual report. Missing from the report was Mick Jagger. In *West of Eden*, Frank Rose recounts the gifting of Jagger.

" ... Jobs and Mike Murray and Andy Hertzfeld and Bill Atkinson all flew to New York to present one to Mick Jagger, whom Jobs had met at a party. They went to his brownstone on a weekend afternoon and were directed by the bodyguards to a third-floor room where Jagger sat in a T-shirt and Levi's. There were keyboards in various corners of the room; Jagger looked like any other middle-aged musician practicing his craft. He didn't seem too interested in the Macintosh. His daughter Jade was, however, so Bill and Andy gave her a demonstration while Jobs and Murray chatted with Jagger. After a while they left."

CALIFORNIA NOTES

Although I lived in Los Angeles for two years in the mid-eighties, most of my life was spent in Minnesota—where I grew up and now live again. So, to write about computers, I commuted to California—a lot!

These are a few notes from those commuting years. By the way, the brilliant programmer is Macintosh programmer Bruce Horn; the freeware author is the greatly missed Andrew Fluegelman, founding editor of Macworld; *the editor is Paul Mithra; and Kevin Goldstein used to be Peter Norton's ghost, but now—I'm pretty sure—is Kevin Goldstein again.*

Kevin Goldstein and I are having dinner in LA. After taking our order, the waitress says, "Excuse me. Are you computer guys? I couldn't help overhearing your conversation earlier." We admit it. She then asks for advice. She wants to buy her child a computer, but she's not sure which one to buy. We ask her a bunch of intelligent questions, and finally ask how much she wants to spend. "Well, gee, not over a hundred dollars," she says, then waits for our reply.

The young man is a brilliant programmer. He was, and is, a whiz at math. He's also an ardent environmentalist, a lover of wild things, and a liberal Democrat. He's upset at the division between liberal arts types and science types. "Hey, I listen to music, I read books, I can appreciate art. Why don't they try to appreciate what I do? There's a lot of beauty in math."

The editor is also a punk musician and an accomplished Basic programmer. "Why don't you write about the fact that computers aren't good for anything?" A beat. "They're not?" I ask. "Well, nothing important," he answers.

It's the last year for Applefest. Next year it's going to be an Apple/IBM fest. The Apple stalwart is trying to salvage some pride. "But notice which name is first," she says. "For now, anyway," is the reply.

It's not the way that programming is explained in college. "It's really, really simple, " the programmer says. "These guys hold the screen stuff, and this guy, just one byte, actually, points to these other guys, and *those* guys have all the disk stuff that, you know, is like just hanging around. Neat, huh?"

It sounds like total nonsense, but for some strange reason it makes sense. Afterwards, you realize that you understand a tricky programming feat for the first time. These guys?

Don Knuth, Obi Won-Kanobi of Computer Science, is visiting Apple before the release of Macintosh. He's just received a software demo. He's floored. Later, he says, "I used to believe that the best programming was done in the university environment, not in private industry. Now, I think it's the other way around."

The freeware author pleasantly puts aside the question of how much he's made from his program. At the computer companies, it's bad form to inquire about salaries, possibly the only remaining conversational taboo. When salaries are mentioned, they blush and change the subject.

At Grid Systems, the woman that answers the phone is stonewalling. You're trying to reach the marketing director, with no success. Unfortunately, you don't have a name, only a title. If you know the person's name, you get through. If you don't, you don't. "Company policy," she says. The frustration is incredible. Is this how the Japanese do things?

It's evening in Los Gatos and everyone is partying. Everything's great. The conversation moves to housing prices, which are astronomical. Someone says, "What about the waitresses and the guys that pump gas? Where do they live?" Silence. The thought hasn't occurred to them before, and they have no answers.

The male flight attendant owns an Otrona Attache and does contract programming in C. The man in the seat next to you manufactures 100 megabyte disk drives. The woman at the hotel's front desk is learning dBase in her spare time. The family physician takes you aside for advice about 1-2-3 macros. You wonder what life's like in Fiji.

"Remember how everyone said that software needs to catch up with hardware? That happened long ago. Now the hardware needs to catch up."

The banker has come to the user group meeting for help. He's having trouble generating reports with his database program. The questions begin, users intent on pinpointing, then solving, the problem. What's he trying to do? He's trying, he says, to keep track of mortgage foreclosures. Oh.

The computer store salesman is angry. "Why do they keep coming out with new stuff? I haven't learned how to work the stuff we've got now! How am I supposed to sell this stuff? *Do you think it's fun looking like an idiot?*"

If you look closely at the top of the Intel building, you'll notice a TV camera sweeping the parking lot, hour after hour, non-stop. Inside, there is surely a person whose job it is to watch a parking lot, hour after hour.

— Doug Clapp: *MacUser* magazine

TALKING WITH KOTTKE

DOUG CLAPP, PAT RYALL, AND DANIEL KOTTKE

This is one of my favorite interviews. It took place in 1984, a few months after the release of Macintosh. It doesn't require much set-up, other than noting that "AppleBus" became "AppleTalk," then "LocalTalk."

In all, a very good time. Dan remains a great guy to hang out with. And I was so impressed with the interviewing skills of Ms. Ryall that I married her the first chance I got. In the years that followed, Apple shipped the products discussed here, and Patti and I shipped Katharine Evelyn, Haley Mae, and Devin Charles Finnegan Clapp.

Who to interview? Burrell Smith was out; he was too busy designing secret projects and recovering from media overload. Donn Denman was out, for now, because he hadn't finished MacBasic when this interview was scheduled (maybe next time). And Steve Jobs hardly talks to anybody, and Apple president John Sculley, even if available, probably wouldn't divulge any juicy tidbits, so …

Who to interview? After long minutes of furious thought, the name Dan Kottke leapt to mind. Dan is a hardware engineer on the Macintosh project, one of the original Apple employees, knows lots of interesting Apple stuff. He's quick with an opinion, is neither blindly "Apple Forever" or "Everything's Junk," and is just generally a fun guy to hang around with.

With that in mind, writer Doug Clapp and *St.Mac* editor Pat Ryall went to Cupertino for two marathon sessions with Daniel Kottke. The subjects ranged widely, from Apple's unreleased networking system (called AppleBus, which allows computers to be tied together and communicate directly), to the magical SCC communications chip in the Macintosh, to "early Apple," Alan Kay, laser printers, pricing, marketing, hard disks, color Macintoshes, and more.

What follows is not the official word from Apple, but we think you'll find it interesting nonetheless. We did. And we found that, just as we suspected, Dan *is* a fun guy to hang around with.

Kottke: I don't know if you've got any good ideas for an angle on this interview. Because I'm not involved in any hot projects right now, and even if I were I couldn't tell you about them. But you know that AppleBus and the laser printer are the big upcoming products, and I really shouldn't say much more than that.

DC: That's okay. AppleBus is boring anyway.

Kottke: AppleBus is not boring, it's really exciting!

DC: Really?

Kottke: I think it's one of the neatest things we've ever done.

DC: Well, it doesn't really affect the typical home user or the hobbyist.

Kottke: Potentially it does affect the home user with regard to getting extended use out of Mac's serial ports. But beyond that it's exciting in terms of the marketplace. It's like a whole new level—it gives a whole new dimension to the machine [Macintosh].

DC: And it's a great attack on IBM.

Kottke: We're not doing it just to attack anyone. We're doing it because we're able to do it. In a sense, we're doing it because we've got this great chip called the SCC that makes it possible, in the same way that the 68000 makes the Macintosh possible.

DC: Let's talk about the SCC chip. Is the Macintosh the first computer it's been used in?

Kottke: I don't know, but it's a very new chip, and Burrell [Smith, Mac's hardware architect] found it—I don't know who tipped him off to it. Zilog makes it. It hasn't been out very long.

DC: Tell us about "bandwidth." Because there's been a lot of talk about the speed of the SCC chip, saying that it's fast enough to handle both voice and data at the same time.

Kottke: I've never heard anyone say that. In fact, I don't think it necessarily makes sense. Let's just look at the rough numbers. What are the bandwidths of audio or analog signals? On the low end, you have telephone-grade audio, considered to have a 3-kilohertz analog bandwidth–by bandwidth here I mean highest frequency component. If you digitize that, which is what voice-mail companies do, you get a bit stream with a baud rate or digital bandwidth consisting of the word size times the sampling rate. Recognizable speech can be as slow as eight bits times 6 kilohertz, or about 180 kilohertz—almost four times better. Digital audio disks run at about sixteen bits times 50 kilohertz, which comes to 800 kilohertz, or four to five times better still. The Mac Sony disk transfers six bits every sixteen microseconds, which gives you about 375 kilohertz, which is twice as fast as Apple's Disk II.

But what does all this mean? Well, was our comparison against the SCC chip itself or AppleBus? Let's look at both. The SCC chip will run flat-out at 1 megahertz, almost as fast as the Mac's bus cycle. Software can't keep up for long with data at that rate. I heard that the Tecmar hard disk for Macintosh runs at about 700 kilohertz. AppleBus runs at 230 kilohertz. Since we said that Mac sound runs at 180 kilohertz, that means that theoretically, you could send a continuous sound channel over AppleBus with room left over for data—and no useful time left over for the processor!

Anyway, the thing that's particularly great about the SCC is that it allows "header recognition." Header recognition means—I'm trying to think of a good analogy. It's like a receptionist at a desk screening your calls.

DC: What's a "header"?

Kottke: When you do any kind of local area network, the basic data structure is the "packet." As in "packet-switched network," a common phrase.

DC: Right.

Kottke: And every data packet has a header. A packet is basically like a sector of data on a disk. Sectors are usually either 256 bytes or 512 bytes, and it makes sense to have uniform sector size on a disk to efficiently fill the space. On AppleBus, packet size will be variable, but no greater than 600 bytes and at least 3 bytes.

DC: And that's the header? So the smallest packet is just a header?

Kottke: Right. And what the header tells you is "where it's coming from," "where it's going to," and "how long it is." Okay? And, when you've got a network, there're millions of bits flying by, all the time. You can't go interrupting your processor for every single message. So you really need what's called "header recognition." And, generally speaking, that's done by an entire circuit board. But all that's built into the SCC chip. The SCC chip is always looking at the data line; it's always taking in data. Every time it sees data, it takes in the first couple of bytes and compares them with a register it has, which has its own address. And if the address doesn't match, it says, "Oh, well, not for me."

DC: So the SCC's like a processor? It's got registers …

Kottke: It's got registers, and it's very complex. It's not really like a processor; it's a *communications controller*. It doesn't have the same architecture a processor does, by any means, but it has "smarts." So anyway, we have this chip, and it's always looking at the AppleBus. The only time it interrupts your Macintosh is when it finds a packet that's addressed to you. Having a secretary answering your phone is a good analogy. It's as though people are calling your number all the time, but a lot of the calls are not necessarily going to be for you personally. But anyway, back to the subject. Have we got any interesting things we can talk about?

PR: I want to hear about laser printers!

Kottke: Well, quite honestly, I don't know much about the laser printer project we're doing. We've got one guy doing it, and he's doing it in a closed room, and it's locked, and the guy doesn't talk, so I don't know much.

PR: It was more of a personal question anyway.

Kottke: Well, I can tell you what I think they're good for without having any specific references to our products. Laser printers will enable people to do a lot of work themselves without requiring a typesetter.

PR: I've love to see typesetting made obsolete.

Kottke: Typesetters are very concerned!

PR: I do a *lot* of typesetting at work. (*laughter*)

Kottke: Typesetters are going to go out of business!

PR: We could all go into designing fonts. None of the Macintosh fonts are anything we could use for body text in the magazine. Somebody needs to get everything that's on a typesetting system onto a computer.

Kottke: The main thing is that the laser printer does for typesetting what the computer did for writing text. On your desk, you can compose with your Macintosh or Lisa or whatever, and you can print out things that are acceptable camera-ready artwork.

DC: How fast?

Kottke: Acceptably fast. I think almost anything is acceptably fast. Speed was never that much of an issue. It's like—if you're printing out a hundred copies of a letter, you should get a Xerox machine! But that's the whole thing. A laser printer is a Xerox machine. *It is!* It's a Xerox machine that's independently addressable with a laser. So you can use it strictly as a Xerox machine, or you can dump down into it from your computer.

PR: Well, we have an understanding at work: we can't get a laser printer until they're less than $4,000.

Kottke: We hope to do that by the end of the year. Seriously. You know, that's what Steve Jobs is really good at: visionary product direction. And he's really right on. He's the one who's pushing for laser printers. But the people that make the printer mechanisms deserve most of the credit. Those things are really hairy. It's hard to get those things to work. And we're taking the mechanism, and attaching a computer to it, and making a package out of it. It's the same way that Sony should get credit for the 3.5-inch drive. We didn't make that drive, and we would *not* have done it. We tried making 5.25-inch drives and it didn't turn out to be a smashing success.

DC: True enough.

Kottke: In fact, I would say that the "Twiggy" drive [used in Lisa before being discontinued by Apple] was not a bad thing. The Apple III's not a bad thing. But the technology moves so fast. It you're doing kind of "evolutionary" product, you fall behind. You have to take leaps. And the Twiggy was basically a re-engineering of products that had already existed. It was great, five years ago, when it started, but the whole project just dragged on.

DC: Five years?

Kottke: Yeah, and Apple's main product stream is not making disk drives. But we're making our own hard disk drive that we're shipping in the Lisa, and from everything I've heard, that drive is just great. We designed and built it from the ground up, so ultimately it should be cheaper than anything else we can buy.

PR: That's the ten-megabyte drive?

Kottke: Yeah, and it's working real well. It's not in high volume yet. We're shipping it in the Lisa 2/10, and I think at some point we may introduce it for the Macintosh. I hope that works out because, eventually, all our computers are going to want hard disk drives, or a very large percentage of them. The technology is clearly here to stay. I don't see any huge magical breakthroughs coming along the line to replace that technology.

DC: How did you get involved with Apple?

Kottke: I was always interested in electronics. But the funny thing was, for the first couple of years that I knew Steve [Jobs], I didn't know that he was interested in electronics. Steve was my friend on kind of a literary-philosophical level. He was the friend of a dorm-mate and had these Bob Dylan tapes playing one day, so I just sat down and listened. At the time, I never even knew he was involved with "blue-boxing" [illegally making long-distance phone calls with the aid of hardware cleverness]. That was a secret, I guess.

DC: You were in college when Apple first started?

Kottke: I was a junior at Columbia in New York City when Steven started Apple. And I just came out for a summer job.

DC: Who was here when you came out?

Kottke: At Apple? Nobody!

DC: You mean it was just Steve and his sister?

Kottke: Literally. When I came, Steve's sister was plugging chips onto the Apple I logic board, and not doing a tremendously great job. So I started doing that: I assembled Apple I logic boards, and I tested them.

DC: You got paid?

Kottke: Oh, yeah, I got three dollars an hour!

PR: What year was that?

Kottke: 1976.

DC: This was when Steve Wozniak was at Hewlett-Packard?

Kottke: I didn't know Woz for quite a while. Woz was never around the garage. He'd come by every week or two, but he never hung out there a lot. I think Woz was intensely busy at that time. The Apple I had already been designed—that was when he was working on the Apple II, though I didn't know it at the time. He was staying up late nights, prototyping the Apple II, writing code for it, writing Integer Basic, writing the Monitor routines. That's why I never saw him.

DC: This is after Paul Terrell's ordering the Apple I's for his Byte Shop?

Kottke: Not long after.

DC: The first order was how many in a month?

Kottke: I'm not sure. I think $30,000 worth.

DC: At $600-something each?

Kottke: That was the retail price. I don't know what the wholesale price was, so I don't know how many systems that entailed. As a ball-park figure, say $400 wholesale? That's a good markup. From $400 to $660? I think I came in on the tail end of filling that big order.

DC: Legendary numbers.

Kottke: And there was no daily production. It was just a batch job. You got a bunch of boards—you got 'em all stuffed at once—and then they all sat in a pile. One by one, a day at a time, we'd get around to testing them. It was very spotty work; we weren't working at it full-time. I was getting paid by the hour, and just a couple of hours a day; that's all it was. If I had been seriously looking for a job, I wouldn't have hung around. I liked the computer. I did my best, all summer, to learn how it worked.

DC: The summer of '76?

Kottke: In between my last two years of college. I went back for my senior year. I didn't have a full-time job at Apple anyway. At that point, Apple was in partnership and hadn't incorporated yet. And, during my senior year at school, Steve would call me up and tell me how things were going. He'd say, "We've got this great company started, you've got to come and work for us!" So, the same week I graduated, I immediately came out. They'd incorporated in January 1977. And sometime in the fall of '76 Steven had met Mike Markkula, and the business plan coalesced. Markkula put in $90,000 and they formed a corporation. They had to get the case designed, to get Rod Holt to design a power supply, and then they had a product.

DC: So when you came back that summer, how many people were there, and who were they?

Kottke: There was a real, functioning company. Mike Scott [then president of Apple] was the skipper (he's always reminded me of "The Skipper" on *Gilligan's Island*), and there were twelve people there. I was the twelfth employee. Rod Holt was chief engineer. Scott, Markkula, Holt ... Wozniak had a number but didn't work there full-time ... Sherri Livingston, who was Mike Scott's secretary... Jim Martindale was production supervisor, he came from Atari ... then there was Jobs ... I don't know how many we're up to.

DC: Seven.

Kottke: Randy Wigginton ... Chris Espinosa—both of them were kind of working part-time, helping Woz out—and Don Breuner, who was hired just days before me. And Bill Fernandez. And I was number twelve.

DC: Wigginton's the author of MacWrite, but what did he do in the early days?

Kottke: Well, his first big claim to fame was working on Applesoft. At that point, Woz was personally having a hard time, and Randy was very helpful in getting Applesoft ready, which was important, because Integer [Basic] has many limitations. And I immediately started screwing together power supplies and base plates and keyboards. That was my first job. I had a screwdriver in my hand. Because it needed to be done.

DC: When did things really take off?

Kottke: The important milestones, to me, were around the fall of '77. Well, we shipped our first unit in June, then quickly jumped to ten, twenty, thirty or forty a day for a long time. I was in production for the whole first year, and when I left production we were still doing only fifty or sixty a day. The first manual was just a folder—Mike Scott threw it together in a hurry. The logo was black. And I remember seeing the first color Apple logo that fall. And I recall thinking, *This is significant.* It was such a great logo! And I just knew that the company was on good footing. It was just intuitive. It seemed like a good omen. God, a rainbow logo! Why doesn't everybody have a rainbow logo!

DC: Okay, how did the Macintosh get its start?

Kottke: Well, Steve got Macintosh to happen. He didn't start it— he kind of took it over from [Jef] Raskin—but he had the vision. And that's what he really sees as his job: he's Apple's visionary. Now, I think it's way too sanctimonious to put it that way, but, on the other hand, that's what he does best. He sets the general direction. And Macintosh was right on. No one else was responsible for it.

DC: What did Raskin originally have in mind?

Kottke: It was the idea of a small, personal, "appliance" computer, as opposed to a "hobbyist" computer. Now, the concept of an appliance computer has many issues, because in order to be an appliance it has to be simple, easy to use, and non-threatening. You could almost say that, by implication, it has to be graphic. Now, Jef's machine was less than half the price [of the Macintosh]. On the other hand, it started in 1979, so ...

DC: There were tremendous arguments, before release, about pricing the Macintosh.

Kottke: Personally, $1,200 was my limit. Now, again, I'd revise that, because that was years ago. But I'd still say that, if I didn't work at Apple—if I were a student—I'd say $1,500 to $1,600. I could see spending that much. If I were in a consortium school, I'd be really happy. Even then, you get the computer and printer and the modem and you're talking $1,600. But students don't have much more money than that.

DC: If they have that much!

Kottke: Yeah. It's like a car. But I think that Macintosh is the first product that Apple's made that I'd buy, even if I didn't work at Apple. Well, not unless I had a good job.

PR: Is Apple on the right track selling Macintosh as a business computer? We get a lot of letters from people complaining, "I bought one because I thought it was a 'business computer,' and it isn't!"

Kottke: The word "business" has a lot of connotations. "Letter-quality printing" is a pretty big part of it. If you go into the Macintosh building, you'll see many letters posted on cubicles that people have sent in, and they're basically business letters. Letterheads and so on. All printed with a Macintosh. And I think they look great.

And yet the laser printer is going to put the whole letter-quality issue to rest. The whole thing of "letter quality" is like wearing a tie and jacket to work. It's the same ethic. The real question is flexibility and "niceness" and aesthetics, and whether it makes your job easier. The ImageWriter is such a beautiful machine; the ImageWriter and Macintosh go together so well that I don't have a lot of sympathy for people who say, "It's not letter quality!" But I do have sympathy for people who already had daisy-wheel printers and can't run them with the Mac. That's real bad. It took a while to convince Steve [Jobs] of that. But now we're fixing that, and that's a very high-priority project.

PR: This is way off the subject, but a friend realized the other day that the Macintosh doesn't have a Monitor [a ROM-based program that allows users to examine, change, copy, and disassemble blocks of memory]. And was he pissed off!

Kottke: Actually, what the Macintosh does have is a debugger called "Macbugs."

PR: "Macbugs"?

Kottke: Yes. It's the general-purpose Monitor and debugger program that we originally got from Motorola for the 68000 and that was extensively rewritten for Lisa, then crunched down somewhat to run on Mac. You get into it by hitting NMI or having a break point in your code. The name comes from Motorola Advanced Computer Systems: (MACS). There's also a desk accessory I've seen that just lists memory. I think when you have an integral disk drive like Macintosh does, it's not much of a disadvantage to have something like that on disk instead of in ROM. It's not used that often.

PR: So how can you get Macbugs?

Kottke: It isn't generally for sale—at least not yet—but you can certainly get if it you're a developer or a persistent annoyance. Or even a sincere seeker.

DC: And the nonmaskable interrupt instruction … ?

Kottke: Well, it's not an instruction. It's a button connected to a pin on the 68000. And all it does is send the processor to a specific address in memory from which it jumps to wherever you want—similar to the reset button. I don't think that's too technical for people to know. And the concept of a Monitor program is something people would probably like to know about also. Because that's—well, I was exposed to mainframe computers in high school. And I was not inspired, in any way, to deal with them. They were unfriendly, big boxes that were inaccessible. There was *no monitor!* There were switches and lights on the front, but that was way too arcane. There was no simple way you could just go in and examine memory locations. And that's what was refreshing, and eye-opening, about the Apple II: all of a sudden the machine was yours! You could sit there, turn it on, and you had access to every byte of RAM. And that was what got me, personally, interested in the machine.

DC: And that's what a lot of people don't like about the Macintosh.

Kottke: That you can't do that. Yeah. But, the fact is, you can! It's just a different way of going about it.

PR: But with an Apple II, you can just buy one, then go in the Monitor, and …

Kottke: That's true. And, in some ways, the Apple II is a better instructional machine for that reason, because it's very simple. But it's a whole spectrum, because, at the other end, the Apple II kind of "breaks down" for doing high-level stuff—the processor doesn't even have interrupt or exception vectors. It's a very simple system. Macintosh is a whole order of magnitude up in terms of system complexity. Everything in a Macintosh happens on interrupts. You can have all these different simultaneous tasks—Macintosh can really be a concurrent machine, without much trouble. Your desk accessories are, after all, concurrent applications. You can have seven different applications running concurrently.

DC: On another subject, how's Sculley doing?

Kottke: Sculley's worth the money. I think Sculley's doing a great job.

DC: How much is Sculley doing?

Kottke: A lot. If I think back a year ago about the impressions people had of the Apple II division—"PCS" [Personal Computer Systems]—before Sculley, PCS has really pulled it together. They impressed all of us with the IIc and the IIc monitor. They just really got their act together. That's a great division! I don't know how much of that is Sculley's doing, though.

DC: I remember old PCS jokes. "What's the difference between PCS and the *Titanic*?" "The *Titanic* had a dance band."

(*laughter*)

Kottke: I did hear that the Apple IIc event, in the [San Francisco] Moscone Center, was largely Steve Jobs's doing. They [PCS] were just going to have this modest press announcement for the IIc, and Steve Jobs went in and said, "Hey, c'mon! We're doing great things! Why don't you do great things too? Why don't you go rent Moscone Center?" And I think that's right on!

DC: What would you like to see Apple make that it isn't? What's on the horizon?

Kottke: That's what is most visibly Sculley's influence, from my point of view: the unified product range. And he's the only one who can do that. Sculley is the guy who can unify these various divisions—such as the Apple II and 32-bit families—and then group them together on a spectrum. Jobs can't do that, because he's too partisan, being general manager of the Macintosh division.

DC: But product-wise, what's next?

Kottke: I think we've got our hands full, for at least another year, just building IIcs and Macintoshes and helping the software get out for the Macintosh. You know, we're still unrolling Macintosh. We're still on trial; we've shown what we've got, but we've got to keep pushing it and supporting it.

DC: Apple seems to want to keep the 128K Macs alive, but everyone I know wants a 512K machine. Everybody!

Kottke: The thing to remember is that the 512K Mac is going to be $1,000 extra worth of RAM. And there's no way around that. Not within this year, I'd say. But for new products—well, you know, inevitably there's talk of a "Big Mac," a "Cheap Mac," and a "Lap Mac." If you think about what the "Cheap Mac" is, that's exactly what we already have. The Mac we have is the cheapest thing you could get in terms of a usable configuration. And you could only go up from there: double-sided disks, 512K, color capability, two drives ...

DC: So you keep the "Cheap Mac" and just crunch the price?

Kottke: That's right. And that's exactly what we need to do. The Apple IIe, for instance, is now being discounted to $800 or $900. And it'll get even cheaper.

DC: And to build a Macintosh must cost … under $500, easily.

Kottke: Well, it's hard to say, because it's very expensive getting a factory started up, and you've got massive amounts of overhead.

DC: So what do you include in the cost?

Kottke: Right. What do you include?

DC: Do you include Sculley's salary in the cost of a Macintosh?

Kottke: Another good point. (*laughter*) But the factory is really quite awesome. It's like being in a high-tech aircraft hangar filled with machinery.

DC: Is the romance gone from Apple? It's not like the days of twelve Apple employees.

Kottke: No, it certainly isn't. What I've seen over the years are teams of people that swell up and balloon in order to get a product out the door, then level off and slow down a bit, then eventually disperse. It seems like often the people who contribute the most tend to be the ones who get restless to move on to something else. But, you know, with all due credit to Steve Jobs, it's perhaps getting to be time for him to start putting together another small group. In 1980, it was getting the same way: the Apple III was out, and everybody was exhausted, going on leaves of absence, and Steve went in and started hand-picking people to "go to work on this little project"—the Macintosh. And it was like this new, little company—all over again. We moved out, moved into our own little offices—it was just like being a new company. Except that we didn't have to worry about expenses. Steve could do that again, and maybe he will.

PR: Do you think he'll do it around something Alan Kay's working one?

Kottke: That's a whole 'nother question. I think Alan's great, but I tend to be a little skeptical …

DC: There's not much evidence of his "greatness."

Kottke: My evidence is talking to him. In fact, everyone who talks to him that I know—well, you know Mike Boich [Mac "Software Evangelist" and MacTerminal author]? It was funny—one of the first times that Alan came to Apple, he was by to see Steve Jobs, and Steve was busy and handed him off to Boich—like, "Here, keep this guy busy for a while!" Well, Mike said he took Kay into the demo room and was showing him MacTerminal. But Boich said he could only take it for ten or fifteen minutes because Alan was overwhelming him! It was like, "This guy is just too smart! I can't take it anymore!" (*laughter*) Coming from Mike Boich, that's a compliment, because Mike's a really bright guy.

DC: But is Alan Kay "all heat and no light"?

Kottke: Well, he's *all* light, actually—the guy's brilliant. But one of the things about Alan is that he's very far ahead of the times. And that seems to be where he wants to be. But he doesn't have a reputation for shipping products.

PR: Maybe he doesn't want to make "real products."

Kottke: Which is fine. That's great! It's kind of like being a nuclear physicist—you're so far removed from reality; you're dealing with equations all the time. And yet, your work is very valid and necessary. Actually, I get the impression that Alan sees himself as specializing in user interfaces, which is potentially a very tangible subject. After all, like the Skeptic philosophers said, all you really know or experience is what you see, touch, hear, etc. *That's* user interface! I don't know. Alan worked on Dynabook, which was clearly way ahead of its time, so you can't blame him for not shipping that one! Then he worked on Star 8010, whose fate is surely mired in the monolithic heart of Xerox. (*laughter*)

DC: Let's talk about important new products. Is there color in Mac's future?

Kottke: Well, it's like this. It's not that hard to design a Mac or modify a Mac to put out, say, sixteen-color RGB to an external monitor. You could even use the current Mac CRT and get sixteen-level gray scale and use color-mapping registers to get four thousand colors or so. The additional cost is mostly just in the extra RAM to quadruple your screen buffer from 20K to 80K, and the cost of the RGB monitor.

PR: Then a color Mac wouldn't have the color tube built into the box?

Kottke: Probably not. You'd want to use the same black-and-white tube and have an external RGB video connector. Apple's even announcing an RGB monitor this summer. So, obviously, it would make sense for us to use that monitor.

DC: How big is it?

Kottke: The same size as the IBM monitor.

PR: Twelve-inch?

Kottke: Uh, yeah. I think it sells for five hundred something. It's a pretty good price.

DC: More, more! Is the color Mac … pretty?

Kottke: Yeah, and—

DC: Can you set the background colors and the text colors? Menu bar color?

Kottke: Of course you—

DC: Color, gee! Can you—

Kottke: No, those are—wait, wait, wait! Let's get this straight. The biggest question is how do you deal with all these colors in software—you have to have all kinds of new menu items and options and preset values. And then, relative to other things like disks and modems, is it useful and necessary enough to justify the cost? It's a big software job. And, of course, you can't make a product out of just the hardware, you need a complete package. I think a color Mac would be great, but I'm not sure it would necessarily get more work done. It sure would look nicer … I mean, years ago we all thought that the Apple III was such a great machine because it had that sixteen-color RGB hi-res, which looked so beautiful, and all you needed was an RGB monitor. And yet, how much software do we see exploiting that color? None! In fact, with an extended eighty-column card, you can get the same color out of an Apple IIe. And I still haven't come across much great color software—other than games, of course. Still, I'd like to think that we'll put color capability at least in the hardware in a future Macintosh.

DC: How do people in the Macintosh division feel about Lisa?

Kottke: You know what really bugs me? This is something that I'd like to see in print: I hear talk, even within Apple, about the Lisa being a "failure." And that really irritates me, because I'm proud of Lisa. I think it was a great success, even though it wasn't a "profit center." It made its money back. It wasn't a loss. The fact is that Lisa established us firmly as a technological leader, which is a very important thing. Just think if Lisa hadn't worked. I mean, the Apple III was … kind of embarrassing—for a while, at least.

PR: But how much of Lisa's "failure" was the machine's fault and how much was marketing?

Kottke: Marketing kind of overestimated the extent to which Lisa would sell itself.

PR: That's an understatement.

Kottke: But that's basically the issue—that it was marketing, not the machine itself. Overestimating sales potential leaves you with pricing that's too high in general, and our strategy of bundling everything together made for an uncomfortably high entry-level price. Another thing that hurt was not having the software development Toolkit ready earlier. Developers really needed Toolkit to make third-party software, but the whole thing kind of stumbled and faltered. It was a mammoth project and took everyone's energies just getting the whole package to work in the first place.

DC: Is Macintosh going to "save" Lisa?

Kottke: I don't think there's necessarily a relation. Macintosh is a very good thing for Apple in general. Lisa was a stage we went through that was successful in some ways and not successful in others.

DC: But lots of people go out to buy a Macintosh and decide they need a Lisa instead.

Kottke: That's right; Lisa's a more powerful machine. A lot of people need that megabyte of RAM to deal with very large documents. And a lot of people want the convenience of multitasking. Lisa's also a great Unix machine.

PR: Are the rumors true that Apple's phasing out Lisa and discouraging Lisa software development?

Kottke: I think that makes no sense at all, for the reasons I just described, but if I say any more, it'll be my job that's phased out!

PR: Is Apple going to kill off the ProFile hard disk?

Kottke: Maybe what you mean is will Apple continue to use the current five-megabyte Seagate drive that we build into ProFile? That's like asking if we'll continue to use 64K RAMs in our computers! For years we've all watched RAMs and disk drives get denser and cheaper—and then, of course, the whole point of our own ten-megabyte Widget project (Widget is Apple's name for the hard disk within the Lisa 2/10] was so that ultimately we wouldn't have to go outside the company to buy our drives. If we acknowledge that hard disks are desirable and here to stay, it makes good business sense to try and build our own. The other side of the issue is that hard disk drives are very difficult items to make reliably and in high volume. And do we think we can compete effectively with all the other companies who do *nothing* but make these drives? Hmmmmm ... I would expect that Apple will continue to make a product called ProFile regardless of whose drive is in it.

PR: How close are we to seeing a 512K Macintosh?

Kottke: I think that 256K RAM availability is a questionable issue. Devices that dense are starting to really push the limits of existing wafer-fab equipment. It's a questions of the chip vendors improving their yields enough to bring the price down. The 256K RAMs are still many times more expensive per bit than 64K RAMs.

I heard a curious thing the other day about 256K RAMs. An engineer at the Mac factory was talking about some 512K Macs that we were building up, and the RAMs seemed unusually susceptible to "flyback RFI." The flyback yoke in any CRT produces a big, whopping electric field. Well, the transistors that make up the 256K RAMs are very tiny devices. And the smaller the device, the smaller the currents. And the smaller the currents, the greater the significance of "background noise," such as the electromagnetic field from a fly-back yoke. At some point, the field will cause failures of the device. We're going to have to be very careful when we start making 512K Macs to test them for this type of parasitic effect.

DC: What about the 800K, double-sided drives for Macintosh?

Kottke: That's similar to the 512K Mac question. It's mostly up to our vendors—that is to say, Sony, in this case.

DC: End of the year?

Kottke: Could well be. The double-sided drive is more a matter of gearing up production—it's not a thorny engineering problem.

— Originally published as "The Straight Stuff from One of Apple's 'Grand Old Men'." in *St.Mac* magazine, August 1984.

RICK BARRON UP TEMPO

RICK BARRON

*R*ick Barron is president of Affinity Microsystems, Inc., makers of Tempo. Rick is a true Macintosh pioneer and an absolutely wonderful guy. Remember Club Mac? If so, you, also, are a Macintosh pioneer! (And you'll want to drop me a note to make sure you're included in The Son of The Macintosh Reader.)

How I Got Myself Into All This

I started out in life a government/journalism major, having worked for two newspapers and a TV station by the time I got to college. While there, I discovered advertising and became a copywriter at one of Indiana's largest advertising agencies (though tiny by any other scale, at 35 employees).

After graduating, I cleverly escaped the draft by joining the Air Force. There, I studied Chinese, Korean, and oxymoronicism (MI) for three years so they could get a year's work out of me and toss me back into the labor pool of life.

By the time I discovered the Macintosh, I had already been a speech writer in Congress, worked for Ralph Nader's Center for Auto Safety and the fledgling Environmental Protection Agency (when it was still protecting the environment), published a weekly

Boulder, Colorado, activities guide, created a five-times-daily computer features radio show in Denver, and dabbled at many additional warm-ups to prepare me to become a software publisher.

It didn't.

Part One: Club Mac

On April 1, 1984, Stephen K. Elliott, Wallace Westfeldt, and I formally began an exercise optimistically called "a for-profit Macintosh users group," and became president, technical director, and editor, irrespectfully.

Members received a disk filled with as many goodies as we could put in 400K, including the Mac's first terminal emulator, called (for trivia pursuers) MacAck, written by Kevin Killion and Bob Salita. It also included Bill Atkinson's *Life* game (which prompted the headline in the premier issue of the *Club Mac News*, "Bill Atkinson Discovers New Life Form," which he did). Plus, members got Steve Capps' graceful *Melting Clock*, first written while he was at Xerox PARC, and a MacPaint file of the Club Mac Certificate, replete with Seal of Good Mousekeeping and suitable for ImageWriting.

The *Club Mac News* was my baby. Too literally, since I often stayed up all night trying to get it to bed. As a monthly, its one-week lead time often gave our members the "latest" news. We would receive photocopies of photocopies of the membership forms we included, from island cliff-dwellers ranging from Manhattan to Pago Pago.

The first issue included a center spread of the famous "1984" Super Bowl commercial. That commercial, which attained the highest-ever "remembered" rating in TV history, cost Apple $500,000 for one minute of air time, a bargain compared to this year's $850,000 for a 30-second slot. The medium became the message, and it was hit short for several years.

Other *Club Mac News* features included a periodical listing of Macintosh software shipping or announced. In what can only be considered an epiphany of telecommunications moments for both of us, Apple's Guardian of the List sent me an OverVUE database of every program shipping and announced for the Mac. When I received it on my end, a file complete with icon, it was an electronic justification for this shaky conspiracy we call civilization.

A few minutes of watching a thermometer on the Mac and *voilà!* I had a ton of information. I knew Federal Express was really in for it. Of course, the telecommunications revolution has been neither instant nor pervasive; there are some problems to deal with, even yet. The file, for example, was sent with only *announced* products selected. Hidden within it, though, were also all of the unreleased products and companies with whom Apple was still under non-disclosure. It was quite a harvest for an editor hungry for insider information. Of course, it was never published. But it did make for some interesting phone calls.

Memorable events occurred daily at Club Mac. Our enthusiasm for the Macintosh and its easy access to the power of computing was stifled only to the extent we may have suffered from disk-swapper's elbow. One disk drive and 128K of RAM makes for a lot of work to open a small file.

Still, some people put up with anything to justify playing with this fun machine. Take Habadex.

Please.

We received a critical review of this very popular early program from a member. For fairness, we offered the publisher a chance to air their side of the story. They declined. So I asked Wallace Westfeldt to at least interview programmers at Haba, and we printed an explanation of the problems, side by side with the unflattering review. First the review hit, headlined "Habadebate: FIFO vs. GIGO" (combining the accountant's principle of First In/First Out with the programmer's credo, Garbage In/Garbage Out). Then Haba hit. An unhappy publisher. He threatened to pull his support of Club Mac forever. We felt very badly about that, but would have felt worse if any actual support were being referenced. At least we were comfortable that we'd offered every opportunity to fairly present both sides. (More, he adds ruefully, than some contemporary publishers are willing to do these days!)

In early issues, we attempted to alert our readers to interesting articles in other publications. *The Rolling Stone*, for example, ran one called "The Whiz Kids Meet Darth Vader," in which Chris Espinosa said about the IBM PC, "At first, it was embarrassing how bad their machine was. Then we were horrified [at its success]." And another was from an early Macintosh magazine called *ST.MAC*, in which the "Secrets of the Finder" article was described as "Two fun, irreverent kids, Bruce Horn and Steve Capps, interviewed by a third, Doug Clapp."

Among products reviewed or mentioned early on that year, some stood out. A smooth-riding mouse that rode on air pumped between two plates of glass gave new meaning to floating-point operations. One that came through with plans only was a foot-operated mouse, though it was a diametric precursor of sorts (ouch) to Personic's head-mounted mouse pointer. When Bill Elbring from Purdue University brought out some Las Vegas-style games for the Mac, we introduced one as "And you thought the Mac had no slots."

In July, 1984, we reported Sony working on a magneto-optical 3.5-inch disk that could hold up to 20 megs. Still working. In August, a column by veteran writer Paul Danish called for a better keyboard—noting Steve Jobs' early edict making keyboard cursors a fireable offense. It resulted in one dealer cancelling his subscription after a prospective buyer read the column, realized the limitation, and cancelled his order.

I frequently wrote about our staff meetings, held beside the Club Mac pool, sipping Apple Daiquiris, and retiring finally to the Sauna Room. A number of our readers believed us, as later conversations would reveal, although in fact we never grew beyond our warehouse-like origins, with one closet-sized room insulated from the roar of the industrial-strength heating system. Two modular wall units provided the only break in the interiorscape, except for the furnace room, which we labelled the Sauna Room and used as a backdrop for photo sessions.

In January, 1985, Wallace Westfeldt and I were invited to visit Apple Computer in Cupertino and were given a week's access to a brand new product called the LaserWriter [stet]. We produced the first commercial publication on it—the February issue of the *Club Mac News*. It was a revelation! I had known typesetting for years, starting with lead Linotype slugs, traversing the spinning wheels, disks, drums and strips of subsequent "cold-type" machines, and ending with a 3,000 character-per-second Autologic APS-5, driven by a pair of Dec 11/34s, with which I had become overly familiar.

This LaserWriter was clearly revolutionary. Instead of a $50,000 front-end workstation, a Mac could be had for under $5,000. Instead of two weeks of on-site training, a few hours with the mouse and you were up and running. Instead of bold and slanted stick letters, WYSIWYG!

We put out our largest issue, 64 pages, filled with a list of nearly 350 software products running on the Mac, and, best of all, reprints of Berke Breathed's *Bloom County* comic strips. These featured young hacker Oliver Wendell Jones and his pal, the Banana PC Junior 9000, a Mac Wannabe. We knew Breathed was on our side when the strip led off with Oliver on Santa's lap, saying …

Oliver: "Listen carefully … and do try to keep up, Big Fellow. I want the new 'Banana PC Junior' computer, 9000 series. That's the 32 bit MC68000 microprocessor. Not to be confused with … "

Santa: "…The 16 bit 8088. Total garbage. El Stinko."

Oliver: (Does a double-take.) "Santa Claus is computer-literate!"

Santa: "Natch."

I was both elated to be present at such a time, and apprehensive that it would be my last opportunity to apply this technology to the *Club Mac News*. Bitten by the Apple evangelism bug the previous November, I left in February, 1985, to become a software publisher.

Part Two: On Becoming a Software Publisher

I was present at the sumptuous press rollout in November, 1984, of Jazz for the Macintosh, from Lotus Development Corporation. Jazz was supposed to do for the Macintosh what Lotus 1-2-3 did for the IBM PC. Held in a vastly redecorated airplane hangar at the Las Vegas airport, during Comdex, it was quite a spread! Lotus limoed us press folks from our hotels (or, as in my case, from one they found acceptable) to what would only be called in wetter climes a potlatch.

A Reuter's reporter and I walked in together and immediately headed for the long tables filled with cracked crab legs, stuffed mushrooms, patés de moolah and more appetizers than we could name. It wasn't until we were stuffed that we turned and realized dinner was to follow, with many courses and several wines.

Lotus was a company that knew how to spend money.

Meantime, a Hill and Knowlton (as I recall) rep decided to introduce me to "Leon Novickas," techie product manager for Jazz. "Leon" turned around and turned out to be Steve Jobs, founder of Apple and, fortunately, a fan of the *Club Mac News.* We talked for a moment, then Steve said, "There's someone I want you to meet." He turned and yelled at top voice, "Hey Mitch!"

This managed to catch the attention of Mitch Kapor, founder of Lotus, as well as the other several thousand people there. But Kapor came over and Jobs introduced us, which resulted in arrangements for a private showing of Jazz. I arrived with four other reporters who had handcuffed themselves to me.

It was a good demonstration, but ended with Ron Anastasia of our group noting, "I didn't see the macros in the spreadsheet," to which product manager Eric Bedell, in perhaps the most carefully crafted response in Macdom, replied "Our focus studies have indicated that the Macintosh graphical user interface is not syntactically appropriate for a macro utility." Or something very similar. Enough to let us get on to the next question, anyway.

Down in the lobby, later on, we went back to wondering why they didn't include this critical component of 1-2-3, and several of us decided to look more closely into it. When the flash and smoke of ideas cleared, Affinity was founded in March, 1985, to make Tempo: macros to step up the pace of Jazz.

Before Tempo was released, Jazz shipped with the biggest hooplah of any software product ever, and slipped with the same degree of notoriety. As Lotus President Jim Manzi later noted, "We shipped 40,000 units that very first month. Within a few months, 41,000 came back. Even the pirated copies were returned."

So Tempo was rewritten to work in any application, and even between applications, something lead programmer John Pence pulled off before any other commercial program could claim that ability.

We scheduled the product to release in July, 1985. Then in August, 1985, at the Boston Macworld Expo. Then October, at the Long Beach AppleFest.

When that didn't happen, I sent a card to everyone who had pre-ordered Tempo: Please let us know which you'd prefer. (A) Cancel my order and let me know if you ever ship. (B) Send me a guaranteed-buggy beta version of the software now and the final version when it releases. (C) I'll wait, just hurry up! Among the hundreds of responses, less than five percent wanted their orders cancelled. About half the rest wanted whatever we had, and formed a very large (though not very efficient) beta test base, and the remainder said they'd wait.

We finally released at the Macworld Expo in January, 1986, but not before we ran out of money twice and had to find some pretty creative sources for funding.

One of our first tech support calls came from a company announced to me as "White Horse Communications." I'd never heard of them, and was tempted to have Janet take a message, since I was in the midst of a dozen other matters, but grabbed the phone.

It was The White House. "We're running Tempo on a virtual Macintosh over Ethernet from our Cray," the voice at the other end rattled out. "We haven't tested that configuration," I replied, adding, "but have you gotten our upgrade?" He hadn't, and that fixed it. Thank goodness.

One of our first fan letters came from a woman who used Tempo in Real Time to create a bouncing-ball style guide to teach her deaf students to sing in unison. That technique was later used in the State Department to teleprompt the Secretary of State's rehearsals. But the ways Tempo is used to help "otherly-abled" people have always been my favorite applications, by far.

When I helped out at a March of Dimes camp in the Colorado Rockies, watching a Mac provide such expression for persons who were greatly restricted gave profound evidence of the value of computers to humans. I've always given first priority to such uses of Tempo, and remain awestruck by such customers as one whose only means of communication with the world is through an eyebrow switch. That Tempo could play any role at all in such a life is both humbling and validating for me.

Not all experiences are quite so satisfying, of course. A caller once claimed that Tempo " ... rewrote the microcode in my ROMs." This seemed unlikely, given that ROMs cannot be written to, so I promised to pay the repair bill for any damage Tempo could have caused, if he took his Mac to a dealer. He spent two weeks, altogether, without a Mac, since the dealer would check it out and report no problem, and then he would bring it back to his office and it would fail, not allowing the Mac to boot from his hard drive or allowing a disk to remain inserted at startup.

Turned out it *was* our fault, but marginally. He used a trackball instead of his mouse, which he left attached to his trackball but unused. So when he bought Tempo he placed our manual on top of a stack of books, under which was his mouse. It was just enough additional weight to hold the mouse button down constantly. At the dealer's, everything was fine, but at his office, it would not boot. We were just glad he called to admit the problem.

A long-favorite tech support call to Wallace Westfeldt, who joined Affinity as technical director, concerned the use of Apple's communications software, MacTerminal. It wasn't a difficult problem, but one that required significant experience in telecommunications. When he had finished, and the caller was happy, Wallace asked, "But I missed the Tempo part of the problem."

"Oh, Tempo's great! No problems at all!" said the caller.

"Then why did you call here?" asked Wallace.

"Because Apple doesn't offer tech support and you guys know every program out there," he replied.

Now, as the Macintosh has matured to a true productivity tool, and grown beyond the word and pictures machine of its roots, neither the Mac nor Tempo are as simple as they once were. Batch processing, auto document formatting, and complex database manipulations are the essence of many of its uses.

But one of my favorite Tempo classics came from an Apple user group officer who recorded all his actions in a Wizardry game, saving the correct moves and discarding the missteps. Soon, he had a macro that linked all the right moves together to get him to the eleventh level with a single keystroke. The attorney's work on the Macintosh now has no single-keystroke solutions for the complex puzzles he solves, as he is one of Apple's top attorneys.

And as for Lotus founder Mitch Kapor, he was asked on the Well, a California BBS, if he was still doing any programming. "Only with Tempo," he responded (so I'm told).

Perhaps Apple Fellow Alan Kay was right. In a massive 1985 *Scientific American* article he said, "In the future, all computer users will be programmers."

I was aghast at that thought then. But now, I'm programming my Macintosh. And it's really fun!

— Copyright © 1992, Rick Barron.

BUGS

O ne of the *Great Truths of Macintosh—back in those early days—was that you crashed. Frequently. Today, one of the Great Truths is that you crash. Sometimes. But not often.*

This piece goes back about four years. That puts it after the Early Agonies and well into the Middle Agonies of laser printers, file format confusion and imaging model madness. In other words, about where Microsoft Windows users are now.

Don't you love it?

There you are, cruising along, doing your stuff. Have you saved? Of course you've saved! Not after every keystroke, no. Who does? But once in a while, sure.

Wham. You're dead.

Welcome to Macintosh.

First there's $2,000 or more to get a decent system cobbled together. Then software. What? $200 to $500 a pop? If you're not a criminal, you'll have the cost of your Macintosh—and probably more—invested in software.

Which only increases the joy when you crash, doesn't it?

Who's to blame?

Everybody.

Let's start at the beginning, with the 128K Macintosh. 128K isn't much memory, particularly when you shoehorn in a gaggle of system resources, fonts, DAs—you name it. Worse, you never know when a new resource will be needed, or when a resource currently in memory is no longer needed.

Oh, and there's the application itself! And the application might be larger than the available RAM.

The answer? A tricky memory management scheme. The idea was that all those globs of stuff—fonts, resources, whatever—floated around in memory. Some were "purgeable;" when not needed, they could be ditched. What remained would be crunched together, in hopes of freeing up nice, clean, sizeable chunks of RAM. Chunks to hold more resources, program data, and programs themselves. The programs would be "segmented," with each segment no larger than 32K.

Given all that, you could—in theory—run monstrous programs, even in 128K of RAM.

Theory, though, is one thing. In fact, the scheme placed a terrible burden on programmers. These globs of floating data couldn't be addressed directly, because their future location couldn't be determined. An indirect addressing scheme—based on "handles" that point to "pointers"—was needed.

That's one reason that Macintosh programming is hard. All those pesky handles. Handles that need to be de-referenced, locked, unlocked.

Enough gory detail, with one addendum: the next time you crash, see if the dialog doesn't mention "ID=2." If it does, feel free to curse handles and floating globs of data. One probably just floated away.

Still, an ID=2 is the program's fault. The application programmer's fault, actually. It's hard to program Macintosh, but it can be done. It's just hard, that's all.

I don't beta test much. I'm content with merely crashing in released applications. But I am beta testing one major program, out soon. My last beta release included an update letter. The letter mentioned that "over 75" bugs had been fixed since the previous beta release.

Over 75 bugs! That's great! Or is it terrible? I'm not sure.

But let's not put all the blame on those who program applications. There's a line of potential penitents.

How about compilers? Programmers write code. Compilers turn the code into programs. And yes, Virginia, compilers are also programs. And compilers can have bugs. The code that goes in may be perfect; the application that comes out may be buggy.

Then there's system software: the System, the Finder, Laser-Writer files. All potential culprits.

The compu-media loves to blast Apple for "buggy system releases." I talk with people almost every day who use older System versions because "I read about the bugs in the new System."

There's some truth there, but not much. In general, the newest System is "the best system," unless you're working in 512K, or on a "pre-Mac Plus" Macintosh. It won't be perfect, but it'll be better. Trust me.

Next up are INITs. An idea from hell. Mean, rowdy kids prowling the innards of your machine. Troublemakers. But too useful—let's be honest: too *cute*—to cast away, right?

You've been warned. Next time you've got problems, get rid of all those INITs (didn't think you had that many, did you?) and try it again. It's worth a shot.

Next up? Hardware. If something's askew, it might not be the application. It might not be INITs or buggy systems.

It might be that third-party hard disk. That off-brand Laser-Writer. The bargain basement modem.

Or even that pricey, pretty Radius monitor.

I've got a soft spot for Radius. Nice to look at, delightful to own, but drop it and it's—no, it's more like: drop any one of many applications into it and *it breaks*.

It's the "see how smart we are" school of product development. See how smart we are to tear off menus? See how smart we are to put in tricky "patches" to the Macintosh system? See? See?

See how some applications don't work correctly anymore?

Apple, wisely, tells developers not to be tricky. Tricky stuff may work now, but may break under new system software. And there's always new system software. You've been warned.

Formats next. Graphic formats are the most fun. In the beginning there was "MacPaint format." A noble format. Streams of bits that became 72 dot-per-inch graphics. No color, no gray scales, just black bits and white bits.

A few bites of the Apple later and we have TIFF, RIFF, PICT, PICT2, and EPS. More to come.

But why generalize? Take TIFF files. Please. Never mind that they're huge and unwieldy; that's another column. You may encounter TIFF files that are:

- 1 bit per sample, black and white, uncompressed, or

- 1 bit per sample, black and white, compressed with PackBits, or

- 4 bits per sample (16 grays) uncompressed, or

- 8 bits per sample (256 grays) uncompressed.

Or you might have a file produced by IBM scanners. That would be … let's see … oh, yes! Reverse byte order. Then there's the FAX compression scheme. This one creates a "compressed" file that's larger than the original! The author of that scheme is probably in Hollywood, turning Dr. Seuss books into mini-series.

Variations and permutations exist even within those broad file types. Thirty or more variations, just within TIFF formats!

EPSF? Do you mean EPSF files that contain PICTs? Or EPSF files that don't contain PICTs? The PICTless EPSF files are another personal favorite. They'll print, but you can't see the image on-screen, because there isn't an on-screen representation! No PICT!

Naturally, you'd like all your graphics programs to load (and print!) all the various files and formats produced by all other graphics programs. Who wouldn't?

Which brings us to PostScript. Macs are QuickDraw, Laser-Writers are PostScript. Different machines, different languages. QuickDraw can do things PostScript can't. PostScript can do things QuickDraw can't. Information gets lost, or misinterpreted, in translation.

Are these bugs? Sure, sometimes. Sometimes not. Could be that newest INIT, you know.

It'll get worse before it gets better. If it ever does get better.

The nineties look to be a great decade for finger-pointing. Pointing at and pointing up.

But it's not a new problem. As Buddha said, just before he logged off, "Decay is inherent in all things. Strive to be enlightened."

Speaking for the hardware and software industry, allow me to say: "We're working on it." Hopefully, in the next version ...

— Doug Clapp

MEANWHILE, AT MICROSOFT...

Here's a look at Microsoft Corporation, circa 1987. Today, Microsoft is a juggernaut, one of the world's most successful corporations and increasingly the major player in every area of computing.

Why is Microsoft so successful? Take a look.

I love to get lost in used book stores. I love to buy strange old books. My favorites are travelogues written in the late 1800s and early 1900s. Things like *A Trip Down the Congo*, and *Travels in the Turkish Empire*. That kind of stuff. Journeys to Xanadu.

I've never been been to Xanadu—or Europe, or even Mexico, for that matter. But yesterday I was at Microsoft. Lemme tell you about it.

First, there's a comparison that can't be avoided. The house that Jobs built versus the house that Gates built. They're different houses. Jobs, the visionary former hippie college drop-out turned wildly successful salesman. Gates, the Harvard-educated programmer turned wildly successful businessman. No, make that "shipwright." Microsoft builds ships to sail on oceans dredged and filled by Tandy, IBM, and Apple. Maybe that imparts a touch of humility, or a dose of reality—assuming the two are different.

Then there's location. Apple commands Silicon Valley. Intel is across the street. The air is sweet with stock option money; the parking lots are littered with BMWs and Mercedes'.

Up north in Bellevue, a clean new Seattle suburb, Microsoft is lost in the fog. I wore my favorite gray cardigan to visit; Seattle responded with a hooded gray pullover. They say that the city is ringed with mountains. I didn't see 'em. I did see Microsoft's parking lots. Fords, Toyotas, and Honda Civics. Carpoolers get the good stalls.

On a good day, you can see four modern buildings set in a ring, connected by walkways, surrounded by tall pines. It could be an insurance company, or a stylish hospital. The buildings frame a pool. The pool has a waterfall. Not a big waterfall, a little one. There's little ostentation here. Near the pines is a small outdoor gym; jogging paths wind back through the trees. The setting is cloistered, rural. It's not Silicon Valley.

Inside, it's quietly busy. Brisk and efficient. Unlike Apple, where many (most?) employees work in cubicles, here people have offices, real offices with doors and windows. Not big or fancy offices; small, neat offices: a desk, an IBM—though more often than not a Compaq—a Macintosh.

Other differences are more subtle. Microsoft seems more studious, less frenetic. More facts, less hype. And, although Apple has recently trimmed and streamlined management, Microsoft seems leaner. Whenever I called Marty Taucher, Microsoft's public relations chief, I imagined offices of "Marty's minions"—a slew of PR people, laboring over press releases, announcements, mailings, and events. It turns out that Public Relations consists of Marty Taucher, Sarah Charf, and a secretary. This, for a company with 1986 revenues of $197,514,000. So I promise not to bother Marty unless I really gotta.

Product management is handled by product managers. One product, one product manager. Young, bright overachievers. Nobody smokes. Mostly MBAs, but few blue suits. Each is responsible for … well … everything, it seems, involved with getting the product made, released, and promoted. A staggering workload for one person. I wouldn't want to work that hard.

But still, you know, it's Microsoft. They can do anything they want, anytime, right? They can afford it, right?

But it's not that simple. I said, "I'd sure like to see some templates for Excel. I'm a totally naive spreadsheet user. Anything over twenty cells makes me nervous."

And they could do that, right? Sure they could, but, as I learned, it's a question of money, people, and—most important—time. What's the best thing for Microsoft to do? Write templates, or do a new version of Word? Update File, or redo Lisp? Work on MS-DOS, or Windows? Write little add-on programs, or invent new applications?

To top it off, each manager has to fight for resources: programmers, staff, money. There's only so much of everything, no matter how big the company. Great programmers don't fall from the skies. When you're involved with as many products as Microsoft, you've got to be smart about what to do, when to do it, and how much to commit. Like they say: "If it was easy, everybody'd do it."

One area that gets resources is telephone support. The support machinery is a thing of beauty. Microsoft supports—lemme count—about 65 products. Everything from Xenix COBOL to Softcard for the Apple II. Imagine. Calls get routed, fast, to the best person to help, and the system is designed to make it likely that the first person you talk to is the "right person" to help.

The numbers that result from this are staggering. For example, take the week ending September 9th, 1986. Microsoft fielded 5,600 calls that week—for Macintosh products alone! Each call required, on the average, five minutes. A "Present Problem Analysis" details the reason for each. Was the problem "Software," "Hardware," "Documentation," "Inexperience," "Production," or maybe an "Inquiry" or "Suggestion"?

Whichever, it's dealt with. The knowledge gained is used in future revisions, to improve products. (And by the way: if you write a letter, it gets read. And probably ends up on the bulletin board.)

So what's new at Microsoft? These days, it's Microsoft Works. Sales are great. It's not a glamour product, but it's clean and fast and useful; a bread-and-butter product. Nice. And it's one of those rare products that wasn't developed "in house." Instead, Microsoft

Works was written by the people that wrote AppleWorks. Their idea was to develop Works then put it out on bids. Microsoft went after it and got it, despite that fact that—at least in theory—it might cut into sales of other Microsoft products. But, like they told me, "It's better to lose market share to yourself than somebody else." That's not dumb, I guess. Nor arrogant.

The "Excel story" is also enlightening. Work on Excel began under a cloud of Jazz's impending arrival. At the time, Lotus had never failed. Apple was counting on Lotus to propel Macintosh into the Fortune 1000. Lotus was gonna spend a ton of money to promote Jazz. Microsoft was worried. And hungry. They knew what they wanted—"The World's Greatest Spreadsheet"—but were worried that Excel would be perceived as merely glueing together Multiplan and Chart.

Mike Slade, the Excel product manager at the time, recalls, "So we took everybody—Gates, Shirley, everybody—down to Apple to show 'em Excel when it was still only partly done. And, you know, we're demo'ing Excel to Jobs and Sculley. And Jobs is saying stuff like 'So where's the word processor? Where's telecommunications?' And we kept saying 'No, what we're doing is Appropriate Integration'! Jobs was being really rude that day."

But, like the ads say, "The rest are history." In retrospect, Jazz was the best thing that ever happened to Excel.

And WordPerfect may have been the best thing that ever happened to Microsoft Word. On Macintosh, it's MacWrite or Microsoft Word. Since MacWrite has been "unbundled," Word has easily outdistanced MacWrite in sales.

But on the IBM, it's a battle. Word versus WordPerfect. They fight on the beaches, in the fields, in the trenches. WordPerfect is a stunning word processor. Microsoft Word is a stunning word processor. WordPerfect listens to customers and gives them what they want. Microsoft, in a real battle at last, recently unveiled Microsoft Word 3—a killer word processor. Microsoft, despite being the world's largest software house, doesn't have an ivory castle mentality.

Which is better? Beats me, but it's a slugfest of style, speed, and features. Fun to watch. The winners will be us, the consumers. In particular, Mac owners. But that subject requires an entire article.

That Microsoft "gives good product" isn't surprising. The product surprises will likely come this year, when Microsoft proves it wasn't kidding about CD-ROM technology.

— Doug Clapp; *MacUser* magazine

Microsoft wasn't kidding about CD-ROM in 1987. Or '88, '89, '90, or '91. Now, in 1992, CD-ROM, at last, is coming into its own as a standard peripheral. Microsoft hung in there.

Smart.

HOW I GOT MY MAC

RANDY NELSON

I f they ever play your town, catch the Flying Karamazov Brothers. It's an amazing show: stupendous world-class juggling and fall-down laughing comedy. It will be an evening you'll never forget.

But Randy Nelson won't be on stage.

It was early in 1984 at Apple headquarters in Cupertino and I was getting my first Mac—Steve Jobs himself giving it to me!

Actually, everybody knows there's no such thing as a free Mac. My partners and I were soon to earn ours in a fiery and fearsome display of Juggling and Cheap Theatrics. Good thing I knew the job was dangerous when I took it.

I was one of the founders of the Flying Karamazov Brothers, a troupe of jugglers and professional silly persons. Like many jugglers, I knew computers: I was a systems analyst in an IBM 360 shop before I ran away to join the circus. It turned out that Steve was a fan of our particular blend of hand-made theatre and hands-on physics, and we were hired to do an Apple company party.

A huge series of tents had been set up on the parking lot behind the main office. Robin Williams and Karamazov were to be the entertainment for the assembled Apple employees. Corporate culture du jour.

Barter is the ancient and noble form of commerce where the complex abstraction of money fails to replace the more fundamental exchange of my work for yours. We'd offered to barter A BIG SHOW for A BUNCH OF MACS, but Apple accounting had balked. They countered with an offer couched in money, and eventually a contract was negotiated.

In any small business, you wear a lot of different hats. In addition to performing, the Flying Karamazov Brothers wrote and directed the show, negotiated the contracts, built the props, and even drove the bus. I was the proud co-owner of a 1954 Greyhound SceniCruiser.

As good electronic vaudevillians, we arrived early on the day of the show to case the joint—and discovered to our horror a furious wind whipping the site. Wind is to jugglers what static electricity is to hardware, and we had been invited to a Van de Graf generator open house. The air crackled with hundreds of Jacob's Ladders.

Employees scurried everywhere, tying things down and smiling. None of our utterly cheerful handlers seemed to be able to make a connection between the wind and juggling difficulty. Our idle banter about it being impossible didn't seem to phase them. "Yep, lotta static today, hand me that chip puller … "

That was a pretty good character note for the people we met that day: apparently facing the impossible was commonplace. They were a wonderful cross, all passion and technology, like test pilots for the Peace Corps, Right Stuff meets Right Livelihood. Are you riding with me, Buddha?

At that point we were ushered out of the howling gale, and into the main lobby.

We jugglers instinctively exchanged the LOOK OF GRAVE CONCERN and asked if they could find us a quiet place to talk. We had about an hour before the show, and all we needed to do was invent a really good hour-long show that didn't involve juggling. Or at least, one where juggling dangerous sharp things that are ruthlessly blown from your hands into the audience is funny. We seriously needed to talk.

The cheeriest handler of them all—his hair not even mussed—began to wrangle us a conference room. Being on hold in a panic is typical in show business. Hurry up and wait. Having received clearance to loaf, I watched the afternoon lobby traffic: folks checking messages, the ritual low-impact flirting with the receptionist, the blur of people too busy to stay for the party hurrying out to the parking lot.

I had Mac-envy. I found myself watching the people with oversized, shiny, gray-green Mac bags slung on their shoulders. I noted the preferred carrying technique: the Mac-bag-indoor-counterbalance-and-slouch, a possible demonstration event in the next Olympics.

Years later, I realize that the folks I envied were really people stuck with taking their work home. The new phenomenon of leaving the workplace, but not the work. That's about as much fun as me having to stuff a brace of chain saws into my briefcase in order to work at home that evening. But sometimes other people's tools look like toys.

We're shown into a big cool conference room to the right of the main lobby. We hope it's quiet and empty.

It is neither.

There sits Robin Williams, the antithesis of quiet, in the midst of more Macs than you could easily count. The Karamazovs had opened for him in San Francisco years before, when Robin had first made it big. At the close of the run, he said next time we played together, he'd open for us.

Our handler noted carelessly that it was neat we were being paid in Macs. Our eyes became big like saucers. We never got an explanation. Apparently the accountants had relented, presumably because of a newly-discovered and advantageous tax break, filed on form B for barter.

Robin was great to be around: a regular person run at twice the clock speed. He erupted comedy. He effused. Endless energy, just ahead of the pulse. We relaxed. You couldn't help it.

Between Robin's continuous high-bandwidth comedy dump and the attraction of the rows of neat Macs, printers, disks and bags—shiny gray-green bags just like those I had coveted twenty minutes before—all hope of us jugglers figuring out what to do in order to earn these proffered riches was lost. We exchanged the LOOK OF CERTAIN VICTORY BECAUSE IT IS REQUIRED. We bathed in the excitement of the people around Robin, laid out our instruments of destruction, and waited.

Perhaps because the celebrity meter for the room was already pegging with Robin's output, I didn't notice Steve's entrance. I looked up from stacking clubs and he was in front of me. His eyes were intense.

He carefully introduced himself, something I've found famous people often do carefully, having met a few in some of my fifteen allotted Warhol minutes. I was thrilled and a little tongue-tied. There was a palpable sense of something very intelligent listening very hard, trying to discern exactly what you meant. A warm, intense spotlight of attention.

We gave in to the room. The afternoon passed all too quickly, and it was showtime. Robin insisted on opening for us.

I remember faces in the crowd that afternoon, wonderful smiles and wind-whipped, teary eyes.

We opened with a little introduction called Prayer. Normally we only used it for street shows—proto-theatre in its most raw and beautiful form. In street theatre, average passersbys are changed into an attentive theatre audience, and then are caused to voluntarily hand over dollar bills in response to the interruption.

We hadn't worked the street for years. These days we were playing on Broadway and in the movies, but it was street chops that were going to get us through this one. And that meant starting with Prayer.

We led with juggling clubs, also known as pins—pins when you catch them, clubs when they hit you. By force of will we urged the lightweight plastic clubs to shuttle between us, a game of catch with fifteen feathers in a fan factory.

Our concentration began to kick in. We felt the familiar slowing of time as we began to focus. Given enough time, anything is possible.

An errant club squirts past me and I watch in facination as my hand patiently follows it, snagging the knob, turning it over and putting it back into the pattern. I am as impressed as anyone: look at what that guy's hand just did!

Following a bit of patter, we juggled sickles. The front row laughs heartily as we honestly explain we may not be able to control the sickles. The last thing in the show they'd catch …

Hatchets and apples are served next. Eating the apples at the same time is, as you know, a requirement of the juggler's union.

Blazing torches were then offered, and with them went the remaining hair on the backs of my hands.

We asked the audience for three items to juggle. We bet the already-standing crowd a standing ovation if we succeeded, or a pie in the face if we failed.

Given that one of the objects was a pound of butter, the outcome of the bet was in little doubt. I remember as we juggled and later dropped an offered Apple IIc, that the keys came off like Chiclets punched from a cartoon mouth. I was later told by engineers that the keys were reattached and the IIc worked fine.

We took the loss of the bet philosophically. It was a good day to pie.

We closed with the Terror Trick. Handcuffs clinked together. A single torch hissed and sputtered in the wind. The egg hit the frying pan dead center as the champagne bottle popped.

A pleasant time was enjoyed by all. We exchanged the LOOK OF TREMENDOUS RELIEF.

After the show Steve wanted to share his work. He got Susan Kare, the soon-to-be-renowned Mac artist, to come in and teach me how to use a Macintosh. In a few clicks and drags she mothered an exponentially ever-increasing clutch of rabbits. As they filled the screen I could imagine the same growth for the machine.

In the years that followed, the Flying Karamazov Brothers Mac'ed their way across five of seven continents. I always had a machine backstage: you need something to do between compiles.

When my family was small, they traveled around the world with the show. But as the family grew bigger, it became harder and harder to manage life on the road. With our third child, the center of gravity for my world shifted completely to home and I decided to go back into computers.

I wrote Steve a letter at NeXT Computer. I told him I wanted to be the one he called when there was someone important he wanted the computer explained to, as he had that day of the show with Susan. He must have remembered because that got me the first interview.

Today I work at NeXT, teaching software developers. I still do travel a bit, but now it's rare that I have to drive the bus.

Randy Nelson works at NeXT Computer, Inc. He is a master program-mer, revered teacher to hundreds of aspiring NeXT developers, and co-author of The NeXT Bible.

And boy can he juggle.

PART

III

HEROES & VILLAINS

BURRELL SMITH ON DESIGN

The Macintosh logic board—the heart of the computer—was magic. Never had there been a computer that did so much with so few chips.

Compare the Macintosh to the IBM PC. The PC had a higher chip-count on its video card—on the video card alone— than the entire Macintosh.

Or compare the first Macintosh to Lisa, as Jeffery S. Young did in "The Journey is the Reward:"

"The digital design that Smith had come up with by January of 1981 was extraordinary. The Lisa, which by then had been in development for two years, was a planned product with a team of 24 hardware engineers and countless software programmers. A single working prototype of the Lisa machine existed … to work, it needed five circuit boards and a number of custom components. Over in a tiny suite of rooms in another building … a long-haired, 25-year-old engineer had made a new computer in a few weeks that was twice as fast and could be sold for one-third the price. It relied on a single circuit board and contained nothing but off-the-shelf parts."

Without a magical design, Macintosh could not have existed.

The magician was Burrell Smith: The right man to lead off "Heroes and Villains," a section which, I'll admit, is somewhat—but not completely—short on villains, as you'll see.

We lead with the best. In February, 1992, Burrell Smith put his art into words.

DC: So, could you give me a few minutes on the Macintosh?

Burrell Smith: I'm not really interested in being, ah ... what would you want to do with it?

DC: I'd put it in a book I'm doing that's an anthology of all kinds of things about Macintosh. The really interesting thing to me is why what you did [designing the Macintosh logic board] was so much better than what everyone else was doing at the time.

Burrell Smith: You know, it's been so long ago, it's sort of like, gee whiz, Mr. Smith, designer of the Macintosh ... it's a little dated, for me. But what I'd say is ... that it's having a team of people who have interdisciplinary knowledge.

It [creation of Macintosh] was essentially what Dr. Land [of Polaroid] did with his product. His little girl was using one of his cameras one day, and said, "Daddy, how come the picture doesn't come out immediately?" And he realized that he had solved the problem, because he treated the answer as the problem and the problem as the answer. So that's the answer: you make the film come out developed!

DC: That's the way it should work.

Burrell Smith: And then he worked backwards to figure out "How you do that?"—but that's easy. The basic idea is: what do you want it to do? Essentially, I think with the Macintosh that was the main thing: that what we wanted the computer to do was infinitely more important than how we were going to do it, and that's really true for any discipline. The decision of *what* to work on is infinitely more important than *how* to actually do the work.

DC: So you aren't be limited by anything. You just say, "This is what should really be done now."

Burrell Smith: Well, no. What I'm saying is that you have to distinguish that from the normal engineer, whose job is really to perform a function. To a normal engineer you say, "Okay, Sam, I need a 16-megabit board instead of a five-megabit board," and the engineer never challenges the notion that maybe we don't need a memory board at all! We could do it optically, using Kodak's new film holography or something—and have a gigabyte! So it's a matter of resonating the problems, as opposed to having the problems linearly defined.

And since no one claimed that they were able to completely define the problem space [of Macintosh], that really created the environment where we could resonate to the answer to the problem, and from there to figure out what the problem is.

It's a completely different idea than saying that it'll have this amount of RAM, this amount of ROM, and then going ahead and linearly implementing that. You determine "What is the answer?" as opposed to "What is the problem?"

DC: How did you even get to work on Macintosh?

Burrell Smith: Moxie, basically.

DC: Because today they would never let you work on it!

Burrell Smith: Well, you know, it's hard to say. I don't know if that's true or not. I think the way it works in any corporation is that you get to do the work once you've proven that you've already done the work that they would give you. So if you design a computer first, like me, and get it running, then …

The managers at Apple would come by and look at the original Macintosh computer running and they couldn't say, "Can you do the computer or not?" They would be asking questions the next level down, which are, "Can you make the video invert the screen, so the characters are black on a white background? Can you make the screen bigger or smaller?" You know what I'm saying?

DC: Yeah.

Burrell Smith: See, once the answer's fully defined, then the problem is solvable instantly.

DC: In one of the books about Apple, you're pictured sitting in front of a piece of paper, which is covered chips and components, and just moving them around until "it worked." Is that true?

Burrell Smith: That's essentially how it's done. What I generally do is … I have the chips … I personalize the chips—which is not unusual. By personalizing, I mean that I ascribe certain personality characteristics to the components. Then I determine how the compendium of components would interact, essentially on a social basis or a biological basis, almost. And then I look for places where the interactions are unfriendly.

And that's called … metamorphism is one term. Personalizing, I think, is a better term.

DC: So you're trying to create a "good person," in a sense.

Burrell Smith: Well, no, not exactly. On a chip level, like the serial communications chip and the state machine, it's a matter of getting them to work together in a group. It's just saying, "How do these components get along with one another?"

And the engineer is the manager of the logic board. So I became the manager of the logic board. Okay, so, you, serial chip, talk to this chip, and so on. It's treating microchips more as biological systems that relate. It's just a very right-brained thing. And I'm a very sensitive person, so I can tell very easily when the board, in total, doesn't have the right balance.

DC: It's an intuitive thing, rather than an analytical thing.

Burrell Smith: Well, right. I'm trying to pull together as much of the circuits and concepts simultaneously—you've got multiple levels, don't forget. You've got the user interface level: how will this effect the person using it?

Then, below that, you've got the engineering level: how will this affect the reliability and manufacturing of the boards?

And then below that you've got another level, which is "Can these components actually be purchased, how will the various submodules of the machine relate?"

So those are at least three levels. It's like the Star Trek chess game, where you've got the three tiers of the chess board.

DC: I get it.

Burrell Smith: That's essentially what it is. You're trying to solve the chess game on three different levels simultaneously. And there isn't a good way to do that analytically, because it exists in at least three orders of infinity, if not more!

It's more of a combination of intuitive and analytical, and I place enormous stress on myself. I concentrate very, very hard for eight, ten hours, even 24 hours in a row, just on a single problem. In that case [designing the Macintosh logic board], that's what I had to do … make those different levels work. Because the manufacturing people have to like it, the software people have to like it, the purchasing people have to like it. All these different levels have to be satisfied.

DC: Was there anything you remember as being really hard, or the thing that took the most time?

Burrell Smith: It doesn't take any time. The hardest problem is communications between management and engineering, and getting the actual computer defined. Once the problem, which is really the answer, is defined, the implementation is really instant. I don't take any time to design my products, virtually. Sometimes it takes a few weeks, but normally two or three weeks to do anything. I won't work on it if it's much harder than that.

That was true for the Macintosh logic board, that was true for the LaserWriter—which took even less time. That was only two weeks. It was true for the Radius Full Page display.

The Radius Accelerator took a bit longer … it was very difficult to debug. That took more than six weeks. That's the very hardest one because it has associative memory built into it.

I did the multiple versions of the Mac. I did the 6809 version of the Mac, the 64K with the original 68000 chip, the 128K, the LSI chip … and I had strong feelings when doing the custom chip that they were going to fail, that the team was not integrated well enough and that I'd have to do another version. And so I knew it. When it happened, I just ran home and did it!

Once I'm comfortable with the general feeling I get from everyone, in terms of their finally having defined the problem well enough, then the actual design … it takes me no time at all to do that.

So I do it with—the only way to say it is, with concentration.

DC: How did you learn this? Did you take any classes or just pick it all up from books?

Burrell Smith: Yeah, I took … I started building projects on my own, you know, a Heathkit radio receiver project …

DC: That's what I did when I was in high school.

Burrell Smith: And … let's see, I built a blue box after that, to do research in telephone communications systems—strictly, of course, legitimate. And then I took two courses in computers at Foothill College and took courses in electronics that I liked. A total of about ten courses at Foothill College—they have some very good professors there—and I just built projects.

The most important thing I tried to learn was, what was the psychology of being a good engineer? Their language—engineers have their own language—the way different chips are numbered, "Should I put a Shottky in because the power TTL is too slow?"

I do everything on the right side of the brain, whereas other people use the left side. It's the biggest difference between myself and other designers, because I deal totally on how do I feel about the design. And I can do the detailed engineering on the left side of my brain, but only after my right side says, "Go do it."

With most people, the left side dominates the right side when you're in the engineering field. I think, "How do I like the way the circuit board looks? If I had that chip there, would it make it look prettier?" I just use a free-flowing set of design alternatives.

DC: So there's an aesthetic? It really works better when it looks better?

Burrell Smith: No question. There's no question it does. And now it's becoming more of a science. And back then, that was one of Steve's better notions: that the computer ought to look good.

If you start with that as a filter for any project—that the project has to look good—if you make that the highest level criterion, it will always work.

These days, Burrell is engaged in solitary, scientific research not related, directly, to computers. Someday, maybe, years from now, we'll see his magic again.

VANNEVAR, DOUG & TED; THE BIRTH OF HYPERMEDIA

MICHAEL FRAASE

A*bove all, Macintosh—like all computers—is an information machine.*

Given that, it's time to speak of Vannevar Bush, who envisioned something much like Macintosh before most of us were born. And Doug Engelbart and Ted Nelson, as you'll soon see.

If Macintosh is the center, we're now at the periphery, where both Macintosh past and Macintosh future are found.

Your author is Michael Fraase, another master of media, who here imparts information in a traditional, linear fashion.

Vannevar Bush and the Memex

The concept of non-linear writing and reading of information was first formalized by Vannevar Bush in the 1940s. It has subsequently been elaborated upon by visionaries, including Doug Engelbart and Ted Nelson.

In the mid-1940s, most of America's efforts were focused on ending the Second World War. Vannevar Bush was Franklin Roosevelt's head of the Office of Scientific Research and Development. Bush was deeply concerned about the amount of information being generated by members of the scientific community on behalf of the war effort. More importantly, Bush was concerned about managing the data and making it accessible to those who needed it.

As a result of his concerns, Vannevar Bush made a series of assessments and predictions—including high-resolution screen displays, fast information retrieval, and the mass storage of information—that proved to be remarkably prescient.

As the Second World War was winding down, scientists were able to pursue individual interests not directly related to the war effort. Bush became more and more aware of the overwhelming bulk of the research documents that had been generated during the war, and he was continually confronted with the difficult process of searching across multiple documents for related bits of information.

In 1945, Vannevar Bush wrote an article—"As We May Think" in *Atlantic Monthly*, August 1945—that changed forever the way we look at the organization, storage, and retrieval of huge amounts of information. Bush was well aware that the human mind operates largely by association and that, by extension, man would work best by associative properties of thought. He speculated that an associative selection process could be mechanized, and that such a process, while significantly slower in performance than the human mind, would possess the property of permanence rather than being of a strictly transitory nature, as are human associative thought processes. Any specific bit of data would be accessible by entering a code, and the document would be displayed on the screen. Margin notes and comments could be added at virtually any point, and associations could be freely drawn between any two documents and displayed on adjacent screens.

The "Memex" was the machine that Vannevar Bush visualized as being capable of providing this associative thought functionality. The Memex was based on the then-state-of-the-art technology of the microfilm reader coupled with navigational levers. Although the Memex machine was never manufactured, another of Vannevar Bush's concepts—the Bush Rapid Selector—was developed and marketed by Kodak and others as what we now recognize as microfilm readers with index strips along the side of each film. Bush's concept of trails or marks and sequencing cues are now known as paths, tours, and webs in hypermedia.

Ted Nelson and Universal Hypertext

No discussion of hypermedia or interactive multimedia can be complete without mention of Ted Nelson, one of the most brilliant minds of our time and originator of the term "hypertext."

Ted Nelson, influenced by the work of Vannevar Bush and Douglas Engelbart, first used the term hypertext in the mid-1960s to describe a form of non-sequential writing. His written works, most notably *Computer Lib/Dream Machines* and *Literary Machines*, have served to influence the current generation of hypermedia pioneers more than any other texts.

Project Xanadu

Xanadu, Nelson's project of the past 30 years, is a global information repository and network he refers to as the "magic place of literary memory." Based upon his concept of "universal hypertext," Xanadu will consist of many thousands of nodes throughout the world, some of which will exist as fast-food-franchise-like establishments. Nelson refers to these as "Silver Stands." When Xanadu becomes a reality many thousands of users will have simultaneous access to mountains of information, through which they will be able to create their own knowledge trails and endless document revisions.

The Origins of Hypertext and Hypermedia

Ted Nelson, when referring to hypertext, means non-sequential writing, and by extension, non-sequential information retrieval and perusal. "Well, by 'hypertext' I mean non-sequential writing—text that branches and allows choices to the reader, best read at an interactive screen. As popularly conceived, this is a series of text chunks connected by links that offer the reader different pathways." We can also extend the definition of hypertext to cover hypermedia by simply adding animation, sound, and full-motion video to the recipe.

Quick to point out that hypertext could include sequential text within its realm, Nelson referred to hypertext as "the most general form of writing," since it is not limited by sequence and other external structures and conventions. Hypertext would render a more enjoyable experience for the reader, because the reader would be able to choose a pathway to his or her own liking, rather than the strict one provided by the author in more conventional forms of communication. "Unrestricted by sequence, in hypertext we may create new forms of writing which better reflect the structure of what we are writing about," wrote Nelson, "and readers, choosing a pathway, may follow their interests or current line of thought in a way heretofore considered impossible."

Most writing—and, by extension, most multimedia presentation—is sequential, according to Ted Nelson, because it grows out of speech-making (as opposed to conversation), and because books are easier to read in a sequential manner. In the same breath he assures us, however, that the structure of ideas is not sequential at all, using a jumble of coat hangers as an apt illustration of the interconnectedness of our ideas. He also credits the concept of the footnote as a break from the sequential, but dismisses it because it cannot be extended.

Non-sequential presentation allows the viewer to form impressions and bounce around, trying different tacks until finding the one that's most interesting or germane to the immediate task at hand. Hypermedia allows for an arbitrary information structure, thereby opening doors, rather than slamming them shut.

Ted Nelson foresaw that once we were liberated from the pestilent confines of the printed page, our writing and presentations would flow in a naturally interconnected manner. Additionally, a body of text could be authored without regard to a target market or "average" reader. Any level of detail could be achieved without concern for violating the supposed rules of general interest. Documents would be modeled after an onion, rather than a potato. Layers of detail could be peeled back and the readers could immerse themselves deeper and deeper into the work instead of skimming the most cursory of treatments. Again, Nelson waxes eloquent: "I wanted everyone to see that we were going to the extended, generalized form of writing, no longer held to the convenient sizes by printing and marketing considerations, no longer restricted to a single expository stream, no longer breaking the true interconnections of a subject to make a sequence (like branches snapped into sticks and put into a row)."

Computer Literacy

As much as Ted Nelson saw computers—especially personal computers—as appropriate hypermedia tools, he continually decried the concept of "computer literacy" as detrimental, because the issues taught to the non-computer-literate are often veiled in layers of unnecessary complication. He is quite adamant on this point: "Nearly everything has to be fitted into oppressive and inane hierarchical structure and coded into other people's conceptual frameworks, often seeming rigid and highly inappropriate to the user's own concerns."

Nelson also took a firm stand against the traditional structure of the computer "file," voicing a strong distaste for the "tyranny of the file" as illustrated by the file's detachment from relationships and history that subsequently results in more confusion, not less.

Computer-Aided Instruction (CAI)

A particularly ordinary target of Ted Nelson's venom was the early form of computer-aided instruction (CAI) that began to develop in the early 1960s. Nelson saw CAI as an attempted paternalism on the part of the schools at best, and at worst, fascism. "Though the student was implicitly at some position in a branching text complex, he or she would have no way to see it whole, no way to choose," wrote Nelson in 1988. "The student's only option was to answer questions, and these answers would implicitly make the next choice in a manner unseen." The entire concept of CAI rested on the attempt to control and restrict users, which was in direct opposition to Nelson's position of the promise inherent in freeing people to pursue their own interests, cross-references, and linkages. Always the pluralist, Nelson was adamant: "This was not the tradition of literature. This was not the tradition of free speech. It was the tradition of the most oppressive aspects of the bureaucratic educational system, dandied up to look scientific."

A Framework of Reunification

Nelson's broad-based goal, then, was a form of pluralistically general hypermedia, although he readily recognized that as the bandwidth of the component media grew, so did the potential for confusing disorder. Video, animation, and sound, while drastically increasing the bandwidth of the medium, raised the potential for confusion and greater incompatibility, and was symptomatic of the situation. His proposed solution was elegantly simple: "To unify and organize in the right way, so as to clarify and simplify our computer and working lives, and indeed to bring literature, science, art, and civilization to new heights of understanding, through hypertext."

Ted Nelson clearly perceived hypertext, and subsequently, hypermedia, to be a "framework of unification" rather than just another obscure structure. He duly noted Doug Engelbart's initial concept that hypertext be one piece, not haphazardly scattered about with bits here, there, and everywhere.

In proposing two styles of the organization of material within a hypertext document, Ted Nelson also demonstrated succinctly how hypertext would be much more useful for the reader than standard sequential forms of reading. He pointed out that when we read a work of non-fiction, we generally hop around from section to section to get the most information relevant to our current needs in the shortest possible amount of time.

Presentation and Effect Hypermedia

Nelson referred to the style of hypertext organization that concerned itself with its possible effect on the reader—manifesting itself in a series of interconnected "planned presentations" that the reader would navigate—as the "presentation and effect" style. At the core of a presentation and effect style of hypermedia, the sequences would be designed for their look and feel, and how they communicated their ideas to the reader.

Lines of Structure Hypermedia

The alternate hypermedia style that Ted Nelson identified as "lines of structure" simply represented the organizational pattern of the subject matter. The effect of the material on the reader—in Nelson's lines of structure style—while taken into consideration, was not a major factor and was easier to implement for the author, " ... since the author is only concerned with analyzing and representing what the structure really is, and the reader is exploring the structure as he or she explores the text."

Reader Orientation

Ted Nelson was also fully cognizant of the reader orientation problems within a hypermedia document. He points out that in traditional paper media, the reader is given "incidental cues" as to his or her location in the material: " ... the thickness of a book, the recalled position of a paragraph on the left or right page, and whether it was at the bottom or the top." Nelson went on to propose that new cues must be developed that are equivalent to the cues we subconsciously employ when reading more traditional forms of the printed word.

Nelson was fully aware of the potential of hypermedia to address complex problems, and firmly believed that hypermedia—with its inherent ability to present complex ideas accompanied by their interconnections in the same document—would advance the state of writing and learning. And Nelson envisioned taking hypermedia a step further, to include the pluralistic interconnections of many authors in a many-to-many relationship. "Hypertext can represent all the interconnections an author can think of; and compound hypertext can represent all the interconnections many authors can think of."

Thinkertoys and the Ten-Minute System

Ted Nelson, along with Doug Engelbart and Vannevar Bush before him, perceived our planet's greatest problems as involving "... thinking and the visualization of complexity." Similar in scope to Engelbart's concept of "augmentation of the intellect," Nelson's idea of thinkertoys is more specific, and would include, for example, a computer system designed to help "... envision complex alternatives."

The crux of any thinkertoy is the ability of the device to allow things of varying levels of complexity to be inter-compared, and subsequently inter-comprehended, by way of their interconnections. Nelson gives very specific instances in which such devices would prove beneficial, ranging from alternative designs and theories, to successive drafts of documents, to discrepancies in courtroom testimony. The structure of a geodesic dome, for example, is quite easily understood when each of its connecting nodes is examined in relation to the other nodes.

The underlying concept of the thinkertoy is that although the interconnections between vastly different problems appear themselves to be vastly different, in actuality they are more similar than dissimilar.

Significant differences between types of problems remain, however, leading Nelson to propose the most general of approaches to problem-solving, including a technique he referred to as "collateration."

To Nelson, the guiding principle of any computer system, regardless of its intended function—but extremely important in the case of a thinkertoy—is that any such system must be inherently, even disquietingly, easy to use. "If it is desirable that computer systems for simple-minded purposes be easy to use," he said, "it is absolutely necessary that computer systems for complicated purposes be simple to use."

Patently obvious, yes, but exceptionally difficult to implement. And therein lies what many consider to be Ted Nelson's greatest acumen. Power and apparent simplicity are not mutually exclusive in the eyes of Ted Nelson, and he's always aimed at (and consistently achieved) the demystification of the various hypermedia technologies.

Nelson aims for simplicity to such an extent as to condemn systems as almost useless that are more complicated than what he calls a "ten-minute system." A ten-minute system is one that can be learned by a novice and put to useful application in less than ten minutes. "I believe that interaction with computers can be at least ten times easier," Nelson states. "Ten times more powerful, ten times more vivid; and that these are issues not of hardware but of virtuality design."

Fantics

Ted Nelson's formulated linguistics is seen by many as camouflage to cover for the weakness inherent in his ideas. Nothing could be further from the truth, although I'm sure Nelson would have no problem with being called a vaudevillain. Nelson as vaudevillain is best exemplified by his concept of "fantics." In Nelsonspeak, fantics is simply the showmanship of ideas. "I derive 'fantics' from the Greek words 'phainein' (show) and its derivative 'phantazein' (present to the eye or mind)."

Nelson's concept of fantic antics to get ideas expressed and understood is right on the money. Contrary to closely-held beliefs throughout most sectors of our society, the new media will not require more and more technical specialization, but less.

All computer hardware and software systems have an inherent learning curve, the period of time required to learn how to use the system in question. New approaches to any problem have a learning curve attached to them: automatic teller machines, new cars, food processors, and computers. The beauty of the original Macintosh was its down-sized learning curve. Anyone could be doing something useful on the machine in less than half an hour. Macintosh formed a new paradigm for powerful computing machinery. Software designed to run on the Macintosh helped solidify this paradigm, and cries of "Once you master any Macintosh program you have a great headstart on most others," were heard throughout the land. How did this come to be? Aside from excellent design and the then-novel idea of "evangelizing" the system itself, it had to do with fantics. People were actually enjoying working with computers. So it's not for nothing that Ted Nelson tells us, "I think that when the real media of the future arrive, the smallest child will know it right away (and perhaps first)."

Doug Engelbart and Augmentation of the Intellect

Douglas C. Engelbart was the first of the second-generation hyper-visionaries to follow in Vannevar Bush's footsteps. Engelbart realized straight-away that while hypermedia was going to revolutionize our access to information, some sort of framework was going to be needed to structure the capabilities that we were going to be confronted with. His concept of the "augmentation of the human intellect" sprang directly from those concerns, and provided the framework for not only the budding hypermedia discipline, but also most of the personal computer industry as well.

Doug Engelbart eventually received Department of Defense funding in the 1960s through the Advanced Research Projects Agency (ARPA) to realize his augmentation theories. Many important ideas, familiar to many computer users, were born at Engelbart's Augmentation Research Laboratory at the Stanford Research Institute (SRI), including the mouse, windows, electronic mail, and outlining. Engelbart's augmentation system for the knowledge worker, however, remains to be implemented in a manner he considers to be acceptable.

If Vannevar Bush was the cerebral intellectual of the underlying concepts of hypermedia, Doug Engelbart was the task master, the visionary who dug in and got his hands dirty and got the job on track. Engelbart read Bush's "As We May Think" piece while he was a radar technician in the Philippines during the Second World War. The ideas proposed by Bush simmered within Engelbart until he was 25. Engelbart found himself living in the California of the 1950s, and decided to address, in some manner, the fact that the most pressing problems facing society were growing faster than the tools used to solve them. Engelbart envisioned a tool that would give a small group of people, working together, a better chance at solving problems that were becoming ever more complex.

Engelbart fully understood that what was needed was not a new way to expand knowledge, but new ways of discovering where to look for specific answers, answers that were already in cold storage somewhere. He also perceived a great need for better communications tools between the individuals working together on complicated problems. Although Engelbart's augmentation system and attendant tools remain in process, the underlying framework came to him in a flash:

"When I first heard about computers, I understood from my radar experience during the war that if these machines can show you information on printouts, they could show that information on a screen. When I saw the connection between a television-like screen, an information processor, and a medium for representing symbols to a person, it all tumbled together in about half an hour. I went home and sketched a system in which computers would draw symbols on the screen, and I could steer through different information spaces with knobs and levers and look at words and data and graphics in different ways. I imagined ways you could expand it to a theater-like environment where you could sit with colleagues and exchange information on many levels simultaneously. God! Think of how that would let you cut loose in solving problems!"

NLS and Augment

The notion of hypertext as bits of documents linked to other bits of information that were easily retrievable by a non-expert was only part of a bigger picture in the mind of Doug Engelbart. Engelbart first proposed his system in a 29-page paper in 1962, "A Conceptual Framework for the Augmentation of Man's Intellect."

Six years later, in 1968, a working system was up and running under Engelbart's specification. The system, called NLS (for oN Line System) included advanced features such as electronic mail, computer conferencing, multiple windows on screen, and a mouse. NLS was designed to allow anyone to read material written by anyone else, and make comments and link other documents from any terminal connected to the system. NLS, in basically its original form, is still offered today as Augment by McDonnell-Douglas, and is used mostly by the Air Force, although it is accessible via Tymshare.

Douglas Engelbart has gone on to form the Bootstrap Institute in Palo Alto, California, with seed money provided by an anonymous benefactor from within the computer industry.

The Knowledge Workshop

Concepts from both Augment and NLS comprised what was loosely referred to as the "Knowledge Workshop" envisioned by Doug Engelbart. Within the Workshop, any user could log onto the system via any connected display terminal. Once he or she was logged into the Workshop, all owned files, as well as any files that were shared among a group of users, would immediately be accessible. Files could be read. New files could be created. Shared files could be annotated. In addition, messages that were not connected to any document could be sent—immediately—to other Knowledge Workshop users. Documents were easily transferred to other members simply by "releasing" them. No paper changed hands, and the transaction was perceptually immediate. Documents could be released to others for their comments and annotations, and the Workshop user would have common access to other members' documents that were specified as a "shared" document.

If all of this sounds vaguely familiar to you as a modern Macintosh user connected to a local area network, it should. The basic concept of file service is identical. One of the new buzzwords in the Macintosh community is "groupware." As you can see, that concept is also borrowed from Engelbart's very seminal work.

What separates Engelbart's Knowledge Workshop vision from current workgroup practice is the absence of paper and its attendant paper handling. Paper is eliminated at all levels. If you wrote—especially if you wrote a lot—this meant an end to lost notes that you had scribbled several days earlier on napkins, matchbooks, or other scraps of paper. Within the Knowledge Workshop, all of one's writings were available immediately, right there. Cross-references, footnotes, sidebars, and annotations were instant and painless. The Workshop promised an end to the time-consuming paper chase, an end to looking for that scrap of paper containing last night's brilliant thoughts that just has to be here somewhere.

Intrapersonal computing, in the form of workgroup collaboration, was also a concept firmly embodied within Engelbart's Knowledge Workshop. Two people could work in a collaborative manner on the same document or set of documents. Two individuals, connected via a telephone link, could work together on a common document: changes made by one person on screen were immediately reflected on the other person's screen. No longer were geographically-dispersed workgroup members subjected to the time delays of revision-by-mail. All revisions could take place in real time, or at least a reasonable facsimile of real time.

Augmentation

Doug Engelbart defined augmentation as "increasing the capability of a man to approach a complex problem situation, gain comprehension to suit his particular needs, and derive solutions to problems. Increased capability in this respect is taken to mean a mixture of the following: that comprehension can be gained more quickly; that better comprehension can be gained; that a useful degree of comprehension can be gained where previously the situation was too complex; that solutions can be produced more quickly; that better solutions can be produced; that solutions can be found where previously the human could find none." Not only was Engelbart's intention to define and create new tools, but to define new ways of working with these new tools.

An appropriate example of Engelbart's notion of augmentation is the concept of writing. Before human beings knew how to write they could only transmit ideas by talking with each other. This oral tradition today survives in some cultures and even as part of our own culture, specifically in the folklorists of the southeastern parts of the United States. Once humans learned to write, they could communicate their ideas among themselves and have a permanent archive of their ideas. Writing enabled the culture to become more informed, because the writer could reach more than one audience at a time. Computer screens take the tradition one step further. No longer confined to ink marks on paper, ideas contained as light elements on a display screen, and stored as patterns on magnetic or optical media, can reach much wider audiences and at the same time enhance our individual "reachability."

Central to Doug Engelbart's idea of augmentation of intellect was a redefinition of what we recognize as a concept. For Engelbart, a concept became something that, like thinking itself, evolved. Outmoded concepts could be readily replaced with other concepts. In addition, he felt that human thought processes, and what he called "concept structures," could not only be monitored and studied, but amplified as well. To quote from his original paper: "We view a concept to be a tool that can be grasped and used by the natural mental substances and processes. The grasping and processing done by these mechanisms can often be accomplished more easily if the concept is explicitly represented by a symbol."

This realization—that the human is aided in the grasping of concepts if the concept is represented by a symbol—led directly to the notion of a hand-held tool used as a pointing device for manipulating representative symbols on a computer screen, what we recognize today as the mouse and icon-based graphical user interfaces.

Engelbart went on to recognize that a concept structure most often evolved on a cultural basis, either on a wide-spread or individual basis, and that it was also—although with less frequency—something that could be "designed or modified." Further, through appropriate modifications, these structures would improve an individual's ability to understand the most complex problems, and subsequently make it possible to reach more insightful solutions to these most pressing problems.

Augmentation Means

The "conceptual framework" upon which Engelbart based his work was designed to be a specific plan for his own augmentation research, and he found that the basic principles applied to both the individual and the wider societal levels of experience. Engelbart proposed that a synergy would result by designing appropriate hypermedia systems to work in accord with human thought processes, i.e., systems that worked the way people worked. Fully aware that the human mind is capable of only small steps, and that each successive step relies on and builds upon previous steps, Engelbart felt that the resulting synergy was not capable of producing any larger steps, only more sure-footed ones.

Doug Engelbart referred to the extension of human capabilities within his system as "augmentation means." He further defined the augmentation means into a group of four basic classes: artifacts, language, methodology, and training.

- The artifact class referred to the human capability of manipulation of symbols and physical objects to make persons more comfortable.

- The language class addressed the manner in which the human mind organizes a world view into the concepts that the mind uses to create a model of the world, and the symbols that are attached to those concepts in the thinking process.

- The methodology class spoke directly to the procedures employed by the individual in any problem-solving exercise.

- The training class was comprised of the conditioning needed to make the other three augmentation means work effectively.

Process Hierarchies

Based upon his concept of augmentation means, Engelbart further observed that augmentation means served to break up large, complex problems into more manageable chunks, allowing the individual to approach the problem as a series of small steps. He called the structure of the small steps "process hierarchies." Although he recognized that each small step—each sub-process—was in itself a process, Engelbart also realized that the human being never uses a "… completely unique process every time he performs a new task."

Each time we are confronted with a new problem we don't reinvent the wheel; rather, we build upon what we already know, using what we already know. To Engelbart, it was clear that we have a finite number of "tools" with which to fashion new solutions, but that the finiteness of the number of tools in no way bore upon the solutions to complex problems that could be arrived at.

As one of my generation's mythical heroes, Mr. Natural, proposed, we have to use the right tool for the job. Even with a finite number of tools at our collective disposal, few of us ever become proficient with more than a handful of them; we continue to re-use tools that have worked in the past when confronted with new problems. The down side of this is that many of us tend to look at every problem as a nail if the only tool we're proficient with is a hammer.

Michael Fraase is the proprietor of Arts & Farces, a multi-faceted communications and professional services business specializing in hypermedia production, technical writing, desktop/electronic publishing, and software design. Fraase is the author of numerous books, including Groupware for the Macintosh *(Business One Irwin, 1991),* Structured Publishing from the Desktop:Frame Technology's FrameMaker *(Business One Irwin, 1992), and the* Business One Irwin Rapid Reference Series *(Business One Irwin, 1992, 1993).*

GUY KAWASAKI UNDER THE LIGHTS

W hen I started this book, I had a very short list of people I swore I'd badger until the end of time (okay: until my deadline) to contribute. Guy Kawasaki—evangelist, columnist, speaker, author, businessman—was on the short list.

I looked up his bio on one of the information services the other day. Under "occupation," he'd written: unemployed.

We should all be so unemployed.

Guy's most recent book is Selling the Dream. As a warm-up, he wrote the best-seller The Macintosh Way.

As "Keeper of the Flame," it's only right to put Guy Kawasaki under the lights.

What, exactly, did you do in the Macintosh Division?

I was Apple's second software evangelist. Mike Boich, currently the chairman of Radius, was the first. We used fervor, zeal, and reality distortion, but never money, to convince people to do software for a computer with 128K of RAM, no hard disk, no technical support, no marketing, and no installed base.

Wasn't it tough convincing early developers to write software? Especially when the Macintosh crashed all the time? Mine sure did.

I like to tell people that it was difficult to increase the bravado of our accomplishments and help my book sell, but it wasn't. In most cases, developers started salivating the moment they saw the Finder and MacPaint for the first time.

Macintosh crashing all the time? No big deal. That hasn't changed to this day. Macintosh even crashes spectacularly. So what?

I remember Mike Murray, the director of marketing of the Macintosh Division, telling me, "You'll never need to buy an application."

He must have meant that as a member of the press, you could always shake down developers for free copies. Actually, he was probably alluding to the LISA Division theory that Apple would create and bundle all the software one would need.

What happened to this theory?

The failure of LISA was a blast of cold air in our faces. It became very obvious that we needed third-party software of every sort for Macintosh to be successful. Thus, we evangelists were supposed to "let a thousand flowers bloom."

Was the original price point of $2,495 too high? Was trading profits for market share the right thing to do?

$2,495 seems like a high price now, but components were more expensive then. At the time, $2,495 was a very aggressive price. I don't think we were trading profits for market share at all. We were trying to change the world while still trying to make a reasonable return.

Looking back, what products and companies are you most proud of bringing into the fold?

I am most proud of evangelizing the small companies and startups like Living Videotext, Silicon Beach Software, and Mainstay. They were the ones who got the "religion." The larger companies thought that they were doing us a favor. As an arrogant person, I have a hard time dealing with other people's arrogance.

What companies couldn't you persuade to create Macintosh software?

Ashton-Tate. Software Publishing. I quickly learned Guy's software evangelism algorithm: a company's success on a new platform is inversely related to its success on current platforms. This is a nice way of saying "Rich bozos don't get it."

What's the future of Apple?

No one, least of all Apple, knows the future of Apple. In a world where we are shocked by the destruction of the Berlin Wall and the downfall of communism, how could we possibly know the future of a speck of dust like Apple?

However, if you are agnostic or atheist, you must rethink your position on the existence of God. Apple's continued success and survival is proof that there is a God. Nothing else can explain this. Apple will survive because there is a God.

Is the Macintosh architecture running out of steam?

From the day a computer architecture is shipped, it starts running out of steam. In the case of Macintosh, there's probably steam to go a total of twelve years, so we have four or five left.

Of course, the pundits and analysts will predict the immediate end of Macintosh because of some screwball UNIX strategic alliance announcement. These people get paid to be controversial and newsworthy. Like the Japanese say, "If you can't do, you consult. If you can't consult, you write."

Speaking of alliances, what do you think of the Apple and IBM alliance?

In the short term, it will have one good effect: Apple can tell doubters in Macintosh, "If it's good enough for IBM, it's good enough for you." In the long run, I will be astounded if it produces anything.

Apple and IBM have "jungle fever"—as in the Spike Lee movie. Apple lusts for IBM's legitimacy. IBM lusts for Apple's coolness. Unfortunately, very few relationships based on lust last longer than a quick trip to the bordello.

Mark my words, in 1994 or thereabouts, Apple will announce that "in order to more quickly and effectively serve the needs of its customers, the alliance has been dissolved." And all the analysts and pundits will say, "Gosh, that makes sense."

In a *NeXTWORLD* column, you wrote about Steve Jobs and the future of NeXT. You ended the column with a memorable statement that's been widely quoted. What was it?

Something to the effect that medicine will cure death and government will repeal all taxes before Steve Jobs will fail.

Why? If you have to ask, you just won't get it. Steve is Steve. That's all that need be said.

You've become one our country's leading exponents of The Right Thing The Right Way. What's that mean?

It means that there is an idealistic way to do business—doing the right things for your customers and doing them the right way—that leads not only to customer satisfaction but also to profits. I've never heard of a company going broke providing too much service and support.

What do you think of the Japan-bashing that's going on today?

Wrong thing, wrong way. Americans are turning into over-paid wimps. For the past ten years, all we've cared about is leverage buy-outs and junk bonds. Not the customer. Now Japan is eating our shorts in some industries—what a surprise!

The best thing people could do to rejuvenate American industry is buy the best product they can, whether American, Japanese, Fijian, or Yugoslavian. When American industry understands that consumers will buy "the best," then will they produce the best. Buying American for the sake of buying American is ludicrous.

By the way, whether America or Japan "wins," I come out okay.

What should consumers look for in software?

Good software is like pornography: very difficult to describe but you know it when you see it. Good software is art: you can see the "soul" of a programmer or programmers. Good software is fun: it should bring a smile to your face when you use it. Good software causes an erection in the mind of a software evangelist. (Guy: I may take this last sentence out.) (Doug: leave it in.)

What were the joys and frustrations of ACIUS?

On a much smaller scale, asking me about ACIUS is like asking Steve Jobs about Apple. The memories are bitter and sweet. I have no regrets about starting ACIUS or leaving it.

Why do you hate Microsoft so much?

I don't hate Microsoft *that* much. I have tremendous respect for the company and for Bill Gates. I believe, for example, he is the best person in the world to run Apple.

I simply believe that Microsoft's goal is total domination of the computer industry. That's okay—a company should have that kind of goal. I don't have to like it, and I can try to slow it down or stop it. I like a fragmented, entrepreneurial, eclectic, and scatterbrained computer industry.

What's next for you?

I've figured out that all men are cremated equal; Bill Gates and I will both be reduced to about a pound of dust. I want to foster a new technique for changing the world and making it a better place, called evangelism. I want to be the evangelist for evangelism.

— Copyright 1992 © Guy Kawasaki

You can help Guy achieve financial parity with Bill Gates—in this life—by badgering your local bookseller for: Selling the Dream *(HarperCollins, ISBN 0-06-016632-0);* The Macintosh Way *(HarperCollins, ISBN 0-06-097338-2); and* Database 101 *(PeachPit Press, ISBN 0-938151-52-5). All products, by the way, of the* American *publishing industry.*

BILL GATES KILLS MACBASIC

DANIEL ICHBIAH

MacBasic was a work of power, art, and love. Donn Denman, who previously wrote Business BASIC for the Apple III, developed a version of the Basic language for Macintosh that was remarkable for its time—and would still be a beautiful, remarkable language today. MacBasic didn't require line numbering, could run multiple programs at once (in 1984 on a 128K Mac, remember), had sophisticated control structures similar to those in Pascal and other high-level languages, and offered almost complete access to routines in the Macintosh ROMs. It was really neat.

It never shipped.

In the meantime, relations between Apple and Microsoft grew strained. According to an account in the *Wall Street Journal* (September 25, 1987), the issue of Apple's MacBasic created a rift between the two firms. In 1985, shortly after becoming chairman, John Sculley wanted Apple to develop MacBasic. He hoped this computer language would have the same igniting effect on the sluggish Mac market that Microsoft's BASIC had had on the Apple II market. Bill Gates, however, was strongly opposed to this plan, and threatened to revoke Apple's license to the BASIC for the Apple II, "Unless Mr. Sculley killed MacBasic and signed over to Microsoft the rights to the MacBasic name." Sculley made the painful decision to comply. With morale already low at Apple, this

185

move led several key software engineers to resign in disgust. "He insisted that Apple withdraw what was an exceptional product," recalls Bill Atkinson, an Apple software engineer. "He held the gun to our head."

Apple was quick to respond in kind to Gates' coup. A few months later, Jobs told Gates that he thought it unwise to ship programs like Multiplan, Chart, and File with the Mac. Gates was persuaded, and that contract was voided. Gates later discovered that Jobs had decided to bundle two Apple programs, MacPaint and MacWrite, with the Macintosh. He was furious.

— Printed with permission *The Making of Microsoft*, Daniel Ichbiah © 1991, Prima Publishing, PO Box 1260, Rocklin, CA 95677, $22.95 ppd.

The story has a further end. Two ends, in fact. First, Microsoft released Microsoft Basic for Macintosh. The language did fairly well, for a time. And the winner is … Microsoft.

Not!

Bill Atkinson's HyperCard blew away Microsoft's Basic, ushering in a new era of "programming for the rest of us." Donn Denman's revenge is Atkinson's beautiful and remarkable HyperTalk language. HyperTalk doesn't require line numbers, has sophisticated control structures similar to those in Pascal and other high-level languges, and—through external routines—offers complete access to routines in the Macintosh ROMs. And much more.

For more of Microsoft's and Bill Gates' history, pick up The Making of Microsoft. *It's engrossing, straight-ahead journalism written by a man who obviously admires Bill Gates, and should. Kidding aside, Bill, we love ya. Really.*

WHAT MAKES APPLE RUN?
AN INTERVIEW WITH JOHN SCULLEY

MARY EISENHART

I t's the eighties. 1988, to be exact. A time of yuppies, beamers, and
(ahem) "third-wave" corporations. Apple's on a roll, finally. Sculley's on
a roll, finally. Life is good as Mr. Sculley sits down with MicroTimes'
editor Mary Eisenhart for a love-feast of sorts. What follows is either a
remarkable look at a corporate visionary who will lead us into the next
century, or … a gooey, touchie-feelie, new-age interview that now
seems dated and naive.

You decide.

Apple Computer's had a very successful year. Desktop publishing
has functioned as, in vice president Jean-Louis Gassee's phrase, a
"Trojan niche," winning the Macintosh first a foothold, then an
entrenched position, in the lucrative corporate market. New-gen-
eration Macs have arrived, and a ground-breaking software "erec-
tor set" *HyperCard* has been released and bundled with all new
Macs. The Apple II continues to thrive in the educational marketplace, and the new IIGS is winning wide acceptance.

All in all, things are looking pretty good for a company many
analysts had all but written off a couple of years ago. And while
he'd probably credit the turnaround in Apple's fortunes to its individual employees, much of the change is due to president/CEO

John Sculley's ability to fuse the company's visionary origins and obsession with the "insanely great" with shrewd marketing and a recognition of today's business realities.

Other computer companies will sell you a machine. Some of them might sell you a solution. Apple will do both those things, and rather well, but it's also selling you a piece of the future.

Somewhere in his book *Odyssey*, Sculley makes the point that Apple's statements and presentations are necessarily heavy on metaphor and figurative language, because the essential business of Apple Computer is based on the development of things that haven't been invented yet.

When you watch an Apple commercial, attend an Apple product unveiling, or one of its traveling road shows, you're being invited to participate in a glorious experiment. When you buy an Apple computer, you're not just buying a machine, you're staking a claim to limitless possibilities. For Apple, the hearts and minds of its customers are at least as vital to the company's present and future as are their wallets.

When John Sculley arrived in 1983 as president and CEO of Apple, it was a startling development. He seemed a classic button-down corporate executive (indeed, he was affably introduced to his new colleagues as "the guy from Corporate America"), albeit an unusually successful one who'd become president of Pepsi-Cola at the unheard-of age of 38, and was considered a likely successor to the chairman of all of PepsiCo.

However, *Odyssey* reveals another side to that stereotype—we see Sculley as the breaker with Tradition, the maverick among the Suits, able to create successful marketing strategy around social change. The roots of Apple's masterful use of hoopla, for instance, can be found in one of Sculley's early triumphs, the Pepsi Generation commercials. A campaign to bring Pepsi a new image as the choice of the baby-boom generation, it used beautifully photographed scenes of often-astonishing emotional intensity. It shook up the formerly staid cola company and brought it hordes of new customers. As Sculley says in *Odyssey:*

"Suddenly we had a revived product and a whole new social group who identified with Pepsi as if it were a new religion. The commercials were successful because they articulated a lifestyle to which a new, more affluent, generation of Americans could aspire, a generation which, of course, drank Pepsi. It showed life as people want it to be, without complication or distraction—a young boy playing with puppies in a field or a cute little girl who dropped a piece of watermelon on her dress.

The vignettes of life's "magic moments" captured America's imagination. They evoked cherished middle-American values, of familial love and the innocence of children. The commercials subtly positioned Pepsi as the modern American soft drink, and by contrast, Coke as the old-fashioned cola.

" … Marketing, after all, is really theater. It's like staging a performance. The way to motivate people is to get them interested in your product, to entertain them, and to turn your product into an incredibly important event."

Odyssey offers a vividly-drawn study in contrasts—the rigidly structured world of Pepsi, a highly competitive environment where Coke was The Enemy, and careers made or broken over tenths of a percentage point of market share, compared to Apple's loose structure, impatience with convention, obsession with vision, and ongoing state of creative anarchy.

It tells of the persistent attempts by Apple's mercurial founder Steve Jobs to persuade Sculley to assume the presidency of a young computer company, a campaign that finally succeeded when Jobs threw out the challenge, "Do you want to spend the rest of your life selling sugared water, or do you want a chance to change the world?"

The book chronicles Sculley's acceptance of the challenge, his growing friendship and philosophical affinity with Jobs, the disintegration of the friendship, and peril to the company in the turbulent days of 1985 as the bottom fell out of the consumer market for computers. It continues with the reconstruction of the company to its current prosperous state, and paints a glowing picture of a future in which individuals have powerful, intuitive tools (Sculley postulates one called a Knowledge Navigator) with which to work and learn.

More than just another tale of life at the top, though, *Odyssey* offers a unique perspective on a world in transition. Not unlike Gassee's book, *The Third Apple*, released earlier this year, it evangelizes Apple's perspective on how the world, business and otherwise, is evolving, and what a forward-looking company can do to prepare for it. Thanks in part to talk-show appearances and other strategic promotions for the book, its message is reaching an audience far beyond the personal computer industry.

Apple is, in a sense, its own most important product, and Sculley has proved himself a master at making it "an incredibly important event."

What appealed to you about Steve Jobs' line about sugared water and changing the world? The typical successful corporate type probably wouldn't have cared at all—why did it work for you?

Because I was known to the outside world as the archetypal corporate executive, but I was really a romantic at heart. I had always been interested in things that had very little to do with business. I was interested in electronics when I was young, and I was interested in the arts. And to suddenly be posed with the choice of continuing the life that I had lived as a professional manager, or going off and doing something that was not only radically different, but much closer to what my earlier interests were, really hit home.

What about the world needed changing?

I felt that there was a chance to do something that was different from the heavily institutionalized world that I was a part of. Here was someone [Jobs] who had no baggage at all from the industrial age, and was talking about a whole new age, the information society, and one in which Apple itself had made some significant changes—it created not only the company, it created a whole industry. And I was being given the opportunity to be a part of it. My sense was that we were just at the beginning.

You were pretty successful in the institutionalized world—why were you anxious to leave it?

I *wasn't* anxious to leave it.

But you did.

I think it caught me at a point where I was either going to sit back and enjoy the fruits of my work over the years, which is what most people in corporate America do at some point. But I was about ten years early—I was about ten years younger than most people are in corporate America who have that kind of position. So I wasn't in my middle fifties, I was in my middle forties. The idea of packing it in in my middle forties didn't make a lot of sense to me, and yet I couldn't figure out what else I wanted to do.

And then suddenly I was confronted with a chance to do something that was a complete unknown to me, and which I felt I was very unprepared for, but one which became extremely haunting almost, because it kept coming back to me time and time again as—maybe this is what I was *really* interested in doing. And maybe I never should have gone off to corporate America in the first place. It was only by accident that I really did.

Would it have been possible at the time you went off into corporate America for you to have done this?

Pretty unlikely, because it didn't exist. Silicon Valley was still apricots.

The reader discovers in my book that I was actually very much wrapped up in technology when I was young. I loved it—I never played with toys, I always played with parts from radios and took things apart—I was much better at taking things apart than putting things together (laughs).

What factors enabled Apple to come into existence at the time it did?

I think, like most success in the world, timing in life is everything, and Apple had extraordinarily good timing. Because if it had come out with these ideas ten years earlier, the technology wasn't ready to implement it.

Look at Ted Nelson [who created the Hypertext concept in 1960].

Sure, look at Ted Nelson—there are a lot of people you could look at who had many of the same ideas, back in the 1960s, but the technology wasn't there to be able to implement it. And Apple had just the right mix of people with its founders, and the right skills—Wozniak who could build it, Jobs, who envisioned the company, Markkula, who was savvy enough to be able to set the company up and get a strong board of directors, and Mike Scott, who could actually operate it. So they had, I guess, a combination of the right people at the right time. It happened to be not just the right time to start a company, but the right time to start a whole industry.

You spend a fair amount of time in your book drawing the distinction between second- and third-wave companies.

Well, the idea of second wave and third wave was first introduced by Alvin Toffler with *Future Shock*. It begins with the first wave, which was the agrarian society we had back in the nineteenth century, and then we went to the second wave, which was the industrial age, with factories and mass production.

Now we're in the third wave, where the natural resources are no longer as strategic as they were in the industrial age, meaning oil and coal and iron ore and so forth. Today the strategic resource is information.

In the information age, the technology ramp is so rapid that it requires people to take tremendous risks in order to be successful. So the characteristics of a third-wave company are very different from a second-wave company.

In a second-wave company we look for size, market position, stability, self-sufficiency, and vertical integration. It's largely a world of competition, competing for a share of existing markets that are growing relatively slowly. In the information age or the third wave, we see that flexibility and focus are on, not the quality you can afford, but the best quality that can be built, are key aspects of succeeding. And we're not really trying to compete for an existing market, we're trying to build brand new markets, often using technology to define the products that will shape those new markets.

So the whole thrust of leadership shifts from the John Wayne model of the leader who is invincible to a new definition of a leader who has to be willing to not only take risks, but make mistakes, learn how to recover from those mistakes, and then not lose the courage to go on and take additional risks.

And so I wanted [in *Odyssey*] to show the vulnerability of leaders, that they had to be more human than they were in the industrial age, because they don't have the fallback safety net of large institutional structures to sort of prop them up and to make them look better than they really are.

How is Apple structured differently from the more conventional companies you came from?

The big difference is that Apple is built around the idea of a network, rather than around the idea of a hierarchy.

A hierarchy which is modeled after either the Catholic Church or the military models is the traditional form of organization in a corporation in the second wave. In the third wave, a network is a better metaphor, because what it does is legitimize a thing that always existed informally anyway.

We know that even in the most traditional corporations the informal network is really where most transactions happen, and where most ideas are passed from one group to another.

In third-wave companies, which are really idea-intensive, which are driven by the success of your ideas and turning them into products, it's even more important to legitimize that informal network. So you'll find that there's very little emphasis on layers in the hierarchy, little emphasis on titles, little emphasis on corporate perks, and a lot more emphasis on communications. So at a company like Apple—just yesterday we had a communications meeting with over 3000 people. That would be something that would just never happen in a second-wave company.

People don't have to buy into the vision in a second-wave company, they have to buy into the policy manual. Policy manuals don't mean very much in third-wave companies. What people want to know is, are they committing themselves to something that's going to make a difference, and are they going to have a chance to actually be a part of it. Those kinds of questions rarely come up in a second-wave company.

What advantages does this approach give Apple over some of its competitors?

I think the obvious comparisons are with companies like IBM and AT&T. AT&T is probably the archetypal hierarchical organization, and look at the difficulty they've had making the transition from a public utility into a competitive private enterprise company trying to compete in the computer industry. It's reported that they've lost in excess of a billion dollars a year for several years in the computer industry.

I think that what many thought would be the undoing of Apple Computer just a few years ago, which was AT&T's size, their huge research capabilities with Bell Labs, has not turned out to be the case, because large institutions don't have the flexibility to change quickly. They don't have the ability to make decisions rapidly. And we know that in the personal computer industry things are happening so quickly that the more agile you are, the more driven by a vision that is understood throughout the company, the more likely you are to be successful. I think even IBM, which has been recognized by many people as one of the finest corporations in the world, has had difficulty making that transition. Because IBM, even though it's a high tech company, is clearly a second-wave company, not a third-wave company.

You also introduce the concept of culture versus genetic code in companies.

Well, we've heard so much in recent years about corporate cultures, and yet culture is an idea that looks backward. It has the historical context of saying, "This is where we have come from, this is the set of traditions that the company has." That is probably more relevant for a second-wave company that doesn't have to look forward, but is designing its plans basically as extensions of what it's already done in the past.

The problem is that in the third wave we are creating brand-new companies, brand-new markets, brand-new technologies, brand new products, and therefore you want to have a way of establishing an environment that people can not only recognize, but one which is also going to be extendable into the future, not just have its roots in the past.

So I prefer the metaphor of genetic code, which says there are certain characteristics, certain values, that a company has to recognize from its earliest days, and if you can define what those characteristics are, then you look for those characteristics to be present regardless of how large you may get, or how complex your business may get in the future. Just as the genetic code stays with us throughout our lifetime, as the cells in our body change every seven years.

I think that what I'm trying to do is get people to think about values, more than culture, and think about values in terms of how you take the best characteristics and extend them into the future, but also have the flexibility to recognize that the company's going to be constantly changing, constantly reinventing itself. That's something that is hard to reconcile when you're looking at culture, which is so tradition-bound.

From the perspective of now as a point in a long evolution, what do you think the essential messages in Apple's genetic code are right now?

I think that Apple's code starts with a vision, and the vision is that we're going to change the world by focusing on the individual, and giving individuals incredible tools that are based on technology. And that these tools will be powerful enough to change individuals' behavior, the way they think and communicate and learn. That's the essence of Apple's vision.

Then the values, which are the other part of our genetic code, are that we must be able to attract very talented people who are going to be creative, and give them an environment where they are able to be extremely successful. So it means an environment that is going to put more emphasis on the individual, more emphasis on small teams, than it does on the traditional issues of control and process that you find in large organizations.

Consequently, regardless of how large Apple gets, I believe the company will always have a right-brain tilt to it. It'll always appeal most to the people who would have a hard time finding any other corporation that they would ever want to go to after working at Apple. They might go start their own companies—that happens in many cases. But the likelihood that they would go to another large corporation would be extremely remote, because Apple does put such an emphasis on attracting people who care about the creative side of business.

But in the course of attracting such people you also introduce a considerable chaos factor, right?

Which is the duality that we're finding—not only in business, we find it in the sciences.

I often look for guidance, not from other business people, because there aren't very many role models, but I look for guidance sometimes in very unsuspected places.

As an example, if you look at some of the new physics concepts—for instance, Heisenberg was able to demonstrate that the more you know about a particle's position, the less you know about its velocity. The more you know about its velocity, the less you know about its position. So what we are learning is that it is possible for things to have a duality to them. Einstein amongst others, and Maxwell, pointed out that light is both a particle and a wave, so it can have two existences at the same time.

That's what I think we're finding in the new corporations, that you've got to have an existence that focuses on creativity and gives the individual a great deal of freedom, but you've also got to have a sense of order. And the order doesn't mean control, it doesn't mean rigid policies or hierarchy. What it does mean is that there has to be an environment that allows things to be free, but also has things headed in the same direction.

Directions become very important in a third-wave company, not necessarily goals as tightly defined as in a second-wave company, but more of a Taoist idea, that the farther you head in that direction, the more you learn about where you want to go, and you're constantly pushing the ultimate destination farther and farther out. And that's almost what we have to do in a company like Apple, because we can't say specifically what our world is going to be like five years or ten years or 15 years out, but we know the directions we have to head in, and the farther we go in that journey, the more we never actually reach the destination. We're constantly pushing the destination out.

Well, those are ideas, whether they come from system cell theory in biology, or whether they come from Taoism or holistic ideas in thinking about the world, or whether it's new physics, that are actually better metaphors and better role models for things that we're doing in business. Now, if I were to go back and tell my former colleagues in corporate America that we were using Taoist ideas and holistic concepts in management, they would think that I'd been in California too long. (laughs)

What's the thinking behind Apple's continuing policy not to license its technology and to keep it all proprietary?

We have chosen not to license our technology, and have no intention of doing that in the future. The evidence that we think that that's right is to look around us.

Look at IBM, which used somebody else's technology, Microsoft's, and now finds its share of market being consistently eroded by the clones. Not only is its share of market being eroded, but the whole value of its technology is not well understood, because the clones don't invest in any research to create new technology, all they do is come in and copy what's already there.

For the industry, that's a losing strategy. As we saw with the Macintosh's success in desktop publishing, by taking the technology path where you can do things in a better way, you can actually create brand-new markets.

It was during that very time in 1986, when Apple was starting to grow with desktop publishing, that we saw the rest of the industry languishing. There *wasn't* much growth in personal computers in 1986. It's only been since 1987 that the industry has started to see real growth again, and it's coming primarily when we see new technology breakthroughs.

From our standpoint, we believe that we have a unique opportunity, because we're the only personal computer company, including IBM, AT&T, Compaq, or anybody else, that owns its own technology—for CPUs, for printers, and for all the systems software that we do, which includes workgroups. What we want to do is show that we can continue to innovate by having the control over our own technology, not having to be paced by what someone else is doing.

At the same time, we know it's a multi-vendor world, and we have to be able to integrate into that world, and consequently we are adopting more and more standards, but they're standards that are in the background, that aren't obvious.

They could be printing standards, like PostScript, or they could be networking standards, like Ethernet, or they could be other standards, like the ISO model for communications, or it could be the connectivity into the IBM world through token-ring standards. We don't have to create the standards, though in some cases we've helped do that, but what we really do have to do is to make sure that the individual isn't working with standards, that the individual is working with something that's recognizable to *them*.

Our innovation is totally focused on the man-machine interface, with a lot of standards in the background. We think that we could never afford the proprietary technology that we have unless we knew that we could retain the value of that technology. Because the crown jewel for Apple isn't our hardware, the crown jewel for Apple is our systems software. In 1987 we spent 191 million dollars on research and development. That's more than the research and development of Microsoft and Compaq and Sun and probably a couple of other companies added together.

Is *HyperCard* part of this strategy of supporting the individual and creating an individual work environment?

I see *HyperCard* as one of those extraordinary technologies that somehow got left out. Remember, almost every technology that we have on the Macintosh was created in some form long before Apple Computer was ever founded. At a lot of places.

What we had to look at, as we went out to the 1990s, was, were we going to have all the right root technologies that we could build on in the future? And the one that seemed obviously missing was hypertext. Because hypertext was a way of simplifying the one thing that had not become very human, and that was databases. Databases still required you to be a computer expert in order to do anything useful with them. You had to program in some language.

So what we did was, we said hey, this is the technology that got left out, so now we've got to find a way to bridge it in. Fortunately, Bill Atkinson, one of our real superstars, was excited about hypertext, and was able to create a technology that went beyond an application, but really had the potential of becoming, over time, part of our systems software.

And so what you're seeing today is the Mac 128K version of *HyperCard*. In other words, it's just the beginning of where we think we can take *HyperCard*.

Why did you go to bat for Bill Atkinson on the subject of bundling it, which was a somewhat controversial decision?

To me it was never even an issue. It was logical that if this was really going to be something that was going to be important as a technology platform of systems software, that you had to make it standard with every computer that was out there, or people wouldn't incorporate it.

And that's turning out to be true. As they say in the theatre, *HyperCard*'s got legs. It's really caught on with education, with enthusiasts, with business people.

And remember that *HyperCard* isn't the first attempt at trying to bring hypertext to the personal computer. We had *Owl Guide*, we had other products, *Zoomracks*, things like that, which were less successful because they were looked at as just another application. What we're trying to do is to say that there's a fundamental technology platform that ought to be available for any application to use parts of it, and therefore, making it horizontally available by bundling it seemed very logical to me.

What happened to the notion of one person, one computer?

One person, one computer has never been abandoned. What we have tried to do is broaden our bandwidth of what that idea means to say, that it can't be one person, one computer, isolated from the world, but it's got to be one person, one computer, *connected* to the world. The importance of connecting up to other computers, connecting up to other people, connecting up in a multi-vendor environment, is one of the big changes. So I'd say we say one person, one computer, connected up to the rest of the world. We've added an extension to that vision, which actually adds probably the essential requirement in order to succeed long-term.

When I first came to Apple, I asked, "How are we going to exchange data from one personal computer to another", and someone threw a floppy disk across the room and said, "That's all we'll ever need." With a stand-alone vision, that's all we ever did need. But clearly that's not where the world's headed.

Originally, Apple was very strongly focused on the home/consumer market. How did you become disenchanted with that?

Well, the only logic I think that anyone can use to say why Apple would have ever recruited someone who knew almost nothing about computers, and only had had experience in marketing to consumers, was that the idea was that Apple was going to build a very successful consumer products company. And as we've seen, the personal computer industry has not turned into a consumer products industry. To the contrary, there have been billions of dollars lost by a large number of companies, some of whom aren't even around anymore, just in the years that I've been in the industry.

What we have discovered is that getting computers into people's homes doesn't necessarily mean that you're going to get them to actually use the computers. Today we don't try to sell computers to people unless they have an idea in mind what they're going to do with them. So that we sell to home education, but it's because people know that they can run the software their kids are using in school with Apple IIs. Or we sell to the home office because they know they can run a business out of their home or they can use it as an extension of their office office computer work. But we don't try to convince anybody that they ought to balance their checkbook or keep track of their recipes or things like that. As farfetched as that seems, that's really how the personal computer industry was talking to people only a few years ago.

So the main areas you see growth in are education, higher education, and mainstream business, is that correct?

Yes. It's not that we don't sell computers to individuals, because we sell a lot of them. It's not that there aren't computer enthusiasts amongst them, because we have a lot of enthusiasts, as is evidenced by the strong support we have from user clubs around the world. But it's like Willie Sutton said when asked why he robs banks—because that's where the money is. (laughs)

And it's true with computers—most of the money spent on computers comes from business and from government. And, because of Apple's special interest in education, it's logical that we continue to grow our position, not just in K–12 but also in higher education. So that gives us a very fertile marketplace to focus on, but it's meant a total repositioning of the company.

We were a home computer-education company two years ago. We're now a business-education company, and probably the best evidence of the repositioning of our company is how the marketplace has valued us.

In the summer of 1985 our market value was around 850 million dollars. And before the market meltdown we reached, I think, something like 7.5 billion dollars. Even today, we're still well over five billion dollars in market value. It all can be attributed to the work of a lot of people at Apple. This wasn't a turnaround of any single individual, it was a lot of people at Apple buying into the idea that we could reposition the company, and do it in a shorter period of time than any other company had done that before.

Do you have any problem with the elitism that's inherent in that strategy? Aren't you aggravating the information-rich/information-poor dichotomy by going after the big-money markets, which is certainly different from the Two Steves/Homebrew vision?

Well, I think that what technologists should do is to build the absolute best tools that we possibly can, and then it's incumbent on all of us in society—not just the technologists, but also the business people, the educators, and the government leaders—to then figure out how we make sure that we don't create a class society with haves and have-nots.

But to compromise the products so that nobody gets a product that's going to make a difference, to me, is not a good fallback. I think we have got to get people excited, that we can do so much in changing people's behavior, in revolutionizing our education system, by creating tools that can offload a lot of the monotonous work from the teacher, to have more time for teachers to spend with the students, to take a heterogeneous society as we have, perhaps, in California more than any other area in the world, and say, "How do we leverage the strengths of those differences that people have so they can learn at their own pace and in the way that they learn best?"

These are the things that we can solve with technology, and if we solve them in the best possible ways, then I think it's going to become more obvious to our government leaders in particular that they can't give benign neglect to education.

My sense is that the revolution of education will have to start with the technology tools. It isn't trying to compete with books anymore, because students really don't read that much. It's trying to compete with video arcade games, with MTV, with special-effects films, and so we've really got to introduce the entertainment value in learning, and make it as enjoyable to learn as it is to do any of those other choices.

Therefore, to compromise the technology just to make it cheap, I think, would be like shooting ourselves in the foot. Because we know the technology is constantly getting cheaper, but we need someone to fund the development of it, and the only people that are going to fund the development are the big markets that have a real need for it in terms of improving their productivity, such as business or such as government.

Eventually it'll allow us to get the cost of that technology down, so that we can introduce those ideas into education. But education as a market by itself couldn't possibly afford the research and development costs that we have to spend to get these kinds of breakthroughs.

How successful have you been at convincing educators and legislators of all this?

I think it's amazing how well-understood these ideas are when you get down to the local level with teachers, even all the way up to— for instance, a few days ago I was meeting with the president of the Los Angeles Unified School District, and they really understand. Bill Honig, who's the superintendent of education in California, understands.

Where it breaks down is when we get to the elected officials above that. For some reason they are fast on the clichés, but they're hollow on the answers in terms of what they're really going to do to make education better.

In our own state of California, we have been slipping like a landslide in terms of our rankings of where we stand with the other 49 states, and yet we're not even putting in as much investment in education percentage-wise as we were a few years ago. We're trying to rebate it back to the population.

I think those are very short-sighted decisions our politicians are making, and if you go up to the national level, I think the decisions are even more short-sighted. We're trying to, in effect, disassemble the Department of Education and essentially just hope it'll all go away, and somehow it'll solve itself through a non-regulated environment, and I think that's very naive.

Is the publication of your book and Mr. Gassee's book in the same year part of a campaign to acquire mindshare in the outside world? It seems like what both books are doing, in large measure, is explaining the ideas behind the machines, the "why" rather than the "what."

Yeah. See, I think we have to remember that we're coming up on a presidential election year in 1988, and my sense is that we can't even talk about issues until after the nominating process. No one will get nominated by the Democrats without taking a very far-left position that will meet a lot of special-interest groups, no one will get nominated by the Republicans without taking a far-right position that will meet a number of special interest groups, and yet we know that in the final campaign both candidates will have to come to a more centrist position in order to get elected.

And at that point, since California has really no role in the primary states for the nomination process, we suddenly become very important as a state in terms of who's going to get elected, and the chances are it'll be a close election. So I think there is a real opportunity to capture national attention on the issue of education in the 1988 presidential campaign, after the candidates have been nominated. My sense is that all the candidates will have very positive things to say about education, and I think there'll be essentially hollow answers.

So that's why I think it's time to speak out now and find out how much grass-roots support there really is for education. I think there's extraordinary support for it, because people really do understand, even if our politicians don't—the people understand it, the educators understand it, the teachers understand it, the students understand it, it's amazing that it can't be understood in better ways by people higher up in government.

My sense is that my book and others are going to help galvanize a lot of attention to these issues, and what we need to do in the coming months is to get those people who care a lot about education to start to articulate, in ways that the broad population will be able to understand, that there really *are* choices, we don't have to sit back and watch our education system go into the drink.

Does your ACOT [Apple Classroom Of Tomorrow] experience funnel into this?

ACOT helps, but it's not the total answer. The ACOT experience is that we've taken Apple II computers and put them in the classroom, so that almost all the students can have one available to them, and then give them access to an Apple IIc at home. There have been remarkable changes, not only in their behavior, but also in their test scores.

But that isn't the total answer. The real answer comes when we can get more and more curriculum-based software, get the computer out of the computer labs, stop teaching computer literacy, and start integrating the computer as a basic learning tool that will let individuals work separate from the regular classroom routine, or even get it integrated into the classroom routine where groups of students are working on common projects. We've just barely scratched the surface in terms of the real impact that the computer can have in education.

My big interest is to make sure that it doesn't become the device that frees some of us, but then leaves a lot of us on the outside, and that's one of the risks in the urban areas, because the number of computers in urban schools is discouragingly low. And even the ones that have gotten in there aren't being well utilized, because nobody knows what to do with them.

That's why we have got to get some help from government leaders to say this is a national priority. It seems to me that this country has always had the right leadership at the right point in time—we had the Marshall Plan, we had to reestablish the strength of Europe, which meant a free world back in 1948. We had the highway system put in when we had to have a highway system put in, which opened up tremendous commerce for the United States in the 1950s and 1960s. We had the NASA program to the moon, which gave us tremendous technology throughout the 1970s.

But more recently we haven't had the major investment in the infrastructure of our country that we're going to have to have as we cross over to the twenty-first century. Probably the biggest investment is the investment in our education system. This is the right moment for a leader, regardless of which party that leader's from, it's not important, to say, "What can I do for the education system?"

My sense is that a hundred years from now the people in this country or in the state of California will look back to the late 1980s, and they won't remember what the INF agreement was, taking 3 percent of the nuclear firepower in the world and disbanding it, or they won't even care that we had a tax reform in 1986. What they *will* say is did we, or did we not, do anything about our public education system. Hopefully, they'll say that we seized the moment and took the steps to start to revolutionize it, and that we got some more intelligent people into government, and people who didn't go into government cared about those issues and started to work together to galvanize a lot of support across the country.

Apple has a strong presence in the universities. How do you see that affecting future change?

It's an extraordinary opportunity, not just for Apple but for the whole world, because Macintosh has become a part of many people's college education. What it means is that, after they graduate—and in June of '88 we'll have the first class that will have had Macintosh through all four years of college—when they go out into the world, regardless of what they're going to do, many of them go out with a genuine love affair with their computer. So it isn't as though it's some machine they have to use just to get by. It's a tool that they think gives them an extraordinary advantage over others around them.

The more and more people that go out in the world, regardless of where they end up, with that feeling that they have an extraordinary tool to work with—they're bound to come up with better ways of doing things.

As we've made this transition from the industrial age to the information age, what we've learned is that the old ways of doing things just aren't as effective any more.

So if we can get a refocus back on the individual, and say that we can offset the over-specialization, the over-institutionalization, that we were left with at the end of the industrial age, and give individuals the tools to go out and do things in better ways, my sense is we'll start to not only be more competitive in a global economy, but we'll also be able to show real productivity gains. So those Macintoshes that have been on campuses for the last four years—it's sort of like the invasion of the aliens.

The pods are coming . . .

The pods are coming. (laughs)

Where would you like to see Apple in 1997?

I would hope that by 1997 we will be well on our way towards creating a product like the Knowledge Navigator that I describe in my book. Most of the technologies are already incubating in the universities or labs, some in Apple's own lab. I think this would be an extraordinary product, because it would have the potential of maybe changing the world as much as the printing press changed the world back in the Renaissance. It's got its roots in things that are already present in the Macintosh, and it's got its roots in other things which we aren't doing yet.

But my sense is that, timing in life being everything, that once again, just as in 1977 the timing was right to start the personal computer industry, in the late 1990s the timing will be right to make a dramatic impact on the world, with individual tools that are even more remarkable than the ones we have today. And I would hope that Apple is still the leader and the innovator in terms of shaping what that world might be.

UGLY?
UNPOPULAR?
CAN'T GET *LAID?*

TAKE IT OUT ON YOUR WHOLE WORLD BY
STARTING A REALLY DESTRUCTIVE

IT'S FUN AND *MUCH MORE SATISFYING*
THAN CREATING SOMETHING *USEFUL!!*
SO JOIN HUNDREDS OF OTHER
SATISFIED LOSERS AND DO IT *TODAY!!*

UNDERSTANDING VIRUSES

C.J. WEIGAND

Early on, I realized that any section titled "Heroes & Villains" needed a piece on viruses.

But which piece? I rummaged and rummaged. And came up, finally, with a winner about a loser. It's an excerpt from Chuck "C.J." Weigand's book Using PageMaker, *published by QUE Corporation. It clearly explains what you need to know.*

Nothing is more devastating than to get hit with a malicious viral attack. Viruses are insidious little rascals that enjoy a well-deserved reputation for being able to bring production work to a sudden and total halt. If you do not set up some form of impenetrable defense well in advance, you can expect someday to get ransacked. No one is immune.

The computer viral threat looms large on the horizon for the 1990s. As we enter the new decade, perpetrators actively are waging new assaults on innocent and unsuspecting computer users. And the number of viruses in circulation is escalating. Although no one fully understands what goes on in the minds of individuals who set out to do this kind of criminal mischief, one thing is certain—viruses are going to get worse before they get better.

Viruses are bits of computer code that covertly attach themselves to programs. Unpredictable results may occur after a virus is unleashed. Applications may function unreliably or freeze altogether; routine tasks may take longer to execute; computers may crash unexpectedly and often; start-up disks may fail to boot properly; files may explode in size and eventually become inaccessible; documents may not print properly—in short, your entire system may behave erratically or become totally unusable.

Methods of viral transmission vary, but sharing or downloading public domain or pirated software is still the surest way to become infected. If you download a contaminated file from a BBS or across a network, you easily can infect your hard disk. A virus also can remain hidden in a compressed file. The virus remains completely undetectable (and impotent) until the file is uncompressed. After the virus is released, however, the virus becomes infectious.

Some viruses lie dormant for an extended period (determined in advance by the programmer) only to activate days, weeks, or even months after initial exposure. Keep in mind that the goal of every virus is to go completely unnoticed while replicating until the maximum amount of spread has occurred. Make no mistake—it is all-out war, and you are the target. Even well-intentioned viruses, like the famous "World Peace" message of a couple of years ago, can do extensive damage. After all, you have enough difficulty writing legitimate code without also trying to make viruses "bug-free."

So what can you do? In brief, do not trust any external contact with your computer system. Test everything before using it. That includes commercial software, which may arrive in its shrink-wrapped box already infected (which has happened on more than one occasion). Use good viral-prevention software to unmask invaders and prevent infection.

After you initially verify that your system is clean, install viral-prevention software and keep the software active at all times. Make multiple backups of new programs and continually back up all your work files. Always keep the write-protect tabs on master disks locked. And, most importantly, after you establish an effective system of safeguards, absolutely never bypass the system. The one time you ignore your defenses could be the one time you end up getting clobbered.

A Virus-Protection Primer

Antiviral products generally include one or more of the following kinds of features: virus prevention, virus detection, and virus eradication. These products recognize attempts by viruses to replicate and effectively stop them from spreading.

The best virus-prevention software takes a generic approach to virus identification and thus provides a broad safety net that can unmask new invaders before they gain a foothold. The downside to this approach is that certain legitimate file-altering evolutions occasionally may trigger false alarms.

Virus-detection software can scan floppies and hard disks to search for infected files. They detect viruses based on known characteristics. Virus-detection programs are, by nature, viral-specific and must be upgraded constantly to recognize every new virus that comes along. Although virus-detection programs identify all known viruses, they unfortunately cannot protect you from new or unknown ones.

Consider, for example, a new virus that lies dormant, programmed to activate itself weeks into the future. Even with the most up-to-date version of the very best viral-detection software, you still could wind up with this new virus on your hard disk. If no one has heard of this virus yet, its identifying characteristics cannot be known. Therefore, no viral-specific code can be written to detect the virus. When the dormancy period ends, the virus activates and, of course, quickly infects your hard disk—unless, that is, you previously installed a generic viral-prevention utility. Such a program can block the virus after activating and prevent the virus from spreading.

Viral-eradication software also is viral-specific by nature. After a known virus has been detected, eradication programs attempt to remove the virus and repair any damage that may have been done. This procedure is tricky at best, and often produces "twice altered" applications. Such applications may not perform reliably after undergoing repairs. In a production environment, however, the use of viral-eradication software could make a difference in getting a crucial job out on time. But, even when viral eradication works, you should consider viral eradication only a temporary solution.

Some antiviral products support more than one category of features. Understanding when and how to use which program is the key to establishing an effective protection barrier. Some come with INITs that you install after verifying your disk is free from infection. These INITs prevent subsequent infection (or reinfection) and also include the capability to generically detect new viral strains. Some scan floppies for infected files but recognize only known viruses; they cannot protect you against the unknown variety. To be fully protected from viruses, you need to use a good viral-prevention utility, or you can become infected with a new virus suddenly and without warning.

Proper use of antiviral software can eliminate completely the risk of casual infection. But you do have to use the software. Ask yourself how much your data is worth. Then add to that the cost of your software holdings. Also, assign a value to the estimated time you may spend recovering from an unexpected viral attack. You find that the numbers speak eloquently for themselves.

Pick good antiviral software to use as your first line of defense against viral attack. Check all new floppies prior to using them for the first time and do occasional backup scans of your hard disk. Using an automatic disk-scanning utility also is important when sharing files with others, as within an office or user-group setting. You ensure that any disks you pass along are not infected by known viruses.

Setting up an organized system of defense affords several layers of protection and more opportunities to contain potentially crippling viruses before they spread. Adhere strictly to safe computing practices and you may avoid becoming a victim.

Note

Trojan horses, programs specifically designed to destroy data, also are making the rounds of the Macintosh community. Unlike viruses, which replicate and spread from disk to disk and across networks, Trojan horses are stand-alone programs that do damage only when they are run; they do not reproduce themselves automatically. Trojan horses typically masquerade as ordinary applications, seemingly harmless, but maliciously destructive when unleashed. Most antiviral products block the spread of Trojan horses.

— From: *Using PageMaker: Macintosh Version*, 2nd Edition. Copyright © 1990 by QUE Corporation.

C.J. also publishes "The Weigand Report," a newsletter billed as "The Working Newsletter for Macintosh Professionals." The Chicago Sun-Times called it "Easily worth its yearly subscription price ... 9.5 of a possible 10 points." I agree. Highly recommended.

Subscription price, for 10 issues, is $65 U.S. and Canada, and $75 overseas. Write to: The Weigand Report, P.O. Box 690, Cedar Hill, TX 75104.

PART

IV

WINNERS & LOSERS

DOUGLAS ADAMS ON HYPERCARD

DOUGLAS ADAMS

I have never met—nor even electronically telecommunicated with— *Douglas Adams. From the little I've gathered, he's an Englishman who's an aspiring writer of comic science fiction.*

To bankroll this dicey career choice, Mr. Adams has written some four-odd books about hitchhiking. The fifth of which, I'm told, he's now pecking away at, and which, I'm told, will be titled "Mostly Harmless."

This information comes to me via a Ms. Maggie Phillips of the Ed Victor Ltd. Literary Agency in London, who sent me a very pleasant fax which, among other things, informed me that, "Your readers may also like to know that the videos of the BBC Television series of 'The Hitchhiker's Guide To The Galaxy' will be available in America this year."

※

Mock if you must. But Bach, Mozart, Velcro, and *HyperCard* is not a bad score.

One day we will all blow ourselves up.

Of this, for most of the time, I am pretty much convinced. I hope it's not before Microsoft gets all the bugs out of *Word* 3.0 because I don't think they should get off that lightly. But it will happen. The local Planet Coroner for our Galactic sector will roll up in his official ship, take a cursory glance at the new, faintly glowing asteroid belt now occupying the third orbit out from the sun, nod curtly to himself, say "Oh yes, another freedom and democracy job," tick it off in his little book and zoom off for an early lunch.

But if he's already eaten and has a little time to kill before dinner, then maybe he will sift around in the rubble a little and ponder on what he finds. Perhaps he will be moved by it. It's even possible that he may be quite impressed. I would like to think he will feel impelled to leave a little plaque on one of the larger asteroids saying "Mock if you must. But Bach, Mozart, Velcro and *HyperCard* is not a bad score."

By the time this article actually comes out (why, with so much technology and desktop publishing and so on, does it still take as long to get a magazine out as it does for a pig to gestate?)...where was I? Oh, yes. By the time this article actually comes out you will probably have read dozens of articles on how wonderful *HyperCard* is, and will be praying that I'm going to go for Velcro, but no. *HyperCard* it is.

So why all the fuss about a program that is a less-powerful visual database than *Business Filevision*? A less-powerful painting tool than *SuperPaint* or *GraphicWorks?* A less-powerful hypertext editor than *Guide?* A less powerful object-oriented programming language than *SmallTalk?* A less-powerful file manager than the *Finder?*

Well, I think it occupies the same niche in the evolution of software as human beings do in the evolution of life. A human can't run as fast as a horse, can't climb trees as well as a monkey, can't swim as well as a fish, hear as well as a dog, or see as well as a cat. But we can swim better than a monkey and run faster than a fish. If we need to go as fast as a horse, we can ride one. If we need to go faster still, we can build a car or an aeroplane, or use one that someone else has built. We can find a way of doing just about anything we want to do. We can even invent Velcro.

It's the fact that we are unspecialised but infinitely adaptable that has been the secret of our stupendous success as a species. A cheetah may, after millions of years of evolution, be perfectly designed to run at a phenomenal 70 miles per hour, but it cannot use the phone–which, as we know, is often a more effective way of getting something done quickly. A giraffe that knew where the ladder was kept could dispense with a lot of troublesome vertebrae.

In other words, *HyperCard* is a program that functions in the same way that human beings do. It can turn its hand to any kind of task at any moment and do it as well as most tasks actually need. And if the task is beyond it, *HyperCard* can use the phone, it can go for a ride on *Excel,* and it knows where *Illustrator* is kept.

An awful lot of what we do on the computer doesn't actually require the massive speed of *Excel* (which is a lousy Paint program), or the power of *Illustrator* (which hasn't the faintest idea who my dentist is, or if I'm meant to be seeing her this afternoon). Most of the work we do does not consist of isolated Herculean tasks of calculation, or typesetting, or managing the payroll of General Motors.

The work we do rarely consists of single Herculean tasks, rather it is made up of a large array of comparatively small and simple tasks, all of which relate to each other. It's the relationships between all these little tasks that makes the work that each of us does unique, and which makes the business of trying to find software that actually fits the way we work such a bitch.

Even the desk accessory strategy didn't really solve this problem, because, although they provide a set of readily accessible small tools, they don't allow you to develop all the little pathways and relationships between tools and data that are what your work really needs, and most of the interesting ones don't work with each other, or with the one application you use most of the time, or with whatever the latest release of the system software is.

It occurs to me that there's an echo of this human-like adaptability to be heard in the hardware world at the moment. The idea of the super-powerful, number-crunching central processor has been taken about as far as we think it can by the current generation of Cray supercomputers. The coming strategy, as adopted in the Connection Machine, is to use far simpler and less powerful processors, but connect scores of them in a network and let them all work together, each tackling (relatively) much simpler tasks. Well, perhaps I shouldn't push the analogy too hard.

Somebody said to me that the great thing about *HyperCard* is that it actually does all those things that people who don't know anything about computers assume they ought to be able to do. In other words, the reality is at last beginning to catch up with the fantasy. You remember the fantasy? That getting a computer would solve all your work and organisation problems? It was like the way that fairy tales used to end. The Prince, having given up fighting ogres, slaying dragons or just generally being a frog, has finally won his Princess. The story then ends with "…they got married and lived happily ever after," as if there's some kind of causal relationship between these two utterly disparate occurrences.

I suspect that I am not alone in having been seduced by a romantic fantasy about the Macintosh. I can remember when we first met. Our eyes met across a crowded room. I was at the Infocom offices about four years ago, when I was working on the game of *Hitchhiker's Guide to the Galaxy.* Dave Lebling had come into the room where I was working and said that there was something next door that I might like. Assuming that he meant what he usually meant, which was that he had found a new type of pizza, I went to have a look, and discovered instead a group of people crowded round a small beige-coloured box that looked like a toy. (As it turned out, there was a very good reason why it looked like a toy.) I watched, at first with mild curiosity, and then gradually I began to feel that kind of roaring, tingling, floating sensation, which meant that I had had my first experience of MacPaint. But what I (and I think everybody else who bought the machine in the early days) fell in love with was not the machine itself, which was ridiculously slow and underpowered, but a romantic idea of the machine. And that romantic idea had to sustain me through the realities of actually working on the 128K Mac, then the 512K Mac, and even (let's be honest, now that the Mac II is here) on the Mac Plus.

Well, just as I had finally resigned myself to being older and wiser, the fairy story has confounded all expectations by suddenly and unexpectedly turning into real life. I've had *HyperCard* on my Mac II for a month, and slowly all the old clichés are coming true. By gradually adapting itself into a model of how I work, it has completely transformed my working life, it's beginning to affect the way I think because I can connect anything anywhere with anything anywhere else, I can try out any idea that occurs to me and quickly find my way back to what I was doing (the program provides you with Ariadne's thread through the Labyrinth), and most astonishing of all it has actually physically transformed my office. For the first time in my life I know where everything is. Every letter, every old script, every odd piece of paper. I can find it in seconds. I can find pieces of paper I didn't even know I had.

The romantic idea that was inherent in the first Mac was that software should be designed not for computers, but for machines. *HyperCard* is the first time that that idea has suddenly and dramatically come to life. Well, that's done. I now have a quick article to dash off for *Practical Fabric Fastening* magazine, and I think I know how it's going to start.

One day we will all blow ourselves up ...

— This article first appeared in *MacUser,* December 1987, titled "Pathways and Relationships." It is copyrighted 1987 © by Douglas Adams.

THE WORLD'S GREATEST SPREADSHEET

DANIEL ICHBIAH

Two power business programs were introduced in 1985: Jazz from Lotus Development, and Microsoft Excel. Macintosh magazines were evenhanded in their praise for both. Mac users thought otherwise.

The story is picked up in The Making of Microsoft:

The October 20, 1986, *Seybold Outlook on Professional Computing* published this sentence on the first page: "A year ago, the competition for boss spreadsheet of the Macintosh was between Lotus's Jazz (which arrived first, by several months) and Excel. That contest is clearly over." The Seybold report noted that Excel boosted Macintosh sales.

Once businesspeople saw that, contrary to some popular notions, a powerful, full-featured spreadsheet program tailored to the Macintosh environment was available, a significant number of them may actually have bought Macintoshes for the purpose of spreadsheet work. Prior to the release of Excel on the Macintosh, people who needed to do heavy spreadsheet work may only have considered an IBM PC type of personal computer.

Some of the most noteworthy praise came in the November 10, 1986, issue of *InfoWorld*. "After being loyal and dedicated 1-2-3 users for several years, we've just recently converted all our 1-2-3 files over to Excel. It's that good." Marwick, Main & Co. installed Excel on 10,000 Apple Macintoshes.

At the beginning of 1987, when Dataquest published the figures for the 1986 market for Macintosh spreadsheets, the gap was unprecedented. Excel, with 160,000 copies sold, represented 89 percent of sales. Jazz had captured only six percent of the users, with 10,000 copies sold. (In fact, Jim Manzi, president of Lotus, stated in 1989 that Lotus had had more copies of Jazz returned than it had sold, referring to pirated copies.) Other programs were responsible for negligible market shares.

Microsoft Triumphs in the Mac World

Thanks to Excel and Word, Microsoft became the number one software publisher in the Macintosh world. InfoCorp attributed half of Macintosh software sales in 1986 to Microsoft. In June 1986, when *MacWorld* published its list of best-selling Macintosh programs, Microsoft dominated the list with Excel in first, Word second, File third, and Multiplan fifth.

In 1987, Excel sales continued to expand at the expense of Jazz. While the ratio between Excel and Jazz was still three-to-one in terms of installed base (254,812 vs. 71,305), it was five-to-one in terms of sales for the year (123,462 vs. 24,650). The InfoCorp report said 1.25 million Macintoshes were in use by the end of 1987.

Excel 1.5 appeared in May 1988. It enabled developers to create complete applications in which the spreadsheet was totally transparent.

Excel 2.2, released May 1, 1989, broke the one-megabyte memory barrier. Now spreadsheets could extend to up to eight megabytes. Two competing spreadsheets had also appeared: Wingz by Informix, and Full Impact by Ashton-Tate. Microsoft Excel, however, remained in first place. The research firm Stratagem attributed an installed base of 715,000 copies to Excel, compared to 30,000 for Wingz and 27,000 for Full Impact. To try to catch up, Informix and Ashton-Tate launched promotions allowing Excel users to switch to their spreadsheets. A Macintosh version of 1-2-3 was announced in September 1987, but was later scrapped.

... Excel, however, made Microsoft number one in the realm of applications for the first time. Microsoft had won such a decisive victory over Lotus that for years, Lotus stayed out of he Macintosh world. One important lesson came out of this experience: Microsoft's strength lay in graphical user interfaces. From there, the road to victory in the PC market was clearly laid out.

— Printed with permission *"The Making of Microsoft,"* Daniel Ichbiah © 1991, Prima Publishing, PO Box 1260, Rocklin, CA 95677, $22.95 ppd.

DEATH TO SHAREWARE

*I*s this sincere? Is it tongue-in-cheek? Isn't it a rather brutal attack on well-meaning souls trying to recoup a profit from the sweat of their brow? You tell me. I know this, though, I've never written anything in my life that inspired as much comment and vilification. It was great ...

It's time to end Shareware.

Shareware has become a stupid idea. HyperCard makes it a pathetic idea; one that demeans the purveyor, the user, and— maybe most of all—the creators of HyperCard.

Once, it was a good idea. A good idea dreamt up by Andrew Fluegelman, one of the giants of the personal computer industry. Andrew was a great magazine editor, a damn good programmer, and something rarer than both: a gentleman.

When IBM introduced the IBM Personal Computer, it had potential, but little software: a word processor, a spreadsheet, not much else.

But it had Microsoft Basic, so Andrew wrote PC-Talk, an excellent communications program. Written in Basic, it was fast enough, easy to use, well-designed, good. I used it for years. There's no shame in Basic, or any other language. By their fruits ye shall know them. PC-Talk had great value. It was a smash.

And it was Shareware, a new idea.

I was uncouth enough to badger Andrew about how much he made from PC-Talk's shareware fees. Andrew demurred, but it was clear that PC-Talk reaped shareware fees in six figures. Not the high six figures, but six figures nonetheless.

So Shareware is a good idea?

No.

PC-Talk, like few other shareware programs, was a full-featured application. It could've been packaged and placed on a shelf any-where, to compete with any other communications program.

And it was upgraded religiously, and supported terrifically. Andrew didn't take the money and run. He wasn't that kind of a guy.

Among other things, he was a businessman. And he realized that software's value isn't only on the disk.

With the exception of Scott Watson and Don Brown, no share-ware author is fit to use the term—or the method—that Andrew Fluegelman invented.

Let's talk commercial software. What do you buy when you buy software?

Well, there's the software itself. And the disk, or disks. That's part of it. And you'd expect a manual, however terse.

But you're also buying promises, made (let's hope) in good faith. Promises that there's a company behind the product. Maybe only a one-person company, but a company. A company that will actively support the product. People, somewhere, near a phone, who can answer a question, or help you work through a problem.

Promises of continued enhancements. Companies like to stay in business. If this is your job, and you like your job, it makes sense to listen to users, to improve your products, to be responsive. It's either that or get a real job.

You don't start a company if your product is junk. It may *be* junk, but nobody invests junk with time and effort.

And that's what you're paying for, when you buy commercial soft-ware: time and effort. And belief. Somebody's belief that the product has value, enough value for them to put themselves, their company, and their money at risk, to say, "We think this has value to you."

So what's Shareware? Danny Goodman calls it "Guiltware."

I call it Stupidware.

First, product accouterments aside, shareware programs themselves are stupid and trivial. The exceptions are few enough to prove the rule. Shareware is poorly conceived, usually poorly programmed, often dangerous, never to be trusted, unreliable, and don't you cringe when you see a misspelling in an "About ..." box?

And then, like some bum on the street, the author sidles up beside you, reeking of stupid code, and has the gall to ask for spare change? I don't know what's worse: the bums who righteously demand your money, the bums who make quasi-legal threats, or the bums who grovel for "...whatever you think it's worth."

Can't the government do something about these shareware people?

My best friend wrote a graphics program. It's real software: it's got a box, a manual, and somebody on the other end of the phone. This guy spent almost two years writing the program in assembly language. He wanted it fast.

But even still, he claims that Bill Atkinson wrote two-thirds of his program. Because Atkinson wrote QuickDraw, and everything on the Macintosh breathes by the grace of QuickDraw. Every dot on the screen is there because of QuickDraw.

Given that, how should shareware "authors" (jeez!) feel about bumming change for HyperCard stacks?

They should feel like fools. They are.

Cut it out, people. The rest of us are embarrassed.

So what should these people do? Where should they go?

Two choices. First, they can put their money (and time) where their mouth is. If their product is good, they should sell it. For real.

Too much work? You bet it is!

Then do what authors have always done. Find a publisher. If the product is good, it'll get published. Publishers, everywhere, are always looking for good stuff. And there's never enough good stuff.

If it's a stack, let' em try Activision, or Hezier Software, or (do I get a kickback for this?) Stax. Hell, try any Macintosh software publisher. If it's good, it's good; doesn't matter if it's written in Mandarin.

If it's not a stack, see the previous sentence.

If they want money, that's how to get it: find a publisher.

That wasn't hard, was it?

The other choice has also has virtue, maybe more virtue. The Public Domain.

It's not the "share" in Shareware that's offensive, it's the "ware." There's never been enough freely givens; not here, not anywhere.

It's a good and noble idea. Public domain authors are in good company. With people like Andy Hertzfield, Steve Capps (I'm learning Morse code thanks to Capps "Telegraph" desk accessory), and Richard Stallman, who's creating a public domain version of UNIX (akin to creating a public domain encyclopedia!).

If you're going to be a Capitalist, then be one. And do it right, or find a publisher.

If not, then share. It makes you feel good. You might even make a name for yourself.

And what goes around comes around. Give freely and be surprised.

(I once read an unorthodox explanation of the so-called "miracle" of the loaves and fishes. The idea was that people always brought food with them, when traveling about the country. And this nice man, trying to share a few measly fish with a huge crowd, shamed everyone into sharing what they already had. And it was enough. I guess it was a miracle. The shareware sleazes could do the same.)

But that's mumbo-jumbo, right? The fact is that Shareware authors don't make any money. It doesn't work. It shouldn't work.

So let's end it.

— Doug Clapp; *Macazine*

THE KarenNet ALL-TIME GREATEST MAC PARTY LIST

KAREN THOMAS

K aren Thomas is CEO & President of Thomas Public Relations in East Northport, New York. A graduate in opera from the Juilliard School of Music, Karen won the 1991 Marketing Computers *magazine Marcom Awards for two COMDEX parties: the John C. Dvorak Party and the Micrografx "Chili Cook-Off."*

She sings, she does PR, and boy ... can she party.

I consider myself the first and only Macintosh computer socialite. Of course, as a socialite, that means that I have to go to all the parties (like I don't want to!). But there's more to it than that. Because I do PR for computer companies, meeting a ton of press and other contacts at parties is really useful. The press loves parties and, since I know so many press people, I have an easy time getting articles placed for clients, which is the main job in PR. My clients are happy, and I definitely have a great time doing it.

Anyone can use computer parties held at conferences to get ahead, through the networking and schmoozing that can be accomplished there. But you have to have the right personality for it, and you need to know where the important parties are.

That's where I come in.

How do you get invited to the computer parties? The most important thing you need to have is "The Official KarenNet Party

List," which I publish for conferences like Macworld, COMDEX, etc. This is a listing of all the parties held at the conference. How do I get the information on these usually top-secret parties? I cajole, finagle, spy, and generally pry out the info from Macintosh insiders all over the U.S.

I'll bet you think parties are frivolous and a general waste of time. But, no. I get more accomplished at a party than I could in weeks of phone calls. At a Mac party, you can meet press, financial analysts, researchers, CEOs, user groups, and just about anybody who's anybody in the industry. In fact, almost everyone mentioned in this book I've seen at Mac parties. You can see them busy making deals and schmoozing, even though they act like they're just partying.

Although my main reason for publishing the party list is to give it to my clients, the press, and computer luminaries, "The Official KarenNet Party List" is for the Macintosh computer, which was originally based on the philosophy of computer power to the people. So, if someone sends me a note on MCI Mail or CompuServe, I will send them a copy of the list. (Especially if they sweet-talk me a little.) I think everyone should have the opportunity to network and grow. And, besides, parties are tons of fun.

The Greatest Mac Parties

The Macintosh computer industry, because of its early reputation as rebellious and youthful, has the weirdest and wildest parties. Here's my pick of the most notorious parties in Macintosh history:

- Rocker Todd Rundgren's annual party at his house in San Francisco (during the January Macworld Conference) is known for the numerous people in a drunken stupor. Definitely a rock 'n roll style party. The next morning, I'm sure he discovers the hung-over Mac programmers sleeping in all over the house. One year, I left at 3:00 a.m., but the revelers were going strong. Some press guys were jumping on a waterbed, programmers were playing with a new NeXT computer (which was still news and never seen), and the real nerds were drooling over some girlie magazine Mac game.

- William R. Hearst III's parties attract top CEOs and press. He flies out to Las Vegas on his private plane especially for the parties, and then flies back the same night. Like the movie *Citizen Kane*, his parties have an air of intrigue. You never know who might show up.

- Doug Clapp's Jolt Party in Macworld, Boston 1987, was the coolest because of its concept. Jolt is the soda most drunk by programmers with "all the caffeine and twice the sugar" of any cola. Jolt is reputed to keep any programmer up all night. And since programmers love to program at night, that's what they drink. So Doug Clapp had barrels of the stuff brought in and the party got so hyper and noisy that the hotel shut it down. I was there, so I know. (We all ended up continuing the party for hours in the hotel bar).

- *MacWeek/MacUser* held a wild BBQ party at Las Vegas Comdex in October 1991 at the Sands. The programmers got so crazy there that many of them ended up jumping into the freezing pool, over and over again. Even Bill Ziff, head of Ziff-Davis, couldn't miss this party. (But he didn't take the plunge.)

- The annual Macworld soirees at the Gift Center in San Francisco are great for the sheer size of the event. The hall is packed with hundreds of party-goers. Four floors of delicacies, from chocolate mousse cake (my favorite) to fettucine and champagne. Those Mac people really know how to party. They danced all night to BeBop music from the 50s.

- Journalist John C. Dvorak's secret party is held at Comdex in Las Vegas each year. The location is always mysterious, and misinformation is purposely given out to keep the party exclusive. People will do anything to find out the location of this party, because Dvorak's party is the most infamous award-winning party in the history of computers.

PART

V

BUT SERIOUSLY, FOLKS...

16 REASONS TO BE GLAD YOU HAVE A MACINTOSH 234

(AND 280 USES FOR A MACINTOSH)

16 REASONS TO BE GLAD YOU HAVE A MACINTOSH

C heer up! Things could be worse … much worse. Instead of having a wonderful relationship with the machine of your dreams, you could be struggling with one of those "other" computers. You know the ones: the DOS machines.

Is the grass greener over there, in DOSLand? Well, look at this, then decide. The file, direct from Microsoft, was found in Microsoft SIG on America Online, titled, "Frequent DOS 5.0 Questions and Answers from Microsoft." But we'll call it "16 Reasons to be Glad You Have a Macintosh."

280 Uses for a Macintosh

Write a book	Book a flight
Keep your books	Write your bookie
Draw a Wookie	Chart a function
Find a typo	Learn to type
Type a blood sample	Sample a population
Pop an address	Address an envelope
Enter a program	Program a game
Chart a gameplan	Plan a campaign
Write your congressman	Run for congress
Congratulate a friend	Find a good investment
Invent a faster-than-light drive	Drive a car
Build a boat	Balance an account
Run a planetarium	Plan a flower garden
Guard your home	Train pigeons
Talk to dolphins	Design a bicycle

Here are the most-asked questions on Microsoft's newly-released DOS 5.0, compiled by Microsoft product support engineers. For more information you can reach Microsoft Product Support at 206-454-2030.

1. How do I repartition my hard disk into one partition?

   First and foremost: You don't have to repartition. Then, we must give extremely specific step-by-step instructions.

2. DOS won't load high. Why not?

   Common causes: User has XT. User has 640K 286 system. User has 1mb 286 system with 384K shadow RAM and no

234

extended memory. User needs to use a /machine switch.

2a. When I boot, I get the error message "unable to control A20 line" what do I do? again, /machine.

3. The DOS Shell won't start. Why not?

Common causes: Monochrome detection bug. Corrupted dosshell.exe, dosswap.exe or dosshell.grb—re-expanding both of these files off the floppies often solves the problem.

4. I just got the "mouse driver not compatible" dialog, or I'm having problems using my mouse in the DOS Shell.

Probably an incompatible mouse driver.

5. What's the difference between extended memory and expanded memory? How do I allocate between them?

Common cause: user is using UMBs (which need extended) and, say, Lotus 2.2 or WP 5.1 (which need expanded). They need to (1) use ram, and (2) explicitly allocate some EMS on EMM386 command line.

Also, how do I get expanded in Windows?

Don't use noems. use ram.

6. I can't get programs or device driver to load high. Why not?

First, you need a 386. Explain briefly why we can't do loadhigh on a 286. Describe shrinking driver problem– "my mouse won't go high" is a common complaint because mouse driver shrinks way down.

7. How do I optimize loading programs high?

First, loadhigh is designed to be safe first and optimal second, not the other way

Plan a budget	Build a castle
Play chess	Print checks
Make change	Change your attitude
Attempt the impossible	Succeed
Impress your neighbors	Notify your landlord
Learn a language	Create a language
Draw on the right side	Calculate sidereal time
Time an event	Investigate math
Prove Fermat's last theorem	Catch a thief
Design a house	House some facts
Improve your spelling	Write a song
Write a résumé	Make children smile
Study the world	Dial Boston
Analyze the Boston Pops	Program a PERT chart
Perfect your reflexes	Reflect on nature
Design an ecosystem	Do your homework
Avoid housework	Check your nutrition
Narrow your priorities	Receive electronic mail
Manipulate some figures	Figure your taxes
Eliminate tautology	Take a break
Check your appointments	Apportion your income
Surprise yourself	Swap tales with a guy in L.A.
Sort numbers	Order silver
Check the commodities market	Market your wares
Design a wreath	Get rich at your own pace
Paginate a document	Practice your Spanish
Squander your paycheck	Design a tapestry
Tap into a discussion	Dissect an algorithm
Teach your children	Calculate the wind-chill
Store your chili recipe	Write a receipt
Reconcile a bank statement	Make a statement
State your goals	Study geography
Control a robot	List your talents
Take on a challenge	Plot a recursive function
Have some fun	Plan your vacation
Verify your suspicions	Cut your energy use
Find a better way	Keep a phone list
Draw a Christmas card	Check your mileage
Record a milestone	Navigate by the stars
Learn to fly	Run your darkroom
Read an encyclopedia	Publish a newsletter
QSL the world	Tell a story

Design a stained-glass door
Plan your day
Disseminate information
Train your pets
Stand up for your rights
Stop a war
Write a warranty
Or start one
Pursue the truth
Manage swine
Print a thank-you
Up the organization
Compare notes
Catalog your stamp collection
Start something small
Draw a map
Decide which tree to plant
Work at home
Study for the SAT test
Doodle
Play the ponies
Amortize a loan
List your assets
Hone your skills
Refine your position
Notify your creditors
Compose a speech
Write a love letter
Graph it
Transpose columns
Find a thread of meaning
Save it for next week
Outline your presentation
Try a new approach
Understand the past
Create an index
Turn on the coffee
Balance your checkbook
Improve your grammar
Evaluate your coin collection
Discover Queorffort
Do the payroll

Check your accounts receivable
Help the disabled
Write your mother
Control a greenhouse
Write a play
Think logically
Bug a corporation
Argue persuasively
Design an airfoil
Learn LISP
Think through a dilemma
Solve a mystery
Study organic chemistry
Publish your novel
Shop for bargains
Map your beliefs
Print 1,000 mailing labels
Enter a strange world
Make something easy
Write your will
Conduct a survey
Make a conceptual leap
Attest to a friend's character
Revise a document
Post a notice
Credit an account
Conquer the galaxy
Get it done first
Break it down further
Figure subtotals
Multiply it all by 12%
Make inventory painless
Plan for the presidency
Predict the future
Match wits with a machine
Write your autobiography
Water your lawn
Study your horoscope
Name the baby
Learn geometry
Design a solar collector
Pay your bills

around. Load order is important, but we don't give any specifics in User's Guide. "Load mirror before doskey" is the kind of specific we should give. Also, we should tell people we only map from C800-DFFF, and they can i=B000-B7FFF on most VGA systems and i=C600-C7FF on most systems besides Super VGA.

8. My machine hangs and I am using EMM386. What's going on?

Answer is in User's Guide, but not the answer to the most common problem which is a mapping conflict. Answer is x=C800-EFFF and whittle your way down until you find the area of conflict. Known common causes: Adaptec controllers, Hard Card

9. Windows won't start in enhanced mode. Why not?

Common causes: 2mb 386 using UMBs but defaulting to Standard Mode, EMM386 conflict that requires x= (and sometimes x= in system.ini), VirtualHDIRQ problem.

10. Just locked up my Tandy T1000 or PS/1. What's going on? Boot from ROM problem. Need to provide workaround instructions.

11. Setup is hanging. What to do?

Believe ATI wondercard is a common cause. Look at manual installation procedure, which often does the trick.

12. When I run SETUP to install the MS-DOS 5 Upgrade to the hard disk, SETUP repeatedly asks for the same Upgrade SETUP disk or states that my UNINSTALL disk is not the correct disk. What can I do?

Remove all TSRs and, in particular, disk caches, before running setup.

13. What's WINA20.386? Why do I need it? Can I get rid of it?

Why–if you're running DOS high and Windows enhanced mode. You can delete if you don't use Windows or if you don't use enhanced mode or if you don't load DOS high. You can also move it.

14. Can't get Lotus 3.1 to start.

Problem is with using EMM386 noems. Solution is to use ram.

15. I tried to load Smartdrive and got an "incompatible partition" error message. What do I do?

DM or SS is cause. You can override using smartdrive /d, but at your own risk. don't override if you have >1024 cylinders.

16. When I task swap the system locks up. Why?

Possible solutions: Delete the DOSSHELL.GRB and expand a new one. (Try different ones.) Check properties if it is a program item. Rename DOSSHELL.VID (to run in TXT mode), use the MONO.GRB and boot clean. If this works then there are definite monitor problems. Also, users should not be using the Task Swappers and Windows simultaneously. There's no benefit, burns memory. You can use the shell and Windows, but don't use the task swapper and Windows. Just use Windows to handle your swapping.

※

— Copyright America Online ©1992.

Estimate an amount of paint
Pitch a perfect inning
Pilot a space shuttle
Send a memo
Alphabetize a list
Furnish documentation
Keep a dairy
Encourage serendipity
Cross-reference it
Sharpen your bidding
Write a haiku
Check your pulse
Study by correspondence
Cancel a check
Start a business
Match a phrase
Send a report
Write a column
Think it through
Break a code
Double a recipe
Place an ad
Defend an empire
Center it
Underline it
Animate it
Tune a guitar
Proselytize
Study crystals
Make it STAND OUT
Draw a conclusion
File a report
Run a lap
Determine list price
Appeal a decision
Brief a colleague
Coin a phrase
Eat a Power Dot
Automate a factory
Sign your autograph
Conjugate a verb

Design a needlepoint picture
Boost your income
Program in Pascal
Improve your memory
Run your furnace
Document your accomplishments
Manage a dairy farm
Fight the good fight
Study the Bible
Play a scale
Move a paragraph
Plot a course
Cure cancer
Check out a restaurant
Find a mate
Parse a sentence
Average a report card
Catch a thought
Find a zip code
Convert to ASCII
Rotate your antenna
Admit defeat
Right-justify it
Boldface it
Learn self-hypnosis
Run a camera
Organize
Synthesize
Put a box around it
Make a deposit
Concatenate a file
Run a lab
Study linguistics
Save a princess
Write a brief
Collect quotations
Phone the police
Jot down a thought
Relate to a machine
Grab an icon
Plot a vector

Now you think of a 280 more uses for Macintosh!

— Doug Clapp; *Macintosh! Complete*

© 1984 Susan Kare

PART

VI

MACINTOSH ART

THE WORD ON TRICI VENOLA

Trici Venola's art is found throughout this book. Good, isn't she?

I first met Trici in 1984, at Softalk Publishing in Los Angeles. I had flown down from Apple (where I was hanging around asking stupid questions) to show the then-secret Macintosh to a group of people eager to publish St. Mac; a magazine which became an early competitor to Macworld until the demise of Softalk Publishing about eight months later.

Trici was a stunning, leather-clad, sharp, hip artist. Hipper than I, for sure. She still is—all of those things. (Actually, I don't know if she wears much leather, these days...)

Trici's route had been like this: A child prodigy turned hippie who straightened out, went back to art school at age 30 and found this sign on the bulletin board:

WANTED!
General kickaround paste-up person to abuse
and work hard long hours.
Low pay.
Ask for Kurt Wahlner

Who could resist?

Kurt was Softalk's fearsome art director. Trici did freelance illustration work for Softalk and—for two years—begged to be hired. (Only as an artist; Trici wouldn't do "paste-up.") "After two years of freelancing for them," she remembers, "Kurt called me up and said that they wanted to hire me to do the art direction for Softline *[a computer game magazine] because my work was so weird. They thought it would go with the magazine."*

It did. Trici went on to become St. Mac's first and last art director. And, naturally, married and tamed Kurt Wahlner.

Here's a more formal account of Trici's achievements.

TRICI VENOLA
(Trē´-sē Věn-ō´-lă)

Since 1984 **Trici Venola** has been blitzing the Macintosh industry with bizarre, exquisitely-rendered images. In the early days of the Macintosh, she authored several volumes of clip art, which raised the industry standard and served as inspiration to a generation of aspiring Macintosh artists. Many of these early images have passed into the Macintosh culture, becoming as anonymous and familiar as nursery rhymes.

In 1988 Venola began working in color, producing a series of print and media ads for Claris' MacDraw campaign. She continues to create screen shots, animations and fine art renderings illustrating the continuing progress of Apple computers.

Working out of her home in Santa Monica, Venola uses the Macintosh for her primary medium as a fine artist and illustrator. Current projects include character design for a kids' video on ecology, 3-D rendering, science fiction illustration and *Brazen Images,* a series of paintings, animations and slide shows in which various deities cavort in a seething darkness punctuated by patterns, flames, musical notes, and tiny Egyptian dancers. The *Brazen Images* characters are created separately and assembled in various ways to create the artworks. The images are the recurring vocabulary; the artworks are poems.

Trici Venola's best-known softworks include: *Mac the Knife, Vol. 3; Mac the Ripper, Vol. 5; People, Places & Things; Norton Utilities on the Macintosh* (interface design); *The Comic Strip Factory;* and *Comic People.*

Award-winning ads include: (print) "Nobody Reads Copy Anyway," "If Only Leonardo Had MacDraw II," and "Historic/Prehistoric" (trade nickname: "The Gazelles") for Claris, and (television) "Change of Heart," "Once Burned," and "Information Age" for Apple.

Fine art softworks from the *Brazen Images* book have been published in magazines in The United States and Japan.

Brazen Images has shown in Los Angeles and New York and continues to evolve.

Trici Venola
Brazen Images
410 California Avenue, #3
Santa Monica, California
USA 90403
310-395-5475

© 1986, 1991 by TRICI VENOLA. ALL RIGHTS RESERVED.

© 1984 Susan Kare

THE ART OF SUSAN KARE

Why is a Macintosh a Macintosh?

One reason is Susan Kare. Susan was a member of the original Macintosh team. Her status as "Macintosh Artist" was equal to that Hertzfield, Atkinson, Smith, and the other wizards that crafted Macintosh.

For the first time, an artist was part of a team that made a new computer. And it shows. Susan is responsible for the "look" of much of the Macintosh interface: icons, cursors, title bars, and most of the icons and patterns in the original MacPaint. She designed the fonts Chicago, Geneva, New York, Cairo, Taliesin, Toronto, and Ransom. (Bill Atkinson designed Venice.) Susan created some of the best-known Macintosh images, including

245

"Japanese Lady," the running shoe found in the first advertisements for Macintosh, Gourmet Baby Food, and the friendly MacPaint "Hello." that introduced thousands of users to a computer they could love.

Susan Kare graduated *summa cum laude* in fine arts and English from Mount Holyoke College, then earned a M.A. and Ph.D in fine arts at New York University. Prior to her position at Apple Computer, she was assistant curator of The Fine Arts Museums of San Francisco. She was Macintosh Artist and Creative Director at Apple from 1982-1985, then Creative Director at NeXT Computer, where she managed the development of NeXT's graphic identity and design, and was responsible for NeXT corporate materials, packaging, and collateral.

Since 1988, Susan has been a computer illustrator and interface designer with a client list that includes Apple Computer, BBD&O, Electronic Arts, Farallon Computing, Frox, General Magic, GO Technology, Logitech, Inc., Microsoft Corporation, and Radius, Inc. She lives and works in San Francisco. A few of her favorite works are found in this book.

© 1984 Susan Kare

HO, HO, HO.

Eat, drink, and merrily celebrate the holiday season at a
PARTY on **Friday, December 19** at 4:30 in the Atrium.
If you are so moved, please bring an **ornament** for the tree.

© 1984 Susan Kare

PART

VII

MAC OPINIONS: BUT WHAT DO YOU *REALLY* THINK?

249

WHAT HAVE WE LOST?

JOCK ROOT

Not everyone was happy about Macintosh. The Old Guard of Apple II enthusiasts had decidedly mixed reactions to the little tan guy. In particular, Jock Root had a few words to say in favor of the Apple II. In 1984, he asked: "What have we lost?"

To the old-fashioned hobbyist, the Macintosh is a sad declaration. It says that to break into the future we must break out of the past and leave it behind. The Mac breaks away from microcomputer traditions in a very profound way: it isn't really a "personal" computer anymore. It has become almost too powerful.

The Apple II represents a more traditional kind of microcomputer. Its specialty is generality—simplicity and open-endedness. It seems to say, "Here is the power of computing; you can use it any way you want to."

The Macintosh seems to be saying, "Here is the power of computing. Wait a moment and someone will come along to use it for you." With all its power and capabilities, the Mac cannot do anything useful until you put in an application program disk of some sort.

Traditionally, microcomputers have been designed as much for the hobbyist as for the professional computer user—but not the Mac. The Macintosh has been optimized for the professional or business user; the hobbyist has been firmly shut out.

250

That's a major change in the very concept of the "personal computer," because the personal computer was created by hobbyists. Some years ago, a bunch of computer hackers took an integrated circuit that was designed for something else entirely and made a personal computer out of it; that's where it all began.

The first microprocessor chip (an ancestor of the Z80 family) was designed as an intelligent terminal—a device for talking to a mainframe computer. It was supposed to be only an input-output device, but it could run its own programs in its own memory. This meant that the host system would not have to waste time managing the screen or reading the keyboard.

When this chip reached mass production, the price came down to where hobbyists could afford it. They discovered that you could add some memory, do input with a row of eight toggle switches and read output on eight LEDs, and have your own computer!

It was a complete bitch to work with, of course. You had to learn to think in machine language and do binary arithmetic in your head. But that's what made it fun: you could really get a sense of achievement from making those LEDs light up in a particular pattern.

The hobbyist market began to develop, and kits started coming out: a circuit board and all the chips and hardware you need to make a "single-board computer" (as they used to call them). This made it easier for hobbyists to get started, and the market grew. Then there was the TRS-80, using this chip in a complete, packaged system—and home computers hit the mass market.

It all started because a bunch of hobbyists took an existing design and started using it wrong. Hobbyists are meddlers. They like to take something apart and figure out how it works, then put it back together in a slightly different way. They think of it as "making improvements."

The Macintosh doesn't let you do that. You can't even take it apart, let alone modify it.

Oh, you can run different programs (applications) on it, and they can modify the machine in certain ways, but that's not at all the same. For one thing, you're not really modifying the system, you're just reconfiguring it, adjusting the controls that were built in by the manufacturer to be adjusted by various applications programs.

In an Apple II you can talk to the System Monitor—a built-in program that helps you write and debug programs in assembly language. The Monitor represents the "essential Apple"; it's always there, managing things for whatever application is running. When there's no application running—when you just turn on the computer without putting a disk in it—the Monitor will talk to you and answer questions. It's not very bright, but it can tell you some useful things (if you're a hobbyist).

If the Macintosh has anything like the Apple's Monitor program–that a hobbyist can communicate with and use to program the system, without putting some third party's programming language disk—then the folks in Cupertino have hidden it well. The screen just gives you a blank stare if you turn on the machine without a disk in the drive. You never use the Mac as a Mac, only as a thing to run MacProgram on. There is no entity there, only a superb pipeline: the computer is nothing, the application is all.

And finally, the Mac is much too complex for one person to hold in his head at once. With a simple old machine like the Apple II, if you understand digital circuit logic and assembly language, you can see how the whole thing works, from electronic signals to high-level languages. It probably takes a whole *team* just to understand the Macintosh at that level.

These horseless carriages are all very well—fast, and convenient, and all that—but they don't have the personality of a horse. They're just machines. Sure, they represent the future, and I'll probably get one someday, but for now, I'll stick with my old horse and buggy. I understand how that works, all of it; and the horse and I can talk to each other.

⁂

— This article first appeared in *St.Mac* magazine, August 1984

Now, 1984 is a long time ago.

So I called up Jock Root. And reminded him that, back in 1984, he wrote that he'd probably get a Macintosh someday.

Has he? Nope. But he's about to, he says, soon.

These days, Jock is working on a "programmed instruction package" targeted toward high-school and elementary students. Right now, the software exists on an Apple IIGS, but he's threatening to move it to Macintosh.

Jock still believes that computing is "a highly verbal process ... at best, it just confuses things to present verbal tasks in a visual way."

Finally, here's a Deep Trivia Jock Root'ism. It's like this: Trici Venola's "Astral Byte Comix" are scattered throughout this book. One of the recurring characters is a wizard. The actual name of the wizard is ... The Root Wizard.

Inspired by Jock Root.

BREAKING AND ENTERING

MARY JANE MARA

Daily Intelligence Reports on the Mac, its programs, peripherals and related issues; available Monday through Friday from the SafeHouse nearest you.

Excel, Word, Chart & File

An opinion piece by Cecilia Lutken (page 49 of the June 24th *PC WEEK*) railed against the idea of removing copy-protection from software:

> *Suppose protection were removed from all American software, causing the domestic software industry to languish and stagnate, making it easy for foreign competitors to overtake us technologically and making us dependent on importing software from abroad. Imported software would not only be more expensive, it would—without a shadow of a doubt—be copy-protected, and the user would go from the frying pan right into the fire.*

HMMM ... Naturally, I would fight to the death (well ... to the point of fisticuffs, maybe) for any fellow American's right to express his or her sacred opinion on any issue, and I like to think I'm open-minded enough to listen to both sides of an argument and recognize merits at either end. While I do not doubt there is someone out there capable of making a good case for software copy-protection, Lutken's particular attempt didn't make that grade. For starters, let's examine the syllogism found in the first sentence of the above paragraph:

IF "A" THEN "B" AND "C" AND "D"

IF ... protection were removed from all American software

THEN ... the domestic software industry would languish and stagnate

AND ... it'd be easy for foreign competitors to overtake us technologically

AND ... make us dependent upon importing software from abroad

The weakest link in this chain of logic is the initial jump from IF to THEN. Nowhere in her argument did Lutken establish as an irrefutable fact that the removal of copy-protection from software would cause the domestic software industry to languish. While I agree with a statement Lutken makes earlier ("... *it is simply ludicrous to suggest that people do not copy software all the time*"), she glosses over the known fact that even the most ambitious copy-protection schemes are routinely broken within weeks of software release. It is, therefore, equally ludicrous not to address *this* irrefutable fact when presenting all the moral, legal, economic and technological arguments surrounding the decision to protect or not to protect.

CASE IN POINT: A customer recently prevailed upon Microsoft to provide him with an 800K master of its EXCEL program (which he had legally purchased) to avoid inserting the master disk each time he used the program. He offered to trade his back-up copy for the newly formatted disk—but the company refused. Certainly that was the company's prerogative. Where did it get them? We can safely assume that it didn't improve customer relations. Worse than that (though very little could be worse than that), this customer discovered how to unprotect Excel himself (along with Microsoft's Word, Chart, MultiPlan and File programs)—*and published his findings on CompuServe, to wit ...*

Use FEDIT on a back-up copy of Excel (just Finder-copy it to a new disk) and do a HEX search for 608EBEDD, change to B1036ADD. Write to disk. Now your copy will be Finder-copyable and will boot without the "Insert" routine. While I'm at it, here are some more…

WORD: *Search for DD6084BEDD*

        Change to DD4E71BEDD

CHART: *Search for DD60DD00126081*

        Change to DD60DD00124E71

FILE: *Search for 126082BEDD*

        Change to 124E71BEDD

MULTIPLAN: *Search for 12608007BE*

        Change to 124E7107BE

THE TRUTH IS … until someone comes up with an unbreakable scheme, copy-protection is really just an exercise in futility. Beyond that, even given eventual success in that arena, there are too many brilliant programmers and software designers out there willing to offer unfettered applications to the public.

Here at Mac Underground we've occasionally agonised over putting our own stuff "out there" without a chaperone—but worrying about copy-protection only adds to development costs and increases personal risks of ulcers, heart attacks, and maybe even cancer. So we said *damn* the torpedos, and the result has been that enough people fork over so we can stay in business and forge ahead.

THE MORAL: It isn't copy protection that makes a program profitable or unprofitable; it's software design and the program's ultimate ability to make a user's life *easier* and not harder. *Good* people (and they *are* out there) are willing to fork over *good* money for a *good* program and *good* support.

People who are losing money on their software should take a good look at what they're selling, how they're pricing it, and how they're supporting it—before they assume that poor sales are due to theft. Sure, copies of even the worst programs *are* being boosted by normally upstanding citizens (an act of which *I* certainly do not approve). Yet as an ex-market researcher for ad agencies around the country, I can say from experience that the economic success or failure of any product (including software) revolves around issues of price, performance, promotion, and the product itself. "Users stole my software" is an out-and-out cop-out.

Regarding Lutken's ultimate fear that furriners will take over the market: c'mon, Cecilia. You're breaking my heart. Do you really think that our electronic B&E wizards would blanch at unmanning *foreign* software? No way! This is AMERICA—land of equal opportunity. Is this a great country, or what?

===

That's it for now. CIAO!

꣭

Here's Mary Jane Mara on Mary Jane Mara:

February, 1984 ... Mary Jane Mara's husband plunks a little gray box on her kitchen table and asks, "What do you think?"

Later that same year ... MJ and hubby (the legendary Jerry Daniels) launch MacUnderground, an online information service dedicated to asking and answering JD's original question over and over again.

In the ensuing years ... MJ (along with JD) co-produces MacWEEK, *an electro-mag for Mac junkies (re-dubbed* MacTALK *after Patch Communications buys the name for its paper weekly); writes articles for the trades; speaks at Expos; co-authors two books on HyperCard; establishes Daniels & Mara, an Austin-based Macintosh development firm specializing in custom front-ends to mainframes—and thrives on the authentic Tex-Mex cuisine of the region.*

꣭

TRICI VENOLA'S
ASTRAL BYTE
"CABIN FEVER"

WOW!! THESE **GRAPHICS** FROM THE SIGGRAPH SHOW SURE LOOK GREAT!! MAKES MY OLD BLACK & WHITE MONITOR LOOK LIKE A **JOKE!!** AND **STEVE JOBS** HAS **TAKEN OVER** THE **COMPANY!** HM... MAYBE I SHOULD GET A ...UM... *PIXAR* MACHINE...

"...HAS SIGNED DEALS..TO REPACKAGE THE $122,000 PIXAR MACHINE FOR SALE IN A VARIETY OF MARKETS..."

$122,000!! AAARRRRGGH!

WHAT AM I DOING? TALKING TO A #!%@!! *MACHINE!!!*

AT LEAST **YOU'RE** ACCESSIBLE!!

FEH!! PTOOIE!! ≥COUGH≥HACK≥ I WORK **ALL** THE **TIME!!** I **LIVE** ON **JUNK FOOD!!** IT GIVES ME *ACNE!!* I'M GETTING **HUNCHBACKED!** *NEARSIGHTED!* I HAVEN'T SEEN THE *SUN* IN *WEEK'S!*

continued...

THE LAST MEN'S CLUB

JOHN C. DVORAK

*W*hen I began this book, John C. Dvorak (he requires the "C") was the first person I contacted. Let me use something, I said. You pick.

John's choice was this column: "The Last Men's Club." My choice was another column: "They Sold Their Souls to the Fortune 1000."

John graciously gave me permission to reprint both columns, on two conditions: first, that I write a fawning introduction, and second, that I plug his latest book, Dvorak's Inside Track to the Mac, *published by Osborne/McGraw-Hill and available at all fine bookstores.*

That takes care of the second condition. Now for the first:

*Hmmm. I'm thinking. Okay, how about … no, that wouldn't do. Okay, I've got it: John C. Dvorak is our **most prolific** and opinionated **pundit** whose personality **and pronouncements** in a **plethora** of publications have produced **pleasure** and **wonderment** in people who **use** PCs. And even Macintoshes. And he tells a mean Scandinavian joke and we would miss him if he were gone. I'm outta here.*

❧

The microcomputer scene is dominated by men. Based on statistics provided by major magazines, we can say that in the IBM world there are about 95 percent men to 5 percent women interested in the machines. In the Mac world the ratio is 90 percent to 10 percent.

Over the years I've wondered about these statistics, and realized that we're running a men's club and don't even know it.

This was recently made clear after I did a local talk show to promote an upcoming keynote at the West Coast Computer Faire. On the keynote panel would be Jim Warren, Steve Wozniak , Lee Felsenstein, Gary Kildall, Don Lancaster, and David Bunnell. All of them males (as far as I can tell). Myself, Warren and Felsenstein did the radio spot. The show's host, a male, asked us a lot of dorky questions about the good old days and then took phone calls. All the calls were from men. All the questions were the same old questions about what computer to buy. We all yukked it up and had a great time.

So we go to the show and do the keynote. I check out the audience. Ninety-five percent male, minimum. I counted only a few women in the crowd of about 1000 onlookers.

That's when it finally dawned on me that men are somehow excluding women from their club. It's a last bastion–a men's club. Sure, sure, a female can join if she really wants to. But the guys dominate the conversation and promote the dorkiest side of the scene. This makes any woman with any sense roll her eyes and grimace.

As the keynote, for example, David Bunnell, a guy with lots of dough, felt like wearing a bunch of the dorkiest old badges and buttons and looking like an original nerd. We all oooohed and ahhhhed over some of the obscure buttons he wore.

In certain circles, like amongst the DEC/UNIX crowd, the level of nerdism reaches heights that can be duplicated only in the most horrid of bad dreams to those of us in the semi-normal world of the Mac. There the guys wear ponytails and Portuguese fishing hats and are covered head to toe with dumb buttons. The guys are real fat or anorexic. Hairy, too. All that is missing is a swarm of flies buzzing around their heads. Exactly *why* the swarm is missing is a mystery. I figure some of these guys spray their hair with Raid.

In this woolly world of UNIX, there are no women as far as I can tell. That is, except for Jean Yates and her crowd of UNIX consultants who promote the operating system of big corporations who don't know what they're in for. Soon Yates leaves and the big nerds pour in; their Cokes and cold pizza and a million pens in their pocket. The mostly female secretaries and clerks and female excess all see these guys as computer types to be avoided. Soon the computer itself is associated with them and it, too, is determined to be some vile device to elude. Good work, Jean.

Men aggressively keep women out of the scene. Women aren't welcome as hobbyists, experts, nothing. If they want to, they can do COBOL coding for a bank, or they can host parties, or pretend to be friendly as PR persons. That's about it. If they insist on becoming members of the club, they are usually forced to become dorks, too, and are never taken seriously. The attractive females, when seen at a user's group, are considered dumb. Their job is to shut up.

I'm aware of one or two exceptions to these axioms. Sue Currier, the president of SoftSynch, is an ex-*Vogue* model, and she hangs out with the boys. But she's an Australian, with the Australian penchant to cuss like a teamster at anyone in her way to the top. This confuses the nerds more than a buried infinite loop. She gets categorized as an exception that doesn't count. Besides that, everyone figures her husband does the real work.

The husband-who-does-all-the-real-work syndrome permeates any notion that a woman can be successful in this industry.

The real issue, though, is whether women can even be allowed to participate long enough to attempt success. In other words, are they allowed in the clubhouse? While unwritten, the answer is obviously a resounding "NO WAY! We don't want any girls in here!"

Let's face it, it's hard to code with some female hanging around all the time complaining about what a mess you've made. Besides that, there is no place for a guy to go anymore where he can pal around with other guys like in the old days of the exclusive men's club.

This is the NEW men's club, and it has to be protected from women trying to sneak in. The sure-fire way to keep the women away is to be a complete slob.

Here are Dvorak's men's club tips:

Never bathe. Wear your hair in a ponytail and only wash it when bugs get in it (and only if they are biting bugs, and only if you don't like to bitten by bugs). Never exercise. Avoid eye contact with women and never talk to them. If they insist on a conversation, then stare at their breasts awhile—they hate that. Wear Earth Shoes. Wear glasses that don't fit. Carry a lot of pens. Slouch.

Dining tips are important. When any group that includes a woman insists on going someplace to eat, always be the first to say, "I know a great place." Then take them to the worst roach-infested pizza joint in town and order an anchovy pizza with onions. Make sure to get pizza goo on your face and smile a lot with a mouthful of chewed pizza. Always do your eating with both hands and hunched way over the plate. Once in awhile wipe your mouth with the back of your hand which you then rub on your jeans (top of the thigh area). If you can do it, I recommend belching every so often. This is especially effective if you can do it with some food still in your mouth and while chewing.

If we men are diligent and use these and other tips (just look around for ideas), we can probably stem any further encroachment. Remember, the IBM world is 95 percent men to 5 percent women, and we're 90 percent to 10 percent. If this continues, they'll soon take over!

Then again, you sometimes have to wonder, who wants to be in a club like this?

❦

— This column first appeared in *MacUser* magazine, August 1987. It is Copyright 1987 © John C. Dvorak.

WHY THE MAC IS HARD TO PROGRAM

CHRIS CRAWFORD

C hris Crawford is the brilliant game designer and master programmer. His games for Macintosh include "Balance of Power," "Patton vs. Rommel," "Trust & Betrayal," and "Patton Strikes Back."

Chris takes the stage twice in this book. Here, with an original piece that takes us behind the scenes of the easy-to-use-but-hard-to-program Mac. Later on, you'll find a reprint from Chris's excellent newsletter, where a much simpler task—building a world—is explained.

❧

The Mac has always been hard to program. From the very beginning, programmers have complained about the difficulty they have experienced getting the Macintosh to do its wonderful Macish things. I can provide an illuminating and dramatic comparison that will put this in perspective.

Before I began working on computer games, I held a job as an energy educator. As part of that job, I had to study lots of technical documents on all aspects of the energy crisis, including nuclear power. I visited nuclear power plants, talked to the people who worked in them, and learned a great deal about how they work and how they are operated. Based on my experiences with both technologies, I can state with confidence that it is easier to run a nuclear power plant than it is to program a Macintosh.

In this essay, I'd like to explain just how and why the Mac is so confoundedly perverse, so frustratingly complex, and so damned difficult to work with, and why software meltdowns are more common than nuclear ones.

User Friendliness

The foremost problem for the Macintosh programmer is the requirement of user friendliness. The Macintosh community is utterly intolerant of anything less than absolute user coddling. The Macintosh programmer is required to protect the user from every possible source of error. This can be vexing and most time-consuming. You have to jump through all sorts of hoops to protect idiot users who are too lazy to read the manual.

Here's an example of how difficult it can be. My most recent program, "Patton Strikes Back," is designed to work in black and white or sixteen colors only. For some complex technical reasons, it really is impractical to try to get the program to work in 256 colors. Now, the program is smart enough to figure out whether to use sixteen colors or black and white. However, once it has committed to one or the other, it cannot change the number of colors it uses; it's just too much of a mess. So what happens if, during the middle of a hot game of "Patton Strikes Back," the user pulls down the control panel, selects Monitors, and changes from sixteen colors to 256 colors?

My program simply cannot work in 256 colors. It will crash if it attempts to do so. But I cannot prevent the user from changing to 256 colors. Moreover, Apple's user interface rules explicitly forbid me to interfere with the user's choice. If the user decides to go to 256 colors, I must not stop him, even if it will cause a crash. I must politely explain the situation to him and ask him to return to sixteen colors. So my program checks the overall color situation as part of its event loop. If the color situation has changed (via the user messing with the control panel) then I have to check how many colors are now in force. If the user has indeed gone to a different number of colors, then I have to stop everything, and put up a dialog box explaining the problem and asking the user to return to sixteen colors. Now, at this point, I have to return control to the user and hope that he will be a good boy, go back to the control panel, and return things to their original state. If he does not do so, then the program will crash. If he does fix it, things can be returned to normal.

Now, it took me nearly a week to work out the precise system for handling this. I spent a week trying different schemes, testing their effectiveness, and coping with unanticipated shortcomings (what happens if the user has some means other than the control panel to change the color setting?). All that time spent coping with a problem that really shouldn't arise in the first place! Can you imagine how many ways a dumb or perverse user can screw up a program? There are hundreds of them! And every way has to be anticipated and provided for. That's one reason why programming the Mac can be such a royal pain.

Multiple Target Platforms

Another problem with the Mac is its unfocussed target base. For the first few years of the Mac's life, all Macs were the same except for differences in RAM size. But with the Mac II, things started to get crazy, and they've gotten worse with each passing year. Nowadays, the range of computer systems that go by the name of "Macintosh" is huge. A Macintosh can have a 68000, a 68020, a 68030, or a 68040 CPU running at 8 MHz, 16 MHz, 24 MHz, or 50 MHz. It can have an 800K floppy drive or a 1.4M SuperDrive. It might have an Apple Sound Chip, but then again, it might not. Same thing goes with a floating point processor. RAM can be anything from 1 MB to 16 MB.

But the worst problem from a game designer's point of view is the monitor. A Macintosh can have a 512x342 black-and-white screen (the Mac Classic). It might also have a 512x380 color screen (the Mac LC). Then there's the black-and-white screen on the portable with some other size. And of course the Mac II comes in 640x480 color or 640x480 black and white, or perhaps a large screen color or black and white. And when we talk about a color screen, it could be sixteen colors or 256 colors or perhaps 24-bit color. And then there are the gray-scale monitors.

None of this is a problem if you're designing a word processing program or a painting program or a database program or a spreadsheet. You just open up a window to fit the screen, and show what you can, leaving scroll bars for whatever is left over. But this doesn't work for game designers. The player of a game must see the entire situation. You can't ask the game player to scroll around in the middle of the game. For example, with "Patton Strikes Back," I had to get around this problem with a ridiculous mess of code that handled each possible case directly. The code looked something like this:

```
IF SmallScreen THEN
  BEGIN
    IF Black&White THEN
      {do the graphics for smallscreen black & white}
    ELSE
      {do the graphics for smallscreen color}
  END
ELSE
  BEGIN
    IF Black&White THEN
      {do the graphics for bigscreen black & white}
    ELSE
      {do the graphics for bigscreen color}
  END;
```

I had to go through this nonsense every single time I needed to put something on the screen. In a game, you draw to the screen many times. You can imagine what a mess my code was. You can imagine how many times I cursed those oddball Macintosh configurations.

Lack of Development Tools and Documentation

This was a serious problem in the early days of Macintosh programming. When I began programming the Mac in 1984, you couldn't develop Mac software with a Mac. You had to buy a Lisa and use it instead. There was a Pascal compiler and an assembler. It was all terribly slow.

To test your software, you had to copy it to a Macintosh diskette and then run the diskette on your Mac. And the Lisa hard disk was slower than current Macintosh floppy drives. For all these reasons, the crucial compile-cycle time (how long it takes to make a tiny change in the program and get the result on your Mac) was about ten minutes. This made software development slow and cumbersome, to say the least.

Nowadays, things are much better. We have excellent tools in MPW and the Think compilers. The compile-cycle time is under a minute. But in some ways we are not as well off as those in the IBM PC world. We don't have the variety of tools available, and we don't have a good C++ (yet).

Complexity of the Toolbox

This is a killer problem. The Macintosh has a built-in set of routines to control every aspect of its use. These routines will automatically handle just about every low-level problem that a programmer might encounter. That's one reason for the uniformity of Macintosh applications: they all look and act alike because they're all using the same Toolbox routines. That's good!

What's bad is the fact that there are nearly a thousand of these routines. A Macintosh programmer is supposed to learn every last one of them. You have to learn its name, its calling parameters, and what it does. Of course, nobody can master all this, so there are reference works to help. Big, fat volumes like *Inside Macintosh* or *Macintosh Revealed*. There are even software references that will look up the Toolbox routines while you're programming. Of course, none of this helps you make sense of any of it. The simple truth is, nobody understands every single Toolbox routine. There are just too many of the damn things.

To make matters worse, the list is always growing. When I started programming the Mac in 1984, there were about 450 Toolbox routines. Over the last eight years, that number has more than doubled. Every year, Apple comes up with new and improved things for developers to learn. Every month, I receive a fat package from Apple detailing new technical developments. It contains a

CD-ROM with new and better routines, new system changes, or some other development. Just keeping up with all this is a big job. I don't know how some people get any programs written.

The Toolbox has another problem: individual routines can be horrendously complex. As an example, let me describe one of the most important and heavily used routines in the Toolbox: CopyBits.

The purpose of CopyBits is easy to understand: it copies an image (stored as a bitmap) from one place to another. Think of images as residing on imaginary pieces of paper, and CopyBits as being a kind of cookie cutter that snips an image from one piece of paper and copies it onto another piece of paper, all without destroying the original image. In most cases, one of those pieces of paper is the computer screen. That's how we draw things onto the computer screen.

The following were found on America Online and are copyright ©1991, 92 America Online. Glad that's out of the way.

Subj: Novice stories   91-01-28 00:19:53 EST

From: HaHaHaHaHa

I worked at a computer store for a couple of years ... get some real weird ones at times ...

One lady tried to use 5.25 inch disks on a Mac by, you guessed it, FOLDING them in half ... then she wondered why they wouldn't work.

Another time, someone complained of losing data from his disks ... he'd use them a couple of days and then they'd just die ... After checking the disk drive out quite thouroughly, we found out he'd been storing the disks on his refrigerator with magnets.

We also got a call about the "any" key once...

In its simplest form, then, CopyBits would have four arguments telling it exactly what you want to do. First, you'd have to tell it where to find the first piece of paper. Second, you'd have to tell it where to find the second piece of paper. Third, you'd have to specify which portion of the source image you want snipped out. Lastly, you'd specify where to place that snipped image onto the target image. Not too messy, is it?

Ah, but the Apple engineers wanted the neatest, spiffiest, most powerful CopyBits ever. So while you're at it, you can also scale the image in either direction. That is, you can scrunch it down, or stretch it out either horizontally or vertically. Of course, that takes an additional bit of specifying work to indicate how much scaling you want. Almost all the time, you don't want any scaling (it looks ugly) so you just have to tell CopyBits, "No scaling, thank you."

Then there's the transfer mode. You didn't think we'd simply copy the image over just like that, did you? No, when we copy it, we can also perform logical operations on the bits of the image, such as ANDing and ORing the bits of the source and the target images together. Perhaps you have noticed some of the strange options in some painting programs that permit you to get inverted images that combine with the original image in weird ways. Those weird effects come from CopyBits. We use them once in a blue moon, but every single time we use CopyBits, we have to tell it, "Standard copy mode, please."

Lastly, there's the mask region. This is a way to copy an image in such a way that it doesn't cover up other parts of the image. You specify a geometric shape that your image will fit into. Any part of your image that doesn't fit gets clipped off. Now, of course, your window already has a VisRgn and a ClipRgn that do some of this stuff automatically, but the Apple designers apparently wanted to make sure that you'd have enough clipping possibilities, so they added this new MaskRgn. In over seven years of programming the Mac I still haven't gotten quite straight exactly when you'd use a MaskRgn instead of a ClipRgn, but what the hey …

The upshot is that a simple and fundamental act like putting an image onto the screen has all sorts of unnecessary bells and whis-tles attached to it. Using CopyBits is like going into a hamburger restaurant and saying, "No, I don't want anchovies, bacon, pep-pers, onions, artichoke hearts, mushrooms, or raw egg on my hamburger," and then discovering that you forgot to rule out the baby shrimp topping.

And CopyBits is not the only routine in the Toolbox. There are more than 900 other routines, some of them just as bodacious as CopyBits. Some of them are worse!

The Macintosh Color System

The system used to control color in Macintosh applications is the most extreme example of why the Mac is so beautiful for users and so agonizing for developers. You can take any of the modular Macs and plug in several display cards for several different monitors, and everything will work flawlessly. You can have a big black-and-white monitor and a medium-sized 4-bit color monitor, and a small 8-bit monitor, and the system software will handle everything seamlessly for you. You can grab a window displayed on one monitor and move it so that it straddles all three monitors, and it will display properly on each. That's magic! I have the greatest respect for the geniuses who designed a system that handles so much complexity so easily, and with so little effort from the user.

BUT!

This thing is absolute hell on developers. I cannot convey the complexity of the system in one essay. Whole chapters of *Inside Macintosh* attempt to accomplish this and fail. The color system on the Macintosh is the most inscrutable software design I have ever encountered, a software House of Mirrors in which everything seems to be defined in terms of something else, and you can never find the source image.

Let me take just one tiny fragment of the system: assigning a color. Suppose that you want to put one special color into your program. It's a pretty lavender, and you have its RGB value (the numbers that define the color) all set and ready. How do you tell the Macintosh to use your lavender?

The first thing you learn is that colors are part of color tables. A color table is a set of colors. So you need to put your lavender into the appropriate color table. All you have to do is find the correct color table and store your lavender into that color table. And in fact there are all sorts of Toolbox routines for manipulating color tables. The problem is, you can't mess with the color table that's actually used on the screen. At least, not directly. For that, you have to use color palettes.

What's the difference between a color palette and a color table? Elementary, my dear Watson. A color palette is a color table that doesn't count for anything. If a color table is a set of commands that roar, "First color: red! Second color: blue! Third color: orange!" and so on, then a color palette is a mousey coward who begs, "Could I please have a little red? And maybe some blue? Is there any room for an orange? Please?"

You, the programmer, have to declare the degree of begging (the tolerance level) of each color. If you set a tolerance level of zero, then there's no begging, so nobody I know uses any tolerance level other than zero.

One other thing: the colors in a palette are not necessarily sequenced the same way on the screen. The eighth color in your palette will probably not be the eighth color displayed on the screen. That's because each monitor has its own separate color table, which isn't the same as a palette, remember? However, if you declare your colors to be explicit, then the color correspondence is preserved ... or maybe it isn't. Who knows?

Basically, then, to get your lavender onto the screen, you simply create a color table handle pointing indirectly to a color table, then initialize the color table with the default colors used on the Mac, then use the appropriate Toolbox calls to modify one of the colors in the color table to become your lavender. Then you merely assign your color table to a color palette, taking care to declare the correct tolerance and explicit settings, whatever those might be, with calls such as CTab2Palette. You would, of course, have to create the palette first with a call to NewPalette. You must also compensate for the red shift of the expanding universe. Alternatively, of course, you could bypass the color table mechanism by creating a palette and manipulating its entries directly with GetEntryColor and SetEntryColor along with GetEntryUsage and SetEntryUsage. Or perhaps you could just bring in a palette previously edited in ResEdit, using GetNewPalette and SetPalette.

Got that? Is it set in your mind now?

Oh, be sure to call ActivatePalette every now and then for luck. And if you failed to declare your window as a CWindow, it won't work and you'll never guess why.

Now, wasn't that simple? It's probably wrong, but it worked once for me.

Wrap-Up

So there you have it: five reasons why the Mac has been so difficult to program. The funny thing is, I still prefer to use the Mac for software development, even though it's not where my bread is buttered. If I were smart, I'd dump the thing and develop directly and solely on the IBM PC, thereby saving myself the cost of all that porting between platforms. But for the cutting-edge game design I do, the Mac is still the most powerful development environment.

⽊

— Copyright 1992 © Chris Crawford

THEY SOLD THEIR SOULS
TO THE FORTUNE 1000

JOHN C. DVORAK

T*his is my favorite column by John C. (he requires the "C") Dvorak.*

⁊

A decade of micros has passed. Somewhere it took a left turn as most of the world went right. The microcomputer industry had high hopes for itself in 1976. Those days are over. Last year, most of the original Byte Shops had folded, including the place where I bought my first computer (a SOL-20). It was the Berkeley Byte Shop. By the time it folded it wasn't even a Byte Shop anymore. For some unknown reason the owner changed its name to the Computer Center, and then, finally, to Track Computers. (The latter was the suggestion of a highly paid consultant.)

The coup de grace was delivered to the West Coast scene when the once powerful West Coast Computer Dealers Association pulled up its stakes and said goodbye. Most of its members were out of business or had gone to work for Businessland.

Critics like to think that IBM had something to do with all this. Unfortunately, it's not true. IBM created opportunities with an open architecture computer that encouraged third parties and entrepreneurs. Apple's closed-up Mac and scanty documentation (at the beginning) contributed more to the decline than did IBM. But that's academic, because I don't think either company is at fault.

It's the people in the business who are at fault, with their acceptance of the notion that you have to crawl like a worm to make money. Let's look around at the scene and see what's happened.

First of all, the nifty computer store isn't dead as a moneymaker. Scattered like the lost tribe of Israel, they're here and there. There are new stores that specialize in aggressive sales of clones and zippy little alternative machines. These newcomers are doing quite nicely, thank you. They're selling what the old Byte Shops used to sell—fun computing. The Byte Shops and a lot of the older stores didn't keep up with the changing scene, and many of them folded with an inventory of dusty old CP/M machines. Until the bitter end they were saying, "A Z-80 machine has more performance than an IBM PC." Yeah, and all of 64K of memory. The hottest Z-80 is like owning a supercharged, fuel-injected Chevy with a one-gallon tank.

These guys were stuck in a limbo of their own creation. They didn't keep up because they booted out the hobbyists (the people who got them started). The stores wanted to make the big bucks by selling the business user. Now they're broke. Good move! The net result is that an entire layer of industry leadership has disappeared. This is a tragedy. Where are the wizened sages?

One group partially responsible is magazine publishers. For one thing, you're reading one of the few genuine enthusiast journals when you pick up a copy of *MacUser*. While the owners of this magazine think it's great to be the only game in town, I think it stinks that there aren't others like it. After all, a primary reason for all this stagnation is the stagnant magazines. They used to be boosters for the technology—not boosters in the sense that they were flacks, mind you, but in the sense that they genuinely liked the business. They began to take themselves too seriously. Soon thereafter, they began to hire "journalists" to write for them. These are guys and gals who could care less about the scene, let's face it. Few, if any of them, have any notion about the innards of a machine and most of them want to write cop stories for the hometown daily.

Ten years ago the magazines were your friends, your next door neighbors. They taught you about the innards of the machines: how they worked; why you should program in BASIC; why you should program in APL. The early issues of any magazine are filled with enthusiastic introductory material—the kind of information a newcomer needs to know to be inspired by it all. A generation of enthusiasts and hobbyists and original thinkers was born, and they spread out among the masses to convert more hedonists to learn the way of the machine. Then they disappeared. Where'd they go? Did they all get rich and move to Newport?

They gave up, it seems to me. They finally got tired of explaining the difference between a bit and a byte. Talk was cheap in 1976, when the difference between a bit and a byte was interesting the apostolic micro user. Now it's a bore. "Read about it in a book," they'll tell you. "Computers aren't really good for anything," they'll tell you. "We sell solutions, not computers," they'll tell you.

They've all sold out. Down the river. They've betrayed their own dreams and ideals for a few gold coins. Screw 'em.

If people (who should know better) can't derive usefulness and fun and enrichment from a small computer, then they should retire to Scottsdale and pull weeds for the rest of their miserable lives. The newcomers will eventually pick up the slack. A hundred years from now you can claim to be a founder of the personal computer revolution if you got started in 1995.

But you still have to wonder how today's newcomer will fare with no wizened sages, no Byte Shops, no enthusiast magazines, and nothing but surly chain store dealers who don't know spit from Perrier. Meanwhile, the hapless novice is surrounded by negative press that claims these machines are as useless as fender skirts on a ten-speed bike.

The newcomer has no way of finding out that there are hundreds of useful new products released daily. The stores don't tell them and the one or two decent magazines can't do it all. The promising new product instead finds its way to a reviewer's shelf only to be discovered long after the programmer had to go back to work for Bechtel to pay the rent. The stores, the magazines and the old-timers (who have long since sold their souls) spend all their time crawling on their hands and knees so they can lick the boots of the Fortune 1000 computer user. It's pathetic.

Let's return personal computing towards the direction it needs to head. Towards a person, not a skyscraper.

— This column first appeared in *MacUser* magazine, July 1986. It is copyright 1987 © John C. Dvorak.

ALSOP TO APPLE

tewart Alsop is a prime mover. He publishes and edits P.C. Letter, *a computer industry "insider" newsletter, and is (for the second time) editor-in chief of* InfoWorld *magazine. Smart move by* Infoworld.

Big guy. Big pundit. Big opinions. Usually right.

Here, in a piece reprinted from P.C. Letter, *he takes John Sculley to task, in an open letter.*

※

DEAR APPLE: PLEASE BE NICE TO MOTHER MACINTOSH

TO: John Sculley, Chairman, Apple Computer, Inc.

FROM: Stewart Alsop, Editor, *P.C. Letter*

RE: Apple and the Macintosh

Dear John:

You blew your stack at some comments I made during the keynote panel at Macworld Expo directly before your own keynote presentation. Since you didn't want to share with me which comments made you so mad, it has taken me a while to find out.

But I have found out and, to tell you the truth, I was surprised. I was surprised because I had guessed wrong about which comments set you off, so I've begun to wonder just how close to the bone I must have unwittingly struck. And that's why I'm writing this letter: you seem uninterested in finding out exactly what it is that I was trying to say (as opposed to what you thought I was saying), so I'll have to communicate somewhat more publicly. And what I have to say could tell you something you don't know about how the Macintosh is perceived these days.

The comment that set you off was the one in which I explained to the audience why there would never be an Macintosh III.

You can look at the Macintosh Classic, introduced in its original form factor in 1984, as the Macintosh I—black-and-white screen, no expansion, compact form factor, highly integrated design.

The Macintosh II was introduced in 1987—traditional computer box with expansion slots, integral color and sound, more robust configurations. Each of these configurations generated a different level of software development, because they offered developers different benefits in trying to satisfy their customers. And, even after the Macintosh II was introduced, many developers chose to maintain the Classic as their minimum configuration. The net effect of this phenomenon was to send a message to customers that there was an exciting and interesting upgrade path inside the Macintosh product line.

In other words, you could buy a Classic form factor and still be able to anticipate greater functionality when you could afford or command a Macintosh II.

Along with Apple's relentless drive to introduce more and more powerful versions of the Macintosh II in 1989 and 1990, the company succeeded in generating a tremendous sense of momentum and excitement for its customers.

Now it's 1992, and Apple has refocused itself on selling lower-cost computers. And the truth is that the customers feel as though they are simply getting repackaged versions of what already exists. Okay, so a mainstream desktop machine now costs $2,500 (based on last week's repricing). And you are selling very cool notebooks (I even went out bought one with my own money!). And you are selling really fast Macintoshes, the Quadras, which have built-in Ethertalk and 24-bit color (for a price).

But these new products don't represent a new level of the platform, only new features and extensions. I am speaking as a real customer in this instance, since I did commit my business to using Macintoshes. I had a real reason to replace my "Classic" machines (now relegated to status as servers for low-intensity applications) with Macintosh IIs, which are our corporate standard (all seven of them). I don't have a compelling reason to replace anything with Quadras or IIfx's, since the only significant benefit is speed—which I can also get through upgrades and fixes, if I really need it.

Now I look at Apple and at your public statements about new products and directions. You've spent a lot of time talking about a new operating system and processor architecture that you and IBM are working on. (This is an interesting tactic you've adopted, of talking about a new platform before introducing it; remember that the Apple II didn't have to contend with the Macintosh until it was actually introduced and for sale.) You've recently spent a lot of time talking about consumer products and personal digital assistants. And you've rightly and proudly talked about the success of the Powerbooks and the low-cost strategy.

So what's missing from this scenario?

The future of the Macintosh. The Macintosh III. A sense of momentum and excitement and possibilities for the Macintosh. Something more than a vague notion that you'll be able to run ported Macintosh applications on these really hot PowerPC boxes.

As you can see from the above stories, I believe very strongly as an analyst that you will successfully execute your strategies for the IBM deal and the consumer-products effort. But, as a Macintosh user and buyer, I keep getting this sinking feeling that all the good stuff is going into product efforts that are not Macintosh and that are not due for 18 to 36 months anyway.

Now put that sinking feeling down into the real world, and I watch Windows users beginning to get better applications software on their platform and get it earlier than I am getting it. Sure, the whizzy video-based multimedia stuff is light-years ahead on the Macintosh, but my users do spend 90% of their time banging away on word processing, database management, and desktop publishing software. And, yes, the networking and graphical interface and integration on the Intel side still sucks rocks, but the users are beginning to get better software and the rest will logically follow (particularly now that Microsoft has begun to figure out this platform game).

I'll tell you what's missing right now—a believable, visible, religiously committed Macintosh zealot at Apple Computer. Jean Louis Gassée fulfilled that role for a few years, but there's no one arguing for the Macintosh anymore, at least not as far as customers can see.

If there was such a person, then there would be more going on for the Macintosh customer than a single system-software extension (QuickTime, which is certainly a brilliant extension) and some line extensions of the hardware. There would be a vision of the future of the Macintosh that included on-board video processing, ISDN, voice recognition, and a way to deal with the fact that Motorola seems increasingly unable to upgrade the 68000 processor line. If there was such a person, the Macintosh customer would feel like there was a fighting chance for the Macintosh inside Apple Computer, particularly when the CEO is out promoting all that futures stuff.

This is what I was trying to say on that panel at Macworld Expo. The fact that you got so upset with these remarks indicates to me that you are also very concerned that the Macintosh is being perceived by customers as a dead end, that perhaps you have heard from some customers on that very point and would rather not have it talked about publicly. And that makes me even more worried, because it strikes me that, if you are concerned, then I really do have something to worry about.

ꝛ⃛

THE MAC, CIRCA 1988…
AND 1992

NEIL SHAPIRO

I*n August, 1988, Neil Shapiro wrote a column for* MacUser *(of which was then Editor-in-Chief) titled "The State of the Mac, Circa 1988." The column looked at Macintosh and Apple present, and Macintosh and Apple future.*

Now that the future's here—at last!—I asked Neil to look back on his prophecies, and get on that crystal horse once again.

Well, here I am typing away on my new PowerBook 170. While I've used the PowerBooks before, this one is my own, new, personal machine and I'm finding that it performs even better than I had expected it would …

Whoops.

Hey, *deja vu!*

The past three or four years have proven one thing about the future as related to Apple Computer, Inc. (and the Macintosh), which is simply that progress will continue and that Apple will remain a company driven to excel their past with always-improved machines that poke at the boundaries of wherever the computing field finds itself. The PowerBooks are a prime example. And, at the end of this piece, I want to try to peer into the PowerBook glass darkly and tell you why I think they are so revolutionary in scope.

But before I go into prediction mode (a choice under the Parapsychic Menu) let's see how I did in 1988. Was I Kreskin? Or was I just Uri Geller?

Not A Two-Part Plan

Back in 1988 I had heard rumors of the Apple IIGS development, and said I thought it would probably have a 16-bit microprocessor, a Toolbox ROM, and fantastic color and sound capabilities.

So far, right all the way! I should have stopped while I was ahead.

I then said that Apple was not going to play the two machines against each other, and that they would let each machine become the best within its field (speaking of the Macintosh and Apple II lines).

Wowser, it's hard to be more wrong.

On the other hand, it's also difficult to imagine how Apple's marketing people could be more wrong than in how they have treated the Apple II line.

My idea then was that the Apple IIGS would remain an affordable computer system for the schools and education markets, and that Apple would continue to support it and keep it viable. At the same point, Apple would be moving the Macs into businesses.

Unfortunately, what has happened is that Apple has taken what was a lock on the education market and literally thrown it away. Because Apple has chosen to abandon the Apple IIGS (no advertising, no new CPUs, no true developer support and co-marketing), they have just about succeeded in doing what IBM and others could never have done—they have moved the Apple logo out of view of hundreds of thousands of school kids throughout the nation. Schools are rightfully reluctant to purchase an expensive color Macintosh (even the LC), and color is important to schools.

Apple has offered the Apple II-compatibility board for the Mac LC as a sort of circuit-board band-aid, but it is a solution that is worse than no solution at all. The board enables the LC to run

Apple II software, but not the newer, Desktop-based IIGS software. Neither can the schools then follow a logical upgrade path to a "si" or higher Mac II, as the board only works in an LC.

So, okay, Apple has blown the education market. I thought they would increase their hold on it and I was 180 degrees wrong. Oh, well.

But, on a brighter note, I did say that "They (Apple) will … by 1990, completely own the desktop publishing field …"

Much closer there, wasn't I?

On the other hand, I did not reckon with two factors: the way developers would show little or no loyalty to Apple and cross-develop on other platforms once Apple helped them with Desktop-based ideas, and that IBM itself would travel down the GUI path to Windows Nirvana.

Granted, everyone "in the know," realizes that Macintosh is better at DTP than a Windows-based PC. But you can't tell that from the ads of programs that bear the same name on both platforms. This has meant that Apple has not owned the DTP marketplace, but has only dominated it.

Still, I give this prediction a true-psychic rating. (Hey, Shirley MacLaine, let's do lunch.)

I also pat myself on the back for my prediction that Apple "has to expand (the Macintosh Interface) onto other non-Apple machines in order to triumph." It seems that Apple itself has recognized this with the announced intentions to develop the "Pink" operating system in conjunction with IBM.

Of course, I personally think that Pink will last right up until the first group of Apple programmers is locked into an argument with a group of IBM programmers. I don't think Pink will make it, because I don't think that the vision of those two companies is congruent enough to allow the type of co-authorship needed to make this work.

I reiterate my previous suggestion to Apple: license ROM-based routines to other companies. Make the money and the inroads, and achieve the industry standardization without risk to the ongoing vision.

I predict they won't listen to me.

⠶

Now The Real Future

But now onto something entirely different: a new prediction, and one I am entirely sure about! Yes, feel free to come back to me four years in the future and point out that I said back in 1991 that:

> *Apple's PowerBook computers are not just evolutionary but revolutionary in design, and will change, forever, the way people design computers, the way they use computers, the way they think about computers—and even what a computer is thought of as being. They are the first "metacomputers."*

I have coined the terms metacomputers and metacomputing based on the work of Douglas Hofstadter in his Nobel-prize winning book *Godel, Escher and Bach*. In that book, Hofstadter explains and details the use of the root "meta" in words such as metaphilosophy and metalanguage.

Basically, a meta philosophy or language is a superset, containing within it the subsets of the whole. But the superset itself is often not an obvious one, and this sets up what Hofstadter calls "strange loops." An example would be the two sentences:

1. An Apple PowerBook is one of the world's smallest, self-contained laptop microcomputers.

2. An Apple PowerBook is one of the world's largest, multi-sited microcomputer systems.

On the face of it, the two sentences seem to point illogically at each other, to set up a "strange loop" of lack-of-meaning. If the first sentence is true, how can the second one be true? If the second one is true, then what of the first? Some logicians would say that, in such a case, neither statement could be true.

But they haven't reckoned with Apple Computer, Inc.!

As it happens, the Apple PowerBook can be used simply as a laptop computer with the ability to run Macintosh software, but it can also be used with Apple's System 7.0 software and the Apple Remote Access program (ARA) to take with you, wherever you go, the access to any number of other computers, networks and peripherals. It can become a metacomputer that contains within itself far more power, far more computing ability, than could be squeezed into its slim profile in any other manner.

Imagine that you have a network in your New York City business composed of three Mac IIfx's, a Mac SE/30, two LaserWriter IINTX's, and an IBM PC clone 386/25. You pop your Macintosh PowerBook out of your briefcase in your San Francisco hotel room late in the evening. Thanks to the power of this wonderful metacomputer, suddenly the time difference and the distance between you and your work no longer matters. The problems don't exist. With one simple command you access your faraway network, you work on your datafiles, you print on your LaserWriter, you even leave EMAIL to the fellow at the 386/25 with third-party software.

Or, let's say that you are at an associate's office and you have brought the wrong spreadsheet with you. Again, the PowerBook becomes a window into your office computer from which you access and use the spreadsheet just as if you were at the other keyboard. Metacomputing, that's what this revolution is about.

Well, perhaps you are one of a group of business partners scattered around the country and you can't quite all get in time zones close enough to have a conference call. No problem. The PowerBook comes to your aid and allows you, from anywhere in the civilized world, to meet with, and exchange ideas and work with, your compatriots. You've got the PowerBook, you've got the power of metacomputing!

Or, you simply wish to word-process a letter to your husband—it's a metacomputer and can operate on its own just as any other computer.

There have been laptop computers before that have allowed their owners, after much hassle in learning computer foofawraw (a technical term meaning complex software and hardware interfacing), to network their laptops to their office machines. But the PowerBook is the first computer system that has made networking so automatic, so all-encompassing powerful and yet intuitive, that it could evolve into this idea of metacomputing.

Indeed, the PowerBook puts me in mind of the original excitement that I and many others felt the first time we picked up a mouse and became enveloped in the Macintosh interface. Until that happened, computers—even microcomputers—were the purview of the elite, of the power priests in the data processing department, or of the person who was more interested in what a computer was than what a computer could do.

The Macintosh, in 1984, said: "NO. Computers are for everyone. A computer is a tool and we have made the tool easy to use."

In 1992, the PowerBook is saying: "NO. You do not have to be a genius to network your computers. In fact, start thinking about all of your computers as one computer linked together—a metacomputer that is ready when you are, wherever you are."

Oh, yes, there is room for improvement. The way Apple Remote Access works today, even with a 9600 baud modem, means that it is unlikely you will want to run many applications remotely. It just takes too darn long. Instead you will find yourself accessing datafiles remotely, and perhaps copying applications from the remote computer to the calling computer.

I predict that Apple will recognize this metaphor (if they have not already) and will build upon it much as they recognized desktop-publishing and built on that. So, I think we will see various ways from Apple, and encouraged from third-party suppliers, to make System 7 networking capabilities better than ever and, via the PowerBook, more portable and linked than ever.

I think that, as wonderful as the PowerBooks are today, in the future we will see portable devices from Apple that will allow us to do anything that we could do with the most powerful computer in our networks from wherever we are. And more, much more.

I also feel that as networks become more prevalent and hardware cheaper, and as more people own both a portable and a home machine, or perhaps a few of each, we will see more examples of ways to work on the same data with computer power from different machines all brought to bear at the same time. I can see a day when the power of a Quadra 900 will look perfectly puny as, through new software and hardware, people focus the abilities of multiple-linked computers—their metacomputer—onto a task or tasks.

The PowerBook and the way it works with System 7.0's remote and network abilities is like the Apple II when it came out with 4K of RAM, a cassette drive, and no lower case letters on the key-board. It is a revolution that is happening, it is a technological marvel more powerful than any ever seen before, but which is really just the tip of the iceberg that we call the future.

Well, I started this column by commenting on how happy I was with my new PowerBook 170. Gee, now it looks like a Model T to me ...

A few pages back, Stewart Alsop pronounced that what Apple needs is "a believable, visible, religiously committed Macintosh zealot ..."

I agree. And my vote goes to Neil Shapiro, one of the best-known and most-loved guys we've got. For good reason.

Neil contributed this short bio:

Neil Shapiro was the founding editor-in-chief of MacUser *Magazine. He is one of the few people to have hired Doug Clapp and John Dvorak as columnists on the same day. Neil is the originator and Chief Sysop of all the MAUG® Forums on the CompuServe Information Services network.*

Neil Shapiro, 34 Spencer Drive, Bethpage, NY 11714; 516-735-6924

PART

VIII

TIPS, SECRETS,
& GOOD ADVICE

SECRETS OF SYSTEM 7

DOUG CLAPP

Oh, So *That's* the Limit!

You're probably familiar with System 7's memory settings for applications, "Suggested Size" and "Current Size."

Ever wondered about *maximum size?* A little poking around in ResEdit reveals this message in the Finder's STR# list:

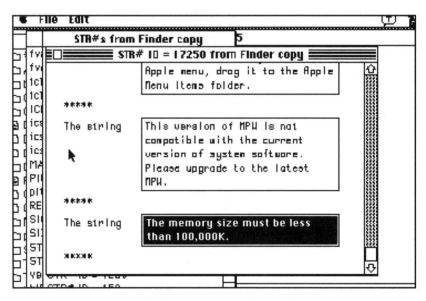

Figure 1. An interesting STR# resource in the Finder.

292

Now, if you're using your mega-gigabyte drive as virtual memory, you can see a familiar dialog, which now reads something like ...

"MonsterApp" prefers 99,999K of memory. 99,998K is available. Do you want to open it using the available memory?

Help! Help!

Why hasn't this been in the *National Enquirer?*

It seems that Apple, long noted for providing a relatively humane workplace, actually *imprisoned* a group of programmers during the development of System 7!

The proof is cleverly hidden on the System 7 Disk Tools disk. Snoop around with your most sophisticated software tools and you'll eventually find this message:

```
Apple Computer Inc.

All Rights Reserved.

Help! Help! We're being held prisoner in a
system software factory!

The Blue Meanies

Darin Adler
Scott Boyd
Chris Derossi
Cynthia Jasper
Brian McGhie
Greg Marriott
Beatrice Sochor
Dean Yu
```

Those imprisoned, we can guess, are the authors of Apple's System 7 software. Hope they've been let out by now ...

The Finder Pays Tribute

The next time you're in the Finder, hold down the Option key and pull down the Apple menu.

The first item is now "About the Finder..." When you mouse up, you'll see a modern take on the famous Finder 5.x "Rocky Mountain" About dialog:

Figure 2. A hidden "About..." dialog in the Finder.

Now wait. Don't click. In a few seconds, the names of the System 7 Finder programmers and helpers will scroll across the bottom of the dialog.

Wait some more. Next come the names of Finder Authors of Days Gone—all the way back to the programmers who created— decades ago— the Lisa Desktop Manager: Bill Smith, Frank Ludolph, and Bill Atkinson.

A Message You May Never See

The System 7 Finder is full of messages, to be inserted in an appropriate dialog at an appropriate time.

But, smart as it is, even the Finder sometimes gets confused. When it does, you may see a dialog similar to this after double-clicking a document:

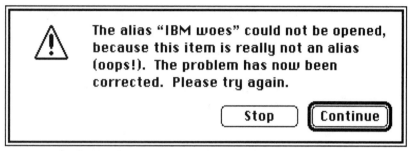

The alias "IBM woes" could not be opened, because this item is really not an alias (oops!). The problem has now been corrected. Please try again.

Stop   Continue

Figure 3. Software chagrin in System 7.

No, You Idiot!

The Finder authors tried to anticipate even the dumbest user actions. If you ever see a dialog with this message:

```
The System Folder cannot be put in the
Trash, because it contains the active
system software.
```

Maybe you should consider using a simpler machine. A typewriter, maybe.

Hypercard 2.1 "Magic"

A crippled version of HyperCard is included with Apple's System 7 software. The trimmed-down HyperCard allows only "typing" and "browsing." The full version of HyperCard adds three more levels: Painting (which allows you to use the Paint tools), Authoring (which allows you to create buttons and fields), and Scripting—

As I was installing a beta version of System 7 on my Mac II, I accidentally selected the floppy as the target disk for installation, the installer came back with:

```
Systen 7.0 on an 800K floppy, ha!
```

HyperCard's highest "userlevel," which enables creating and editing scripts.

But you can turn HyperCard into a full-fledged application with a single word. Here's how:

1. Launch HyperCard.

2. Choose Last from the Go menu to go to the Preferences card.

3. Type Command-m to bring up the message box.

4. Type "magic" (don't type the quotes) and hit Return.

Presto—three new levels are added to HyperCard.

For more insights into hidden HyperCard commands, press Command-Shift-s and read through the Home stack script.

One more HyperCard 2.1 secret: Hold down the Option key while choosing "About HyperCard" from the Apple menu for a dialog of information about your system.

One Reason *Not* to Use 32-Bit Addressing

In the Memory Control Panel, there's this option:

```
32-Bit Addressing
◉ On
○ Off
```

Figure 4. Addressing options in the Memory control panel.

Most people choose "On." It's a good choice if you have a newer Mac, and don't use programs which aren't "32-Bit clean" (in other words, if "On" doesn't cause frequent crashes), or if you have an older Mac and have the "MODE32" init installed—which makes old Mac ROMs, themselves, 32-bit clean.

But, assuming your situation fits the above description, is there a reason *not* to use 32-bit addressing?

Yes. If you have more than 8 megabytes of RAM memory. Why? Because with 32-bit addressing "off," any RAM above 8 megabytes is used as a RAM cache. The result: blisteringly fast screen redraws and overall very snappy operation.

(On the other hand, if 32-bit addressing is on, and you have the appropriate software, you can use that extra memory as a RAM disk. Maybe the real point here is: buy more memory and you can't go wrong!)

The Keyboard Combination You Need to Know

How many keyboard combinations are there? A programmer would probably say the number's a "very large integer."

But here's one keyboard combination you need to know, if you use System 7. It's Command-Option-esc.

What's it do? Forces a "Quit" of the frontmost application. What's it good for? Exiting a crashed application, without having to restart your Macintosh.

We know, we know: you've got five applications running. Each one has open documents, and probably none of the documents have been saved recently. If you Restart, you lose everything.

So remember: if an application crashes, you don't need to Restart and lose everything, everywhere. Just hit Command-Option-esc and you can "kill" the crashed application and can go on with your work. (Although prudence dictates that we now say this: Save your documents in other active applications, quit the applications, *then* Restart, just to be safe.)

The Right Gesture

You're in the Finder, about to edit a filename. You click on the name, it highlights, and then ... and then ... you wait for what seems days (okay, long moments) until the cursor changes to an I-beam and you can begin to edit.

There's a faster way. After you click on the filename, make a "gesture,"—move the cursor just a smudge, just a pixel or three, and the cursor instantly changes to an I-beam.

The whole notion of adding gestures to the mouse action pantheon was discussed during the development of System 7. And at least this one gesture (are there more?) made it into the final release, in a sneaky, non-documented fashion.

Starting up with Style

In System 7, there's no longer a "Set Startup" item on the menu. Instead, you place applications (or more likely the alias of an application) into the Startup Items folder, which you'll find in the System Folder.

Whatever's in Startup Items is launched when you power up your machine. You can also place documents (or, again, aliases of documents) into the Startup Items folders. I always launch Microsoft Word and my phonelist on Startup.

Now for the tip. Not only can you make applications and documents into Startup Items, you can also place folders (aliases of folders, most likely) into Startup Items. If you do, the Folders will be open on your desktop the next time you restart.

Balloons for Power Users

Real power users don't use balloon help, right?

Well, here's one reason to use those pesky ballons. Choose Balloon Help, then choose "About this Macintosh" from the Apple menu.

You'll see the now-familiar bar graphs that tell you—sort of— how much memory is being used by active applications and desk accessories.

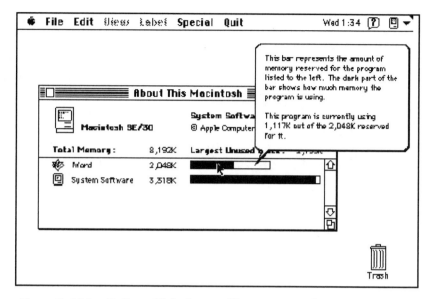

Figure 5. Using Balloon Help for specific memory information.

Now more the cursor over one of the "memory bars." Voila! The balloon informs you of the *specific* amount of memory being used!

It's good information, especially if you're tinkering with memory sizes in Get Info boxes.

Putting Things in Order

To see filenames at the top of "Name" views in the Finder, begin the filename with a space—that puts it at the top. You can also put a space before frequently-used Apple menu items to place them at the top of menus. Beyond spaces, you can experiment with other non-alphabetic characters to achieve marvelous feats of lists designed in the order you wish. To be precise, the order of characters is:

<space> " ! # $ % & ' ( ) * + , - . / 0 (then 1,2,3, etc.) : ; < = > ? @ A (the remaining capital letters, and so on).

Subj: Sys7 Error   92-01-21 17:59:15 EST

From: Kngtut

I got this one a minute ago from System 7.0.1. I was trying to paste a custon icon into a folder. When I let go of the mouse button on Paste, it came back with:

```
The command could be completed,
because it cannot be found.
```

Help Close at Hand

It's a no-brainer, but it's true: the best System 7 hints are always available. Go to the Finder's Balloon menu and choose "Finder Shortcuts." There they are! But they only work if you use them! So read, try 'em out, and force yourself to use the shortcuts, again and again, until they're second nature. This tip is a variation on the timed-honored advice "RTFM."

❧

HOW TO MAKE A MILLION IN THE SOFTWARE BIZ

DENNIS JAMES

T*ime now for The Dennis James Story.*

It begins in Los Angeles, at Rainbow Computer—one of the best, and last, of the great computer stores. A mythic place, filled with neat computer stuff, dark beer on tap, and knowledgeable folks who loved what they did.

There toiled Denny James, a store manager who was crazy nuts about Macintosh. So crazy nuts that he became—it was unavoidable—a great salesman. From Rainbow he went to Egghead Software, and managed several stores on the West Coast. First, two small Egghead stores, then a larger Egghead store—which quickly became one of the most profitable Eggheads in all the land.

From there, Egghead Corporate kicked him upstairs, to create, then rule, their Apple, Macintosh, and book divisions. The result was good for big companies, good for Egghead, and a blessing to small companies with neat products.

Software is a multi-billion dollar industry, the corner of our new Information Age.

While the world wasn't looking, Encyclopedia Brittanica went electronic, software and hardware went on the shelves of major discounters, and Sears began accepting credit applications for Lotus 1-2-3.

Is This Good News?

You bet it is, if you make your living creating, selling, marketing, or doing something with software—like I do. It means that you've just hit The New Gold Rush.

Sometimes I wake up at night in a cold sweat with this thought on my mind:

MILLIONS of people are buying computers at a rate that is BEYOND ASTOUNDING. Apple Computer, Inc. announced net revenue of $1.8 *billion,* and new income of $166 million, for the *quarter* ending December 27, 1991. While that sounds pretty incredible, compare it to Microsoft's fourth quarter!

How profitable is software? To put it in perspective, Bill Gates and Paul Allen (co-founders of Microsoft) each own a Porsche that U.S. Customs says is illegal to drive on any road in the United States. Cost? Probably more than the gross annual income of most South American countries. Fun? Only if you like sitting in a parked car on Saturday night listening to the radio and honking the horn.

How Can I Get Involved?

You ask: Am I too late?

No.

Even though Microsoft and a few other companies own 95% of the software industry, there is still great money to be made writing and selling software. When we're talking about *billions* of dollars, there's a lot of pocket change to go around—the big boys are so concerned with owning North America that they forget about the little pieces.

All the signs are there: star in the east, heavier fur on horses and dogs. We are heading into a fantastic era of computer software sales. Just be careful to avoid the swinging, gigantic tails of the large software manufacturers as they feed on the soft, green, consumer underbrush.

Ah … you're curious. What does it take to create and blow software out the retail and direct sales doors?

Daddy, Where Does Software Come From?

To understand this question, we go back in time to the computer Paleozoic, after the first Big Iron Age, around 1975.

In those days, I honestly think people created 99% of retail computer software for personal reasons. One person needed a software product, so he learned how to program and wrote it for himself. After he finished, he thought, hmm … I wonder if anyone *else* would like to use this?

I wonder if anyone would *buy* this?

No marketing demi-god was consulted. No memo dropped down from on high ("Find a good check-writing program and copy it, no … do a better job with the interface!"). Some frail human being just woke up one morning, learned Pascal or Lightspeed C (or, God forbid, MPW), wrote the damn thing, and it worked!

These days, in the nifty 90s, software publishers actually hire consumer marketing people (shudder), whose last job was merchandising baby powder or Cascade dish detergent. Now it's not enough to just want a product—these folks have brought new highs to product creation. A software publisher must now develop a product strategy before the first line of code is conceived.

Develop a Product Strategy

How do you develop a product strategy? Here's the easy way: go to a computer store and ask them what software sells the most. Copy the best of that software type without infringing on patents or copyrights.

Feel free to copy the way the box looks and feels, and many of the program's best features and functions. They topped #1 for a reason.

Take the best and leave the rest (as Steve Jobs once said). But be aware that you do this at your own risk. The manufacturer may feel that you've stolen their best features—we call this infringing of patents and copyrights—even when you haven't, and sue your pants off. We call this competitive legislation.

Enjoy the fruits of your computing union. If there are several market leaders in a category, there is probably so much confusion that you can get something going. No kidding ... the leader may sell thousands of copies a month and you may sell only twenty, but twenty times $600 is $12,000 a month! You may be able to give up your part-time job. But don't give up your day job.

Crudely put, this is Market Research. If someone sells a thousand of something, we can assume that there's a market. Beware, however, if there is only one top-selling product in a category. There may only be a market for that product (ask Microsoft about WordPerfect on the PC).

Market research may keep you from writing the next aardvark animal husbandry database.

Find a Lazy Software Publisher

Every once in a while, an entire software category goes to lunch and doesn't come back. If you find yourself saying, "I would buy that kind of software if it were cheaper, if ..." Count up the ifs. If there are more than seven ifs, create a product for that category.

Try to be everything your competitors aren't. For example: if the products are expensive, go cheap. If they have large boxes, go small. The more positive aspects you can cultivate, the more successful you look in comparison.

There are times in every consumer's life when they are mad as hell and not going to take it any more. A great example of an opportunity is the spreadsheet market. Most spreadsheets are expensive: $299 and up. Make a low-cost spreadsheet with 80% of the high-end features, and you'll probably have a successful product.

A great example of this happened late in 1991. Microsoft released a minor update of Microsoft Works (the #1 integrated package) when no fewer than *four* competitors released competing products. Any *one* of these hot products would have given the aging Microsoft Works the willies. Four was obsessive behavior. While Microsoft wasn't looking, Microsoft's competitors were.

Invent a New Software Category

This is known in the industry as the bleeding edge. It's being the lead salmon up the river, or the head goose in a flying wedge. You may be right, but you'll be too tired to take advantage of your edge when you finally arrive.

Take another look at aardvark animal husbandry. It may lend itself perfectly to computerization, but you may have too many factors to overcome. What if no aardvark breeders are computerists? You'd have to break in their brains on computerizing before you'd get a chance to talk them into using your program.

Bleeding edge products seldom make it to the end of the race without lots of development and marketing dollars. A great example is CD-ROM. While at Egghead Software, I stood up at the Microsoft CD-ROM conference with Apple and strongly supported CD-ROM development.

I told the publishers in the audience that I'd buy what they developed and stock it on Egghead's shelves. But there were two problems with this particular bleeding edge: software developers wouldn't develop products unless the hardware came down in price. And Apple wouldn't drop the price of their hardware until they were assured that a mass market existed.

What's the Plan, Sam?

Once you've developed a product, you have to create "The Plan."

Having done this a few times, I admit that even if things are going great, a plan is seldom followed. But purchasers in major retail organizations and venture capitalists always seem to want one. There are two ways to write a plan:

1. Do it yourself, or

2. Hire someone to do it.

Writing one yourself isn't hard. Running a business is just that: standard operating and sales costs. The hard part is knowing *who to sell*, but finding the high rollers like Egghead Software isn't all that hard, either. Books can make doing the right thing easier. Highly recommended: *Selling the Dwarf* by Guy Kawasaki. (Just kidding. It's *Selling the Dream.)*

Or get yourself a hired gun. There are two kinds of channel managers (aka Rep Groups):

• Those that sell into the channel, take the money and run, and

• Those who *manage* the channel for their publishers.

Use the first group if you want to get your products into major accounts. Use the latter if you want to get your products into major accounts *and keep them there.*

Market Analysis: Itch the Niche

Next do a market analysis. Figure out what makes your product HOT and what makes your competitor's products NOT. You've probably already thought about this, but now's the time to put it on paper. It's also a good time to fix weak spots in your product.

Pick up reviews of competitive products. Go to user groups and power users and ask what *they* want (a novel idea). Go to large retail outlets and take the salespeople to lunch. If you can, do the same thing with corporate salespeople. It never hurts to get as much feedback as possible, especially if it only costs you lunch money!

Who are you trying to sell? Targets: purchasing personnel in large retail and direct sales organizations, salespeople, and customers. Each of these targets has surprisingly different reasons for purchasing product—and you must reach at least two of them to succeed.

Wrap It Up, I'll Take It . . .

Once you've selected your major account targets and done your market analysis, it's time to create your packaging.

How to: go into any large retail outlet and take a close look at the software packages. I've always liked a package that is 9" x 10" tall, 8 1/2" wide and 1 1/2" to 2" deep. A strong, crush-proof box is a must. It has to survive shipping, handling, customers, elephants, and gorillas.

A blank "candy box" with a different slip-cover for each of your products is more cost-effective than separate boxes. Make sure the contents don't bounce around. Color is necessary, but good design is critical. Also, stay away from nonstandard or overly-large boxes—they don't look right or fit on the shelves!

In retail, the package must sell the product. It has to be attractive enough to pull the customer over and make him or her pick it up. I call this "glance-ability." And the back of the box must fully explain what the product can do: features and benefits.

Corporate sales don't need the same kind of packaging. They don't care what it looks like, just how hard it is to sell and how much pull-through you plan to do. You could put your software in a white, 11" x 17" envelope and they wouldn't care. They don't love this stuff like you and I do. Accept this notion and you'll do fine.

Packaging no-no's are shrink-wrapped manuals with a disk inside, wimpy boxes, bad manuals, hard-to-install software, and boxes with late 60s designs that say nothing, yet tout recycled paper used in the box construction. The right package can make or break you with Egghead Software, and with your customers.

Which Comes First, the Ad or the Order?

Now that you have your package, you have to advertise it. Or do you? When should you advertise, where should you advertise, how much should you advertise, and how much should you spend? The answer to this is, "Yes, you should advertise." But that's as simple as it gets.

One CEO's Conundrum

The Vice President of Marketing thought all available money should be spent keeping the product in the public face. On the other hand, the VP of Sales felt that all available money should be spent putting a sales organization together. Which VP should get the nod?

This is like asking, "When a VP falls in a boardroom, and there's no one in the boardroom but the CEO and the VP, does the VP make a sound when the pink slip hits the trash can?" The obvious answer is that you need advertising *and* a sales organization, but a smart CEO adjusts these figures to take advantage of the the times a product sells best. This is known as the Product Sales Cycle.

When should you advertise your product? Here's a bizarre thought: advertise product when you want to give sales a boost! Market products during the rollout (or subsequent upgrade), and whenever your customers spend the most money buying software.

If your product is a consumer-oriented product, advertise during the December holiday season or any time during an INCREDIBLE SALE!

Should you advertise before you release the product, or should you just take it retail and see what happens? My vote has always been to take it retail and save yourself some money. Why? Because until you get it in the pipeline, your advertising is wasted (unless you like taking orders direct).

OK, I lied to you.

There are actually three times when this is totally untrue:

1. You are Lotus or Microsoft and you have to spend a jillion advertising dollars whether you like it or not.

2. You are a publisher who really doesn't really plan to sell the product into distribution—you actually want to (or need to) sell the product to a larger publisher.

3. You can't get any of the major resellers to bite on your first pass, so you turn to pull-through advertising.

Question: Who advertised a currently-available, integrated product over a year (at least it seemed so) before it was sold to Symantec? Answer: Leonard Development ran full-page ads month after month, then sold GreatWorks before it hit the shelves anywhere. I wrote a marketing assessment for one of the other companies who wanted to buy GreatWorks. Symantec outbid us!

Does this mean I don't believe in advertising in *MacWorld, MacUser, MacWeek,* or the like? (Jerry, I didn't say that!) Just practice smart advertising. Many larger publishers advertise enough to be seen most of the year, then come on strong twice a year. This is called Event Marketing, and it's designed to punch a hole in everyone else's typical monthly advertising.

A great example: Apple Computer advertises strongly two or three times a year. Can you guess when these times usually occur? Here's a hint: MacWorld happens in January and August. When do you usually see five-page spreads of Apple products?

Zig When Everyone Else Zags

There are times when it's great to advertise even though every rule in advertising says you shouldn't. I have an odd habit of advertising when no one else advertises, in June and July. Two great reasons for doing this: magazines and large retailers are dying for advertisers, and no one else of any consequence is advertising during these times.

How about Un-advertising? In 1983, we heard about Steve Jobs' "special project." No advertising, not a whisper escaped anyone's lips about this new computer. All we knew was that Apple had to come back with a sledgehammer to counter IBM's PC-punch.

What happened: Apple invited a group of consultants and large local accounts to preview the Mac. I heard that it operated like a Lisa and used a mouse. But it was much smaller: a 12" by 12" by 12" box. I even took the time to make a cardboard mockup with these lengths in mind. When I didn't know what to expect, my imagination filled in the facts. Seeing a Macintosh was love at first sight. I bought one immediately.

A couple of weeks later, Apple Computer made history with the classic "1984" ad that pitted them against "Big Brother" IBM. Question: How many times did the "1984" commercial run? Answer: only once, during Super Bowl Sunday on January 15, 1984. How many times did you think you saw it? Write this number down, it may have some kind of religious significance someday.

Pearls Before Swine; Or, Time to Drop the Dime

It's time to tell the world about your baby. It's time to send out demos, blow the PR trumpets, and make the pilgrimage to software Meccas across the land. You now have to sell the large account purchasing personnel, the sales people, the media, and, gasp, the consumers.

Plan the product rollout. Create the sales materials and other collaterial. Divide up your resources to attack the different channels: Retail, Education, Corporate, National, and Government. Create PR materials. Send them out! Don't forget your demos, visits to User Groups, and tradeshow participation. And don't forget your Maalox.

If you can, fly out to see everyone. Most of the purchasers for Egghead Software and other large accounts really don't have time to see you, but you'll get a chance to dress up and increase your frequent flier miles at the same time!

Rollin' on the Downside

Sometimes the rollout is a great experience, usually when you've done your homework. It's picturesque. A dream. People offer a standing ovation as you float by on your way to pick up your MacUser Eddy award. However, you have to be prepared for the other side of the coin as well. It can be tough, even when you've done everything right.

Be prepared for suggestions. Everyone will have at least one. How do you handle suggestions? Smile, smile, smile. Don't bother with the real reason you created that feature. Don't even harumph when a well-known media type sees your right-handed menu command from his or her left-handed world. Smile. Thank them. Tell them that it's sure to be included in version 2.0!

Seriously: if you make a mistake, fix it. If you ship the wrong product, take it back and ship the right product. If you jump to the wrong conclusion about a feature, step back and do the right thing. You will be remembered for your prompt attention and support. Likewise, you can lose a lot of friends by hemming and hawing when all anyone wants to do is move your product through the channel.

There's Gold in Them Thar Icons

You've done everything you can. Egghead Software purchasers like your product (even after the changes). Salespeople have been prepped and polished. And the media has sung the praises of this "incredible new kind of software," even taking it to the level of "ground-breaking."

What's left? Consumers have to want to buy it. This is the magic part of the software industry. The Sesame Street character, Big Bird, even invented a term for it: Serendipity. But take heart, consumers are pretty sharp these days.

I think we'll look back on 1992 as the year that consumers really stood up for their computing rights. They told Compaq that quality was important, but not as important as price (ouch!), and told IBM that they may have been big stuff in the mainframe and minicomputer market, but not with microcomputer buyers who feel PC clones work just fine, thank you.

Consumers also placed a big vote for the GUI interface. Windows 3.0 established itself as the #1 money-making software interface in computerdom. And new low-cost Macs ran out the door so fast that it took Apple Computer almost a whole year to catch up with channel sales.

Will consumers want to buy your software product? Beats me! All you can do is put the right bait in the water and hope that Lady Luck (or Lenny Luck, if we're being non-sexist) smiles down from above.

One thing we do know: there's plenty of bucks to be made. You can tell there's blood in the water when old enemies belly up to the bar (Apple and IBM, Tandy and Microsoft, Intel and IBM, et al.). They sense that there's plenty there for all (at least right now), so they're jockeying for position. It's cute to see Big Blue suits with their arms around long-haired, earinged, Macintosh programmers.

With All This, Why Do They Still Do Those Things They Do?

There are those in the Software Biz who have gone through several incarnations as software publishers, channel managers, etc. There is no doubt that many do it for the money (it can be good when it hits). Others do it because they are perpetually driven to organize, like little product-oriented chipmunks. Publishers/gold miners of a new electronic age. Maybe they do it because they don't know anything else …

The Truth? I believe that today's software publishers are entrepreneurs who know there's something dramatic about touching people's lives with a responsible, usable product—and who enjoy making a few bucks besides. Several publishers I know—who have made the big bucks—continue to roll new products down the software lane.

Me too. I'm still here.

Want more? If so, it's time for specifics. We cut to an edited transcript of an on-line conference between Mr. James and members of the Software Publisher's Association:

Working with Egghead Software

A Candid Conversation with Dennis James

This is an edited transcript of an SPA Macintosh SIG America Online conference held on April 11, 1991. This information is private to Macintosh SIG members.

We asked you to come talk with us on this topic as an alumnus of Egghead. When did you leave Egghead?

October '89. I had been with them for five years.

What did you do there?

Larry Foster brought me up to Egghead Software's corporate offices to set up and manage the Mac, Apple, and Book Divisions. Along with Brian Mitchell and Paul Doell, I was responsible for purchasing, merchandising, and promotion of Macintosh, Apple, and Book inventory for 200+ retail locations and 175+ direct sales locations.

Simply said, I found it, bought it, promoted it, merchandised it, and returned/revived it when sales slacked off. I was also heavily involved with evangelizing Macs at Egghead Corporate Headquarters.

What do you do now?

Channel management, sales, marketing, and training consultant— not just for Egghead, but nationally. Negotiate relationships with national accounts and distributors, including old/new product complications. Work with publishers to create, initiate, and implement advertising and promotions. Assist positioning of company and product(s) image. Work with developers on human interface and feature sets. I especially enjoy working with small and medium-sized publishers.

How can people reach you?

My company name is RAVADA at (206) 486-5120, FAX (206) 481-0145. On America Online, I'm DJAMES. By the way, RAVA-DA is part of the seventh unpublished novel of Jonathan Swift's *Gulliver's Travels*. RAVADA is the Land of Perfection.

We've heard a lot of tales about this: how many software titles did you receive per day, really?

Back in '89, not as much as you would think, maybe five to ten Macintosh titles a week. You'd be surprised how many times I called someone for a demo. Since I'm a Macoholic and a voracious reader of all Macintosh weeklies and monthlies, not much got by me. What was more horrendous were the phone calls–maybe 40 to 200 a day. Never under 40 a day.

How did you proceed in your selection?

First, gut reaction. (1) Will it sell? Who will buy it, consumer or corporate (large account) sales? (2) Next, packaging. (3) Next, money for marketing, promotion, and support.

Did demos help your decisions?

Demos are critical, but they have to be delivered with care.

What are the three worst things to do when submitting a package?

Some of the worst things are: (1) Not checking the market needs, thinking, "I need a software package for aardvark animal husbandry, so everyone needs one." (2) Not checking packaging needs. (3) Having an attitude. (4) Not having a plan. (5) Not having financial backing. (6) Not partnering up with an experienced crew.

Do gimmicks and "freebies" (coffee mugs, train whistles, Rolls Royces) help a submission?

I always liked 'em, but they never influenced a purchase. And "freebies" that were obvious bribes were returned along with the demo product(s).

How about T-Shirts ?

A Mac developer who writes a program without designing the T-shirt first is not a real Mac developer.

Tell us about a success story. A package that got picked up in a record time. What did they do right?

Truthfully, they were usually big companies with a lot of money and lots of products. But that doesn't mean a little company can't do it too, like Paul O'Brien, who dogged me for six months, taking my suggestions and continually reworking his product until I gave in and purchased Synchronicity (which still sells well).

What influences you more: good reviews, lots of advertising, or great PR?

PR over advertising, any day. A good review can make or break you.

So do as Guy Kawasaki says: "Get the cult to like your product."

Exactly.

Let's play this scenario. I send you my product. You like it. Then what?

I check out your company, is it going to be around next year, do you have more than one product? Even so, I will probably buy through a distributor. I call you to see what your plan is: will you advertise, what is your national plan, do you plan to do strong PR?

What do you mean by strong PR?

Articles in *MacWeek*, *MacUser*, etc. Also in columns on "the grapevine." Deals with other publishers.

What about these monster first orders we all heard about?

The days of the mindless huge first orders are over (except for Christmas sales). A 500-600 piece order is not out of line. I have sold in 1,000-piece orders before, but not without a plan for moving the product through. All bets are off for Christmas. A great product with a smart marketing plan can clean up. You will sell a minimum of three to four times the software at Christmas than you sell during the rest of the year.

Is walk-in traffic most of each store's bread and butter?

This will blow you away. Ready? Most Egghead customers go into an Egghead an average of once a week. That's higher than a supermarket. They are married and have 2.3 kids, and they live within ten minutes.

Do they spend money each time? How much?

You had to ask that! They spend, on the average, $1,100 the first year. It tails off after that. At Egghead, that is. Also, impulse buying has to be considered. The impulse level for PC buyers may stop around $100, but Mac buyers go up to about $250.

Mac buyers may spend more than PC buyers, but there's many more PC buyers, so the overall PC software sales dwarf Mac sales. In a $300-million-plus company, that still is a large chunk of change.

Tell us about products that really surprised you, and why you think they did differently than you expected ...

My favorite story is about ATM. All I had seen was a horrible beta and wouldn't see the product until it shipped. I popped for a big order, and set up nationwide advertising the weekend just before it was released, and had it overnighted to the stores. I gutted the price so that we nipped the direct mailers by five bucks. I made a will and sat down to wait.

Just as ATM shipped out the door to us and someone else—I think it was ComputerWare (these people are MacGods)—the SF earthquake hit. For all the bad things we can say about that earthquake, I was one of two major retailers with *tons* of ATM in stock, for three weeks, at an incredible price. Needless to say, the earth moved in more ways than one. Want another?

Please.

A small company named Visionary Software (Paul O'Brien) sent me a product: the I Ching, of all things. He got me on the phone one night right after five, and I told him he didn't have a chance of selling any of these things.

But I said I'd help him if he really wanted. Over a six-week period, he would send me his new box (I told him he needed a box), and various gamma versions of his product. Finally, he got it the way I wanted it (even though I was sure it was going to be a dud). So I bought a few and put them in the stores.

And, crazy enough, the product began to sell, and continued to sell strong for over a year.

What do you think sold that package?

Some products are easy to see, others are real sleepers. It captured the imagination of a great number of people: me, the salespeople, the writers and critics, and finally, consumers.

It was fun to use. It was pretty and had great sounds. Even today, his upgrade rate is great.

Thanks, Dennis!!

Thanks for having me. Feel free to call any time.

༄

— Copyright 1992 © Dennis James & American Online, Inc.

Dennis James is CEO & President of RAVADA, based in Bellevue, Washington. He subsidizes his fascination with computers by helping software publishers create, market, and sell software.

CHANGING COMMAND KEY SHORTCUTS IN FINDER 7.0

ALEX NARVEY

*I*n earlier versions of the Finder, it was easy to change menu item short-cuts—a quick trip to ResEdit, open the MENU resource, and have at it. System 7, though, did away with that resource scheme, making custom shortcuts … impossible? Nah, just tough. It can still be done, and here, thanks to Alex Narvey, is how.

Finder 7 has a new scheme for menus, and cannot be edited like the former MENU resource. However, there is a way to add command keys in the Finder for System 7.

1. Make a copy of the Finder.

2. With ResEdit 2.1 open the "fmnu" resource. You will see numbered resources. The main Finder menus are as follows:

    #1252 = FILE Menu

    #1253 = EDIT Menu

    #1254 = VIEW Menu

    #1255 = SPECIAL Menu

    #1256 = LABELS Menu

    (In this example we will give the "Make Alias" Command in the FILE Menu a Command Key of "L").

3. Open up #1252—the FILE Menu resource. Locate the Alias Command by doing a Find ASCII "Make Alias". You will notice that three hex bytes preceding this is "00". Change the "00" hex to "4C". ("4C" in hex is equivalent to the "L" character in ASCII). It should look like the following:

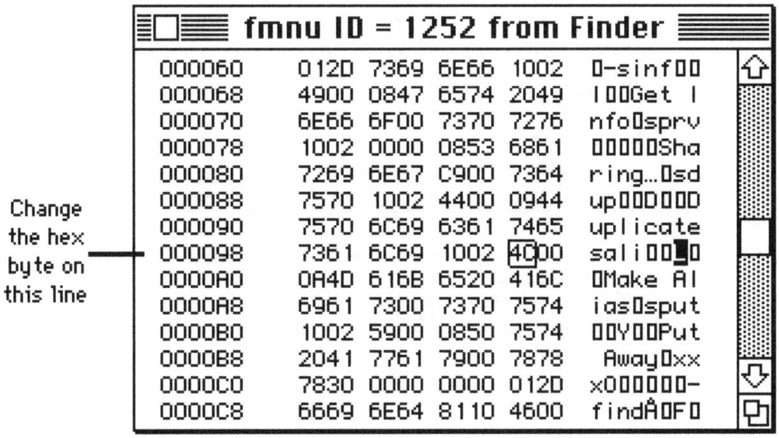

Figure 1. Adding a Command L shortcut to the "Make Alias" Command.

4. Quit ResEdit and save changes. Drag the operative Finder out of the System Folder and into another folder. Put the new Finder into the System folder and reboot. Voila! "Make Alias" = Command L.

Other possible changes are the ever-popular:

Restart = Command R

Shutdown = Command S*

and for the slightly more courageous:

Empty Trash… = Command T

*The Shutdown Command looks a little different and requires a slightly different approach. Instead of "Shutdown" you will see the word "shut" FOLLOWED by three hexbits. Change the third hex bit to the S character (number 53). Please see the diagram below:

```
▤☐▤▤  fmnu ID = 1255 from Finder ▤▤  ⇧
000028    7074 8006 5400 0C45   ptÄ0T00E
000030    6D70 7479 2054 7261   mpty Tra
000038    7368 C900 7878 7830   sh…0xxx0
000040    0000 0000 012D 7365   00000-se
000048    6A65 1002 4500 0A45   je00E00E
000050    6A65 6374 2044 6973   ject Dis
000058    6B00 7365 7261 1002   k0sera00
000060    0000 0B45 7261 7365   000Erase
000068    2044 6973 6BC9 7878    Disk…xx
000070    7830 0000 0000 012D   x000000-
000078    7265 7374 8100 5200   restÂ0R0
000080    0752 6573 7461 7274   0Restart
000088    7368 7574 8104 0000   shutÂ000   ⇩
000090    0153                  0S         ◰
```

```
▤☐▤▤  fmnu ID = 1255 from Finder ▤▤  ⇧
000028    7074 8006 5400 0C45   ptÄ0T00E
000030    6D70 7479 2054 7261   mpty Tra
000038    7368 C900 7878 7830   sh…0xxx0
000040    0000 0000 012D 7365   00000-se
000048    6A65 1002 4500 0A45   je00E00E
000050    6A65 6374 2044 6973   ject Dis
000058    6B00 7365 7261 1002   k0sera00
000060    0000 0B45 7261 7365   000Erase
000068    2044 6973 6BC9 7878    Disk…xx
000070    7830 0000 0000 012D   x000000-
000078    7265 7374 8100 5200   restÂ0R0
000080    0752 6573 7461 7274   0Restart
000088    7368 7574 8104 5300   shutÂ0S0   ⇩
000090    0153                  0S         ◰
```

Figure 2. Adding a keyboard equivalent to the Shutdown command.

To add an S shortcut to the System 7 Finder, change the second last line from example of the left to the one on the right.

The corresponding ASCII characters and hex bytes are:

A = 41	J = 4A	S = 53
B = 42	K = 4B	T = 54
C = 43	L = 4C	U = 55

D = 44	M = 4D	V = 56
E = 45	N = 4E	W = 57
F = 46	O = 4F	X = 58
G = 47	P = 50	Y = 59
H = 48	Q = 51	Z= 5A
I = 49	R = 52	

The existing menus and their command keys are:

A   Select All (EDIT)

B   —————

C   Copy (EDIT)

D   Duplicate (FILE)

E   Eject Disk… (SPECIAL)

F   Find… (FILE)

G   Find Again (FILE)

H   —————

I   Get Info (FILE)

J   —————

K   ————— (NB: This is used by Suitcase II in the Apple Menu)

L   ————— (Try "Make Alias" / FILE Menu)

M   —————

N   New Folder (FILE)

O   Open (FILE)

P   Print (FILE)

Q   ————— (Try "Shutdown" / SPECIAL Menu—or "S")

R   ————— (Try "Restart" / SPECIAL Menu)

S   ————— (Try "Shutdown" / SPECIAL Menu—"Q")

T   ———————— (Try "Empty Trash…" / SPECIAL Menu)

U   ————————

V   Paste (EDIT)

W   Close Window (FILE)

X   Cut (EDIT)

Y   Put Away (FILE)

Z   Undo (EDIT)

(This tip was developed out of comments made by Mel Beckman, 75226,2257 in the MacSEVEN Forum on Compuserve)

❧

Alex Narvey
THUNDER ENLIGHTENING PRESS
P.O. Box 332, 905 Corydon Ave.
Winnipeg, MB, CANADA R3M 3V3
(204) 253-2627
Compuserve # 71041,132

AN EVENING WITH
THE MEANIES

F*rom the vaults of America Online, here's the edited transcript of a on-line conference with members of Apple's System 7 development team. Those who aren't on-line savvy should note that :-) and similar creations are smiles.*

❧

6/1/91 11:03:01 PM Opening "Blue Meanie Chat" for Chat Log recording.

OnlineHost: Welcome folks. We'll be starting in about five minutes.

OnlineHost:

```
: |_____   ////      T h e
: |                       |_____
: | *   *   *   *  |_____         ////  M a c i n t o s h
: |   *   *   *    |
: | *   *   *   *  |_____         ////  U t i l i t i e s
: |   *   *   *    |_____
: |_____|_____         ////     F o r u m
: |
: |_____         ////  W e l c o m e s
: |_____
: |_____
:  _____         ////        Y O U !
```

OnlineHost: Good Evening, and welcome to the Macintosh Utilities Forum Saturday Night Conference. Tonight, we are holding this event in conjunction with the folks from Apple who have been contributing to the America Online System 7.0 Support Forum. Your host for this evening is AFL Bear, MUT's Forum Leader. AFL Bear is assisted tonight by our own AFA John, tonight's Technical Director, and Sue Borg of the System 7 Resource Center.

OnlineHost: We have a special program tonight about Apple's new System 7. We are fortunate to have as our guests members of Apple's esteemed "Blue Meanies" team! Blue Meanies with us this evening are Chris Derossi (C Derossi) and Greg Marriott (JusSomeGuy). Chris, Greg, & other Meanies did a lot of searching for the bugs that nobody else could find. Among their duties, Greg focused on hunting down scores of obscure application incompatibilities, while Chris was responsible for integrating the different pieces of the software into a coherent whole, while making sure that the result was buildable and runnable. These folks are the people who truly made System 7 deserving of the phrase, "7.0 - Rock Solid!" They, and other Blue Meanies, actually wrote a lot of the code that's in 7.0, but not the large and obvious pieces. More often, they wrote the little tricky bits that fixed particularly difficult problems.

OnlineHost: Chris, Greg, and John Sullivan (who was unable to make tonight's chat due to a previous engagement,) have been online answering many of the queries and comments—over 3,500 so far—posted in AFL Ferino's System 7 Support Forum. Just last week, Chris signed onto America Online for the first time and has already joined the fray, answering questions from his first day online! And now, these gentlemen have kindly consented to answer your questions about System 7, right here in real time!

Now let's give Chris and Greg a chance to say hello and we'll start taking your questions immediately.

C Derossi: Hi gang! I hope that we'll be able to answer all of your questions tonight. (That means that you can ask only easy questions, okay?) Jim Reekes is also with us tonight. Jim worked on the Sound Manager for System 7, so you can blame him for all the sounds that come out of that box on your desk.

JusSomeGuy: Chris is my boss, so I'll just let him speak for me. He doesn't let me talk to strangers. Okay, okay. We're all tired from working hard to make System 7 available, but it's really great to get your feedback in a forum like this one. I hope we can help make your System 7 experience an enjoyable one! :)

AFL Bear: Thanks, Greg! I know you folks have been quite busy! And now, could our surprise guest, Jim Reekes, tell us few words?

JimR72: I've been working in MacDTS supporting developers for the past few years, and recently joined Mac System Software specifically on the Sound Manager. I think I can handle most any question, so let go!

AFL Bear: Alright! We've got a lot of questions already ... so we'll turn right to them!

AFA John: Our first question comes to us from DavidIIci ...

Question: Is there some "physical" change made when System 7.0 is installed which makes it difficult/impossible to re-format to System 6.0.x? Someone over on Prodigy's Mac BB claimed that a drive's boot blocks are re-written when System 7.0 is installed, and suggested that this makes it difficult, or impossible, to return to System 6.0.x.

C Derossi: System 7 doesn't do anything like that. As a matter of fact, we go back and forth between System 6 and System 7 all the time during our testing. It does move things from your desktop to a folder called Desktop Folder, which is only visible under 6.0. And it moves your DAs out of the System and into the Apple Menu Items folder, but it doesn't change anything fundamental about your drive or hardware.

AFL Bear: That was a great question, David! Be sure to carry the correct news back to Prodigy! :)

AFA John: Our next question is from TonyM19 ...

Question: Hello. May I first say that you've done a wonderful job with S7! Two questions: 1- Does Sys7 load 32-bit QuickDraw automatically in those Mac IIs that don't have it in ROM? 2- Speaking of ROM, is Apple going to upgrade those IIx, IIcx and SE/30 ROMS?

JusSomeGuy: 1) 32-bit QuickDraw is built into System 7. You get it on all color machines. 2) Apple has no current plans to provide a ROM upgrade to Mac II class machines. We are, however, looking into the possibility of doing so in the future. Watch MacWeek for ship dates:)

AFL Bear: That's great! It's good to know ... MacWeek can keep us up on the news, too!

AFA John: This question comes to us from AFC GeneS ...

Question: I gather that some features weren't included when system 7 was released, such as printer manager improvements. When do you intend to tackle these matters?

C Derossi: A lot of things that were planned for System 7 had to be dropped in order to ship. We had to make some trade-offs during the whole process. Those things that did not make it into System 7 are being worked on for the future, but you know the line about not talking about: future, hypothetical products.

AFL Bear: Of course, this lets you guys keep your jobs having something to do on System 7? ;)

AFA John: GearsRuss asks ...

Question: are the rumors that the 8*24GC won't run with system 7.0 true???

JusSomeGuy: The 8*24GC card will work in unaccellerated mode (i.e., as an 8*24 card) just fine in 7.0. But we added a couple of new Quickdraw modes to System 7, and the GC card implementation of them wasn't done by the same team that worked on 7.0. We should have a new version of the control panel by fall.

AFL Bear: Thanks, Greg! That's good news. And our next question, please? :)

AFA John: Our next question is from GShapiro ...

Question: Will there be a maintenance release to fix bugs found in the Golden Master release of 7.0? Also, have many confirmed bugs been reported so far?

C Derossi: At this time, we have no plans for an emergency bug-fix release. On the other hand, we are committed to fixing bugs in our software, and we're still working. But there's no immediate new version pending. As far as reported bugs go, we've mostly gotten comments that 7.0 is the most stable release we've ever had.

OnlineHost: I guess that's what they mean by "Rock Solid"!

AFA John: MicroPhone asks ...

Question: How did the Blue Meanies get their name? Related to the fact that System 7 was code named "Blue"?

C Derossi: I named the group. The name "Blue Meanies" was invented because we didn't want to be tied to any particular project. The Blue part does come from the fact that the System 7 team was called the "Blue" team at one time. The "Meanies" part comes from Greg's attitude.

SueBorg: I'd like to thank you all for coming (a little late for that comment, I know. ;) And invite you to come visit the System 7 Resource Center. You can download a copy of System 7, if you wish, or get help at either the Developer or End User discussions.

AFA John: Our next question is from JZacharia ...

Question: Why does printing a document in Monaco 9 print much slower on my ImageWriter II ? There is about a 10 sec.pause between about every 3 lines.

JusSomeGuy: Well, none of us are printing experts ... I can't think of an obvious reason why Monaco 9 would print slower than under 6.0.x. I guess it could be because TrueType is being used to image characters at a larger size to take advantage of the resolution of the printer.

AFL Bear: Thanks, Greg! This may be a good time to plug the System 7 Upgrade AnswerLine. Don't forget, folks, if you purchased the System 7.0 Personal Upgrade Kit, you are entitled to 90 days of free support for transition-related questions!

AFA John: LesT asks this question about 7.0 disk seeks ...

Question: From reports it seems that Sys7 requires an exorbitant number of disk seeks. Is this a flaw or dependent on the processor or just Sys7?

JimR72: System 7 does nothing more or less about disk seeks. It may be true that more files are being accessed. Fragmentation of the disk is likely to slow down any such system, but System 7 isn't the fault here.

AFA John: Our next question is from Diamante ...

Question: When I asked an Apple "Senior SE" about LW+ problems (drops in and out, disrupted BG printing, etc.), he said "Known problem - no fix planned. LW+ will not be supported next year." ACK! Tell me this isn't true, and that there IS a fix coming!

JusSomeGuy: I don't know who this guy is, but he's dead wrong. There was a problem with beta versions of 7.0 on a MacPlus, but those were fixed for Golden Master.

OnlineHost: Rumors squelched here! Just ask! :)

AFA John: Our own AFC JimW has this to ask ...

AFL Bear: Thanks, Jim! And we have lots of questions ...

Question: Does System 7 present new opportunities which can be exploited by viruses?

JusSomeGuy: We've taken some steps along the way to make several of the existing viruses impotent in System 7 and we've been pretty careful not to add any new ways to allow the entry of unwanted code.

AFL Bear: This is good to hear, Greg! By the way, folks, our guests will be staying awhile longer to tackle the many questions waiting.

AFA John: SilkWah steps up to the microphone next ...

Question: I am configured with 14 MB RAM on a IIsi. 5MB in the IIsi and the balance in software virtual. How will this work with Sys 7 ?

JimR72: Works great!

C Derossi: If you're talking about the product "Virtual" from Connectix, we're not sure that it works with System 7 in its current version. If you're talking about the virtual memory feature that is part of System 7, then it should be fine. You will notice a performance decrease, though, since more than half of your RAM is out on disk.

AFA John: Willi asks a question that I bet many people are wondering ...

Question: I am interested in running System 7, but I want to keep Sys6.0.5 as a backup. I have only one hard disk and am wondering if there is a way to partition it to run either as startup.

C Derossi: We don't know of any partitioning software that will let you set either one as the ...

OnlineHost: You got them thinking on this one,
Willi!

C Derossi: We don't know of any partitioning software that will let you set either one as the startup disk. The startup disk control panel can only
select between different disks. There are some par-
titioners that might work, though. I've heard of
one that starts from the partition which comes
first alphabetically. There may be other solutions.
You might want to ask a dealer about products that
could do this for you. On the other hand, you could
just keep multiple System folders on your disk and
switch between them with one of the "Blesser"-type
utilities. Be careful, though, as multiple System
folders can lead to trouble if you're not knowledgeable in how to deal with them.

AFL Bear: Thanks for those ideas, Chris! And AFC
BigDan wonders about something he noticed ...

Question: I find that System 7 requires significantly more disk changes when doing a floppy-to-
floppy copy with one drive.

JusSomeGuy: The copy engine in the Finder was completely redesigned for System 7. Along the way we
noticed that our good ideas about how to make copying go faster worked fine for hard disks, but not
as well for floppy disks. This is definitely an
area we plan to address in a future version.

AFA John: Our next question is from MicroPhone ...

Question: Will we ever see support for tearoff
menus in future versions of Sys 7?

JusSomeGuy: We don't know. We only work here.

JimR72: Important future direction.

JusSomeGuy: "Unannounced products", and all that
...

AFA John: Our next question is from AFC Carey ...

Question: What printer drivers for System 6.0.x are compatible with 7.0?

C Derossi: None of ours; we have new versions that come with 7.0 (which work under 6.0.x, too, so you can use the same LaserWriter driver for all your networked machines). As for third-party drivers, you'll have to contact them on a case-by-case basis. We didn't do anything in System 7 that should break old drivers, though.

AFA John: This next question comes to us from JD Minard ...

Question: Could Jim give us an overview of what the new sound manager does? Will it work on older Macs that don't have the new sound chip?

JimR72: Well, the "new" sound manager works on all existing Macs. For the machines that have the Apple Sound Chip there are additional features such as multiple sound channels, play from disk, etc. We've also added Sound Input which is device-independent so that you can even use the Farallon MacRecorder as part of the System. We're continuing to work on even more features and to support the high volume/low end machines even better. If you have suggestions send them to us!

AFA John: This question comes to us from AFC DaveAx ...

Question: Will our guests tell us what is planned for System 7 as regards background printing for serial devices?

C Derossi: This IS something we're working on. But you know the mantra, "If it hasn't been announced yet, I can't talk about it".

OnlineHost: Where have we heard that before? :)

C Derossi: BTW, the Personal LW LS (which is a serial printer) does do background printing today.

AFA John: This next question is from DaveWarker ...

Question: Are there any reported cases of developers being killed by falling copies of IM Vol 6? :)

OnlineHost: Duck!

JimR72: No, only hernias carrying it home from the bookstore. There was one rumor about a case of IM falling from the 5th floor on top of someone's head knocking him out. Another person saw this and was so shocked he had a heart attack and was hit by a car. But other than that I haven't heard of anything bad happening.

OnlineHost: WoW!

AFA John: OceanCoMU asks ...

Question: Hello. Chris, you and your staff have done a fantastic job with System 7! Did the development team use the Cray and a lot of CASE (Computer Aided Software Engineering) for the large codes in S7?

C Derossi: Thanks for the compliment! The only thing WE used the Cray for was ray tracing pictures for startup screens. :) Actually, the Cray gets used mostly for plastics molding analysis so that the insides of our Mac cases don't get too hot.

AFA John: Shekar 5 asks ...

Question: Why hasn't the system heap status been improved for 7.0? I think there should be a control in the Memory CDev for System Heap control... the heap is always full even when I startup!

OnlineHost: Good question, Shekar!

JusSomeGuy: The system heap status in 7.0 is greatly improved over that of 6.0.x. It automatically expands and contracts as necessary during the boot process (and also while you are using the machine). Users should never be subjected to a control they can't hope to understand, so putting a system heap adjuster in a control panel would be a waste of time. So, we just made it work. The system heap will always appear full, because it will shrink down as space in it is released.

AFL Bear: Now you've got the straight poop, Shekar! Spread the word!

AFA John: AbbyD steps up to the mike next and asks ...

Question: Will we be seeing 'AppleScript' soon, or is the Userland product, 'Frontier', going to be the main(?) language of AppleEvents?

C Derossi: I'm afraid that I can't talk about Apple's scripting solution, just that we're working on one. For now we're working with third-party companies like UserLand and others to make sure that what they do will work with our future designs.

AFA John: Our next question is from ThinkingMac ...

Question: Is there some known bug that causes icons to disappear? Everytime I reboot, some applications get "de-iconed", and all I see are the generic application and disk icons. The affected apps change with every desktop rebuild.

AFL Bear: Thanks, Chris!

C Derossi: There have been reports of this, but we can't point you to a specific cause. You might have one of a few problems that we know about. First, if you used an early version of System 7 (one of the alpha or beta copies), then you might have corrupted part of your disk structure. Run Disk First Aid and if it reports unrepairable problems, then you'll have to backup and reformat. If your disk is okay, or you didn't use pre-release copies of System 7, then you might have some files that have "Bundle" bits set incorrectly. This is hard to find unless you're skilled with ResEdit or MPW, or have a utility like BundAid (sorry, don't know who makes it). You might be low on disk space and the Finder couldn't store your icons into its desktop database. Finally, you could try rebuilding your desktop; there's a slim chance that you have a corrupt desktop database. (Delete the desktop files (both old and new) first, using ResEdit to rename them and make them visible.)

JimR72: BundAid by Jim Hamilton, 2914 Aftonshire Way #13102,Austin, TX 78748 GEnie: J.HAMILTON10, CompuServe: 71640,235

AFA John: AFC Chuck asks ...

Question: If I am switching from System 7 to System 6 should I rebuild the desktop? Will this be advantageous or a waste of time?

JusSomeGuy: Yes, you should rebuild the desktop if you go from 7.0 to 6.0, since 6.0 needs to know if you have moved applications from one place to another, etc.

AFA John: Our next question is from Lund1 ...

Question: The System 7 Bible (from the people who wrote the Mac Bible) make mention of a performance slide bar to vary the performance of the local user and the sharing users for a shared volume or folder. Is the a feature that was left out?

C Derossi: Back in early versions of System 7, there was a slider that let you choose whether you wanted your Mac to give preference to the local user, or to people who were logged on across the net. Then, we decided that it really didn't make that much difference. Next, we found out that people who setup other people's Macs REALLY liked having the control. Finally, we found out that the slider was completely useless, since a bug in the code caused the value that actually got used to be totally random! In the end, we opted for leaving it out since we could make the interface easier without sacrificing any really important functionality. Of course, we could always ship an extension that would give you the slider back like it was before (that is, when it didn't really do anything).

AFA John: Sumatran asks ...

Question: What's being done to address the performance of S7 on the Plus?

JusSomeGuy: We are working on improving the performance of System 7 across the product line. In the case of the MacPlus, I'm not sure how much effort we will be expending on it, since it is a very small part of our installed base at the moment, and dwindling fast.

AFA John: This question comes to us from MicroPhone ...

Question: Are their any hidden wonders in Sys 7.0 that the Meanies might tell us about. Even a clue or two?

C Derossi: Clue #1: Yes, they're in there. Clue #2: Try everything.

JimR72: The Sound cdev and the Scrapbook supports copy/paste of sounds.

JusSomeGuy: Try pasting a picture into the Puzzle DA.

OnlineHost: Are we talking smiley faces and credits? ;)

JimR72: Try pasting the color map in the Mac cdev.

JusSomeGuy: There's a new city in the Map called Middle Of Nowhere ...

OnlineHost: Go on, guys! Tell us more! This is good stuff!

JusSomeGuy: Try using Clear on the Puzzle to get the numbers back ...

JimR72: Solve the puzzle and listen closely for the voice of Chris...

AFA John: This next one comes from AFC JimW ...

Question: Will Desktop Manager under 6.0.5 use the same desktop database files as System 7?

C Derossi: As a matter of fact, we made a change late in System 7 so that the desktop file formats would be compatible. BUT, there is more information stored in a 7.0 desktop which won't be in a System 6 desktop. We made the file formats the same so that CD-ROM which are going to live on file servers will work on 6.0 AppleShare servers and 7.0 File Sharing servers with the same desktop file (which obviously can't be changed on a CD-ROM).

AFL Bear: Folks, we are at the end of the questions, so I will open up the floor and you can all congratulate these fine folks for a job well done!

JusSomeGuy: I agree. I want to thank all of you for being such great customers! Thanks for all the great feedback and bug reports during the development of System 7. <tap><tap><tap> Is this thing on?

AFL Bear: How about it, folks? Was this a good piece of work or what? :)

AFL Bear: Tons!

OnlineHost: We hope you enjoyed this stimulating discussion with The Blue Meanies, some of people who brought you System 7! We owe a big debt of appreciation to them for being our Special Guests here at MUT and look forward to seeing their continued presence in the System 7 support area.

OnlineHost: Please join the MUT staff in giving Chris and Greg a rousing round of AOL applause. Thank you, guys!

OnlineHost: We would also like to thank you all for coming tonight and for your questions and interest. Without you we wouldn't be here. There were some terrific questions! :)

OnlineHost: Don't forget to look in the "System 7" area of America Online, and also the Macintosh Utilities & DA's Forum for the latest information on System 7 utilities.

6/1/91 1:01:00 AM Closing Chat Log.

⤜

MORE SECRETS

It Takes Longer That Way

The first Apple Macintosh user manuals were as artful as the computer. They were lovingly designed, lush with white space, lavishly illustrated and—in a first for computer manuals—strewn with color photographs.

Chapter 1 begins with a classic Apple "lifestyle" photograph. Here, in a two-page spread, is a young blond student, seated before his Macintosh. He's California handsome—a very hunky guy, actually. Behind him is a blackboard covered with scientific diagrams.

His moody gaze is rapt on the Macintosh screen. We don't see the screen, because the Mac is facing the student, not the camera.

So the *back* of the Macintosh is facing the camera. And there, on the back, is the power switch.

Which is off.

Paranoia is Job 1

A member of the original Macintosh software team told us this Steve Jobs story.

Taken with the idea of a vanity license plate for his Mercedes, Steve ordered up plates that read "Jobs1."

Naturally, driving a Mercedes in Cupertino with a "Jobs1" plate attracted attention. People chatted up Steve wherever he stopped: the gas station, convenience store …

Soon, paranoia crept in. *What if I'm kidnapped?* the young millionaire began to fear. It happened to Getty. They cut off his ear, for Chrissake!

Finally, Steve took off the plates and stashed them in the trunk. Not long after, the California Highway Patrol stopped the plateless Mercedes.

Needless to say, Steve's plates are now vanity-less gibberish.

(As a postscript, it should be mentioned that John Sculley, in his autobiographical *Odyssey*, writes of what seems to be an kidnapping attempt on himself during a jogging outing. So let's not dismiss too quickly what might be justifiable paranoia on Steve's part.)

❦

The Mystery Mac Classic Disk

Hidden away in the ROM of every Mac Classic is a mystery boot disk that contains System 6.0.2 and AppleShare. To see this disk, hold down the Command, Option, X, and O keys and start your computer. This key combination boots directly into the System files stored in the Classic's ROM boot disk. At one time, Apple had considered offering the Classic as a diskless workstation and built in this feature to allow booting without a floppy or hard drive.

— *COMPUTE* magazine, February 1991

❦

The Macintosh SE Hidden Slide Show

There a four-frame "slide show" hidden in the Macintosh SE ROM. To see it, you'll need to have the MacsBug debugger in your System folder, and a programmer's switch attached to an SE.

Ready? Make sure you don't have any applications open—you're about to interupt (read: crash) the active application. Being in the Finder is a good idea. Now press the interrupt button. The debugger window will come up. Now type G   41D89A (make sure to type the space after "G") and press Return.

The slide show, showing the SE development team, begins, and continues until you reboot.

☙

DR. MAC'S TOP TOP TENS

Bob "Dr. Macintosh" LeVitus' Top Ten Power User Hints

10. R.T.F.M. (Read the #*&@^# manual!)

9. Read about the Mac. (*MacUser, MacWeek, Macworld*, etc.)

8. Learn to type faster. (More important than you think ...)

7. Join a user group. (Call the Apple User Group hotline at 800–538–9696 Ext. 500 to find the group near you.)

6. Don't be afraid to experiment. (But see tips 1 and 2 before you start!)

5. Get more RAM. (4-5Mb minimum, 8 is better, 20 or more is the best.)

4. Rebuild your desktop regularly—at least once a month. (Hold down the Command and Option keys at startup until you see the "Are you sure you want the Desktop rebuilt on the disk 'Your Hard Disk'?" dialog box. Then click OK.)

3. Invest in cool utilities like MasterJuggler, QuicKeys II, and Now Utilities.

2. Back up your work.

1. Back up your work AGAIN!

Bob "Dr. Macintosh" LeVitus' Top Ten Power User Utilities

10. After Dark/More After Dark (Berkeley Systems)

   The ultimate screen saver. Prevents phosphor burn-in and makes your Mac look cool at the same time! Groove on the flying toasters and tropical fish while doing something nice for your monitor.

9. Last Resort (Working Software)

   Captures every keystroke to a text file, so you'll never lose another word, even when you crash or the cat chews through the power cord! I just used it to recover this paragraph when Word "quit unexpectedly."

8. ResEdit (Apple Computer)

   Powerful juju. Customize anything. Standard warning applies: never use ResEdit on a master or original file; always work on a copy.

7. On Location (ON Technology)

   The most awesome search-your-disk(s) utility ever. Find any word in any document on any disk in seconds.

6. Norton Utilities for Macintosh (Symantec)

   The Rolls Royce of file and disk recovery. You may not need it right now, but trust me, someday you will …

5. (Tie) Retrospect (Dantz) or Redux (Microseeds)

   Two fine backup/archive programs. Choose Redux if you back up to floppies or other removable media, Retrospect for all tape drives.

4. (Tie) DiskTop (CE Software) or DiskTools/File Director (Fifth Generation Systems)

   A pair of Finder substitutes that let you move, copy, rename, or delete files or folders, launch programs or documents, get information on the size and number of files or folders, erase, eject, or unmount disks, and search for files using more flexible options than Apple's Find File.

3. MasterJuggler (AlSoft)

The Swiss Army knife of utilities. Load fonts, DAs, and sounds without installing them in your System, compress fonts, resolve font ID conflicts, and much, much more.

2. Now Utilities (Now Software)

The ultimate collection—ten utilities for all occasions, including classics like SuperBoomerang (makes Open and Save dialog boxes much easier to use), NowMenus (hierarchical Apple menu), and Startup Manager (turn Extensions and Control Panels on and off quickly and easily).

1. QuicKeys 2 (CE Software)

Macro and keystroke recorder par excellence and the most useful utility you can get for your Mac. If you only buy one utility this year, this should be it.

❧

Bob "Dr. Macintosh" LeVitus' Top Ten Desktop Diversions

10. Creepy Castle (Reactor)

Arcade-style game in the genre of Beyond Dark Castles, which was one of the great arcade games of its time. Added bonus—unlike most games these days, it's in black and white—looks and plays great on a Classic, SE, or Plus.

9. The Talking Moose and His Cartoon Carnival (Baseline)

The moose is back and he's funnier than ever in his latest incarnation. New characters include Puck the Bardic Dragon, P.T. Penguin, and Stinko the Evil Clown.

8. 3 in Three (Inline Design)

A tour de force of animation and sound from Cliff Johnson, creator of the award winning Fool's Errand. An interactive treasure hunt featuring 80 mind-boggling word puzzles, logic dilemmas, and brain teasers.

7. Oids (FTL)

One of the best space-war arcade games ever. Awesome color graphics (works fine in B/W as well) and superior game play make Oids a game you'll play again and again.

6. Spectre (Velocity)

A blazing shoot-'em-up. You control a battle craft called a "Spectre." Your objective: survival. Cruise around shooting enemies, and collecting ammo and flags. Totally addictive and even more incredible on a network with one or more friends.

5. Sherlock Holmes, Consulting Detective (ICOM Simulations)

A fascinating game with over 90 minutes of full-motion video. Match wits with Sherlock and Watson; guide them through London, interrogating suspects and solving three intricate murders. The game is afoot! (Requires a CD ROM player and 256-color Mac, but worth it.)

4. Kid Pix (Broderbund)

I don't know who likes Kid Pix better, my three-year old daughter Allison, or me. Kid Pix is the cutest application I've ever seen—a wild, wacky paint program packed full of sound and animation. A delight for kids (and grown-ups) of all ages.

3. Rise of the Dragon (Dynamix/Sierra)

The year is 2053. Los Angeles has entered the Age of Decay. The air is thick with pollution; drug abuse is at an all time high. The mayor's daughter has been murdered with a dose of bad drugs. The mayor is depending on you, William "Blade" Hunter, Private Investigator, to save the day. If you're a fan of sci-fi movies like *Blade Runner* or *Alien(s)*, and you have about thirty hours to spare, Rise of the Dragon will knock your socks off. Lush hand-painted 256-color graphics and stunning animations combine with a pulsing original soundtrack to provide a richly compelling and thoroughly interactive experience.

2. Spaceship Warlock (Reactor)

This is the CD that pushed me over the edge—after seeing it at Macworld Expo, I ran out and bought a CD player. A cosmic space opera drawn by Mike Saenz (MacPlaymate, Virtual Valerie, ComicWorks, Shatter Comics, etc.), with animation and music by the multi-talented Joe Sparks, this epic drama is the one by which all interactive fiction will be judged for years to come. (Requires a CD ROM player and 256-color Mac, but worth it. Don't forget to pick up a copy of Sherlock Holmes Consulting Detective [see # 5 above] as well!)

1. Wallpaper (Thought I Could)

What can I say? This little $59 utility has captured my heart. Wallpaper allows you to create, edit, save, and display an unlimited number of large desktop patterns. Comes with hundreds of gorgeous patterns, and you can easily create your own. You've gotta see it to believe it! As Steven Bobker said, "Wallpaper is nothing less than revolutionary. Now your desktop can be prettier than your screen saver."

❦

The Top Ten Ways to Tell the Difference Between Bob "Dr. Macintosh" LeVitus' *Stupid Mac Tricks* and Guy Kawasaki's *The Macintosh Way*

10. *Stupid Mac Tricks* is the one with the Moose and the Fish.

9. *The Macintosh Way* is the one with the scholarly footnotes.

8. *Stupid Mac Tricks* doesn't bash Ashton•Tate or Apple.

7. *The Macintosh Way* doesn't bash Moose or Fish.

6. The chapter on Sexplosion is in *Stupid Mac Tricks*.

5. The chapter on dating and marriage is in *The Macintosh Way*.

4. *Stupid Mac Tricks* only mentions Apple twice.

3. *The Macintosh Way* has the quote from Apple's Jean Louis Gassée.

2. *Stupid Mac Tricks* has the quote from Night Court's Harry Anderson.

And the Number One way to tell the difference between *Stupid Mac Tricks* and *The Macintosh Way* (drum roll …)

1. *The Macintosh Way* can't make your Mac emit a disgusting barfing noise!

❧

About Bob LeVitus

Bob began his professional career in the early 1970s as a roadie and lighting director for the Jackson 5. Bob is still capable of a hiphop rendition of Dancing Machine even though he left the show biz world to get a degree in marketing from California State University.

Bob was a partner in a market research firm for four years, but headed out on his own when his partner could not appreciate the wonders of desktop publishing on the just-developed Macintosh computer. Approaching a new monthly publication, MACazine, *to pitch his market research services, Bob instead joined the publication as the editor-in-chief. Since 1989, Bob has been a contributing editor of* MacUser, *but is best known for his popular book,* Dr. Macintosh: How to Become A Macintosh Power User.

In the fall of 1990, Bob LeVitus launched Stupid Mac Tricks *on unsuspecting computer users. Published by Addison-Wesley, SMT became a word-of-mouth hit, with more than 40,000 copies sold to date. The sequel,* Son of Stupid Mac Tricks, *has also gone on to become a bestseller.*

Bob lives in Austin, Texas, with his wife Lisa, daughter Allison, and assorted dogs and cats.

❧

SOMETHING TO TRY WHEN YOU CRASH

BOB LEVITUS

Here's more of Bob LeVi—er ... Dr. Mac. This time from his newest book. What book? (Clever segue into publisher's required notice, which must appear on first page of excerpt. Therefore:) From Dr. Macintosh, Second Edition by Bob LeVitus. Copyright © 1992 by Bob LeVitus. Published by Addison-Wesley, 1 Jacob Way, Reading, MA 01867, (617)944-3700. Suggested retail price $24.95. Reprinted by permission of Addison-Wesley Publishing Company.

Fortunately, the book is a better read than the permission notice. Dr. Macintosh is a grand how-to tour of Macintosh power userdom, full of tips, tricks, and sage advice from the good doctor, including

❦

Here's a little trick you can try when your Mac crashes (that is, when you get a System error).

Most Macs come with a little piece of plastic called the *programmer's switch*. (Among those that don't—the Classic, LC, IIsi, Portables, and PowerBooks). Although the Macintosh *Owners' Guide* warns that it's for use only by programmers, that's not necessarily true. It can be a time-saver for anyone. It came in the box with your Mac; install it according to the directions in the documentation that came with your Macintosh. If you can't find it, an Apple dealer may sell you one.

On compact Macs (Plus, SE, SE/30) and full-sized Mac IIs (II, IIx, IIfx), the front switch is the reset switch; the rear switch is the interrupt switch.

On the Mac IIcx and IIci, these switches are installed on the lower left side of the front panel, under the Apple logo. The left switch is the reset switch; the right switch is the interrupt.

The reset switch works the same as turning your Mac off and back on with the power switch. If you need to restart your Mac after a crash or freeze, you can push the reset button instead of turning the power off and on.

> **Subj: More Novice Stories 91-02-05 16:06:00 EST**
> **From: LadyMacBth**
>
> Yep, I've heard of people storing their disks on the side of the computer with magnets.
>
> Other favorites:
>
> - Person picking up mouse and physically moving it back and forth across monitor screen.
> - Lady typing disk labels by running the label through the typewriter ... while it's attached to the disk!
> - Conversation: "I teach UNIX."
>   "Oh really? What do you teach them?"

The interrupt switch can sometimes return you to the Finder after a crash, if you follow the steps listed below. (By the way, the interrupt switch really *is* a programmer's switch. They use it to escape from crashes, too.)

Technically, you're invoking the Mac's built-in debugger when you press the interrupt switch. Typing the suggested sequence into the debugger window (shown in Figure 1) can sometimes allow you to recover from an otherwise hopeless system crash.

I find it's occasionally worth the effort to try this trick, especially if you're running System 6 under MultiFinder or System 7. Even though you will usually lose any unsaved work in the application you were working in when the crash occurred, you may be able to save work in other applications you have open. For example: let's say you're running MultiFinder, have documents open in MacWrite and MacPaint, and crash while working in MacWrite. Press the interrupt switch and type the sequences in the next section. If it works, and you're returned to the desktop, you will probably be able to go back into MacPaint and save your work. You'll lose any unsaved work in MacWrite, but at least you will have saved something.

The method given in the next section works only with certain kinds of system errors. There's no way to tell beforehand whether it's going to work; but if you've crashed, you might want to give it a try.

Crash Recovery

In the event of a crash or freeze, press the interrupt switch. It sometimes brings up an empty box with a caret (>) prompt. If it does, try typing the following:

```
SM 0 A9F4 <Carriage Return>
```

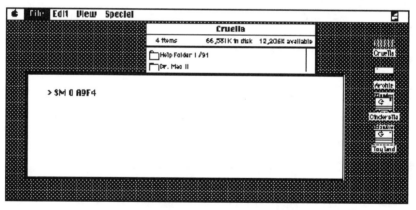

Figure 1. Recovering from a System error (crash) after pressing the interrupt switch.

The zeros in this line and the next one you'll type are all numeric 0 (zero). Type the characters exactly the way you see them, spaces and all (see Figure 1).

After the carriage return, the box will fill with characters but the first line and prompt will remain blank. Type:

```
G 0 <Carriage return>
```

That's all there is to it. If it works, you'll be returned to the Finder. If it doesn't work, you'll either get another Bomb dialog box, or the box will fill with characters. In either case, press the reset switch to reboot.

Using this trick leaves your Mac in an unstable state—it will probably crash again if you don't restart it real soon. If the trick did work, do whatever housekeeping you need to do (that is, save any unsaved documents), then restart your Mac using the Finder's Restart command. The Finder's Restart sequence is infinitely better for your Mac than a crash. Using it minimizes the chance of damage to your Desktop file or disk directories.

I've got one of those little yellow sticky notes posted to my monitor to remind me. You might want to do the same. Mine looks sort of like this:

Figure 2. A little yellow sticky-note reminder on my monitor.

PART

IX

HERE & NOW

A BOY, A DAD, A LAN

JAMES HORSWILL

Welcome to the Here and the Now. Not the past, not the future, but what's happening now: networking, world-building, interface-crafting, telecommunicating, brain-frying, and a few well-chosen words to a particular Macintosh.

We begin with an article that first appeared in The Computer Buyer's Resource. It happened like this: I'd just finished—I thought—this book. So I decided to take a nap; it's two in the afternoon, I'm beat. I laid down and grabbed something to read, aimlessly began flipping pages, and started to read, "I'm inordinately proud of my son."

This, I think to myself, is a great way to start a computer article. And it got better. So I got off the bed and on the phone, and now have the great pleasure to introduce you to a piece by James Horswill, in which System 7, LANs, passwords, and file sharing come home.

❧

I'm inordinately proud of my son. I'm not talking about the mildly inflated pride one expects from any normal father. I'm talking about a particularly fulsome smugness that drives me to work him into any conversation—I worked him into this article didn't I? This year he was interviewed for a piece in *Smithsonian* magazine, and I carried that issue around for weeks, showing it to everyone I knew.

Like any father and son, however, there is a certain degree of rivalry between us. We are both inveterate punsters, for example, and constantly try to out-awful each other. One day in the car, our local FM station was playing Bach's *Air on a G String*. I suggested that if a performer makes a mistake while playing it, he should call it *Err on a G String*. Ian objected. "No, Dad! *Ur on a G String* is the book by the woman who worked her way through Sumeria as a stripper." At this point, my wife, Carol, threatened to get out of the car, even though we were doing 55 at the time.

Ian doesn't stop at trumping my puns, however. He also has a penchant for setting little tasks for me. He's working on a doctorate in artificial intelligence at MIT, and he'll say things like, "Hey Dad, here's a good book on LISP. You ought to know something about programming. Why don't you take a look at it?" He's even got me making a faltering attempt to learn LaTex, a page markup language that only a programmer could love.

Last summer, when he was visiting us, he suggested that I should network the two Macs in the house. (Carol has a Mac in the spare bedroom on the second floor, where she can work in peace, while I have a Mac in the basement, where I can create messes that won't bear sober contemplation.)

I said there wouldn't be any point in creating such a network. He argued that Carol could use the DeskWriter that I have in the basement, rather than the ImageWriter she has in the bedroom, while I could work upstairs when I could no longer stand our windowless nether regions. "It would be easy with System 7," he pointed out, "and anyway, it would be fun, and you ought to have some experience with networking."

He didn't convince me then, but by the time he came home for Christmas, I'd decided to give it a try. Ian suggested that we might be able to use the two unused wires in the existing telephone cables, but would have to make sure that there was a continuous circuit between the bedroom and the basement. That approach seemed a trifle Byzantine to me, so I chose a more conventional approach.

A friend of mine was selling PhoneNET connectors for $20 each, and I bought three. These allowed us to use ordinary telephone wire for the connections. I had a pair of phone jack crimpers around the house somewhere, along with some extra jacks, but of course I couldn't find them. We had to go to Radio Shack to buy a new pair of crimpers, some jacks, and a hundred feet of phone cable. Ian gave me a hard time about not being able to keep track of my tools.

Stringing the cable from bedroom to basement went fairly smoothly, though at one point I needed my ViseGrip pliers and couldn't find them. Ian sneered. "Hey, Dad, don't you have a tool box, or tool caddie, or something?"

"Yes," I said, "but I never remember to put anything there." After another ten minutes of searching, I found the pliers—in the tool caddie.

Once we'd strung the cables and attached the PhoneNET connectors to the printer ports of the two Macs, setting up the actual network was rather straightforward. Since both machines were running System 7, we didn't need to install any special networking software. System 7 includes built-in file sharing.

Our first job was to name the two machines, so that they could recognize each other over our network. To do this, we used the Sharing Setup control panel. (See Figure 1.)

We had to give each Mac a name, and also an owner. We named the basement Mac "Downstairs Mac," and the bedroom machine, "Upstairs Mac." I called the owner of the Mac in the basement "Downstairs," and that of the other, "Upstairs."

Since Carol and I were the only people on the network, there was no earthly need for passwords, but I was like a kid who had just gotten his Captain Midnight decoder ring, and so, of course, I had to assign them anyway.

I gave myself "Jim" as a password, and gave Carol, "Carol." Now, when I want to log onto Carol's Mac, I sign on as its owner, with the password "Carol." When she wants to log onto my machine, she uses "Jim." By logging on as owners, we assure ourselves of full access. By the way, passwords are case sensitive, so if

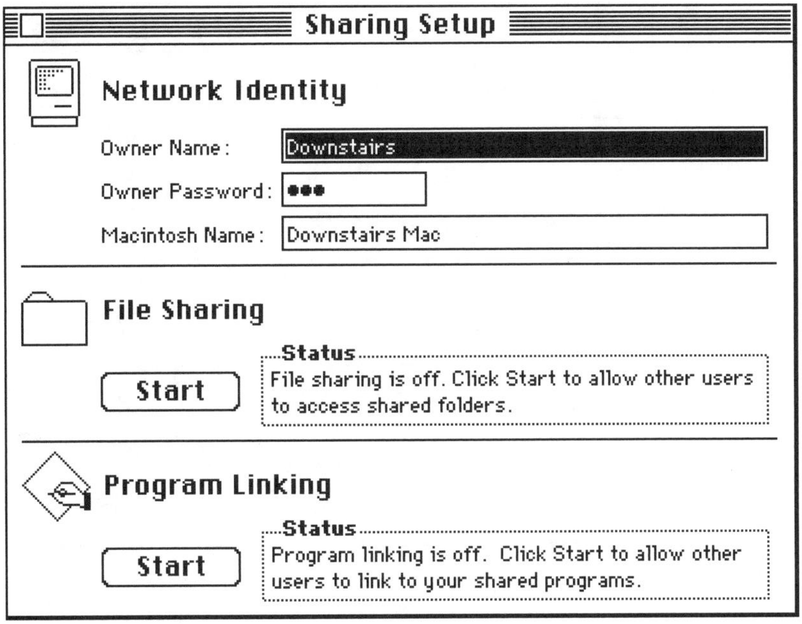

Figure 1. The Sharing Setup Control Panel.

Carol wants to use my machine, she must sign on as "Jim," and not "jim." And I must sign onto her machine as "Carol," not "carol."

To start file sharing, we simply clicked the file sharing start button. We didn't worry about program linking, as we had no programs to link. After initiating file sharing, we had to determine which folders and/or hard disks were to be shared. In this case, we wanted to grant full access to all volumes on both machines. Users can share up to ten folders, CD-ROMs, and hard disks at one time. We went to the Finder, selected a hard disk, and chose "Sharing … " from the File menu. (See Figure 2.)

We clicked the check boxes for "See Folders," "See Files," and "Make Changes," so that when Carol or I signed on as the owner of my Mac, we would have unlimited access. Ian and I did this for each volume on my Mac, and we did the same for Carol's hard drive. Of course, we had to go up to the bedroom to set file shar-

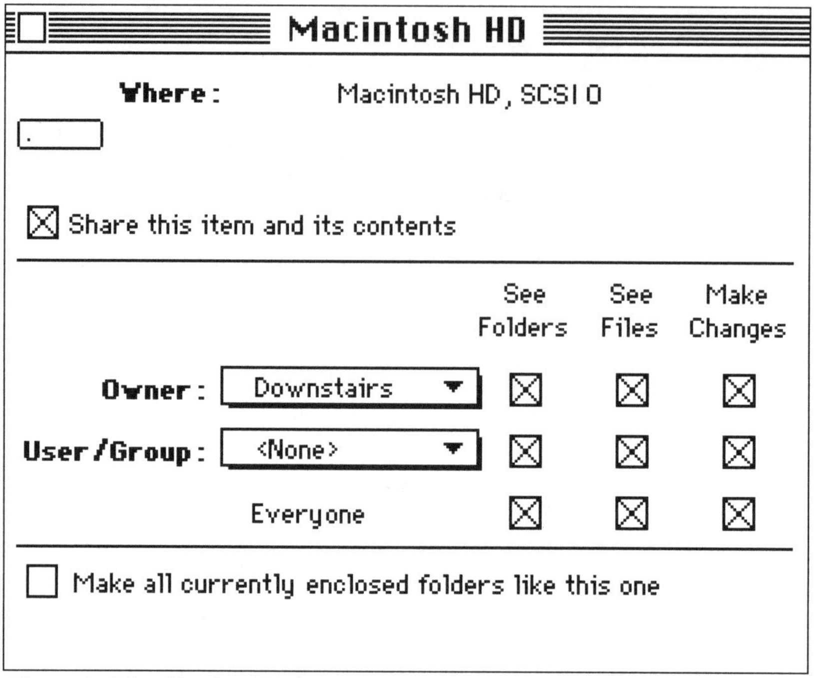

Figure 2. The Sharing Dialog.

ing on her Mac. It would have been possible to set up limited access privileges for other users, but since Carol and I were the only ones who would be using the network, there was no point in doing so.

Now, whenever I'm in the basement, and I want to get a file from Carol's hard drive, I just choose AppleShare from the Chooser. (See Figure 3.)

I select Carol's machine (since there are only two computers on the network, it's the only one listed) and type in *her* password in the dialog that comes up. I don't use *my* password because I'm signing onto her machine as its *owner*. The icon for her hard drive appears on my desktop, just as if it were mounted on my machine. However, the icon has AppleTalk cables connected to it, to indicate that it's a shared volume. In the same way, if I go upstairs, I can log onto my Mac from Carol's.

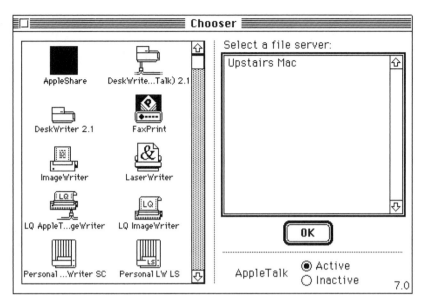

Figure 3. The AppleShare Chooser Dialog.

If I don't want to share files, I turn AppleTalk off by clicking the Inactive button in the Chooser. This frees about a 100K of memory. I can free even more by turning file sharing off. I do that by opening the File Sharing control panel and clicking the Stop button.

I can use Carol's hard drive just as though it were attached to my SCSI chain, though more slowly, because the process involves a form of telecommunications. I can open and change files, save new ones, and trash old ones. I can even run the programs that reside on her hard disk, though at a considerable penalty in speed. Note that most publishers license their software for one machine at a time, so running some programs over a network is impermissible. To turn file sharing off, I simply drag the icon of Carol's hard drive to the trash.

Printing over the network is even simpler. We have a DeskWriter in the basement, and it has built-in AppleTalk. When Carol wants to print to it from upstairs, she just selects it in the Chooser, and prints as she normally would. That's all there is to it. She doesn't even have to have file sharing turned on. The only catch is that she has to go down to the basement to collect the hard copy. Sometimes, if I'm feeling particularly sheepish about something I've done, I'll even bring it up to her.

This doesn't work the other way around. I can't print to Carol's ImageWriter II from my Mac, because it doesn't have AppleTalk. If you are planning to use your printer on a network, be sure that it has that ability. Some printers are intended for a single user.

Incidentally, when I installed System 7 on Carol's machine I encountered a printing problem that I initially attributed to an INIT (Extension) conflict. When Carol tried to print to the ImageWriter in Best mode, printing was excruciatingly slow. It became glacial with Adobe Type Manager installed. I spent an afternoon of hair pulling, trying to find the problem, and eventually posted a question on a local bulletin board. I soon learned that System 7 prints slowly to some devices, especially ImageWriters and StyleWriters.

Apple has now released a patch called the System 7 Tune-up. I've installed it on both my machines, and the ImageWriter problem seems to be largely cleared up. Apple makes the following claims for the new patch:

Memory is managed better, resulting in fewer "out of memory" messages.

Printing is faster and more reliable.

There is more memory available for application programs on computers that are not connected to a network (such as a PowerBook computer being used on the road).

I installed the patch a few hours ago, and ImageWriter printing is, indeed, faster. I also found that I can now use Canvas to trace the edges of a scanned image that used to give me an "out of memory" message. If you're running System 7, it might be a good idea to get a copy of this patch from a dealer, bulletin board, user group, or information service, and install it on your Mac.

Once we had the network up and running, we installed a shareware INIT called BroadCast, and sent insulting messages to each other, like two kids with a tin can telephone. Ian insisted that we download NetTrek from a bulletin board, and have at it. We did so, and he sat at the upstairs Mac while I sat in the basement, and we went where no man has gone before. I am hopeless at arcade games, or anything else requiring any degree of eye-hand coordination, so I spent most of my time spinning helplessly, while Ian decimated me with phasers and photon torpedoes. I loved every minute of it. What greater joy for a proud father, than to sit in his own home, and be pummeled electronically by his son?

Since Ian returned to Boston, I have found the new network quite useful. I hate sitting in the basement all day, with no windows, and it's pleasant to occasionally go up to the bedroom and work at the Mac while I watch the birds in the backyard. I started this article up there, but had to move back to the basement when I found myself becoming too distracted.

Carol has had no difficulty printing to the DeskWriter over the network, and I'm sometimes startled to hear it begin printing quietly, seemingly unbidden, as if it had suddenly acquired a mind of its own.

The network that Ian and I established is extremely simple, and should not be used as a model. However, if you have two or more Macs in your home or office, and they're running System 7, you might want to consider investing in some PhoneNET connectors, and setting up a network. Of course, it will be more fun if your "kid" is working with you, needling you about taking better care of your tools.

❧

— Copyright 1992 © James Horswill

James Horswill is a freelance writer, Macintosh tutor and electronic publisher. When asked for a short bio, he responded with:

James Horswill was born and raised in Minneapolis, and graduated from the University of Minnesota in 1960, with a degree in Theatre Arts. He has been a professional character actor in Twin Cities theatre for many years. He is sole proprietor and only employee of The Moving Finger (no, it's not from the Bible, it's from the Rubáiyát) through which he makes faltering attempts to market his skills as a freelance writer, electronic publisher, and Macintosh tutor. He is a regular contributor to the Computer Buyer's Resource, *a computer monthly in the Twin Cities market. He is survived by his wife, Carol, and his son, Ian.*

This article first appeared in Computer Buyer's Resource, *a monthly tabloid produced in Minneapolis, Minnesota. If you'd like to subscribe, a year's subscription is $19.95. Send the check to Subscription Manager,* Computer Buyer's Resource, *P.O. Box 18305, Minneapolis, MN 55418.*

EMPOWERING THE USER,
NOT THE PROGRAM

BRUCE TOGANZINNI

F irst the bio, then the article, then the pitch.

The bio:

Bruce "Tog" Toganzinni is Apple employee #66. He began Apple's human interface effort fourteen years ago by developing and publishing Apple's first Human Interface Guidelines. Since then, he's done human interface design for scores of applications and many of Apple's computers. He hacked together his first computer in 1957 and has been designing interfaces ever since. Tog is Apple's Human Interface Evangelist; a design consultant to Macintosh Research and Development, and key members of the developer community.

Tog lives with his wife, two kids, three dogs, six cats, and 80,000 head of bees, on a small farm in the redwood forest, overlooking San Francisco Bay. As required by law in California, he does most of his design work while steeping in his hot tub. Normally this would seem like heaven, but not when you are being dive-bombed by 80,000 bees.

My wife, the Doctor, recently switched handling the data for a medical research project she's doing from a popular power-user spreadsheet application to pencil, paper, and calculator.

She is now more productive.

Yes, the math is slower, but she is not longer spending 95 percent of her time trying to figure out what power-user feature she needs to get the spreadsheet to stop suddenly filling entire columns with number signs, or how to "trick" her spreadsheet into building a graph with the important data on the X axis, instead of on the legend. Is she alone in having these problems? No. They have become so endemic that *Business Week's* cover story for April 29, 1991, was entitled, "I Can't Work This ?#!!@{ Thing!"

What is going wrong here? Somewhere along the line, many technology designers lost track of the real goal: empowering our users. Whether it's for VCRs, computers, or clock radios, designers are adding every button, switch, and other power-user feature they can in the mistaken belief that the true power of technology is to be measured in the number of specifications and controls, rather than impact on people's lives.

When it first appeared, the Macintosh computer was a counter-force to this mad race. In fact, it made technology so accessible, so simple, that people at first assumed the machine was weak and underpowered. It was only after people began to see what they could accomplish with it that they recognized what a powerful beast it really was. But now, as our programs, operating systems, and computers continue to grow in power, our users have begun to feel less powerful and less in control. This is partly because the tasks have become more complex, but something else is leading to the increased difficulty of using our machines, something we need to address.

The Myth of the Power User

Many of us have stopped designing for anything resembling our real user population, in favor of designing for people remarkably like us. Yes, we learned years ago that we should not design software for ourselves. Instead, we were to seek out typical users from our target population. Many of us soon found, though, that dealing with a large number of typical users was a real bother, so we gradually zeroed in on a handful of people with whom we got along well, who would really play with our new software, and give us the very best feedback. In other words, people just like us.

I came across one developer a year ago who had, as his sole target user, a guy so much like him they could have been twin brothers. He designed his entire system around what this guy liked and didn't like. His software had more controls on it than the Space Shuttle. Worse, no one on the entire planet other than he and his user could make the application work.

Based on the demographics of computer programmers, designers, and product managers, it is of little surprise that our new target audience too often now consists of bipedal, testosterone-based life forms between the ages of 18 and 39.

Yes, I said testosterone-based life forms. At the risk of offending certain politically-correct parties, there does appear to be a difference, however minor, between boys and girls. And the overwhelming majority of power users I've come across are definitely male.

There are female power users, of course. I must have met four or five of them myself. And before everyone goes nuclear, let me explain what I mean by power-user: A "power user" is a person driven by hormones to want complete and utter control of every function of his or her computer, even if having such control seriously degrades efficiency and productivity.

Tim Allen's character on *Home Improvement*, the ABC Tuesday night comedy series, is the prototypic power user. He's the only guy in the neighborhood with a 120-horsepower lawn mower that will do 0 to 60 in less than seven seconds. It's not much use on his suburban lawn, but it makes a really neat noise when you start it up.

I know several guys at Apple who have so many weird public-domain extensions in their system folder that virtually none of their applications run properly. Accomplishing the least task is like walking through a mine field. So what? As far as they're concerned, it merely increases the challenge! They wouldn't think of parting with any of their extensions. They even have the temerity to claim the extensions make them more efficient.

My experience has been that most women do not "play around" with their machines. Rather, they see their machines as serious productivity tools, there for the express purpose of helping the women accomplish their task. Women, in general, want to do their work, not "play computer."

A lot of men don't want to "play computer," either. Far from it. But the power users do, and they, right now, are having a grossly disproportionate effect on the direction of design. Our computers are becoming unapproachable to children, women, older men, and males between the ages of 18 and 39 who are not particularly enamored of machinery. In other words, we are beginning to design systems that will alienate the majority of our current users, as well as virtually all the "hold-outs" who have failed, thus far, to embrace our wondrous revolution.

Designing for Productivity, not Power

I went shopping for a battery-operated drill this month, eventually choosing between two models. One I will label a wimp drill: Tim Allen's character wouldn't touch it with a ten-foot pole. The other was a true power-user dream:

Wimp $^3/_8$" Model	Power-User $^3/_8$" Model
Compact in size	Big, with popular assault-rifle styling
"Regular" power	35% extra power for those tough jobs
Two speeds	Infinitely variable speed
Single, built-in battery pack	External battery pack: use one while a second one is charging
Small charger	Large, heavy charger
1 hour charge time	1 hour charge time
Built-in trickle charge	Who needs it? We're powerful!
5-position clutch	5-position clutch
Reversible	Reversible

Wimp ³/₈" Model	*Power-User ³/₈" Model*
Wall-mount charge stand	Table-top charge stand
2 lbs. 6 oz.	4 lbs. 6 oz.
$84.95	$159.95

I wanted to buy a portable drill because I wanted to avoid having to drag around extension cords to use my existing power drills. (A battery-operated drill is a poor choice for a first drill.) Therefore, I was looking for:

- Power
- Portability
- Availability
- Accessibility
- Functionality

The power-user drill had 35 percent more power than the wimp one. An important difference? Not really. My plug-in drills sport more than five times the power of the most powerful battery-operated drill. 35 percent more may be an impressive claim on the side of a box; it makes little difference in practice.

Both drills offered portability, but the wimp drill is significantly lighter and better balanced, enabling a person to carry other tools at the same time, with greater comfort.

The lowly wimp drill wins hands-down when it comes to accessibility: the charger base screws to the wall and the drill is simply dropped into it, whole, always there to be found when needed. The power-user drill, its battery, and its charger are all permanently loose, and can be conveniently scattered all over the house.

The power-user drill has two superior areas of functionality: first of all, it has variable speed, a handy feature, particularly when trying to start screws. Having a clutch helps, but doesn't solve the problem. I'm pretty good at starting screws, so using the two-speed wimp drill wouldn't be as much of a problem for me as for the new user. This is the same paradox that the Macintosh Classic finally addressed: the most casual computer users need the most sophisticated computer and software. The $666 Apple One of 1976 was a fun toy for hackers, but useless for the average user. It took a $1000 Macintosh to finally put a usable tool in the hands of "common folk."

The power-user drill's second advantage is its ability to have one battery pack charging while the other one is installed in the drill and being used. All that would mean to me would be that I have to remove the battery every time I wanted to charge it. I would drag out my corded drill were I to be doing so much drilling as to kill a battery pack.

Both drills charge their batteries fully in one hour. (The fact that the power-user drill's charger weighs more than twice as much doesn't seem reflected in its capabilities, even if it makes it seem more impressive.) But the lower-priced model also has a trickle charger to keep the battery ready-to-go over time. With the power-user drill, the battery I charged three weeks ago is likely to be dead now when I need it. For all practical purposes, a battery-driven drill not used every day and lacking a trickle-charger requires a minimum of one hour to drill a hole.

"Yes, but its supposed to be used every day. It's a *power-user* drill!"

Stripping off supposed non-essentials because power tools or software are to be used professionally doesn't cut it. Carpenters get sick. They go on vacation. They don't want to have to stand around for an hour charging their drill when they return. CAD package users and word processor users also go on vacation. They don't want to have to spend their first three days back trying to re-memorize 1400 different esoteric commands that have taken the place of a well-designed visible interface.

Attention to detail could be found in every aspect of the smaller drill. Its clutch is a ring wrapping around the front of the motor housing like the focus ring on a camera, labeled so either left- or right-handed people can read it, then move it easily with a quick twist of the wrist. The clutch on the power-user drill is a small knob buried underneath the drill, requiring the user to stop work, turn the drill upside down, and hurt his or her fingers trying to clack the knob into a new position. (This for the convenience of the mechanical engineer who designed it, not the user who would work it.)

I ended up buying the wimp drill, because when they built it, the design team for this drill was thinking about me and how this drill would fit into my life. I knew it would be there, available, accessible, ready to go with no fuss, and that I would be comfortable and efficient when using it.

That's what I want in software. I don't want heavy, clunky, half-thought out "features" screwed into the side of lumbering software with all the grace of a badly hot-rodded car.

Let's get back to designing simple, functional, elegant software. And I don't mean weak and ineffectual, either. Take a look at the new Vellum 3D. A snap to learn, easy to use, and leaves a whole bunch of power-user packages in the dust.

We need to return to designing for our real users. We males, in particular, need to seek out people who are not just like us. We need to try ideas out on women, older people, younger people, handicapped people, and, most important, people who are not power users.

Having design sites and beta sites is a great idea, but your sites should include people who really don't want to be sites, people who will only be willing to be a site if you put in more effort and offer more goodies. Otherwise, you will be selecting solely for power users, because no one else in their right mind will play around with buggy software for free.

⚜

— Copyright 1991 © Apple Computer, Inc.

If you liked that, you'll love Tog on Interface, *published by Addison-Wesley. The piece you just read isn't in the book, but everything you ever wanted to know about interface is. It's a great, fun read and only $26.95—about one-third of what'd you pay for a "wimp" drill.*

IN WHICH WE LAY THE
SPEED ISSUE TO REST...

You've got your Macintosh Classic, Classic II, assorted PowerBooks, ci's, fx's and Quadras. And on the other side, your 80286s and 80386s in a variety of speeds: 16 Mhz., 20 Mhz, 33 Mhz, and so on.

Which is faster? This is a question reminiscent of "Is it closer to Chicago or by bus?" Still, we're happy to answer the question. Better yet, we'll let Banana6000 answer it, once and for all.

Subj: Speed   91-09-30 10:23:46 EST

From: Banana6000

Just to quell the rumors flying here, the Flight Sim Forum on CompuServe ran tests against a IIci and a 386/33 running the 4.0 versions of Flight Sim for the Mac and the PC. Each was running the same modes, same scenery. They reported that, although the Mac version was just slightly slower (and they reported it was barely noticeable), they also said the Mac had much better resolution for the scenery.

— from America OnLine, Games SIG. Copyright 1991, 92 © America Online.

A further comment stated that if Macintosh (digitized) sound was turned off, the Mac version ran about twice as fast the the version running on the 386/33 Mhz PC. So there.

HOW TO BUILD A WORLD

CHRIS CRAWFORD

Finally, an article with practical applications!

If you like this article—and you will—consider subscribing to The Journal of Computer Game Design, *where this first appeared. The* Journal *is a six-times-a-year newsletter full of fascinating and feisty stuff hosted by (and mostly written by) the best game designer of them all, Chris Crawford. It's good entertainment, and a revealing "insider" view of the complex and changing computer games industry.*

Mail your $30 check to: The Journal of Computer Game Design, *5251 Sierra Road, San Jose CA 95132.*

Global Dilemma (my title was *Guns & Butter*) was not one of my better games. It had some severe problems integrating economics with the military portion of the game. But it did contain a number of elements of which I am proud. One of these was the continent-generating algorithm. World-building routines have been part of a number of games: *Seven Cities of Gold, Starflight, Empire,* and others sported world builders. The basic task is simple to state: generate a unique terrain map from a random seed, insuring that the map contains interesting yet functional terrain. Achieving it, however, can be quite a challenge.

For *Guns & Butter*, I wanted to make a world builder that would go beyond current technology, a world builder that would support complex terrain types, yet look good and not concoct impossible terrain. In this article, I will describe the world builder that I designed.

Specifying a World

I began by determining that my world would consist of a single continent. My game did not need naval forces, and I thought it best to avoid the complication of maritime rules. Next, I defined the size of the rectangle into which the continent would fit. The continent itself would be composed of fundamental units called provinces. Each province would be an irregular region with a single city as provincial capital. Countries would be collections of provinces. Straight roads would connect adjacent provinces, but not all contiguous pairs of provinces would be connected by roads.

To lay down the continent, I simply laid down provincial capitals randomly. My random number generator randomly selected points in the available space, the only restriction being that no new point could be placed within 64 pixels of an already-existing provincial capital. This prevented overcrowding of provincial capitals. I laid down 64 provincial capitals. These were the skeleton of the nascent continent.

With the capitals in place, my next task was to form the provincial boundaries. The boundaries had to divide up the existing territory among the various provinces, and then assign nicely meandering boundaries. After all, provinces that looked like polygons would never do. I decided to tackle the problem in two steps: first, to assign polygons that divided the territory, then to "meanderize" the polygon sides.

Drawing the Polygons

The task of making a clean set of polygons out of a set of points is quite tricky. After I had solved the problem, I discovered that it is addressed in *Sedgewick Algorithms*, second edition, pp. 408-410, although his discussion is even more hand-waving than this essay.

The problem can be simplified by casting it into a different form. For the set of cities, create a set of spokes connecting the cities such that (1) all cities are connected by spokes; (2) no two spokes cross each other; (3) every pair of cities that could be connected with a spoke is connected with a spoke; and (4) the total length of all spokes is minimized. I'll show you how these spokes can be used to make provinces later. For now, I shall concentrate on building the spoke set. Consider the following diagram:

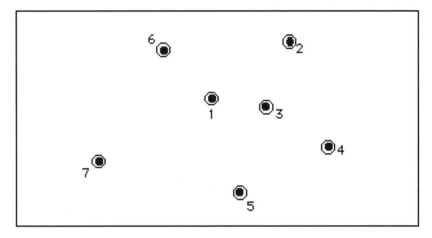

Figure 1. The Spoke Set

I shall create the spoke set for City 1. I first create a list of the nearest cities, ranked in order of their distance from City 1. In this case, the list has cities 3, 6, 2, 5, 4 and 7. Starting at the top of the list, I begin adding cities to the spoke set of the City 1, but two factors could exclude a city from the spoke set. In this case, City 4 is masked from inclusion by City 3. The spokes are too close together, and the subsequent border will be too seriously deformed. Therefore I must reject City 4. The obvious way to do this is to calculate spoke angles and look for spoke angles that are too close together. As it happens, the use of trigonometry in this calculation is prohibitively slow, so I used another, more complex, system that runs faster. This other system is too messy for me to explain here. It used analytic geometry to calculate whether any of a set of lines intersected.

Building a Province from Spokes

The result of all this calculating is a set of spokes for each city on the map. Those spokes break up the space of the continent into triangles. This is important, as quadrilaterals will cause this algorithm to fail. Note that condition (3) of the above set of requirements for spokes insures that all the shapes formed by the spokes are triangles. To form a province around a city, we create two sets of midpoints: the midpoints of the spokes themselves, and the midpoints of the triangles. We connect all these midpoints to make a province:

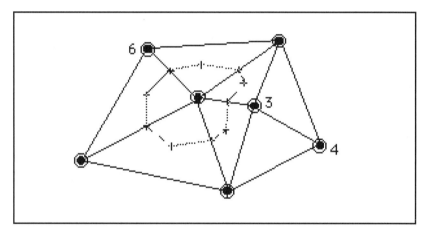

Figure 2. The Province

Randomizing the Province Boundaries

We now have a set of polygonal provinces. The borders are straight lines, which looks much too artificial. We need a reliable way to make those borders wiggle realistically. Moreover, there's a nasty restriction: we have to have the same wiggling on both sides of the border. That is, when we create each province's final shape, the zigs and zags of its border must match the corresponding zigs and zags of its neighbor's border. This, it turns out, is a major problem.

My solution to these requirements was to create a deviation table 1,024 elements long and stock it with random numbers between -7 and +7. The algorithm begins at one vertex of the polygon, and prepares to walk down the edge of the polygon. First, it selects the starting table index from the deviation table that it will use. This selection is based on the coordinates of the vertex and the direction (clockwise or counterclockwise) in which the polygon is being drawn. This guarantees that the same deviation table entries will be accessed, regardless of which side of the border is being drawn. This is what insures that we get matching borders for the two adjacent provinces. This trick also insures that different sections of the deviation table are used to draw different borders, so there will be no telltale pattern to the deviations.

The algorithm takes many small steps down the polygon edge towards the next vertex, at each step wiggling the border in the x and y dimensions by the amount given in the deviation table. The result of all this is a beautifully irregular province.

Adding Mountains, Forests, and Deserts

My final task was to add terrain features: mountain ranges, forests, and deserts. I decided that I wanted these terrain features to act as apparent blocks to roads connecting provinces. You will recall that all adjacent provinces are connected by spokes. Well, not all spokes became roads. Some spokes are left empty. The spaces created by these non-road spokes are the spaces that I wanted to fill with terrain features.

To define these terrain regions, my algorithm traces a complex polygon by laying down a right-handed path. It first grabs some non-road spoke. It then lays down an initial point one-quarter of the way down the non-road spoke.

If the spoke on its right is not a road spoke, it draws a line to the one-quarter point on that spoke. It continues this process until it encounters a road spoke. When that happens, it draws a line to the midpoint of the province polygon edge emanating from the road spoke. It continues drawing to the midpoint of the line connecting the city in the opposite province to the end of the province polygon edge that it had just bisected. The process described in this paragraph is iterated until the algorithm returns to its starting point.

The result is a polygonal region occupying the non-road areas between provinces. Depending on whether it is a forest, a mountain range, or a desert, I randomly scatter the appropriate icons inside the region. Although they are created in random order, they are drawn from top to bottom so that the base of one mountain or tree does not obscure the top of a lower one.

Results

A typical end result is shown in Figure 3. As you can see, the continent is quite pretty. It takes about five minutes to build this continent on a Mac Plus.

ક

— Copyright 1991, 1992 © Chris Crawford.

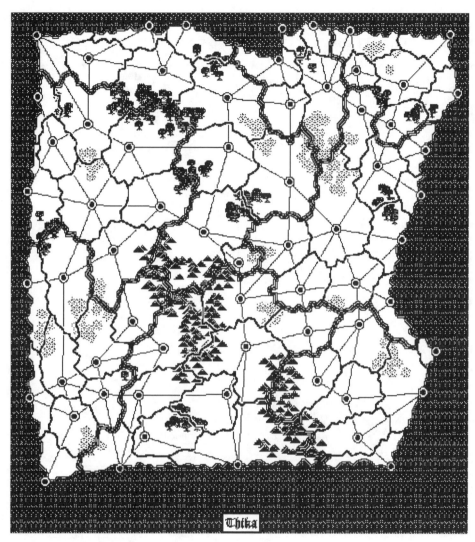

Figure 3. The Finished Continent

DIALING MACINTOSH

G ot a modem? Great! Don't have a modem? Get one!

The reasons are given below: 3,273 reasons in all; Macintosh bulletin boards of every stripe and kind. Unless you live in Ghana, there's probably at least one BBS that's only a local call away.

I love CompuServe, I love America Online, I love MCI electronic mail, but hey: most of these BBSs are free!

From: Dennis Runkle

To: *The Macintosh Reader* readers

Subject: Dialing Macintosh

Hello, MacCommunicator!

This is a listing of bulletin boards that have at least some portion dedicated to things Macintosh. I hope it provides new sources of information and electronic fellowship for the modem-endowed.

I started keeping the list sometime in 1985, soon after I discovered micros, Macs, modems, and electronic bulletin boards (necessarily in that order). I find the BBSs and message networks to be the best source of current information on just about anything relating to the silicon-based life-form in front of which so many of us spend so much bleary-eyed quality time.

Though I get some information from my own browsing online, much of the list results from feedback I've received from conscientious folk who believe in putting as much energy into the system as they receive. If you have more recent information on *any* Mac BBS in the list, or new boards to add, please notify me so I can pass the word. I post updates on Compuserve, MacComm DL9, and America Online.

Thanks,

Dennis Runkle

NOTE: PLEASE! PLEASE! get a message to me if you find out a listed board is no longer in operation. 'Tis unpleasant indeed for a new voice line owner to get carrier-wave crank calls at all hours of the night! I've purged most listings older than 1/1/89, based on not hearing anything more recent about the boards.

NOTE 2: Be gracious in your BBS visitations and respectful of the Sysop, who in most cases is donating hardware, software, a phone line, and mountains of time to provide a forum for communications.

BBS List (Macintosh orientation or subsection) — Version: 24
Version Date: 3/10/92
Date of last update: 2/24/92

- Sorted by phone number.

- Most of these are unverified first-hand, many may now be extinct.

- Dates refer to most recent mention I've seen on some other board.

- Times are LOCAL time zone for the BBS.

- 2400 baud usually means support for 300/1200 as well.

- HS denotes capability for high-speed transfers at 9600 baud or higher; where known, the type of high-speed protocol is noted in parentheses: (DS) dual standard, (v.32), or (HST).

- V = validation required.

- RedRyder Host (RRH) and Second Sight (SS), WWIV, Hermes, MacMansion, MacCitadel, Novalink, and MEBBS are Mac BBS programs; TBBS is IBM-based.

- TeleFinder and FirstClass are GUI-based BBSs; users generally download interface software on initial login.

- FidoNet boards are listed if they carry Mac-specific message bases; the individual board doesn't necessarily have a significant Mac file base.

- Sysop names listed with [Compuserve],<DELPHI>,{GEnie}, or /AOL/ IDs if known.

- This list was first posted to Compuserve MacComm DL9, and America Online.

- Entries which have not been verified since 1988 have been purged.

- Try communication settings of 8-N-1 as a default.

Please contact me if you know of corrections/updates/deletions/etc.

Dennis Runkle — Compuserve: [76174,374] AOL: /Drunkle/

InterNet: ag266@cleveland.Freenet.Edu

aa049@medina.Freenet.Edu

===

Note: Entries/updates which are based solely on Ed Edell's list of Red Ryder Host/Second Sight boards (from 6/90) are denoted by EE. Thanks Ed!

A portion of the current updates were based to some degree on info from: Mike Stark, Marc Ziegler, Wendy Marchuk, Steve Levinthal, Dave Slotter, Jerry Ronchi, Michael Scott, Phil Nickerson, Bill Stewart, John Gallaugher, Roger Lai, Rod Whitten, James Brost, Ron Weber, Robert Sawyer, Kevin Christy, Andrew Claxton, Paul White, Fritz Kass, and Rick Barrett.

Thanks for conscientious communications!

BBS Name	Phone	Date	Sysop	Comments
Sintel	0039-11-596274	2/14/92	Marco Civra	Italy; 2400 bd; NovaLink Pro; FidoNet 2:334/103
Prolink BBS	0039-382-27622	2/14/92	Massimo Senna [71531,32]	Italy; 2400 bd; NovaLink Pro; FidoNet 2:331/313
Eastern Telecom	0039-444-301687	2/14/92	Roberto Venditti	Italy; Hermes; 9600 HST; FidoNet 2:333/202
TeleMACo BBS	0039-51-341537	2/14/92	Cristiano Verondini	Italy; 9600 v32; Maximus 2.0; FidoNet 2:332/406
MLink/MacMusic	0039-59-599369	2/14/92	Stephen Head	Italy; 2400 bd; SS; FidoNet 2:332/105
Nezumii Land BBS	011-81-52-776-4922	3/21/91	Kazuhiko Nakano	2400 bd; Telefinder; Nagoya City, Japan (formerly listed as Nagoya Mouse Club)
Dhahran BBS	011-966-3-874-1355	2/28/90	Bill Strazdas	SS; 2400 bd; HS; Dhahran, Saudi Arabia; EE
Sydney A.U.G. BBS	02-498-7084	9/10/88	Bruce Stanley	Sydney, Australia
ClubMac RemoteMaccess BBS	02-73-1992	9/10/88	Jason Haines	Sydney, Australia
Integra TEx BBS	02-746-1109	9/11/88		Sydney, Australia
Apolloline BBS	02-869-8349	9/10/88	Richard Heppell	Sydney, Australia
Asian Express Net	03-5375-2852	11/18/90		2400 bd; HS (HST); FidoNet 6:730/10; Japan
MacContent BBS	03-848-2915	7/24/91	Paul Liu	Australia
Scottish Opus	041-880-7863	12/16/90		Glasgow; Opus 2:259/2.0
InterHuet BBS	055-557436	7/28/90		Voor XRS in Apeldoorn; FidoNet 2:512/29
Rhein-Main Macintosh BBS	06-101-41471	5/23/91	Duncan McNutt	2400 bd; FidoNet 2:243/100; Germany
Night Fantastic	06-254-7779	9/5/90		Canberra, Australia; FidoNet 3:620/249
AMDA-Link Mac BBS/Linz	0732-2468-9412	8/17/90		Linz, Austria; 2400 bd; FidoNet 2:31/41
MacNews	0733-232-446	5/31/89		SS; Italy
Oracle PC-Network TBBS	08-234-0791	10/17/90		FidoNet 3:680/804; Australia
Hackers' Retreat	08-266-2408	9/1/88		Opus 3:681/857; Windsor Gdns S.A.
Full Metal Straitjacket	08-272-2291	11/25/89	Alastair Rankine	Australia; 2400 bd; FidoNet 3:680/820; EchoMac gateway OZ/USA
New'Ave	081-633-274	5/31/89		SS; Italy
Publishing Shop!	091-261-5228	8/26/90		Newcastle upon Tyne; Opus
NJ MacLaw BBS	201-235-0121	3/7/92	Stuart Kurtzer	SS; 2400 bd; lawyer board, $150/annual fee
Digitbits	201-288-7269	3/7/92		2400 bd
Shadow Spawn BBS	201-293-7778	3/7/92	Charlie Teufert	FidoNet 1:269/203.0
EEE's BBS	201-340-3531	6/2/90	Ed Edell [74216,1312]	2400 bd; SS; HS (HST); maintains master list of SS/SS BBS's; FidoNet 1:107/563
Power Strip Mac BBS	201-348-0576	3/7/92		2400 bd; Hermes
Rock Pile	201-387-9232	3/7/92	Tom Heffernan	9600 HST/DS; Mansion; FidoNet 1:2605/158
Microcosm BBS	201-398-1133	3/7/92		2400 bd; 9600; FidoNet 1:269/202
Phantom of the Mac BBS	201-460-1673	11/12/90	Nick Matejko	2400 bd; HS; Hermes
CFONJ TBBS	201-486-2956	3/7/92		FidoNet 107/332; HS; 2 lines; SEE 908-486-2956
Mac Atlantic BBS	201-543-6950	11/12/90	Bill Trubeck	WWIV; 2400 bd; FidoNet 1:269/403
NITEMAER BBS	201-569-4074	11/12/90		2400 bd; Hermes

BBS Name	Phone	Date	Sysop	Comments
Macintosh BBS	201-666-2013	3/7/92	Robert J. Gallo, M.D. [75465,1411] {DR.GALLO}	SS; 2400 bd; 9600 HST/v.32; FidoNet 1:107/525; HS (v.32)
Electronic Pen BBS	201-767-6337	3/7/92	Maria Langer [70461,1663] /MariaL1/	9600 HST/DS; Mansion; FidoNet 1:2605/157; MacList 6:6001/9; Writers & Points SIGs
Finishing Technology Hotline	201-838-0113	3/7/92	Ted Mooney {E.MOONEY}	2400 bd; SS; PCB mfg. special interest BBS
RockBoard	201-857-8880	11/26/90	Adam Curry [73320,1524] /ADAMCURRY1/	music SIG; NovaLink; new number
Quick Facts	202-289-4112	2/1/89	Fred Stinson	2400 bd; SS; 9am-Noon SS,24hrs M-F; EE
Castle Anthrax	202-298-8151	1/15/91	Greg Humphreys	Hermes; Mac & IBM areas
Mac OnLine	202-547-0435	1/18/90	Marvin Miller /MicroChap/ {M.MILLER47}[76655,2646]	MacONLINE!; Hermes; MacONLINE! magazine; 2400 bd
Empire BBS	203-226-6694	11/12/90		2400 bd; Hermes
Sixth Sense BBS	203-371-7073	11/21/90	/IvanW1/	Mac/IBM/][GS; D&D; 2400 bd; Hermes
Elm Shore MUG BBS	203-458-2071	7/1/91	Karl Etter [76517,2772]	Hermes
Bit Bucket	203-569-8739	2/19/91		Hartford Mac Users Group (H.U.G.E.)
Pretend BBS	203-761-1469	11/12/90		2400 bd; Hermes
Wilton Woods OPUS	203-762-8481	8/21/90		2400 bd; HS (HST); Opus 1:141/250
Earth Network	203-763-3485	4/26/91	Dale Ulrich	2400; HS (HST); SS; FidoNet 1:142/500
Web	203-790-6612	7/19/90		FidoNet 1:141/735.0; 2400 bd
T.S.C.	203-854-9716	8/18/90		2400 bd; Opus 1:141/245
Greenwich High School Online	203-863-8866	11/12/90		2400 bd; Hermes
Headboard BBS	204-269-4343	6/25/90	James Waschuk, Sysop of Mac sub-board	2400 bd
AdventureLine	204-656-2996	11/12/90		2400 bd; HS (DS); Hermes
Speed of Light	205-262-3735	4/26/91	Daniel Brown	2400 bd; FidoNet 1:375/15; new number
SmorgasBoard	205-745-3989	12/14/90		2400 bd; HS (HST); FidoNet 1:3613/3
Lyceum	205-826-9205	6/18/91		2400 bd; FidoNet 1:3613/13
(TBD) BBS	205-882-2995	6/2/90	Tom Konantz {T.Konantz}	2400 bd; SS; survey validation; $24/annual for full access; EE
Lerxstwood Mall	206-232-7426	9/7/90	/BubbaSmith/	2400 bd; Hermes; HST line -7556
Mac-A-Mania Nut	206-242-8028	11/29/90		2400 bd; HS (HST); FidoNet 1:343/75
Bumbershoot BBS	206-282-3065	7/15/90	Tam Keltner	2400 bd; HS; SS; FidoNet 1:343/43; new number
Slumberland	206-283-6771	9/10/91	Wendi Dunlap aka Little Nemo [76702,1251]	MacCitadel; multi-computer areas; 2400 bd
Abraxas Information	206-323-7578	11/12/90		[10pm-8am PST]; 2400 bd; Hermes
MAChine IE	206-329-0304	2/1/92		FidoNet 1:343/83
Port Angeles/ Evergreen Micro Network	206-452-2012	11/12/90	Lance Rasmussen /Lance EMCN/	SS; 2400 bd; FidoNet 1:354/1; HS (DS)
KTOL Radio Point BBS	206-459-4609	11/1/89		2400 bd; FidoNet 1:350/11
Beyond BBS	206-475-0402	7/23/90	/Regulus3/	2400 bd; Hermes
Mac Venture	206-487-2823	2/25/89		
Mac Cavern	206-525-5194	2/25/89		
Uneasy Alliance	206-562-1223	11/12/90		2400 bd; Hermes
dBBS	206-624-8783	1/25/91	Dave Schnuckel	Seattle Downtown Business User Group; Novalink; $35 first year, $25/yr sustaining

BBS Name	Phone	Date	Sysop	Comments
Mac Castle	206-630-4728	2/25/89		
SeaSoftNet	206-637-2398	9/10/90		Fido 1:343/8.9; new number; 2400 bd
Pac/Mac	206-641-6767	5/31/91		HS (DS) node; Hermes; FidoNet 1:343/91; see also 206-643-4826
Library	206-641-7978	1/30/89	The Flying Kiwi	TBBS; Mac section; 2400 bd; 5 lines
Pac/Mac	206-643-4826	5/31/91		2400 bd; Hermes; FidoNet 1:343/91; see 206-641-6767 (HST node)
Sea/Mac	206-725-6629	7/2/91	Jim Creighton	2400 bd; HS (HST); FidoNet 343/31; Mansion BBS
MAChine BBS	206-726-1484	11/12/90		2400 bd; Hermes; 2 nodes
Homework Hotline	206-859-7271	1/25/91	Bob Horlick, Derry Lyons	SS; education orientation
Bunny Board	206-863-8662	12/19/90		2400 bd; Hermes; FidoNet 1:138/134
Crystal Cavern	206-883-1383	8/28/90		2400 bd; FidoNet 1:343/105
Mac Exchange	206-889-9802	6/2/90	Tom Fitzsimmons	FidoNet 343/49; 2400 bd; HS (HST)
Basic Training BBS	206-964-4149	11/22/90	Sean Fuery /Sean Fuery/	Hermes; 2400 bd; FidoNet 1:138/140
ICON-NET SDMac/EuroGate Mac	207-725-8533	8/1/89		Opus 1:132/206
Lyons Den	207-799-2374	9/24/89	Henry Lyons	2400 bd; EE
JJHS-BBS	208-455-3312	4/28/90	Jim Smithers, Mike Hoffman, Andrew Gerber	2400 bd; HS (HST); Jefferson Jr. High; SS; EE
MacStudio California	209-333-8143	7/29/89	Christopher Watson, Cecil Ramirez	2400 bd; SS; annual $25 fee; EE
Fresno Connection	209-432-9778	11/12/90		2400 bd; Hermes
U.I.E. Communications	209-529-1141	4/15/90		2400 bd; FidoNet 1:208/106; WWIV
Ellipsis BBS	209-575-1411	5/11/90		Hermes; 2400 bd; FidoNet 1:208/107
MMUG BBS	209-825-8537	10/16/91	Don Leister	Hermes; 2400 bd
Dorsai Diplomatic Mission	212-431-1944	12/2/91		Usenet link
Frontal Lobe	212-439-6126	12/12/91	Tim Degraye	2400 bd; HS (HST); FidoNet 1:107/747
Metro Area MUG	212-597-9083	12/2/91	Frank M. Ventura	2400 bd; HS (HST); SS; FidoNet 1:278/705
NYMUG BBS	212-645-9484	12/2/91	Darryl Peck [71131,1760]	2400 bd; SS
Sappho's Exchange	212-697-3713	12/10/91		2400 bd; SS; women only; voice validation req.
Apple Sauce	212-721-4122	12/12/91		2400 bd; Apple II & MAC
Apl Pi	212-753-0888	2/1/88		Fido 107/103; 2400 bd
Links_II Midi_Inn	212-877-7703	11/29/89	Billy Arnell	FidoNet 1:107/711; multi-user; TBBS; MIDI users; members only
Jeff's BBS	212-982-4444	12/12/91		
Glassell Park BBS	213-254-4133	2/24/92	Pete Johnson [74035,466]	2400 bd; SS; HS; V; music section; FidoNet 1:102/863; $24/yr for full DL access
Glassell Park BBS	213-254-4852	11/10/91		FirstClass
Olympus II	213-275-6975	12/15/90	Frank Price [74156,1307]	Hermes support board; 2400 bd; HS (v.32)
Manhattan Transfer	213-372-4800	8/4/90	Michael Scott	2400; HS (HST); FidoNet 1:102/135; SS
Kirk's BBS	213-376-2150	8/2/90	Kirk Crawford	2400 bd; 7am-midnight PDT; SS; FidoNet 1:102/132
Legendary Pirates BBS	213-379-2080	11/12/90		2400 bd; Hermes
MacAttack	213-414-2009	11/12/90		Hermes
RADIO FREE FREZBURG	213-432-4139	11/12/90		2400 bd; Hermes
Mac-HACers	213-549-9640	7/27/90	Bud Grove	2400 bd; HS (HST); SS; V; FidoNet 1:102/141; Hughes Aircraft BBS, some public sections

BBS Name	Phone	Date	Sysop	Comments
LAMG BBS	213-559-6227	1/29/91	Reed Hutchinson /MacReed/	2400 bd; HS (HST/v.32); TBBS multiline; V; Los Angeles Mac Group membership required $25/yr
Big-Mac Attack BBS	213-791-7060	11/12/90		2400 bd; Hermes
Digital Dungeon	213-820-4320	9/4/91	Glen Heinz	MacCitadel BBS SW
Nibbler's Node	213-936-6923	11/12/90		2400 bd; HS; Hermes
Chrysalis	214-349-9397	2/22/92	Garry Grosse	2400 bd; 4 lines; FidoNet 124/4214
MacExchange	214-394-9324	2/22/92		2400 bd; HS (HST DS); FidoNet 1:124/1009; SS
Mac Shack	214-644-4781	2/22/92	Charles E. Taylor	2400 bd; 9600 bd DS; SS
MACRO Mouse	214-739-0645	2/22/92	Bob Winningham	2400 bd; HS (HST); SS
Garden State Macintosh	215-222-2743	5/27/89		2400 bd; HS; WWIV
SATALINK	215-364-3324	8/4/90		2400 bd; FidoNet 1:273/203
PennMUG BBS	215-387-8095	12/9/91		2400 bd; Hermes; Node 2; see also -9684
PennMUG	215-387-9684	12/9/91		Node 1; see also -8095
HyperCity(tm) BBS	215-440-7558	6/19/89	Mayor Klaus	SS; EE
Bob's Mac	215-446-7670	9/14/90	Bob Ferrill	2400 bd; SS; FidoNet 1:273/402; $10 one-time fee for level 2 access
Illusions BBS	215-584-4756	11/10/91		FirstClass
Typesetters' BBS	215-626-4812	1/24/89		for typographers and type professionals; Mac & IBM
StarLine	215-635-2341	4/26/91	J Ehrlich /JEhrlich/	2400 bd; HS (v.32, MNP-5); FidoNet 1:273/922; NovaLink Pro
Outer Limits BBS	215-638-7391	9/4/90		2400 bd; FidoNet 1:273/217
Computer Paradise	215-657-5427	8/27/89		2400 bd; WWIV
Turbo-386	215-745-9774	11/11/90		2400 bd; HS (HST/DS); FidoNet 1:273/906.1
Drexel University Library	215-895-1698	5/27/89	Tim LaBorie	SS
DragonKeep IV	215-895-2579	12/9/91	Dave Slotter	9600 bd; SS; Drexel U, World's First Mac Group
Power Down Inn	215-943-9624	7/29/89	John Grabowski	SS; EE
Appleholic's BBS	216-273-1340	2/24/92	Bob Abbott	2400 bd; FidoNet 1:157/511; aka Buzzard Board
Cleveland FreeNet	216-368-3888	2/24/92	multi-SIG	2400 bd; multi-line; message boards & information; CWRU sponsored; link to InterNet; Usenet conferences; part of NPTN
Steel Valley BBS	216-545-0093	1/13/89		Opus 1:237/505; 2400 bd; HS
Hal's BBS	216-587-3435	12/24/90	Tom Huff	online games
Medina County FreeNet	216-723-6732	2/24/92	multi-SIG	2400 bd; multi-line; msg boards & info; community sponsored; alt ph. 225-6732, 335-6732; Internet access; part of NPTN
Monsterous Mac	216-752-4921	2/7/91	Carlin Wiegner	SS; 2400 bd; HS; fee required after trial; alt ph. 216-752-4925
Monsterous Mac	216-752-4925	2/7/91	Carlin Wiegner	SS; 2400 bd; fee required after trial; alt ph. 216-752-4921
NEO Apple Corps	216-942-3389	9/3/90		2400 bd; Mac section; Fido 157/700; NEO Apple Corps members only

BBS Name	Phone	Date	Sysop	Comments
Frayed Ends of Sanity II	216-943-2788	5/23/90	Adam Purcell	3pm-8amM-F,24hrsSS; Hermes
Avalon (CUMUG)	217-384-3128	9/12/90	Russ Jacobson	2400 bd; FidoNet 1:233/14; SS
Friendship Inn	217-443-1860	8/27/89		2400 bd; HS (v.32); FidoNet 1:233/6
Information Exchange	217-875-7114	5/2/90	Robert Williams [76174,1110]	SS; EE; Central IL Automated Message System
RCN	219-237-0651	11/1/89		4-Lines; 2400 bd; FidoNet 1:227/2
MCN 1	219-282-1054	11/01/90		2400 bd; multi-line; FidoNet 1:227/2
NDG Technical Forum	301-345-2098	10/17/90	Bob Pulgino	4th Dimension SIG
Dog's Dwelling	301-384-5847	8/26/90	E. Kasic	Mac & IBM; 2400 bd; HS (v.32); Hermes
AIR Net	301-467-7814	10/10/91	Johns Hopkins [71477,507]	discussion SIGs; Johns Hopkins area
Eastern Mac Exclusive	301-471-4263	5/17/90		MacCitadel
CRABBS	301-553-6929	2/1/92	Barry Connor, Bill Arndt	2400 bd; SS; FidoNet 1:261/1053; Annapolis Apple Slice UG
John's BBS	301-566-1336	8/27/90		FidoNet 50:5301/1083, 1:261/1083
Capt Peg's	301-570-4590	11/25/90	/Zoso G/	2400 bd; Hermes
MacCity BBS	301-599-9116	11/12/90		2400 bd; Hermes
MacSachel Printing	301-649-7019	11/12/90		imagesetting svc bureau; 2400 bd; Hermes
Chronic Town	301-681-5579	2/8/90	I. Soberoff	2400 bd; messaging board
BlackDog BBS	301-730-3264	7/23/90	/BusyBD/	Mac/Amiga/IBM; 2400 bd; Hermes
Mouse Event	301-747-7820	3/10/90	Ed Perrine, Tim Winders [70711,16]	2400 bd; HS; WWIV; new phone number ??
Nut House	301-764-6889	11/12/90		2400 bd; HS (HST); Hermes
Divinity II	301-854-3680	2/27/90	/SeanM12/	2400 bd; HS
FireStation BBS	301-866-8613	8/10/90		2400 bd; FidoNet 1:261/1044
Yucca's Domain BBS	301-869-1365	1/25/89	Bruce Clark, Lao Saal, Justin Hersh	Mac & IBM
Twilight Clone BBS	301-946-8677	9/9/90	Paul Heller	2400 bd; RBBS; FidoNet 109/421; 8 lines (1 HS); $25/yr dues; new number
Hitchhiker's BBS	301-992-6839	9/12/90	Bart /EMSumner/	2400 bd; HS (DS)
Double Nut BBS	301-997-7204	10/1/90		2400 bd; FidoNet 261/627
Dragon's Lair	302-738-0345	9/22/91	John Morgan [70372,152]	
Christian Connection II BBS	303-352-5013	10/05/90		2400 bd; FidoNet 8:77/23
Fort Mac	303-361-6965	5/12/90	Greg Shaw	2400 bd; SS; HS; FidoNet 1:104/617
MacLeisure	303-444-5175	2/15/91	Paul Echternacht	2400 bd; SS; V
HappyLand BBS	303-447-3934	11/8/91		HS
On-Line Consulting BBS	303-449-5251	1/13/89		Opus 1:104/45; 2400 bd
Dream Park	303-530-2571	7/9/89	Paul Meyer	2400 bd; SS; EE; mostly 24 hrs
Boulder Mac Maniacs	303-530-9544	1/25/91	Ed Fenner	Fido 1:104/49; 2400 bd; $25/yr local users, $15/yr LD users
Mile High Mac Meet BBS	303-758-9159	2/15/91	Jon Taylor	2400 bd; HS v.32; $15/yr fee; Hermes
MAGIC	303-791-8732	2/15/91	Steve Sande	2400 bd; HS v.32; Hermes; Mac & GS Info center
Chatfield Armory BBS	303-972-9023	12/21/90		2400 bd; FidoNet 1:104/602.0
Check-In	305-232-0393	7/9/89	Dave Game	2400 bd; SS; EE; FidoNet 7:43/11; 2 lines
Ganas BBS	305-235-6247	10/15/89	Mauricio Ardila [71271,3041]	
Sunshine Online Service	305-378-6828	6/2/91	Louis Oaken	2400 bd; FidoNet 1:135/92; MacList 6:6032/1

BBS Name	Phone	Date	Sysop	Comments
Gameport BBS	305-386-9626	6/4/90	Chris Alvarez	game section
MACabre BBS	305-673-4083	4/20/90		2400 bd
NatMAC BBS	305-748-7993	11/12/90		2400 bd; Hermes
MACATTACK! BBS	305-753-4605	11/12/90		2400 bd; Hermes; Mac and PC areas
Fluid Power	305-763-7743	9/25/90		2400 bd; FidoNet 1:369/4
Regina Fido (V12)	306-777-4493	9/7/90		2400 bd; FidoNet 1:140/20
WYNET - Wyoming Dept of Education	307-777-6200	4/28/90	Steven King	2400 bd; SS; EE
Genealogy BBS	309-692-0786	11/12/90	Robert Wilton [72447,1475]	Hermes; sponsored by Central IL Computerized Genealogists
MouseCapades	309-755-8274	4/28/90	Bob Young	2400 bd; V; SS; EE
Spider BBS	31-15-158-300	10/1/90	Roel Wigboldus [73040,1720]	Netherlands; Telefinder
MacBBS	31-71-318-678	8/21/90		FidoNet 2:512/114
Manhattan Transfer	310-372-4800	12/30/91	Michael Scott [72435,327]	SS; FidoNet 102/135
Northwestern	312-491-3892	9/5/89		
Convolutions	312-583-7679	8/7/90	Rick Duff	2400 bd
Inferno	312-752-3674	10/17/89	James Powell	WWIV; online Tarot, games; 2400
MACaritaville	312-766-2636	9/5/89		
20/20 TBBS MultiLine	312-769-2020	7/29/90		2400 bd; FidoNet 1:115/769
Data-Mania	312-923-1932	8/30/90		2400 bd; BBSX (Atari)
Galapagos	312-943-3498	11/12/90	Sal Bernstein	Hermes; 2400 bd; HS (DS)
MCMUG/MacMania BBS	313-278-8578	9/15/91	W. Marchuck	Free; 2400 bd; 24hrs.; SS; 9000 files; FidoNet 1:120/282
Mikie's BBS	313-477-9652	12/8/91	Mike Savu [75206,3305]	9600 bd; Apple & IBM
MaxMac BBS	313-572-9536	9/26/90	/MaxMac/	2400 bd; NovaLink Pro
Cheswick's RBBS	314-349-5344	7/16/90		2400 bd; FidoNet 1:100/375
Odyssey	314-821-4957	6/3/91		2400 bd; FidoNet 1:100/415
Mac Paradise	314-846-8929	10/2/90		9600 HST line; 2400 bd access line -8982; Hermes
Mac Paradise	314-846-8982	10/2/90		2400 bd; 9600 HST line -8929; Hermes
Control Panel	314-867-3939	1/13/89		2400 bd; Opus 1:100/545; HS
Show Me More Stacks BBS	314-997-6912	10/2/90		2400 bd; Opus 1:100/255
Nightshift	315-457-3144	8/1/89		Mac section
Digital Visions	315-492-8765	2/25/91	Tom Loomis	2400 bd
Shockwave Rider	315-673-4894	12/1/90	Eric Larson	2400 bd; Fido 260/330; HS (DS); QuickBBS; well-run BBS, active sysop
Enterprise BBS	315-682-4043	8/1/89		FidoNet 1:260/332
Bird's Nest	315-685-3367	2/4/90	Tom Dodson	2400 bd; SS; V; FidoNet 260/337; EE
Galaxia!	315-695-4436	4/26/91	Chris Zazzara	TSAUG MUG; Mac section; 2400 bd; FidoNet 1:260/328
X-tronic Connections	316-793-8819	11/6/90	/RolandH/	2400 bd; Adult BBS; Hermes
B-Line BBS	317-288-5569	2/1/92		FidoNet 1:231/440
MacConnections BBS	317-290-1762	9/7/91	Barry Skidmore [70216,27]	SS
Falx Cerebri QBBS	317-290-9070	8/28/90		2400 bd; FidoNet 1:231/80
Some Place BBS	317-353-9981	8/1/89		FidoNet 1:231/120

BBS Name	Phone	Date	Sysop	Comments
IndyServe QBBS	317-849-4007	12/05/90		2400 bd; HS (HST); FidoNet 1:231/250
Circle City Mac	317-924-2784	10/20/89	David Herren	2400 bd; SS; EE; down 4-5 am; FidoNet 1:231/220
CajuNet Connection	318-235-3207	11/1/89		2400 bd; Opus 1:396/201
Swampland (Node 2)	318-238-0251	9/26/90		Novalink Pro
Swampland (Node 1)	318-239-4536	9/26/90		Novalink Pro
Golddust Plantation	318-424-0375	6/10/91	Ralph Wade Phillips	2400 bd; FidoNet 1:380/20
Lawboard	318-981-3373	9/10/89	Mike Durand	2400 bd; SS; EE
Mouse College	319-365-4775	4/28/91	Bob Cramer	2400 bd; Hermes; FidoNet 1:283/119
DarkSide (Antwerp, Belgium)	32-3-235-5144	4/19/90		FidoNet 2:295/27.2707
Bomb Shelter	358-084-4970	11/12/90		Finland; 2400 bd; HS; Hermes
Lands of Adventure	401-351-1465	5/27/89		Nova Link BBS; alt number 351-5211
Lands of Adventure	401-351-5211	5/27/89		Nova Link BBS; alt number 351-1465
MacNet Omaha	402-289-2899	2/1/92	Jim Redelfs	2400 bd; Hermes; FidoNet 1:285/14; BBS for Omaha MUG (OMUG)
Wind Dragon	402-291-8053	9/9/90		2400; FidoNet 1:285/637.0
Moon Base Alpha 1999	402-476-3886	11/12/90		2400 bd; HS; Hermes
TKG BBS	402-895-7419	11/24/90	Terry K. Gutierrez [72446,2566]	2400 bd; SS
Student Exchange	403-228-9525	6/22/91		2400 bd; HS (HST); FidoNet 1:134/49; Calgary
SunValley/MicroLink	403-246-4504	8/26/90		2400 bd; HS (HST); FidoNet 1:129/34; MicroLink 8:7500/16.1
Mac_Xen_Link	403-274-4503	11/12/90		2400 bd; HS; Hermes
Calgary's Resource...	403-277-4658	12/29/90		ST/IBM/Mac areas; HS (HST/DS/v.42bis); 2400 bd; FidoNet 8:7500/11
MacLORE BBS	403-284-1059	11/3/90	/MoonStream/	FidoNet 1:134/54; alt. ph. -2465
MacLORE BBS	403-284-2465	11/3/90	/MoonStream/	FidoNet 1:134/54; alt. ph. -1059
Calgary Online	403-284-9274	12/29/90		some free areas, fee for full access
Nimbus BBS	403-433-7540	11/12/90		2400 bd; Hermes
M.O.U.S.E. BBS	403-436-4566	3/16/91		2400 bd; Telefinder
TimeWarp Tavern II	403-475-1444	8/6/90	Sean Peterson [76526,374]	SS; 2400 bd
Arctic Online	403-983-2123	12/10/89	Stephen Bedingfield	2400 bd; SS; EE
Swizzle Stick	404-250-4366	11/27/89		FidoNet 1:133/11; 2400
Infamous Basement BBS	404-354-0560	8/29/91	Robert Sawyer [70253,1076] /RobertS402/	Hermes; 2400 bd; Mac & IBM
Atlanta MUG BBS	404-447-0845	12/24/91	Robert Story, Ron Patterson, Scott Anderson, Bill Stewart	2400 bd
USS Republic	404-664-1075	8/13/90		2400 bd; HS (HST); FidoNet 1:133/1371
Shoe's CPU	404-882-5445	9/9/90		2400 bd; HS (HST); FidoNet 1:3621/425.0
Plasmatic Info Exchange	405-624-0006	1/13/89		2400 bd; Opus 1:19/41; HS
Fort Knox Fido	405-843-3545	12/26/90		2400 bd; HS (HST); FidoNet 1:147/49.0
Cybernation	405-943-3178	9/1/89		FidoNet 1:147/54
BIKENET	406-549-1318	9/8/90		2400 bd; Opus 1:346/5
Pyrotechnic's	407-254-3655	11/29/90		2400 bd; FidoNet 1:3610/55
Space Coast BBS	407-269-2169	2/1/92		FidoNet 1:374/3

BBS Name	Phone	Date	Sysop	Comments
Data Exchange	407-297-8043	11/1/89		2400 bd; FidoNet 1:363/31
NCC-1701	407-380-1701	2/1/92		FidoNet 1:363/1701; 9600 bd HST
Cornucopia TBBS	407-645-4929	11/02/90		FidoNet 1:363/18; 2400 bd
Abacus Information Center	407-774-3355	9/9/90		OPUS 1:363/7
File Cabinet	408-224-6004	2/3/92		9600 bd; IBM/Mac files
Backboard	408-226-3780	1/25/92		2400 bd; SS; HS
Mac Outpost	408-245-0207	8/1/91	Andy /Andy s12/	2400 bd; HS (DS); Hermes
FirstClassKitten	408-245-9209	1/29/92		FirstClass BBS; 9600; 2 lines
Crumal's Dimension	408-246-7854	1/23/92	Great Crumal	2400 bd; HS (HST); FidoNet 1:204/557; SS
Ringworld	408-247-3986	8/1/91	Ringworld Engineer	2400 bd; Play-by-Mail gaming, Society for Creative Anachronism
MacDaze-II	408-252-6801	2/3/92	Bob Murrow	2400 bd; FirstClass BBS; 4 lines; HS (v.32/v.42 DS/HST); SS; FidoNet 204/33; fee for extended time/access
Digikron	408-253-1309	2/3/92	Douglas Thom, Rudy Rugebregt	2400 bd; HS (v.32); SS
MacDaze	408-253-3926	8/1/91	Bob Murrow	2400 bd; HS (HST); SS; FidoNet 1:143/33, Eggnet 99:9403/33; messages only, no files; formerly Phoenix 2 BBS
Klub KAT	408-261-1606	1/14/92		2400 bd; FirstClass BBS
A32 User's Group	408-263-0299	1/22/92	John Griffen	2400 bd; SS; $35/yr fee
Positive Image	408-270-8916	1/27/92		2400 bd; Mac/IBM files
South Bay Soaring Society BBS	408-281-4895	8/1/91		R/C Sailplanes; 2400 bd; Hermes
Inferno	408-395-5378	7/15/91		25 lines; 2400 bd; HS; alt. ph. 395-3721, 289-1431; also entry in 415 area code
Portal BBS	408-725-0561	7/15/91		2400 bd; fee-based service ($10/month); UUCP, ARPA, Bitnet access; Telenet node access
AllNet	408-736-2607	1/29/92	Alfred John Frugoli	2400 bd; FidoNet 1:143/205; SS; FirstClass BBS; 9600; formerly Sphynx BBS
Sunnyvale Fido Connection	408-738-1119	1/22/92	Mike Steiner	2400 bd; messages only, no files; FidoNet 1:143/207.2
THE MouseHole	408-738-5791	2/24/92	Larry Nedry [71566,650]	2400 bd; Galacticomm BBS; programming/tech info; MacTutor magazine code disk downloads; see also -5793 (19200 PEP), -6699 (9600 v.32 only)
THE MouseHole	408-738-5793	2/24/92	Larry Nedry [71566,650]	19200 bd PEP; Galacticomm BBS; programming/tech info; MacTutor magazine code disk downloads available for fee; see also -5791 (2400 bd), -6699 (9600 v.32 only)
THE MouseHole	408-738-6699	2/24/92	Larry Nedry [71566,650]	9600 bd v.32 only, MNP 1-5; Galacticomm BBS; programming/tech info; MacTutor magazine code disk downloads available for fee; see also -5791 (2400 bd), -5793 (19200 PEP)
SuperMac BBS	408-773-4500	7/15/91	Dina Sakahara, Fabian Ramirez	2400 bd; HS; SS; tech-support for SuperMac products

BBS Name	Phone	Date	Sysop	Comments
MacScience! BBS	408-866-4933	7/15/91	Ray Terry N6PHJ	2400 bd; HS (HST); SS; FidoNet 1:143/36
Symantec BBS	408-973-9598	7/15/91		2400 bd; Symantec product support
Major League BBS	408-997-8591	2/1/92		2400 bd; HS; IBM & Mac areas; FidoNet 1:143/313
Johns Hopkins U BBS (JHUBBS)	410-467-7814	11/24/91		Hermes; online games
Whitegold!	410-922-7569	10/22/91	Timothy Waire	TeleFinder; $50/yr for 120 min/day; see also -7743
Whitegold!	410-922-7743	10/22/91	Timothy Waire	TeleFinder; demo login GUEST, pswd GUEST; $50/yr for 120 min/day; see also -7569
Pgh Computer Connection	412-765-0532	11/23/91		2400 bd; FidoNet 1:129/29.0
Pioneer Valley PCUG1	413-256-1037	4/26/91	Mort Sternheim	2400 bd; FidoNet 1:321/109
Baudville	413-562-1870	4/26/91	George Brooks	2400 bd; HS (HST); FidoNet 1:321/304; SS
SpaceMet South	413-592-0942	8/1/89		FidoNet 1:321/302
Moonrise	413-665-1158	2/1/92		FidoNet 1:321/117
Macintosh Only BBS!	413-746-3202	4/26/91	Matthew Jongh	2400 bd; TBBS (running on Mac II under SoftPC); FidoNet 1:321/307
SpaceMet North	413-772-2038	11/1/89		2400 bd; Opus 1:321/151
Digital Bimmers	414-264-6789	1/25/91	Jenni Morgan	WWIV
PC-Express	414-327-5300	11/27/89		FidoNet 154/200; 2400 bd; multi-line; HS
Radio Free Milwaukee	414-352-6176	8/22/90		2400 bd; HS (HST); FidoNet 1:154/414
Forecast Office	414-541-9426	7/13/90		2400 bd; FidoNet 1:154/970; HS (HST)
Milwaukee Metro Mac BBS	414-682-7427	2/1/89	Steve Weinert	2400 bd; FidoNet 154/154; HS
Jasmine Support BBS	415-285-6862	3/27/90	Scott Gaidano [76117,3055]	
221BBS	415-329-1703	5/1/89	Brian & Charlotte Erickson	2400 bd; SS; EE
Draco Redux Apple Info System	415-342-0511	10/3/91	Mac SysOp:Rod Whitten /AFA Game/	2400 bd; Hermes; Mac,] [,] [GS; alt. ph. 415-342-3661
Draco Redux Apple Info System	415-342-3661	11/15/90	Mac SysOp:Rod Whitten	2400 bd; Hermes; Mac,] [,] [GS; alt. ph. 415-342-0511
Mac F-X BBS	415-349-7322	8/3/90	/Waddy/	2400 bd; Hermes
Nwonknu HQ	415-365-4194	7/18/90		2400 bd; HS (HST); FidoNet 8:914/701.0
Leviathan RBBS	415-387-5117	12/24/90		2400 bd; FidoNet 1:10/8, 8:914/204
Records Department TBBS	415-426-0470	9/11/90	Bill McCauley	FidoNet 1:161/42; 2400 bd
Leading Technology	415-462-3347	8/14/90		2400 bd; FidoNet 1:161/91
MacCircles	415-484-4412	12/21/90	Patricia O'Connor	SS; 2400 bd; Mac XL; FidoNet 1:161/555
Inferno	415-490-1170	11/23/90		25 lines; 2400 bd; HS; alt. ph. 856-8746; also entry in 408 area code
Twelfth Night (or, what you will)	415-567-0217	3/16/90	Jono Smith [74676,1625] /JonoS/	2400 bd; HS (HST); Hermes; FidoNet 1:125/17, 8:914/214
Dimension X	415-574-4544	11/12/90		2400 bd; Hermes; NUP = Juillet, Awesome
Dream Machine	415-581-3019	1/25/91		2400 bd
Macademe/Emma	415-681-9594	6/1/91	William Sommers	2400 bd; Opus 1:125/222
Billboard	415-686-4338	2/1/89	Bill Maginnis	SS; 8am-8pm; V; EE
Stanford MUG BBS	415-723-7685	1/25/91	Greg Whitten	2400 bd; SS; FidoNet 1:204/445; EE; music, DTP, Mac II groups; Delphi,Usenet & Info-Mac digests

BBS Name	Phone	Date	Sysop	Comments
MacWARP BBS	415-751-8396	11/12/90		2400 bd; HS (HST); Hermes
TOPS Support BBS	415-769-8874	3/1/90		2400 bd
Bay	415-775-2384	7/13/90		FWB support (HD Util); 2400 bd; HS (v.32)
MACINFO BBS	415-795-8862	6/1/91	Norm Goodger [70167,2316]	2400 bd; HS (HST); V; SS; FidoNet 1:204/555
Harry's BBS	415-824-7809	9/11/89	Harry Chesley	2400
Berkeley Mac Users Group	415-849-1795	4/26/91	Raines Cohen <BMUG>	2400 bd; TBBS; limited access for non-BMUG; voice line 415-849-4357; FidoNet 1:161/444; HS; new number ?
Psychic Link BBS	415-849-3539	8/7/90	/Arcana/	Mac/Amiga; 2400 bd; Hermes
Coconino County BBS	415-861-8290	2/1/92		FidoNet 1:125/28
Fog City	415-863-9697	9/9/90		2400 bd; FidoNet 125/100; Gay Mac Users Group
HayMUG BBS	415-881-2629	2/12/89	Nick Barcet [71071,3036]	Cal State U Hayward MUG
MicroLINK	415-898-1696	4/28/90	Jeff Baudin	2400 bd; SS; EE
Macintosh Tribune	415-923-1235	8/1/89	Vern Keenan MacWEEK [76077,1351]	2400 bd; Fido 125/444; new name
Thought Plane	415-932-8293	11/25/90	/LeGarre/	NovaLink; temporarily down
OneNet BBS	415-948-1349	2/3/92		FirstClass BBS; 9600; 4 lines
Sound Mind	415-965-1525	1/29/92		9600 bd
Zone BBS	415-965-3556	8/27/89	Ron Schultz	2400 bd; WWIV; FidoNet 1:143/202
EGS/Philo	416-286-6191	09/15/90		2400 bd; FidoNet 1:250/416
Magic BBS	416-288-1767	11/7/91		FirstClass BBS; 2400 bd; 5 lines
Daily Planet BBS	416-336-6159	4/14/90	Dennis Richards [73500,657]	V; annual fee
Club Mac	416-462-2922	2/23/91		2400 bd; SS; Club Mac members only
Logic Now	416-487-9771	2/23/91		receives feed from Argentic
Emergency Ward	416-499-7475	2/23/91		2400 bd; Hermes; V
Apple Techlink	416-513-5544	2/23/91		Apple Canada tech support
InfoSource	416-574-1313	11/1/89		2400 bd; Fido 148/264; HS; 8 LINES,10 LASERS
Argentic	416-593-4025	2/16/91		2400 bd; SS; formerly Real Mac, Eh?
Arkon InfoSystem	416-593-7460	2/23/91	Michael Alexander, Ernie Reimer, Jeff Avery	2400 bd; SS; Mac & Apple //; EE
SoftArc	416-609-2250	11/10/91		FirstClass support BBS
Towne Crier	416-646-0263	8/1/89		FidoNet 1:250/11; Wildcat
Far Jewel BBS	416-690-2464	2/19/91	Robert Radford [76354,535]	2400 bd; HS (HST); SS; V
Land of Oz	416-767-9385	2/23/91		2400 bd; Hermes; V
LOGIC Information Systems	416-922-1626	4/1/90	Geoff Ghaerty, Blari Angus, Jim Low	2400 bd; SS; $45/yr; EE
TriStar BBS	417-887-3282	8/9/90	Ned Wilkinson [71477,322]	HS (Telebit); 2400 bd; various computer SIGs
Bab-O-Manie	418-663-4312	6/27/91		2400 bd; HS (DS); FidoNet 1:240/99
Mac's R Us BBS	419-535-8722	2/1/92		FidoNet 1:234/32
POST Office BBS	419-536-8967	11/12/90		2400 bd; Hermes
College Crier	419-537-4110	7/9/89	Les Elsie	EE; SS
Zephyr BBS/SASS	419-893-0121	12/22/90		FidoNet 1:234/4; 2400 bd

BBS Name	Phone	Date	Sysop	Comments
AMDA-Link Mac BBS	43-222-712-4737	8/31/90		Vienna, Austria; 2400 bd; FidoNet 2:310/16.70
MacTel_HQ	44-602-455444	2/1/92	David Nicholsoncole	2400 bd; FidoNet 2:253/200; Nottingham, UK; HS (DS) line 0602-455497
Buz Board RyBBS	44-81-202-9175	12/31/90		IBM, Mac, Amiga, Apple] [areas; 2400 bd; HS (HST/v.32/v.42bis); London (UK)
MacTel_Metro	44-81-543-8017	12/24/90	John Lockwood	2400 bd; FidoNet 2:253/202; London, UK
MacBaud	44-865-514466	10/5/91		UK; 9600 v21, v22, v22bis, v32
Plutten & Cat's BBS	46-480-14302	6/30/91		2400 bd; FidoNet 2:200/301; Europe(?)
The Front	49-40-381149	12/11/90		NovaLink Pro; 8 lines; alt. line -3894409; Hamburg, Germany;
Wildbox BBS/Heidelberg	49-6221-799500	11/23/90		FidoNet 2:247/9; Germany
MegaBoard	501-521-0547	2/1/89	Mark F. Carter	2400 bd; SS; EE
LinguaBase	503-222-9774	2/22/90		Hermes BBS
Toolbox BBS	503-344-7387	7/11/89	David Ellsworth [71410,1666]	
PC Technics	503-393-0998	5/27/89	Steve Poole	GIF pics; 6:30 pm to 8:30 am M-Sat, 24 hrs Sunday
Rogue Valley ElectroMail	503-535-4692	6/30/91	Chuck Flickinger	2400 bd; SS
Outlet BBS	503-648-6462	10/02/90		2400 bd; FidoNet 1:105/333
Central Point Support BBS	503-690-6650	3/1/90		2400 bd; Copy II Mac, PC Mac Tools support
Greyland BBS	503-747-6098	4/24/91	Steve Ebener	2400 bd; HS (v.42bis); FidoNet 1:152/42
Corntown Connection	503-753-7250	2/1/89		2400 bd; Opus 1:152/203
Tech-Line BBS	503-754-7613	10/24/90		FidoNet 1:152/215
LateNight BBS	503-757-8968	5/9/90		FidoNet 1:152/208
E-CMUG	503-967-4250	12/24/90		2400 bd; Opus 1:357/3
High Concepts	504-391-2925	10/18/90		2400 bd; FidoNet 1:396/16
Health Education Electronic Forum BBS	504-588-5743	11/30/89	Michael Pejsach	2400 bd; SS; HS; V
New Orleans MUG BBS	504-837-8188	6/2/91	Bob Nordling [70521,1327]	2400 bd; HS (PEP/v.32); FidoNet 1:396/13; membership reqd for downloads; new number
The \/\/ave	504-866-7710	12/05/90		2400 bd; HS (HST); FidoNet 1:396/40
Drawing Board	505-525-0844	10/1/90		OPUS 1:15/2
Macintosh^2	505-678-1318	12/4/89		2400; FidoNet 1:381/401
Call BBS	505-891-3840	9/8/90	Joseph Emmanuel	SS; FidoNet 1:301/4; HS (DS)
Caesar's Palace	507-895-8619	2/4/90	Kevin Capwell	2400 bd; HS; SS; EE
Cul-De-Sac B&G	508-429-1784	11/01/90		2400 bd; FidoNet 1:322/360
SoundStage BBS	508-453-0392	7/10/90	Walt	NovaLink
Sounding Board	508-474-8950	3/13/91	Jonathan Gourd /Sound Man8/ {J.GOURD} [72627,370]	2400 bd; HS V.32/V.42bis/MNP1-5; Mac files & GIFs
Greyhawk BBS	508-650-1292	3/24/90		2400 bd; HS; Mac & IBM
Think Tank	508-655-3848	1/7/90	Bill Heiser	2400; HS
Macro Exchange AMIS	508-667-7388	8/20/89	L. Hajinlian	Mac section; area code change
Mystic Tribunal	508-689-4493	8/1/89		FidoNet 1:324/131
Odyssey Part 1: Atlantis	508-820-1861	8/23/89		2400 bd
Main Street U.S.A.	508-832-7725	4/26/91	Chris Silverberg	2400 bd; FidoNet 1:322/575; SS; 3pm-7:30am M-F,24 hrs SS

BBS Name	Phone	Date	Sysop	Comments
Odyssey Part 2: Aquarius	508-875-0413	8/23/89		
Odyssey Part 3: Apocalypse	508-877-0768	12/19/90	Wenyao Tsai	2400 bd; HS (HST); Hermes; FidoNet 1:322/349
MACS BBS	509-924-5364	2/1/92		2400 bd; Hermes; 9600 bd DS; FidoNet 1:346/6
Acey BBS	509-966-8555	9/11/90		FidoNet 1:347/12.0; 2400 bd
'02 Register BBS	512-250-2279	11/12/90		2400 bd; Hermes
Outlandos d'Amour	512-288-0914	11/12/90		2400 bd; Hermes
Mac Securities & Exchange Center	512-323-2429	11/12/90		2400 bd; Hermes
ZenWedgie	512-332-0265	1/11/91		2400 bd; Hermes
Bull Creek BBS	512-343-1612	2/1/92	Mark Bryant [75146,2345]	2400 bd; HS (HST); FidoNet 1:382/54.11; SS; Appletalk/MacServe network; $15/yr
ForeignDesign-EliteTexan BBS	512-345-9469	11/12/90		2400 bd; HS (HST); Hermes
M.S.I. After Hours	512-366-0556	8/24/90		FidoNet 1:387/304
Soft World BBS	512-383-9898	6/28/91	Michael Skurka	2400 bd; HS (HST v.32); FidoNet 1:397/2.1
Impact Crater BBS	512-392-4366	11/07/90		2400 bd; Hermes; FidoNet 1:382/15
UTA School of Nursing (SON-NET)	512-471-7584	8/1/89		Opus 1:382/18
Necropolis of Dreams	512-472-6220	11/12/90	/DavidN39/	2400 bd; Hermes; alt ph -6905
Necropolis of Dreams	512-472-6905	11/12/90	/DavidN39/	2400 bd; Hermes; alt ph -6220
Hellhole	512-474-1512	11/12/90		2400 bd; HS; Hermes
Akbar & Jeff's BBS Hut	512-482-9183	11/12/90		FidoNet 1:384/64; 2400 bd; Hermes
Cygnus Interstellar Info	512-641-2063	6/29/91	Bruce Tomlin	2400 bd; FidoNet 1:387/555
Mac Exchange	512-658-3212	6/19/91	Greg Lewis /Greg93/	2400 bd; TeleFinder; V; 2 phone lines
Arcane Dimensions	512-832-1680	7/9/89	Vincent Parsons	2400 bd; EE; SS
Diner	512-836-1420	7/9/89	Joe Coleman	2400 bd; SS; EE
Atlantis	512-836-8777	8/1/89		FidoNet 1:382/36
Motorola Freeware BBS	512-891-3733	8/21/90		2400 bd; Motorola support
Stomp'n Brew	512-993-7595	11/12/90		2400 bd; Hermes
Currents!	513-253-2476	6/1/91	Randall Brown /RandyBrown/	2400 bd; HST v.42; FidoNet 1:110/430; MacList 6:6026/1; Hermes; member K12Net Int'l Education Network
Mac Mania BBS	513-561-2225	7/9/90	/Jason29/	Hermes; 2400 bd; HS (v.32)
Grand Finale	513-683-1686	7/19/90	/ChuckW16/	2400 bd; Hermes
Mega-Mac	513-779-3722	4/7/91	Kevin Clark /Kevin 5575/	2400 bd; HS v.32/42; Hermes
Queen City Mac BBS	513-831-6079	11/12/90		2400 bd; Hermes
BetaBoard I BBS	514-486-3454	11/1/89		SS; 2400 bd; FidoNet 1:167/183
Mac a Mac	514-766-3653	09/23/90	Maurice Tringle	2400 bd; SS; primarily French msg base; FidoNet 1:167/113; $25/yr for DLs
MAC-LINK	514-935-1652	9/4/90	Mark Smith, Henry See, Patricia Sullivan, Brian Chamberain	2400 bd; HS (HST); FidoNet 1:167/182; SS; FidoNet 1:167/182; $60/yr; new number
Quebec Online	514-935-4257	2/1/92		10 lines; FidoNet 1:167/182
PComm	514-989-9450	8/29/90		2400 bd; FidoNet 1:167/1.0
Zoo System	515-279-3073	7/2/91	Mark Toland	WWIV; password: PLEASE; 2400 bd; FidoNet 1:290/2.1; HS (v.32)

BBS Name	Phone	Date	Sysop	Comments
Enchanted Mansion BBS	515-279-6769	09/13/90	Michael Pester	MacMansion; HS (HST); 2400 bd; FidoNet 1:290/628
Cyber-Net	515-628-4992	11/12/90		2400 bd; Hermes
FOG-LINE	515-964-7937	8/1/89		Opus 1:290/627
Apple Corp Elite	515-989-4514	5/27/89		
Mac's Delight	516-499-8471	1/13/91	Bob Taub [71641,1303]	2400 bd; HS (v.32); Hermes
Lighthouse BBS	517-321-0788	11/1/89		HS; 2400; (Opus1:159/950)
][the MACS	517-655-4605	7/7/90	John Endahl /JEndahl/	2400 bd; NovaLink
Wolverine	517-695-9952	2/1/92		FidoNet 1:239/1004
Wizard BBS	517-783-1059	3/7/91	Jeff Kirkpatrick [76630,2126]	Mac section; Sharp Wizard users
MECCA/ENVIRONUS	518-381-4430	6/2/90	Don Rittner	2400 bd; V; SS; AlterNet 7:526/305; FidoNet 267/102
Wonderland Regional Macintosh BBS	519-672-7661	9/4/89	Erik Sea	2400 bd; HS (HST); SS; FidoNet 1:221/109 (London Hub); $20/yr; EE
MacHaven BBS	601-992-9459	4/26/91	Ray Leninger	2400 bd; HS (DS); SS; FidoNet 1:3632/6; $10/yr
Stacks R Us/WCTV	602-252-7928	1/25/91	Mike Atanasio	2400 bd; Hypercard stacks; $30 annual fee
Carpe Diem!	602-277-8846	2/28/90		HS; 2400 bd; FidoNet 1:114/50
BioSPHERE	602-336-0744	11/10/90	Joe /JoeBruni/	NovaLink; 10pm-8am
??	602-461-0772	12/3/89		FidoNet 1:114/67; 2400
Arizona Macintosh User's Group BBS	602-495-1713	4/26/91	Michael S. Bean	2400 bd; SS; FidoNet 1:114/56; HS (DS); AMUG members only; $30 annual fee
Tucson Apple Core (TAC)	602-577-6393	2/4/90	Lawrence Lee	2400 bd; HS (HST); SS; FidoNet 300/15; $20/yr
Mactivities	602-722-2924	2/4/90	Roger Gibson	2400 bd; HS (HST); SS; $ req. for DLs; EE
Kitty's Sandbox	602-829-7522	12/23/90		2400 bd; FidoNet 1:114/110
Phoenix Red Ryder Host #1	602-870-1810	6/2/90	Joe Tvedt	2400 bd; HS; SS; V; EE
First DIBS	602-881-8720	2/4/90	Jesse Tharin	2400 bd; SS; FidoNet 1:300/7
Arizona Macintosh User's Group Preferred BBS	602-926-4026	4/26/91	Michael S. Bean	2400 bd; SS; FidoNet 1:114/121; HS (DS); AMUG members only; $30 annual fee
EyeNet *HS*	602-941-3747	7/9/90	Leo Bores	2400 bd; OPUS 1:114/14; HS; aka Mac Shack, Stack Shack, Mac Wizards
4th Wave / AMUG2	602-947-0587	8/13/90	Alan Heflich	licensed NewsBytes source; 2400 bd; FidoNet 1:114/53; SS
The Lion's Den	602-985-1861	09/17/90		2400 bd; FidoNet 1:114/64
Tiger's Den	602-996-0078	9/1/90	John Gillett	2400 bd; HS (HST); SS; FidoNet 1:114/27; $25/yr for DL access
Recovery BBS	603-228-0705	7/28/90		2400 bd; HS (HST); FidoNet 1:132/131.0
Jungle	603-233-1474	9/26/90		NovaLink Pro
Apple Power BBS	603-424-0371	1/31/91	Kevin McLaughlin /KevinMcL/ {Norsk}	HS (v.32/v.42); Nova Link; second line 603-429-1309 (2400 bd); formerly MacSNAC
Apple Power BBS	603-429-1309	12/31/90	Kevin McLaughlin /KevinMcL/ {Norsk}	2400 bd; Nova Link; second line 603-424-0371 (9600 bd); formerly MacSNAC
Doppler/Deep Cove BBS	604-277-9920	7/29/91	Wayne Duval, Ron Weber (Mac Lib) [72040,542]	2400 bd; V; TBBS; FidoNet 1:153/915; IBM/Mac/Amiga/Atari; multi-line, see also -9940, -9960

BBS Name	Phone	Date	Sysop	Comments
Doppler/Deep Cove BBS	604-277-9940	7/29/91	Wayne Duval, Ron Weber (Mac Lib) [72040,542]	9600 HST; V; TBBS; FidoNet 1:153/915; IBM/Mac/Amiga/Atari; multi-line, see also -9920, -9960
Doppler/Deep Cove BBS	604-277-9960	7/29/91	Wayne Duval, Ron Weber (Mac Lib) [72040,542]	9600 v.32-14,400 HST; V; TBBS; FidoNet 1:153/915; IBM/Mac/Amiga/Atari; multi-line, see also -9920, -9940
Macintosh Way BBS	604-574-1199	7/29/91	Eric B. Poustie	FidoNet 25:4604/132, $20 donation for DL access
Ebenezer Christian BBS	604-826-6607	8/1/89		FidoNet 153/508; 1:7501/0
Carihi Secondary School BBS	604-923-3118	9/4/89	Howard Harding	2400 bd; SS; EE
Sunshine BBS	604-943-1612	6/2/90	Bob Cotter	2400 bd; SS; EE
Hogs Hollow	604-948-0272	2/1/92		FidoNet 1:153/928
Radio Station WFXY/ Cumberland Post BBS	606-248-6397	5/1/89	Warren Pursifull	2400 bd; SS; EE
MacCincinnati BBS	606-572-5375	6/2/90		
Memory Alpha BBS	607-257-5822	5/15/90		
Mutual Net *QNX*	607-533-7540	1/13/89		2400 bd; Opus 1:260/405
MadMacs BBS	608-221-3841	9/12/90	Jerry Pophal	2400 bd; SS; $15/yr for DL access; Madison WI MUG
Mac Line BBS	608-233-9487	3/15/91	John Allen /JohnA79/	2400 bd; SS
Buyer's Review	608-244-0852	9/9/90		reviews SIG; Opus 1:121/6
Caesar's Palace BBS	608-782-1036	7/29/89	Kevin Capwell	2400 bd; SS; EE
Funeral Home	609-345-8631	10/29/89		
Discordia	609-497-0883	6/18/91	Greg Oberfield	2400 bd; FidoNet 1:266/45
Stockton State College BBS	609-652-4914	11/19/89	Jay Paul, Mac sysop	2400; multi-line; HS line 652-4923
Desperate BBS	609-737-2876	11/22/89	Dan Norcross	SS; 2400 bd
Armoury II	609-985-4750	4/18/90	Robert S. Mason	2400 bd; HS; Hermes
MacExchange II	612-290-9777	11/12/90		2400 bd; Hermes
System BBS	612-338-8844	11/15/90	Jeff Iverson /J5RSON/	HW/SW sales; 2400 bd; six lines
Railway Post Office	612-377-2197	11/12/90		2400 bd; Hermes
Tower Exchange BBS	612-420-7811	11/12/90		2400 bd; HS; Hermes
The Real American BBS	612-535-3196	10/25/90		2400 bd; FidoNet 1:282/71
Creative Solutions	612-546-1624	1/25/91	Ira Wald	2400 bd; Hermes; $25 annual fee
Glacier BBS	612-557-8925	11/12/90		2400 bd; Hermes
Macintosh Exchange	612-561-2747	12/31/89	Lincoln Bovee	
ExchangeNET	612-571-7774	10/21/90		2400 bd; FidoNet 1:282/65; UUCP
Syndicate	612-572-8370	11/12/90		2400 bd; Hermes
Desert Oasis	612-636-4285	10/25/90	/MJannusch/	Hermes; 2400 bd; HS (HST); FidoNet 1:282/72
DTP Exchange	612-636-7580	9/8/90		2400 bd; HS; DTP only; FidoNet 1:282/61
Conus BBS	612-642-4629	6/1/91	Scott Christensen	2400 bd; HS; V; FidoNet 1:282/24; 6pm-8am CST M-F,24 hrs SS; SS
Caverns of Depth	612-778-1222	11/12/90		2400 bd; HS (DS); Hermes
Bloomington BBS	612-888-3712	10/11/90		2400 bd; HS (v.32/v.42bis); FidoNet 1:282/22.1

BBS Name	Phone	Date	Sysop	Comments
Great MacHouse (Australia)	613-03-562-2624	10/1/91	Matthew Simpson	2400 bd; HS (v.32); SS; FidoNet: 3:633/204
JUNGLE_electric	613-233-1474	12/20/90	/KenroyH/	NovaLink; 2400bd; HS (HST); FidoNet 1:163/151; 3 nodes; design & DTP support
Whole BIT News	613-521-3690	11/1/89		2400 bd; Opus 1:163/206
MacOttawa	613-729-2763	8/30/90	Graydon Patterson	2400 bd; SS; 10 day trial, $45/yr; FidoNet 1:163/124
EntrNet-Q	613-739-1030	8/25/90		2400 bd; FidoNet 1:163/224
Beta Traders	614-385-3870	8/27/89		2400 bd; WWIV; HS
Aurora Borealis	614-471-5733	12/25/90	Mike Lininger	2400 bd; HS; SS; FidoNet 1:226/200; alt. ph. -6209
Aurora Borealis	614-471-6209	12/25/90	Mike Lininger	2400 bd; HS (HST); SS; FidoNet 1:226/200; alt. ph. -5733
Nashville Exchange	615-383-0727	2/1/92		FidoNet 1:116/19; 2400 bd; 20 lines
Zoo BBS	615-426-2214	5/30/91		
INFO*LINK	615-434-2551	12/5/90	Mac SysOp: Greg Whitfield [76066,516]	Mac/DOS/others; 2400 bd; 3 lines; alt. ph. lines -2995, -2875
INFO*LINK	615-434-2875	12/5/90	Mac SysOp: Greg Whitfield [76066,516]	Mac/DOS/others; 2400 bd; 3 lines; alt. ph. lines -2995, -2875
INFO*LINK	615-434-2995	12/5/90	Mac SysOp: Greg Whitfield [76066,516]	Mac/DOS/others; 2400 bd; 3 lines; alt. ph. lines -2995, -2875
Shadow Keep BBS	615-435-0446	5/30/91		
MacClique BBS	615-691-7094	5/30/91	Phil Butler	Telefinder
Muon BBS	616-534-7149	11/30/89	Doug Gosciak	2400 bd; FidoNet 1:228/23; SS; HS (HST)
Dr.Theopolus	616-949-1321	8/1/89	J. Kuiper, D. Fletcher	2400
BCS Info Center TBBS	617-227-7986	9/4/90		FidoNet 1:101/121
WOLF'S DEN	617-266-6370	11/12/90		2400 bd; Hermes
OnRecord Music/Midi BBS	617-324-7310	4/28/91	Ogie Tudor	2400 bd; MIDI/Music; professional & amateur musicians; multi-line; music SW sales; $30/annual fee; FAX service free to members; NovaLink; FidoNet 1:101/280
Nova Central	617-367-2427	9/26/90	Greg	NovaLink Pro BBS support
Tom's BBS	617-471-0542	5/29/91	Tom McGee	2400 bd; SS
PhotoTalk	617-472-8612	7/26/90	Robert Gorrill	2400 bd; Opus 1:101/206
4th Dimension BBS	617-494-0565	6/16/91	Zeff Wheelock [75776,211]	2400 bd; Mansion BBS; Mac/IBM/Apple/Tandy; FidoNet 1:101/450
NPI III	617-592-5772	6/23/90	Charles Carley	2400 bd; Opus 1:101/193
Reflections	617-593-7228	6/19/91	Bill Reed [73757,3243]	2400 bd; FidoNet 1:101/270; new number
NewWorld Magic	617-595-5626	1/1/89	Doug Dupree	FidoNet network 101 host; alt. number 595-5627
NewWorld Magic	617-595-5627	1/1/89	Doug Dupree	FidoNet network 101 host; alt. number 595-5626
BCS Mac BBS	617-625-6747	6/5/91		FidoNet 101/485
Mac's Diner	617-643-2882	1/29/89		
Mac Users at Berklee (MUB) BBS	617-739-2366	11/5/89	Joe Zobkiw, Ira Horvitz	2400 bd; also IBM, Commodore, Atari support; MIDI; College of Music, Boston; $20 one-time fee

BBS Name	Phone	Date	Sysop	Comments
BCS Telecomm	617-786-9788	7/27/90		2400 bd; Opus 1:101/122; HS
Graphics Factory	617-849-0347	5/29/91	Noel Gouveia	2400 bd; SS; 12am-6pm
Crystal Palace	617-859-9478	4/3/90		NovaLink Pro; 2400 bd
Buckman's Tavern II	617-863-8502	6/16/91	Larry Wolf	2400 bd; Mac & IBM
MacEast	617-868-7987	1/25/91	Holden Smith	2400 bd; HS (HST); SS; $25/yr for DL access; EE
Newton's Corner	617-964-6088	1/25/91	Curt Morrison	2400 bd; SS
Prism	617-965-7816	1/25/91		SS; one-time fee for access
Emerald Keep	618-394-0065	1/1/90		Ami Fido; 2400 bd; HS; FidoNet 1:288/601
Systems Support Group BBS	618-549-1129	11/1/89	Mike Harrell	2400 bd; SS; FidoNet 1:288/528
MacUG SafeHouse	619-272-2059	9/8/90		2400 bd; FidoNet 1:202/710
Kittyhawk	619-371-4776	12/12/90	Robert Wright	2400 bd; HS; Mac, DOS and music sections
Telemac BBS	619-576-1820	1/25/91	Richard Parcel	2400 bd; HS (DS); SS; EE; $18/yr DL access; San Diego MUG
Fun House	619-697-8714	3/17/90	/DanielK3/	SS
Mystic Passage	619-726-1591	7/25/89	Patrick Martin, Sam Norris	2400 bd; HS; formerly MacBonsall; closed system
MacNERDS	619-758-1700	11/12/90		Trust Deed Sales Info; 2400 bd; Hermes
Mac INFONET	619-944-3646	5/27/89		WWIV
We the People BBS	702-258-0660	2/1/92		2400 bd; FidoNet 1:209/765
Mac+ BBS	702-293-4655	11/12/90		2400 bd; Hermes
Nevada Mac-Home of A/MUG	702-359-4999	12/20/90		FidoNet 1:213/777; 2400 bd; HS (HST/DS); Northern Nevada Apple // and Mac User Group; $30/annual for full access, $15/annual for NetMail & Echos
Western Type BBS	702-366-9107	09/28/90	Dave Gardner	FidoNet 1:209/720; 2400 bd
Shadetree	703-231-3806	9/21/89	Randy Minton	A/UX users; 2400 bd; HS (HST); SS; EE
Craig's Place	703-241-5492	6/1/91	Craig Vaughan	2400 bd; FidoNet 1:109/342; RBBS; Mac programmers
Northern VA Astronomy Club	703-256-4777	4/29/90		RBBS; FidoNet 1:109/118
ASTEC Support BBS	703-338-6025	1/2/92	Rod Paine [72017,117]	Telefinder; 2400 bd; HS (Hayes ULTRA 144 units 14,400 bd V.32bis, 9600 bd V.32, V-series 9600 LAPB); BMUG vol II PD CD-Rom online; download Mac user interface application on first call; some free areas, annual fee for full access
Brewster's Barn BBS	703-352-1502	3/29/90		2400 bd; HS; FidoNet 1:109/30
Mount Olympus	703-524-7312	8/13/90	Nick Firsow /NicFirsow/	2400 bd; Hermes
BBS THALIA	703-533-3938	11/10/90	/HABBERTON/	2400 bd; show business/actors/agents; Hermes
Bull Board	703-631-8772	2/11/90	P. Simerly	IBM, Atari, TI, Mac, OS2, Unix; FidoNet; HS
MainLine Mac [Node 1]	703-658-0086	11/12/90		2400 bd; HS (HST); Hermes; alt ph -0087
MainLine Mac [Node 2]	703-658-0087	11/12/90		HS (DS); 2400 bd; HS; Hermes; alt ph -0086
Mormac BBS	703-709-9381	7/20/90	Jeff Pearson /JPearson/	2400 bd; Hermes; FidoNet 1:109/348
End of the Line	703-720-1624	11/29/90		2400 bd; FidoNet 1:274/16

BBS Name	Phone	Date	Sysop	Comments
Silver Island	703-759-7038	5/23/91	Miller	2400 bd; Hermes; FidoNet 1:109/330, 6:9001/1; aka Mac Den, Tower of Illusion
Culpeper Connection	703-825-7533	7/27/90	Clyde /Clyde2cx/	2400 bd; NovaLink
Macintosh Network	703-860-1427	10/30/90	Garner Miller /Bear/	FidoNet 1:109/328.715; 2400 bd; MacVirus echo origin
Cluster BBS	703-893-3632	8/22/90		5pm-7am; Opus 1:109/131
Mirror BBS	707-485-0987	9/10/90		FidoNet 1:125/26; 2400 bd; HS (HST)
Sonoma Online	707-545-0746	6/19/91		2400 bd; HS (HST v.32); FidoNet 1:125/7
K9 BBS	707-745-6225	8/27/89		2400 bd; WWIV
Byte out of the Apple	707-747-0306	7/27/91	Gregg Phillips	2400 bd; FidoNet 1:161/508; Node 1, Hayes Ultra 96 V.32; see also -5406, -2121
Byte Out of the Apple	707-747-2121	7/27/91	Gregg Phillips	Node 3, ISDN; see also -5406, -0306
Byte Out of the Apple	707-747-5406	7/27/91	Gregg Phillips	FirstClass; Node 2, USR_DS v.32bis/HST; see also -0306, -2121
MacComm Connection	707-795-1721	10/26/90	Ren Just	2400 bd; FidoNet 125/14
WALL BBS	707-874-1135	11/12/90		2400 bd; Hermes
Working With Works	708-260-9660	8/30/90	Michael Sloan	2400 bd; SS
The Rest of Us (TRoU) BBS	708-291-6660	2/1/92	Steve Levinthal	2400 bd; V; USR Dual Std v.32; new number; FidoNet 115/400; TROUMUG user group members only, $40/annual fee for MUG
Ephemeral Hedgehog	708-293-1886	8/30/90		
MACropedia (tm)	708-295-6926	4/26/91	Dave Alpert KB9CNU	2400 bd; HS (DS); SS; $30/yr for full access; FidoNet 1:115/295
Macinations	708-352-9282	12/25/90		2400 bd; HS (DS); FidoNet 1:115/352; Mansion
Inverse Universe	708-395-4914	8/30/90		2400 bd; HS (v.32); Hermes
Northwestern U BBS	708-491-3892	3/1/91		
Shangri-La	708-596-3648	7/5/91	Chuck Ross	Hermes; 2400 bd; HS (HST); fee for full time/access; verified quality Sysop-ping!
Sedation Exclamation!	708-654-2064	11/12/90	Chuck Remes	2400 bd; HS; Hermes
Hangar 18	708-655-4952	6/11/91	Mike [72230,3604]	Hermes
Spectrum MacInfo	708-657-1113	8/10/91	Steve Levinthal	2400 bd; FidoNet 115/729; HS USR Dual Std v.32bis; no required fees
Prime Time	708-741-1995	8/19/90	Art Wittenauer	Hermes; 2400 bd; HS (HST)
TrendTec	708-759-9214	3/1/91		DTP & Graphics; 2400 bd; HS; Hermes
Alliance Computers BBS	708-831-1142	3/1/91		
FamilyNet Int'l. Echogate	708-887-7685	2/1/92		FidoNet 1:11/50
Polymorphic BBS	708-910-3814	12/12/90	Josh Stein	Hermes
Mad Macs	708-948-7008	9/14/90	Jason Fried /Reflex/	Hermes; 2400 bd; HS (HST); on-line store
Brain in a Pan	713-480-7422	2/16/91		OPUS 1:106/260
MacEndeavour	713-640-2533	2/16/91	Brian Hall <BOS1A::HALL>	2400 bd; TBBS; FidoNet 1:106/6268
HAAUG Heaven BBS	713-664-9873	4/8/91	Clark Johnson [76077,2673]	2400 bd; 2 lines; 9600 v.32bis; Houston Area Apple Users Group members only, membership $35/yr

BBS Name	Phone	Date	Sysop	Comments
Galapagos	713-799-9016	2/16/91	Sal Berenstain	2400 bd; HS; Hermes
CMS BBS	714-222-6601	4/25/91		support board for Mac/Apple products
CMS Support BBS	714-259-4390	6/3/90		CMS Mac product support; 2400 bd
Mountain Air BBS	714-336-6080	11/19/91	Paul White [70202,157]	2400 bd; WWIV; Mac & IBM
Gentle Rain BBS	714-593-6144	8/9/90		2400 bd; FidoNet 1:207/111
Spider Island Software BBS	714-730-5785	8/16/90		demo of Mac-like comm interface (Telefinder)
Nymphotic Zitron	714-827-2018	11/12/90		2400 bd; HS (DS); Hermes
SIGnet.Canada	714-858-5322	10/09/90		2400 bd; FidoNet 1:103/328
MacVille USA	714-859-5857	1/25/91		formerly Ancient Rome
Mac Exchange	714-860-1805	7/29/89	Tom Fitzsimmons	2400 bd; HS; SS; V; FidoNet 1:103/337; EE
The Desktop	714-898-7269	9/11/91	Mark Murphy	9600 bd; Hermes
Grandpa's	714-952-2312	2/4/90	Frank Bolan	2400 bd; SS; EE
La Habra Connection	714-992-0716	1/19/91	Tom Galland	2400 bd; HS (DS); FidoNet 1:103/345
MacCursor	716-225-5189	7/23/89		
Mac's Last Stand	716-248-0694	9/11/90	James Vangeyten	2400 bd; SS; FidoNet 1:260/211
AARDVARK Burrow	716-383-1635	2/4/90	Bruce Peters	2400 bd; SS; EE
E F X Systems	716-396-2699	10/22/90		2400 bd; FidoNet 1:260/610
MacSpence	716-594-1344	7/23/89		
MacGallery BBS	717-252-3227	12/8/91	Wayne Jaeschke [72600,1150]	Mac & IBM; GIFs
Mouse House BBS	717-285-2535	7/9/89	Dan Schwartz	2400 bd; V; SS; EE
Hackers Corner	717-597-7105	2/1/89	Jim Diller	2400 bd; SS; 8pm-8am; EE
Forest Hills BBS	718-268-1240	12/2/91	Tommy Brown	2400 bd; HS (DS); SS
Wall	718-278-2120	6/2/90	Robert Lanza, Frank Sullivan	2400 bd; HS (HST); FidoNet 1:107/604; SS; EE
Armageddon	718-459-8230	12/12/91		
NY NovaLink	718-493-4430	6/24/91	J Edmund	2400 bd; FidoNet 1:278/635
Laserboard	718-639-8826	12/2/91	Adam Wildavsky [76670,3070]	2400 bd; HS (9600 USR & v.32); $18/yr for DL access; SS
New York On-Line	718-852-2662	12/2/91	William Bowles	2400 bd; SS; FidoNet 1:268/607; $10/yr for full access
Not Even Odd	718-997-1189	2/1/92		2400 bd; FidoNet 1:2603/204
Onion Patch BBS	719-570-6805	10/30/90	Douglas Vanroeder	2400 bd
Eagles' Nest	719-598-8413	10/25/90		2400 bd; HS (HST); FidoNet 1:2210/518, Opus 1:128/18; School Dist. #20
Scorpion	719-637-1458	9/28/90	Chriss Koch	2400 bd; SS; FidoNet 1:128/46; HS (HST)
Online with Hayes	800-874-2937	8/21/91	Toby Nixon [70271,404]	Hayes modem support; nationwide BBS directory
Mainly Macintosh	801-374-5438	11/12/90	Steve Trottier /STrottier/	2400 bd; Hermes
Transporter	801-379-5239	7/9/89	Tim Myers	2400 bd; SS; V; EE
Mac Plus BBS	801-634-3655	8/2/90	Tracy Peek	2400 bd; SS; 3pm-8am MST; FidoNet 1:15/10
ACSU BBS	802-388-3959	2/1/92		FidoNet 1:325/202
Green Mountain Mac	802-388-9899	7/2/91	Jim Wright, David Herren	2400 bd; HS (DS); FidoNet 1:325/201
ShadowMacs BBS	802-425-2332	7/18/91	Jason Hyerstay	FidoNet 1:325/124
CVU BBS	802-482-2110	12/01/90		2400 bd; HS; Multi-Line; TBBS; FidoNet 325/107

BBS Name	Phone	Date	Sysop	Comments
Fort Mill BBS	803-548-0900	7/2/91	Bill Taylor <FMBBS> [73057,1207]	2400 bd; HS (DS); FidoNet 376/24; SS
MacMoore	803-576-5710	11/12/90	Don Davidson	2400 bd; HS; Hermes
Carolina Networx	803-788-8039	8/1/89		Opus 1:376/10
Macinternational	803-957-6870	1/1/89	Ralph Yount	2400 bd; SS; EE
CFI BBS	804-422-1109	1/5/91	Rusty Werntz; Ray Kallman (Mac CoSysop)	FidoNet 1:275/328; new number
Halen's Haven	804-480-0506	10/28/91	Andre Doles	HST 14.4, 3 nodes
Virginia Data Exchange	804-723-1663	12/21/90		2400 bd; RBBS; FidoNet 1:271/270
Ye Ole' World BBS	804-784-3771	11/21/90	Wilbur M. Sims III [76447,3367]	
Virginia Data Exchange	804-877-3539	2/1/92		2 lines; Free; FidoNet 1:271/270
SubZero II	804-978-1076	11/12/90		2400 bd; HS (v.32); Hermes
Gold Coast Mac	805-494-9221	7/27/90	Jim Dynes	2400 bd; HS (HST); $24/yr for full access; FidoNet 1:206/2811; online murder mystery
Fred's Place	805-687-1001	11/24/90	/Columbus/	2400 bd
Farside BBS	805-986-1277	11/12/90	L Lewis /Uncle GS/ {L.LEWIS3}	Mac,] [,DOS; 2400 bd; HS; Hermes; NUP: Adobe
WhistleStop	806-791-3210	3/7/92	Todd Knowlton /ToddK13/	SS
MacBBS	808-456-8498	7/1/90		2400 bd; FidoNet 1:345/21
Ghostcomm Tele-Services	808-456-8510	12/23/90		2400 bd; HS (HST/v32/v42bis); FidoNet 1:345/8
MacBBS	808-486-6673	2/28/90	Dennis Mitchell	2400 bd; SS; EE
Apple Grove	808-595-3228	6/15/91	Ivan Gum [73527,3652]	2400 bd; Hermes; Hawaii; Mac, GIFs, Music SIGs
Opus Amicus BBS (San Juan, PR)	809-724-0621	11/1/89		2400; FidoNet
Caribbean Breeze	809-773-0195	7/9/89	Douglas E.Canton Jr.	2400 bd; SS; FidoNet 1:367/12; EE
AVXIA BBS	81-3-355-4395	9/13/90		Tokyo, Japan; 2400 bd; HS (v.32); FidoNet 3:730/9.0
Mercury OPUS	813-327-3556	8/5/90		FidoNet 1:3603/20.0; NEW NUMBER
Grapevine BBS	813-371-3600	12/02/90		FidoNet 1:137/201; 2400 bd; HS
ENTREvous II	813-542-5482	8/28/90		FidoNet 1:371/1302
CRASH 'N' BURN BBS	813-733-3666	11/12/90		2400 bd; Hermes
Mystical Mire	813-745-2666	8/1/89	David Davids	FidoNet 1:137/7; 2400 bd; HS
Magical Mystery Tour BBS	814-337-2021	6/2/90	Glenn Rudolph	2400 bd; HS (HST); FidoNet 1:237/503; SS; EE
Castle Glen Finnain	815-332-3014	12/18/90		2400 bd; Hermes; FidoNet 1:143/207.2
Six Macs over Texas	817-346-9552	9/1/90		2400 bd; FidoNet 1:130/13
DAMUG BBS	817-383-3268	11/12/90		2400 bd; Hermes
The Spectrum	817-428-0578	1/13/91	James Mike Myers II	2400 bd; HS (HST)
ATION BBS	817-540-1142	2/22/92	Jim Heath	2400 bd; SS
Cleburne BBS	817-641-4842	9/1/89		FidoNet 1:130/14.0
WendellNet BBS	817-794-5641	10/13/90	/Clay Bongo/	Univ. of Tex.; 2400 bd; HS; Hermes
Obligatory Hendrix Perm	817-924-2922	11/12/90		2400 bd; Hermes
Mac BBS	818-332-3783	12/4/91	Organized Chaos	
Ionion Polises	818-335-0738	11/12/90		2400 bd; HS (HST); Hermes; NUP=Sleeze

BBS Name	Phone	Date	Sysop	Comments
CVMUG BBS	818-704-1365	12/21/90		FidoNet 1:102/804; 2400 bd; HS; Hermes; alt. ph. -5476
CVMUG BBS	818-704-5476	12/21/90		2400 bd; FidoNet 1:102/804; alt. ph. -1365
Realm of the Darkness	818-792-1661	11/12/90		2400 bd; Hermes
Red Dwarf Node 2	818-794-4943	11/12/90		2400 bd; Hermes; alt ph -5843
Red Dwarf Node 1	818-794-5843	11/12/90		2400 bd; Hermes; alt ph -4943
Apple Bus	818-919-5459	12/17/91	Mark Chally	2400 bd; Hermes; programming
Mac Valhalla	818-951-4445	5/23/91		2400 bd; FidoNet 1:102/942; HS (DS)
Drawing Board	818-965-6241	5/29/91	Char Rice	2400 bd; SS; FidoNet 1:102/885; DTP; fee for PS Art DLs; Laserprint svcs
HOUSE ATREIDES	818-965-7220	11/1/89		2400 bd; HS; (Opus 1:103/602)
BEAR'S LAIR	818-988-6694	6/2/90	Bruce Gerson	2400 bd; HS (HST); FidoNet 1:102/823; SS; $25/yr for full access; EE
DUBBS	885-634	12/30/90		FidoNet; alt number 831-908; Dublin, Ireland
DUBBS	885-908	12/30/90		FidoNet; alt number 831-634; Dublin, Ireland
Daniel's Den	901-362-5313	8/1/89		FidoNet 1:123/11
USA-Net	901-396-7300	7/14/90		2400 bd; HS (HST); FidoNet 1:123/25
NiteMare BBS	901-754-9823	5/23/91		2400 bd; HS (HST); FidoNet 1:123/13
Memphis Online	901-795-3453	1/7/90	/DRAlbaugh/	
MENSA BBS	902-466-6903	5/1/89	Peter J. Gergely	2400 bd; SS; EE
Traders Tavern	904-434-8679	5/4/89		2400 bd; WWIV
Rickards High School BBS	904-488-9344	8/8/90	Cathy McQuone	FidoNet 1:3605/40
LOCAL Paper	907-225-1240	7/9/89	Bob Kern	SS; EE
Apple Diggins (line 1)	907-333-4090	9/26/90	Bobby Diggins	2400 bd; Novalink Pro; alt ph 907-338-4373
Northermost Node	907-452-1460	7/30/90		FidoNet 1:17/38; Fairbanks, AK
Rice Paddy in North Pole	907-488-9327	12/1/90	Al Rice	5pm-9am PST M-Sat.,24 hrs Sun; SS; 2400 bd
ORPHEUS	907-694-0963	4/15/90	T-Bone (Ted HocHSatter)	musician SIG
Phantasm	908-291-4134	8/15/91		9600 bd
NJMUG BBS	908-388-1676	3/7/92	Mike Bielen	9600 HST/DS; SS; FidoNet 1:107/947
Dragon's Cave BBS	908-469-3450	3/7/92	Ralph Merritt	9600 HST/DS; FidoNet 1:2605/602; new number
CFONJ TBBS	908-486-2956	3/7/92		FidoNet 107/332; HS; 2 lines
Milky Way	908-580-0486	8/15/91		9600 HST
Realm of Insanity	908-741-5208	3/7/92	Mr. Insanity (Adam Scott [72357,1673])	2400 bd; WWIV
Underworld	908-840-4463	3/7/92	George Burdell [70357,476]	2400 bd; 9600 bd
Castle Tabby	908-988-0706	8/20/91	Michael Connick	2400 bd; HS (HST); formerly Mouse's Cottage; Mansion; FidoNet 1:107/412
MicroLine	912-764-7701	6/9/91	Mel Etheridge [76056,706]	2400 bd; HS line 912-764-9430 v.32/v.42/ bis; Hermes
Lawrence News Center	913-841-2752	8/28/90		multi-line; FidoNet 1:280/102
Battleship Armageddon	913-841-3059	8/2/90	Will McLean /Ozymandius/	WWIV; 2400 bd; HS; FidoNet 1:280/101
Mid-Hudson Mac	914-562-8528	9/4/89	Phil Leahy	2400 bd; HS (HST); SS; PELCO Computer Services; D&D game

BBS Name	Phone	Date	Sysop	Comments
Info-Center BBS	914-565-6696	12/27/91	Sam, Fred, & Fritz Kass /SamKass,FredK,FritzK/	2400 bd; SS; HS (Hayes Ultra 144)
Village BBS	914-621-2719	11/22/90		2400 bd; HS (HST); FidoNet 1:272/1
Dead Deckers Society	914-682-0404	11/12/90		2400 bd; Hermes
Health Professions BBS	915-590-9798	7/28/90		2400 bd; HS (HST); FidoNet 1:381/61
NightLine-1	916-362-1755	8/1/89		Opus 1:203/39
UNICOM BBS	916-365-5600	11/12/90	/HaroldB52/	Hermes
hd industries BBS	916-446-0926	3/11/91	Bill Davies /BDavies/	2400 bd; HS v.32/v.42; Telefinder; FidoNet link; 6pm-8am PST
MacNexus	916-448-5348	1/25/91	Ken Matley	2400 bd; SS; FidoNet link
DynaSoft	916-753-8788	11/1/89		Opus 1:203/955; HS; 2400
Now and Zen Opus	916-962-1952	5/23/91	John Lamb	2400 bd; HS (HST); Opus 1:203/34.0
TUMS BBS	918-234-5000	2/1/92		2400 bd; FidoNet 1:170/404.2
First MidAmerica MultiAccess	918-250-8495	8/1/89		FidoNet 1:170/605
Palindrome	918-743-8347	7/9/89	Kirk Kerekes	2400 bd; SS; EE
Computercenter Multiuser Online Services	918-747-0250	8/19/90		multi-line; 2400 bd; FidoNet 8:7104/9600
Mac Tonight	919-469-4838	9/17/89	Charles Boyer [71210,414]	2400 bd; WWIV
Home by the Sea	919-639-9728	8/1/89		FidoNet 1:151/122
Micro Message Service	919-779-6674	9/3/90		TBBS; 2400 bd; FidoNet 151/102
N.C. Central	919-851-8460	11/1/89		HS; 2400 bd; FidoNet 1:151/99
NC Public Safety Officer's BBS	919-886-8826	8/1/89		FidoNet 1:151/40
Homestead BBS	919-929-0974	8/18/89		
Cynosure	919-929-5153	09/26/90		2400 bd; HS (HST); FidoNet 1:151/501

❧

And here's Dennis Runkle on Dennis Runkle:

I found the one true path to computers by way of the back roads; moved from mainframes to micros fortuitously at the time of the Mac's first roll-out, and have had a mouse in-hand ever since. I'm currently a Manager of Technical Services at BP America in Cleveland, Ohio (America's North Coast). (Manager of Technical Services = "Probably caused the problem with the computer in the first place but knows how to fix it.")

❧

THOSE PESKY ELFs*

DOUG CLAPP

hat about low frequency electromagnetic fields—that invisible stuff that radiates from your Macintosh?

Are they bad? Will they hurt you? Can they kill you?

It's a controversy. Experts are divided. As a layman, I only know a couple of things. First, doctors now tell pregnant women not to use electric blankets—which makes me suspicious. Second, my mother, graced with a heart pacemaker, studiously avoids microwave ovens when they're "on."

But, in the spirit of fairness, here are two points of view. The first is a barely coherent, paranoid rambling. The second piece is from Apple. Apple's doesn't think there's any problem at all, but they're—ahem—looking into it.

First, the paranoia.

Sunblind

Here I am, the product of millions of years of evolution, staring into the sun.

We weren't made for this, you know? I remember reading a book about art—great painters, and how they did it. A sentence struck me and still remains: painters only paint light. There isn't

*Referred to EMFs by Apple

anything else to paint! Only light reflected off objects. Light reflected off the world. Shades and shadows, bright and dim. The world as reflection.

Whew.

It started with movies; but even movies are reflections. The sun's up in the projection booth.

Then TV. And we all started staring into the sun. In the early 60s there were cautions about not letting the kids sit within five feet of the TV. That's not heard anymore.

It's a perverse national ritual: every night millions of TVs flicker on, and millions of Americans sit. Rapt, looking into the sun where images dance.

Now there's a company that sells undergarments made with metallic threads—to keep monitors from turning your unborn children into Flipper. Rays—Zap: a mutant.

I've got a friend who's a throwback. Doesn't eat meat, wears jeans, smokes dope. Lives in the country. I called him once when I lived in LA. "How are you?" he asked. "Ah ... " I said, "I feel sorta listless; not much energy. Don't know why." "*Of course you feel lousy,*" he said. "Look where you live! You got any idea how many microwaves are pouring through your body *this very moment?*"

Microwaves pouring through my body? Do I need that? Wait— it was right on the tip of my ... musta been zapped by Channel 4, boring another hole through my cerebrum!

Sunblind. In the last years of this century, the sun is everywhere. My face is into the sun this moment. Above, a flourescent fixture pours "clone-light" into the room. With a shortwave radio, we could listen to Moscow or Lima or Rome or Peking. They're in the room too. Just think: Moscow in your brain, this instant!

Can't let the paranoia take over. Gotta keep control. Now it's big screens though, isn't it? Full-page displays! Why do "they" want us to have large monitors? Maybe they know ... what? Maybe Burrell Smith doesn't like us. Maybe that's why he designed that big

"Radius Full Page Display" monitor? He doesn't like us. Wants to make us all sunblind! Maybe Burrell isn't really designing hardware. Maybe he designing a new race. A race of *Burrell Smith Mutants*!

— Doug Clapp; *MacUser* magazine

❧

Now, here's Apple's statement on exposure to extremely low frequency electromagnetic fields. It begins …

Apple Computer, as a major user and manufacturer of personal computers, is committed to making products safe. That's why we closely follow scientific developments that can guide our product design efforts, and test our products against international safety standards. Our aim is to meet or exceed all safety regulations in every country where we do business.

Recently, questions about the possible health effects of prolonged exposure to extremely low frequency electromagnetic fields (EMF) have been raised. The issue encompasses not only computer monitors, but also all other EMF sources, such as electrical wiring, televisions, and household appliances.

Because Apple values highly our customers' trust, we take seriously any question of product safety. We have reviewed the scientific reports, and sought the counsel of government regulatory agencies and respected health organizations. Based on the prevailing evidence and opinions, Apple believes that the electric and magnetic fields produced by computer monitors do not pose a health risk. We are actively encouraging further research so that we can continue to ensure the health and safety of our customers and employees.

Although the body of scientific research has not defined a health problem or established safety limits, Apple offers a variety of lower-emission products for customers who want to reduce their exposure to EMF.

Apple has announced the Macintosh 21" Color Display, and has recently begun shipping new versions of the Macintosh 12" RGB Display and the AppleColor High-Resolution RGB Monitor. These products join the Macintosh Classic and Macintosh 12" Monochrome Display in offering customers display products with magnetic-field emission levels below the Swedish MPR-2 guidelines.

Apple products with magnetic-field emission levels below the Swedish MPR-2 guidelines are listed below:

Product	Part number
Macintosh Classic	all configurations
Macintosh Classic II	all configurations
Macintosh 12" Monochrome Display	M0298LL/A
Macintosh 12" RGB Display	M0297LL/C
AppleColor Hi-Resolution RGB Monitor	M0401LL/B
Macintosh 21" Color Display	M5812LL/A

More information—including information on the Swedish MPR-2 guidelines, Apple's ongoing testing activities, and a list of other documents regarding display emissions that are posted to AppleLink—is included in a document entitled "Apple Displays Have Lower Magnetic Emissions," posted on AppleLink –> Apple Sales & Mktg –> Apple Programs –> Health and Safety Information.

Here's another opinion: buy a portable or forswear cathode ray tubes altogether. A little prudence never hurt.

TALKING TO MY MAC

CARL PHILABAUM

A few paragraphs down, Carl says that human interface is one of his main interests.

That's overly modest, but I can take care of it. Carl is a leader in the field of computer-based instruction. He was deeply involved in Control Data's famed "Plato" project, and went on—with two other Control Data employees—to start Authorware, Inc. He was the principal designer of Authorware's "Course of Action," a Macintosh application that's arguably the best—and certainly the most sophisticated—courseware software available.

Today, Authorware is a multi-million dollar company. Back when Authorware was three people, Carl was "the interface guy." He crafted a marvelous interface, which included a nifty control that hadn't yet occurred to Apple: the pop-up menu.

A year ago, Carl left Authorware and bought a big spread in Wisconsin. These days, he uses his Quadra to design his woodland paradise and does consulting—he's a prince of multimedia—for museums around the country. Currently, he's helping to craft a landmark multimedia health education project encompassing tuberculosis, and HIV and other sexually-transmitted diseases.

Carl's living room is graced with a completely white, partially-melted bicycle. It's perfect.

❧

ar·tic·u·late *adj.* 1. Endowed with the power of speech. 2. Spoken in or divided into clear and distinct words or syllables. 3. Capable of, speaking in, or characterized by clear, expressive language.

"Open the pod bay doors, HAL."

"Open the pod bay doors, HAL!"

It's 23 years ago and I'm in college. *2001: A Space Odyssey* has opened at the only Cinerama in town. I'm toying with majoring in computer science. I'm drawn to the movie because of wild, psychedelic color sequences in the film, reported by several of my friends.

Today, 23 years later, human interface is one of my main interests. I recall the research reports from Xerox's Palo Alto Research Center in the 70s. They introduced me to pulldown menus, windows, icons, and the mouse interface. Then there was the Apple Lisa and, in 1984, the first Macintosh. It took me about ten minutes to be pretty good with the mouse. I saw a few different speech recognition products—for other computers—during this time. They typically recognized only a very limited vocabulary, required a master's degree in electrical engineering to install, and were over-priced.

Three years ago, I had the chance to work, briefly, with the original Voice Navigator created by Articulate Systems. I had built a simulation of a 35mm camera that used mouse interaction to change the lens aperture, shutter speed, take a picture, and so forth. After loading the Voice Navigator software and attaching the hardware box, it only took fifteen minutes to add voice controls to my simulation. "Open aperture." "Faster shutter." "Shoot!"

I was wowed! At a business presentation the next morning, my co-workers and I used a wireless microphone to control the simulation. The audience was impressed.

I bought a Voice Navigator II a year ago. It immediately provided that "first one on my block" excitement. It also looked great. I could now explore "Voice User Interface" in detail for myself. My first inclination was to use voice for every pulldown menu command, every dialog box option … everything.

Articulate Systems provides a set of languages for controlling many popular Macintosh programs. A language—to Voice

Navigator—is a file of commands for controlling an application. Each command consists of one or more mouse movements, clicks, or keypresses.

You can customize the languages provided and create your own. You need to create a voice file that contains the sound of your voice saying the commands of a language. This is called "training" the commands. You can say *anything* to train a command. The Voice Navigator doesn't understand English or any other language. It simply matches your voice to the voice patterns you trained it with.

I won't go into details of setting up and using the software, but rather what happened to me during my explorations. The manuals are well-written and I needed to use them to accomplish my objectives.

The main goal of advanced interfaces is increased productivity. I quickly found that simply substituting voice for *all* keyboard and mouse actions didn't give me the increased productivity I expected.

Sometimes, a little analysis goes a long way. So I started analyzing how I use my computer each day. I identified those frustrating situations where my thinking got ahead of me because of an excessively tedious action I had to do. I also studied my new combined interface—keyboard, mouse, and microphone.

Here's what I found:

First, there are standard Macintosh actions I use in every application. These, by now, are second nature, but require me to hit command keys—or move the mouse and click—when I'm mentally already thinking about my next action. So I created voice commands for *Open, Close, Save, Page Setup, Print, Cut, Copy, Paste, Delete, OK, Cancel, Quit, Scroll up,* and *Scroll down.*

Close is used both to close documents in an application and to close folders in the finder. I was amazed at how wonderful it was to have voice commands for *OK* and *Cancel,* since they are used in almost every dialog box.

Because I use a small set of applications and utilities every day, I set up voice commands to quickly launch them from across the room. I'm fortunate to have an office in a separate room, with few distractions. (There is a dog that barks outside my open window sometimes on warm days.) The Voice Navigator comes with voice commands to *Activate* and *Deactivate* the microphone; I have these set to respond to "Listen" and "Voice Off."

I use the standard, sleek, desktop microphone that comes with Voice Navigator. Articulate Systems sells other microphones, including a headset microphone with a noise-canceling feature for environments with much ambient noise.

My printer and scanner are a few feet from my Mac, so I have to move to them to insert a page to be scanned, or an envelope or letterhead for manual printing. Soon after I got my Voice Navigator, I needed to scan a large number of text documents with OCR software. Here's how I did it: I started the software, walked over to the scanner and put in the first page. I said "OK" to start the scan. I spent the rest of the time feeding the scanner when needed, and rambling around my office working on other tasks.

I scanned and saved all the documents without ever touching my keyboard or mouse—or sitting down.

For word processing, I have a few often-used text phrases set up as voice commands. Things like my name, address, phone number. Many of you probably use macros to do the same. I can imagine my attorney really taking advantage of the Voice Navigator.

Most of my work is with graphics or multimedia. This is where I've found the greatest gains with voice. Voice allows me to maintain my creative context and work much, much faster.

Here's an example. I'm doing detailed work in a color paint program—without voice—and I need a different tool. So I zip across to the tool palette with the mouse, click a new tool, and zip back to my work. Granted, moving to the tool palette *is* fast and easy. Picking a new tool is also fast; tools in a palette are typically 20 x 20 pixels or larger, and it's easy to hit one of 400 pixels.

Moving *back* to the work is what takes time; especially when I need to zero in on a single pixel. It's a case of "leaving and returning to the context of your work."

With Voice Navigator, I keep my cursor and eyes on the work and simply ask for a new tool. I also use voice for *Bring to front, Send to back, Rotate, Change color,* and commands buried in hierarchical menus.

And then there are dinner parties. Every once in a while, we have guests who don't use a Macintosh. They're not quite sure what to make of my Voice Navigator—or should I say they don't know what to say?

Here's what I say: "I love it."

If you want one, contact:

Articulate Systems
600 West Cummings Park, Suite 4500
Woburn, MA 01801
(800) 443-7077

৯৳

— Copyright 1992, © Carl Philabaum.

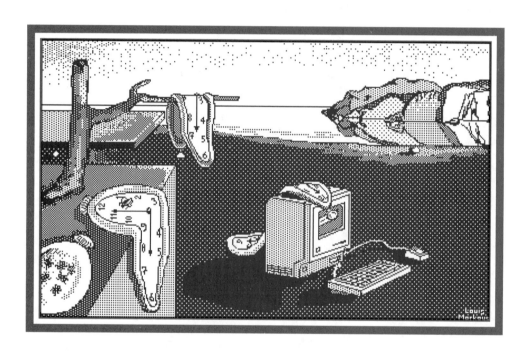

PART

X

SOON OR NEVER

411

APPLE ON BLUES POWER

TONY BOVE & CHERYL RHODES

W elcome to the future.

Maybe.

A world of multimedia, heavy-duty corporate computing, AppleIBM, high-speed data networks, and nifty little handheld guys that work with radio waves (or something similar) to do amazing things in a Mac-like way.

Maybe.

The future is an iffy thing. Probably because the future doesn't exist. Nonexistent realities tend to be iffy. It's a trueism.

Luckily, we don't need to concern ourselves here with global warming, the destruction of the rain forests, America's growing underclass, or the Twin's chances to win the World Series again.

Instead, we have weighty matters to delve into. The heaviest topic of all is the Apple/IBM alliance. And the best people to take on the complex and gritty prospect are Tony Bove and Cheryl Rhodes, two journalists who know what they're talking about.

Listen:

Apple and IBM Agree to Develop a Standard Platform

The industry was taken by surprise, right before the fourth of July, with the announcement that Apple and IBM are getting together to jointly develop a new computing platform. The announcement stated that the two former rivals will "...work to create powerful new open system software platforms for the 1990s." The gist of the letter of intent is that the companies intend to develop and market new technologies that will be used in existing and new products. The companies intend to offer these new technologies to other vendors for incorporating into other computers.

It didn't take long for the industry's leading columnists and pundits to pronounce or denounce the relationship. One columnist compared the relationship to Madonna and Sean Penn (as in big name relationships rarely last). Comparisons were also drawn with IBM's acquisition of Rolm, General Motors' acquisition of EDS, Apple's own stillborn relationship with DEC, IBM's "strategic" partnerships with various companies such as Novell, Borland, and Lotus, and so forth. The reading was engaging, but practically none of these columns or reports touched upon the nitty-gritty details of the technology. This was not necessarily the fault of hyperactive writers or headline-mongering editors: Apple and IBM released precious few details about the technology. Besides, for TV coverage of this famous superpower pow-wow, who cares about details?

Perhaps the reason why many of the critics could see no real benefits is that few believe that the two companies can actually get down to business and deliver a new platform. Cynics see only the jockeying for position of the new companies, the stillborn efforts of the previous partnership between Metaphor (Patriot Partners) and IBM, and the failed marriage between IBM and Microsoft. Many cynics point to a culture clash that will happen when Appleniks mingle with the blue suits. Perhaps they forget the culture clashes in the relationship between Microsoft and IBM, which took nearly an entire decade to unravel.

But it is the technology that brings these companies together, not the headlines. Just as IBM, when it introduced the PC, needed a new operating system to represent the new paradigm for personal computing, so now do both IBM and Apple need a new paradigm for the RISC platform. The technology in question is the object layer that separates the system software and APIs (application program interfaces) from the actual hardware. The fact is, Apple is further along in defining this object layer than either Patriot Partners or Microsoft.

The intent of the partnership is nothing less than an effort to redefine the personal computing environment of the next decade without Microsoft's involvement. Microsoft's chairman Bill Gates alluded to this problem in the recently-leaked internal memo from Mr. Bill to his troops, in which he said, "IBM is proposing to take over the definition of PC desktop operating systems."

Apple has prepared itself for this venture. One reason why System 7 was so late was that Apple planted the seeds for a processor-independent version of the system that would eventually work on top of this new object layer. Apple had acknowledged that, as a result of playing a proprietary fiddle in the computer market, the company was ultimately heading for obscurity in the margins of the industry, and that a change of strategy was in order. IBM had already acknowledged some of its failures in the personal computer market, and the need to consolidate the benefits of various operating environments such as OS/2, NextStep, and OSF/Motif. The idea now is to implement these APIs on top of this new object layer.

Both companies also recognized that they needed to implement a short-term strategy to bring the Mac OS and interface to a wider audience of users, especially multimedia users. Apple may also have realized that it can't operate with low profit margins and high volume manufacturing operations and still compete effectively with Japan Inc. on the home computer front.

The Japan-bashers in this country may be pointing to the IBM-Apple deal as the ultimate patriotic deal of the decade, but we would not be surprised to see the resulting IBM-Apple multimedia software environment promptly licensed to Sony and other Japan manufacturers for the next generation of home machines. IBM may be expanding its domestic manufacturing operations and making more of its own components at Japan's expense, but the end result will likely be participation in this platform by Japanese companies, with system licensing revenues pouring back into the company that is marketing the IBM-Apple system.

Open Now Means Blind Faith

Critics who say the IBM-Apple technology is not "open" are confusing openness with the status quo. A technology is open if anyone can license it—and it is the stated intent of this partnership to license the object-layer technology the companies co-develop. Part of the intent is to also create a standard multimedia platform that would be licensed to other vendors. We think it is very possible for Apple and IBM to co-develop technology that is "open" by every definition of the word.

When we ask customers what openness means to them, in most cases it means the ability to choose many different types of machines (workstations, laptops, desktops, etc.) that will run the same software. This answer sounds more like the definition of "scalable" with the added benefit of multiple sources. DOS is scalable down-market from desktops into laptops; OS/2 is scalable from desktops up into workstations; Unix is scalable from workstations up into mainframes but not down into laptops; and the Macintosh OS remains locked in a single vendor's platform with no real choices (yet) for laptops or workstations. Many customers have said that they prefer an "open" (read clone-able) technology largely because they expect components for mixing and matching to be available at lower prices, due to competition.

Software developers have a notion of openness as a state in which a system can be licensed to many different vendors to provide a larger installed base than before. Scalability becomes important as these developers try to extend their reach into categories such as laptops and workstations. The IBM-Apple partnership addresses both issues (openness and scalability) by creating an object layer that would run on everything from mainframes to laptops, and be freely licensed; this object layer could then support multiple APIs. How is this message any different than, say, Sun Microsystem's message about Unix and SPARC? It is now important for Sun to transform Unix into an object-oriented system.

What is confusing to the mainstream users is that throughout the 80s, "open" technology has been synonymous with IBM-compatible technology, with Microsoft getting the credit and the licensing revenues because Microsoft's DOS was literally the only common denominator. We rarely hear any customer or software developer claim that Microsoft's technology is "better" than the Mac; more often they simply dismiss the Mac because it is "proprietary."

But in the 90s, it is plausible that Apple could take Microsoft's place as the "open" systems vendor, and the Mac look and feel could take the place of Windows as the preëminent graphical user interface. IBM's acquisition of Metaphor (which ties IBM into the original Xerox research on graphical user interfaces) and its agreement with Apple removes any legal obstacles for IBM to advance the state of the art of graphical user interfaces, borrowing freely the best ideas of the previous interfaces.

Pink Pride and Blue Money

What exactly are the terms of this partnership between Apple and IBM? It represents the union of Apple's expertise in product development and marketing, and IBM's muscle in financing and in the MIS/enterprise computing world. The IBM-Apple agreement covers four areas:

1. The companies plan a joint venture to co-develop "open" object-oriented system software based on Apple's Pink project, which will span a wide range of computing platforms and include everything from laptops to large servers. A separate company will be created to market and license this system software widely, avoiding the issue of a single manufacturer's control over the technology. The Patriot Partners effort will be rolled into this new effort as "complementary" technology. Metaphor (recently acquired by IBM) will be responsible for integrating the efforts of all three companies.

2. IBM and Apple will work together to integrate Macs into IBM's enterprise systems and client/server architecture, by means of new communications and networking products and

an enhanced AIX (IBM's version of Unix) that would include the Macintosh Toolbox for running Mac applications. It is expected that Apple's A/UX would evolve into AIX.

3. Apple will adopt IBM's POWER RISC architecture (in a single-chip implementation by Motorola) for use in future Macintosh computers. This "Power PC-based" Mac could be available within three years and be priced between $2,000 and $3,000. It will run the Mac OS, A/UX, and Pink operating environments, all running on top of the object layer.

4. Apple and IBM will co-develop a common multimedia platform by creating and licensing platform-independent software environments in an effort to provide a market for multimedia content. This platform will include Apple's QuickTime technology, and possibly a more "object-like" version of the Mac OS.

Each one of these areas is important for software vendors, desktop publishers, and multimedia content developers. However, the last one—a standard multimedia platform—has never been addressed before by such powerful manufacturers. Only Microsoft has promoted the concept of a standard multimedia platform, the MPC (Multimedia PC), and Tandy has all but shipped a machine that conforms to this standard, but multimedia developers have not been impressed by it, and Microsoft is not in a position to improve upon the hardware.

In addition, Microsoft still faces a legal challenge from Apple over the look and feel of Microsoft Windows, upon which the MPC is based. IBM, with its optical disc technology and ownership of Metaphor, and Apple, with its superior graphical user interface, are in excellent positions to get together and define a new standard for multimedia.

One misconception making the rounds of industry debates is that the multimedia platform requires Pink, and that both companies, which have histories of system software delays, will be unable to take advantage of the window of opportunity to create a multimedia platform as a standard.

But Pink, the object-oriented environment built upon the object layer, is only one aspect of the IBM-Apple agreement. The Power PC/RISC workstation, the Pink operating environment, and the enterprise-wide integration are significant ventures for laying the foundation of object-oriented computing for the future business computing market. Software developers will no doubt queue up to receive information about developing for this platform. But it is true that Pink is a long time coming.

On the other hand, the multimedia platform, which can be developed more quickly with today's technology and with the Mac interface, can have more of an immediate impact, focusing today's multimedia content developers, and opening a new home market in two years (perhaps replacing VCRs everywhere) that is potentially far more lucrative than the desktop computing market in the long run.

Another aspect of this agreement—the integration of Macs into the IBM enterprise computing model—does not have to wait for any new developments other than some communication and networking products. Macs are already integrated to some degree through the use of Novell networks. Neither Pink nor the RISC architecture are necessary for this integration to be strengthened.

Sitting on Top of the Object Layer

The most important aspect of this agreement is the object layer upon which all these technologies may sit. True, a new operating environment should not be saddled with the APIs of the past—this is Microsoft's game plan, all but discredited because no one wants to buy a new environment simply to run old programs. But with new environments, it takes time to develop new applications that are better than the old ones.

Moreover, the multimedia content titles, even more so than applications, have to run in this new environment.

What is unique about this object layer is that it runs older APIs and it also runs Pink, which has a totally new interface. Pink could eventually become the foundation for new types of computing machines—the DOS of the late 1990s. Although the details have not been announced, Pink is rumored to be a new approach to computing, and a system that will be implemented directly in silicon. The "objects" in Pink make it possible to mix and match components with ease. If the rumors are true, Pink may be even more object-oriented than GO's PenPoint (another interface and API that IBM has licensed). It is unlikely that Pink will look anything like today's Mac interface.

(One software developer explained that the need for a File menu, with Open, Save, Quit, and other such commands, would be eliminated. Another suggested that a truly object-oriented environment could run on anything, given the capability to modify the code of lower-level objects that link the system to the hardware.)

Pink could therefore be attractive as a scalable environment for any type of computing device, be it a hand-held communicator or a mainframe. It could then act as the glue that binds the computing and consumer electronics technologies into one industry and market. We envision a future RISC-based platform that could run several operating system interfaces, including OS/2, the Mac OS, and Pink, linked to a common object layer.

Speculations aside, everyone knows that Apple will have to spend a great deal of time and effort bringing Pink to market. But IBM and Apple have time on their side: with the Mac interface (which is superior to Windows right now), IBM and Apple can deliver a multimedia platform within two years that does not need Microsoft's present or future versions of Windows. IBM can also point to a new object layer that will support the OS/2 API, providing a consistent upgrade path for developers that is less confusing than the current OS/2-to-Windows "path" that Microsoft is promoting.

The key to success for this agreement is the positive attitude of everyone involved, if this attitude can be maintained. Microsoft has already shown how a negative attitude about IBM can ruin a good thing. The culture clash that everyone expects to occur between Apple and IBM occurred already between IBM and Microsoft; perhaps IBM learned culture lessons from the failings of this relationship. Now Apple and IBM have to combine their Pink and Big Blue cultures to come up with a royal purple.

A Purple Rain on Microsoft's Parade

This year has been a bad one for Microsoft's image, though excellent for software sales. First, IBM and Microsoft had to put a flimsy happy-face mask on their deteriorating relationship over the fate of OS/2. Then the Federal Trade Commission (FTC) launched an investigation of Microsoft, prompted by the happy-face agreement, which in retrospect seems ridiculous now that IBM and Microsoft have all but divorced. The FTC expanded its investigation when it heard tales of so-called abuse from many of Microsoft's competitors, and even from some "partner" firms. Apple recently gained another legal victory in its lawsuit against Microsoft and Hewlett-Packard over the look and feel of Windows. Finally, Microsoft had to back off TrueImage (a PostScript clone) and try to repair its relationship with Hewlett-Packard.

Still, it is not likely that anyone will feel sorry for the world's largest software company, which is enjoying tremendous sales of its applications and of Windows. The company's system software dominance does not sit well with competitors on the application side, where they feel Microsoft has an unfair advantage due to advance knowledge of the inner workings of its system software. Microsoft has competitors in nearly every level of the software business, so it is not surprising to see many large software vendors willing to jump ship from Microsoft's plan to upgrade DOS users to Windows, and eventually to Windows NT (New Technology), a fully 32-bit version of Windows.

Predictably, Microsoft officials reacted to the IBM-Apple agreement with scorn and paranoia. On the one hand, Microsoft is understandably bent by the notion that IBM and Apple are joining forces to compete directly with Microsoft, and that Apple is trying to remake itself into a company that primarily sells system software (like Microsoft).

On the other hand, IBM's new direction casts doubt on OS/2 itself, leaving Microsoft sitting pretty with the only operating environment (namely, Windows) that presumably will be consistent from Intel-based DOS PCs on up to RISC-based workstations. Microsoft officials are quick to point out that IBM's commitment to OS/2 is now in question, and that customers will be confused.

Microsoft's answer is to push the development of Windows NT. Formerly, Microsoft was committing to provide compatibility for the OS/2 2.0 API (application program interface) within Windows NT (which at the time was simply called "OS/2 3.0"). Now, Microsoft has announced that it is dropping the OS/2 2.0 API, forcing application developers to choose between the Windows and OS/2 APIs. Microsoft is poised to drop OS/2 altogether, and push Windows NT as the future operating environment for all platforms.

The shift in marketing gears at Microsoft is likely to produce even more tension between Microsoft and IBM. (Microsoft is still under contract to provide something called "OS/2 3.0" to IBM.) The IBM-Apple agreement points to a development path that starts with the OS/2 2.0 API and proceeds directly to the new object layer, bypassing Windows completely.

The ACE of Clubs

The IBM-Apple deal certainly has the Mac third-party developers dancing in the streets. These developers—some of the most innovative in the industry—already know how to make a Mac program sing, and presumably they will not have to reinvent their advantages with a different API. These developers have stood behind what Marc Canter of MacroMind has called "the best computer in the industry," and they are hoping to be vindicated. As Dave Winer of UserLand points out, nothing would be finer than to see the Mac OS appear on IBM platforms.

For publishing software users, the "professional desktop" computer is the next step that combines personal productivity with workstation-like distributed processing, and application developers want to be ready for this next wave. Competing for the developer's attention are the proprietary NeXT workstation, the "open" Unix-based Sun SPARC workstation, the OSF/Motif environment developed by the OSF consortium, and the recently formed ACE (Advanced Computing Environment) platform endorsed by a consortium of PC-compatible manufacturers and workstation vendors, led by Microsoft and the Santa Cruz Operation (SCO). With all the talk of openness and standards, the workstation side of the computer market enters the new decade more fragmented than ever before.

ACE includes Compaq, DEC, Microsoft, MIPS, NEC, Olivetti, SCO, Silicon Graphics (SGI), Wang, and Zenith. This club is characterized not so much by a progressive attitude as by an attitude of wanting to hedge all bets. The group will use the ARC (Advanced RISC Computing) spec for MIPS RISC processors, but also will continue to support Intel's 386, 486, and x86 (future) processors. One progressive component of the ACE spec is the high-performance graphics system services, the Iris API and Graphics Library, from SGI.

Upon this foundation rests support for two operating systems, according to the specifications: Microsoft's NT environment (formerly called OS/2 3.0), and SCO's unified Unix implementation with the Open Desktop interface (which is based on OSF/Motif and X Window). Again, the proponents are hedging their bets, unwilling to settle on one or the other environment. Programs written for DOS, Windows, OS/2, and Posix (an industry-standard definition of a Unix API) are automatically accommodated on ARC and Intel high-performance machines. The APIs for these environments are glued on top of Microsoft's NT kernel, which essentially acts like an object layer.

Unfortunately for the group, the specs are not yet completed and a schedule of products has not yet been announced. However, the basic elements (the EISA bus, and a DOS-compatible and Windows-compatible API) suggest that the ARC/Intel platform will enjoy at least moderate success, appealing to customers who need to maintain backwards-compatibility with existing DOS and DOS/Windows machines.

Pair of Macs Beats an ACE?

The ACE platform is a direct challenge to Sun Microsystems, which has enjoyed great success with SPARCstation sales; to NeXT, which has started to become a player in the workstation market with its second generation machines; and to IBM, which now has its own advanced computing environment on a drawing board shared with Apple.

Apple has felt for some time that it had a good chance at providing a competitive high-level system software environment for future

RISC machines that are not made by Apple. In addition, the leverage of having system components to license puts Apple in the catbird seat for directing the development of the new generation of multi-media player machines. (This is where NeXT wanted to be, but the company could not get IBM to commit entirely to NextStep.) All that was needed was something to push IBM toward Apple.

We have always been enthusiastic about Unix with a Mac-like interface, even though A/UX never took the market by storm. IBM appears to like the combination also. Part of the agreement calls for IBM to use the Macintosh Toolbox so that IBM's version of Unix, AIX, can sport the complete look and feel of a Mac, plus the ability to run standard (32-bit clean) Mac applications, plus support for 32-bit Color QuickDraw. AIX thus inherits all the benefits of Apple's A/UX.

Apple is already committing to provide a Power PC RISC plat-form that runs the Mac OS, A/UX, and Pink. We would not be surprised to also see on a future IBM RISC machine the APIs for the Mac OS, AIX, Pink, OS/2, and OSF/Motif. Throw Display PostScript and NextStep into the mix, and the machine would run nearly all of the progressive software environments that are attrac-tive for all forms of publishing and multimedia. Thus, what NeXT had promised in the way of a professional desktop, Apple (with IBM's help) may actually deliver.

Enterprise Computing: Beam Me Up from Armonk

IBM so far has licensed other technologies far and wide with little to show for results. NextStep went nowhere; PenPoint-based lap-tops are not yet available; Patriot Partners did not get off the ground. Meanwhile, IBM's OS/2 strategy was in trouble. OS/2 2.0 is a solid product, but the wind has been taken from its sails by Windows. IBM's current strategy of demonstrating how Windows applications can run on top of OS/2 looks more like capitulation than compliance.

OS/2 Presentation Manager (PM) has always been the linchpin in a strategy to establish SAA (Systems Applications Architecture) as a smooth and consistent set of operating environments that spans mainframes to personal computers.

But IBM is changing the way it produces personal computer software by taking the small work group approach. Its Personal Software division is cranking out Windows programs, and will probably now start cranking out Mac programs. IBM is embracing the Mac operating environment for its RISC machines at a time when Mac developers are working on advanced versions of their products. This is good news for Mac users.

Apple has sued Microsoft and H-P over the look and feel of Windows; now IBM has sidestepped the entire issue by making a deal with Apple to adapt the same look and feel over IBM's RISC product line. IBM has also acquired Metaphor, which gives the company a legal-proof license to use any part of the original Xerox interface. The next step (pardon the pun) is for IBM to incorporate the Mac and Metaphor interfaces directly into SAA; or, if that is impossible, to abandon SAA or redefine it as something new. (Pity the poor MIS departments that have been trying to standardize on SAA—it is once again a moving target.)

Thus, the Mac interface that launched thousands of individual entrepreneurs and small businesses through personal empowerment will be used to bridge the gap between the individual and the MIS bureaucracy. They call this "enterprise-wide" computing, and it spurs the development of tools for managing electronic publishing and distribution of documents, video teleconferencing and mail, and other enterprise-wide activities.

Mac Multimedia: Ticket to Ride

The IBM-Apple agreement is the best news that multimedia content developers have heard in a long time—better than the Microsoft-specified Multimedia PC (MPC). It means that the Macintosh installed base will grow faster in the short term, and that the MPC is not the only game in town. In short, their pioneering development efforts on the Mac will pay off.

With over two million installed Macs capable of upgrading to System 7 and of displaying color graphics, the Mac is right now the largest potential platform for interactive multimedia—all that is needed is for CD-ROM drives to sell in larger quantities, or for some media technology better than CD-ROM to be introduced.

Windows isn't growing the multimedia market (yet). Although the number of copies of Windows going into the channel has surpassed four million, insiders estimate that only about one million copies are actually in use for the specific purpose of running several Windows applications, not merely to switch between ordinary DOS programs, or to run just one Windows program. As for MPCs, the multimedia extensions to Windows are not yet shipping to anyone.

One year from today we should be writing about the IBM-Apple multimedia platform as an area of explosive growth for multimedia developers. The agreement between IBM and Apple to endorse a common multimedia platform reflects the basic complementary nature of their strengths. Apple captured the mind-share of the industry with respect to graphical user interfaces; IBM captured the mind-share with respect to enterprise-wide computing. Neither has a significant share that would block the other's success.

The agreement points out that with both companies, the only road to success is to cooperate against a common enemy and forge a new standard with the best technology they can muster. For Mac users, this path represents the best hope to save them from eventually succumbing to a world dominated by Windows.

— This article first appeared in the *Bove & Rhodes Inside Report on Multimedia*, issue #56, July 1991. It is Copyright © 1991 07/16/91 by Tony Bove & Cheryl Rhodes

Tony Bove & Cheryl Rhodes edit several newsletters, including the Bove & Rhodes Inside Report on Multimedia *and the* MacroMind Developer Letter. *Bove & Rhodes are also columnists for* Publish *magazine, the* Prodigy *service, and* Computer Currents. *For details, contact them on MCI Mail (TBOVE), CompuServe (70105,722), or AppleLink (D0493), or write to Bove & Rhodes, Box 1289, Gualala, CA 95445.*

APPLE IN THE PINK?

DENISE CARUSO

*T*ony Bove & Cheryl Rhodes, in the previous article, pretty well wrapped that whole Apple/IBM thing, right?

If it's a great deal for both companies, does that mean Apple's in the Pink?

❧

September 29, 1991

Once again, or maybe I should say "finally," the spectre of the Apple Computer-IBM Corp. agreement is hitting the papers. John Sculley of Apple and Jim Cannavino from IBM have been batting their eyelashes at each other in public, and the rumormeisters are saying the duo will be making their agreement public this coming week.

The behind-the-scenes machinations on this deal are absolutely terrifying to behold. Never have so many intelligent people's hours been squandered on something that seems to make so little sense.

At first I thought the deal was a semi-good idea. I liked the part about joining together to make a fresh start with object-oriented software (apologies for using that hideous buzzphrase, but that's what it is). But now, rumor has it, there will be no joint development of an OS. Instead, Apple may just finish its own operating system, called Pink, and the two companies will work together to make it run on IBM's RS/6000 RISC workstations.

Excuse me? This grand and glorious Apple-IBM thing is about putting software on a workstation? Those kinds of deals get cut

426

every day in Silicon Valley. And if I remember correctly, Apple is also developing a RISC workstation, maybe even based on this same chip. Cooperation and competition do kind of look alike on a page, if you're not wearing your glasses, but they are not the same word. As someone's bottom line will no doubt attest after a year or so of this nonsense.

I'm sure there's more to the deal than that—Apple and IBM are preparing some equally grandiose agreement about multimedia as well—but the noises I hear coming out of Cupertino are not sighs of ecstasy. They are groans of torture. If Apple employees don't "get" the benefit of the IBM gig, they will not go gently in that big, blue night.

In fact, there is a sign posted in some Computer-tino cubicles —no, never mind, I can't tell you about it. It's humiliating, and for once I'll spare the parties involved. I'll tell you instead about the T-shirts seen at Macworld Expo in Boston last month, which are basically the same idea, only less personally vicious.

Front of T-shirt: Apple logo, with text underneath, "This is your brain." Back of T-shirt, Apple and IBM logo together. Text underneath: "Your brain on drugs."

And indeed, I have to say, this deal seems more and more surreal to me the more time goes on. No matter how good it sounds when Sculley and Cannavino talk about it, there is a gutter-level reality that I think Sculley, at least, has completely missed.

Over the years Apple has been touted over and over again as a "marketing company," due no doubt to its lavish product announcements and such, but from day one it has never been able to effectively sell its technology, which has always been superior, against IBM or Microsoft.

While I was traveling in Europe, I chatted up a lot of people on the Apple-IBM thing. I was met with one big universal rolling of the eyes, and more than one person said it was the death knell for Apple.

Already, they said, IBM's sales force is using the agreement as a crowbar against its so-called partner. When making sales calls to large accounts, I heard, the question invariably comes up: "What about the Mac? We like the Mac." In the past, IBM would say, "Forget the Mac. It's not compatible with anything, it's a toy, blah blah blah." Standard sales BS.

But now they're saying, "Oh, you don't need to buy a Macintosh. We're going to have everything the Mac has."

A joke I heard in London pretty much sums up the whole thing: What do you get when you cross a Macintosh with an IBM? Answer: An IBM.

꙳

— Originally appeared on America Online as "Pink on the RS/6000? Is that all there is?" © Copyright 1991 Denise Caruso and America Online, Inc.

Denise Caruso has been involved in the electronics industry for nearly a decade. Her articles and columns have appeared in the San Jose Mercury-News, Personal Computing *magazine, the* Business Week Newsletter for Information Executives, *the* San Francisco Examiner, *and other publications.*

Today, she's editor of the industry newsletter Digital Media: A Seybold Report.

Digital Media *focuses on the convergence of personal computers, telecommunications, and consumer electronics, and the digitization of all media, including sound, video, graphics, animation, and photography. Caruso joined Jonathan Seybold's organization in March 1991, and launched the newsletter—to an overwhelmingly positive reception—at Seybold's Digital World conference in June. Digital Media's editorial offices are located in San Francisco.*

Digital Media: A Seybold Report
Subscription office:
428 E. Baltimore Pike
P.O. Box 644
Media, PA 19063
(215) 565-2480

THE CRABB PAPERS:
A CRITICAL LOOK AT THE CORPORATE MACINTOSH

DON CRABB

A nd now for the real world, where people in corporations use—and mis-use—their Macintoshes every day.

Here's the world as it is, and the world as it should, and may, be, brought to you by Don Crabb, one of the true heavy-hitters in the Mac community.

ᴈ⃨

The Real Multimedia Revolution: QuickTime

Perhaps no computer-based technology has been so hyped in the last couple of years as multimedia. Even though many corporate Mac users can't even agree on what the concept means, we've had a veritable explosion in multimedia authoring products and multimedia future shock predictions.

Unfortunately, what we haven't had much of is a cogent explanation of why multimedia should be important to us. Indeed, most managers I've talked with have been left with the impression that multimedia is only of interest to shops that have a substantial committment to the graphic arts. Managers want to know what multimedia can do for them. They want to know what business problems multimedia can solve.

Even if you strip away the hype that has attended the multimedia lovefest in the last two years, you'll still find a serious technical problem—multimedia authoring systems are way out in front of their delivery systems. Who cares if you can create a multimedia application if it takes $20,000-worth of computing and video equipment to make the sucker come to life on someone's desktop.

Because multimedia has not yet become mass media, it's a tough sell to most managers. This delivery problem is so serious that it has tarnished multimedia's potential as well as its current state of the art.

Apple has realized this, of course. Even though their signal-to-noise ratio hasn't always been high when it comes to explaining multimedia to the market (can you say Helocar? I knew that you could), a group of Applelites have had their eyes on the prize for a while. The result of their efforts, of course, is QuickTime.

QuickTime manages events that happen over time, like sound and video, much like the way that QuickDraw manages the drawing of still images on a Macintosh's screen. In short, QuickTime is a new System software architecture extension for the integration of dynamic media within Macintosh computers. For most corporate Mac users, and their users, QuickTime consists of a system extension you plop into your System 7 system folders.

Once that's done, you've just turned your Macs into true multimedia delivery systems (even B&W displays like those on the Classic and Classic II will be able to take advantage of this technology—albeit at a less realistic level than an 8- or 24-bit color display). While you probably won't be authoring QuickTime-based applications on minimum Macs, you will be able to display the fruits of those developmental efforts without having to add expensive frame grabbers, laserdisc players, sound boards, or other media esoterica. With a single piece of technology Apple has managed to solve the basic delivery problem in the Macintosh world (and hopefully Kaleida will extend this technology to other platforms).

QuickTime promises to change the kind of information that managers deliver to their users and that information systems deliver to those managers. How? Because that information will no longer be limited to text and graphics. Adding moving pictures, video, and sound to any application ratchets up its level of information transferral. In fact, QuickTime should allow corporate

Mac users to create new in-house applications that will themselves become strategic resources that can be displayed across corporate Macs (without needing fancy video equipment).

Consider, for example, the case of the factory manager who is designing a new critical assembly system. With the incorporation of sound and video into the system, assemblers will be much better informed as to what is happening in the assembly process. You could postulate hundreds of other similar applications, such as decision support systems, or inventory systems, or even accounting systems that will be more communicative with the addition of multimedia components. And all of these will be made affordable (in terms of both time to develop and cost to display), thanks to QuickTime.

QuickTime will ship as a standard part of System 7.1 sometime during 1992. This system software, more than even System 7, shows corporate Mac users just how good Apple can be when their hearts and minds are in right place.

QuickTime and Workgroup Computing

I've been thinking a lot lately about different technologies and what they really offer us in terms of better work environments and professional growth. One of those technologies that keeps popping up in my head is workgroup computing.

Workgroup computing (at least the term, if not the reality) was a hot topic a few years ago. The very idea that computers and software would make it easier for people to work together was a bit revolutionary. I can remember many articles in the computer press, of course, but the subject was so fascinating to people outside the immediate computer community that it fostered discussions in the general press as well. What has happened to workgroup computing in the last couple of years? Has it made a difference to most corporate Mac users?

After spending some time researching the subject, I came to a couple of initial conclusions: (1) workgroup computing is still ill-defined, and (2) workgroup computing has fostered precious few new tools.

Although academic researchers have done a pretty solid job of looking at how people work together and interact, with the exception of the efforts at M.I.T. and their work with Lotus (and the Lotus Notes product), little workgroup computing software has been written, or even proposed.

Notes, of course, is probably the one case where the technology that might make workgroup computing really work has been explored. But because Notes is very expensive, doesn't run on the Macintosh, and has not been a tremendous success, it hasn't done anything for corporate Mac users, and their users.

Instead, the Mac has fostered some decent, if uninspired, "groupware" applications—mostly of the shared document variety. Working over a LAN, these shared document programs (like Mainstay's "MarkUp") allow more than one person to view a document and add copymarks and editorial comments. The idea is that such multi-person documents will foster some of the inter-group communications that workgroup computing promised from the beginning.

There are other Mac examples of course, including "Meeting Maker" from On Technology, but the workgroup thrust on the Mac has been to provide basic tools, not to define a truly new category of software with new points of view.

Perhaps the problem with today's workgroup computing applications is that the idea of using computers that are hooked together on a LAN as a substitute for real interpersonal communication is flawed. Even when people share marked-up documents, how much new information is gained by this sharing? Is the amount and quality of this shared information worth the cost of the LAN and the software? What kind of people-to-people contact gets lost when we resort to a software tool?

Some other corporate Mac users and myself are beginning to have our doubts, at least about today's state-of-the-art in workgroup computing. We see that the basic tools we have on the Mac work okay, but they don't seem to be giving us the big improvement in the way people work because of them. The great flow of ideas back and forth that workgroup software has promised to create just hasn't happened yet.

Part of the problem with today's workgroup software on the Mac is its limited mission and scope. Fortunately, that's likely to change over the next few years as several new technologies come online in an affordable way—voice annotation of files, and real-time video and sound data.

Think about the improved communication that a workgroup application, designed around these two technologies, could provide. You could create documents with extensive voice comments on them in the voice of the document's author. The documents could also contain explanatory video clips to further improve their communications quality among a group who can't always meet face-to-face.

Apple, of course, with their QuickTime extensions to System 7, make much of this new workgroup technology possible. As things start to shake out for Macintosh workgroup computing over the next few years, expect to find workgroup computing tools finally hitting their stride. And QuickTime will lead that charge.

The Truth of Enterprise-wide Computing and Apple's Role

When was enterprise-wide computing invented? 1991? 1990? As early as 1989, perhaps? Wrong on all counts. Try about 1965, when IBM began to sell its first time-sharing terminal access system for its new 360 mainframe computers.

Enterprise-wide computing is simply the 90s' name for what first was called mainframe timesharing; later minicomputer timesharing (invented by Digital); and eventually shared workstation networks, popularized by Sun. Understanding this simple fact will help all corporate Mac users get a better grip on building competent enterprise-wide computing systems in their companies. Know thy enemy, so to speak.

Reducing the BS factor inherent in enterprise-wide computing is essential for corporate Mac users who expect to get something out of the vendor-specific tools and software implementations that promise improve the whole shebang in this decade. Any vendor who tells you that they invented the best enterprise-wide computing solution is either "full of it," or badly misinformed. Take either stance with many grains of salt.

With a pedigree as old and well-conceived as enterprise-wide computing, you'd think that the tools being offered to make the thing work in different environments would be fairly straightforward.

Unfortunately, confusion reigns supreme among as many vendors as it does among corporate Mac users. About the only thing everyone agrees on is the importance of SQL—yet SQL should only be the starting point of any enterprise-wide computing environment.

Not even Apple has told us just which technologies should be the backbone of an enterprise-wide system. While connectivity tools and multimedia extensions will help all corporate Mac users to make better use of their enterprise-wide systems (by enabling a richer form of information to be exploited by all their Mac staffers and Mac workgroups), the base these products are supposed to extend is still undefined by Apple and many Mac vendors.

Just what, then, is the "enterprise" in enterprise-wide computing? The corporate database, of course. All of those mainframe disks full of terrabytes of information. Most of it so badly organized that some companies can't begin to exploit it.

Enterprise-wide computing should be all about taking this gold mine of information and reusing it in ways more easily accessible to everyone in the corporation who needs it. More importantly, each of these ways of using the data must be tailored to the particular audience. A middle manager, for example, working in international sales hardly has the same needs as a engineer in product development, yet both need access to the full corporate data resource—not just some preselected subset.

The reason so much precious corporate data goes unused is that the access tools and user environments are lousy. Mainframe and minicomputer database companies have done a crummy job over the last ten years in reacting to the needs of their customers. That's why microcomputer databases have grabbed so many of their customers. Departments were willing to spend money to take data from the corporate database and stuff it onto a micro running something as mediocre as dBASE, just to have it close at hand. Think of the costs in doing this, both in terms of the local dBASE applications, and in terms of the loss to the corporation in strategic decision-making capability because managers in those depart-ments were working with only a fractional subset of the available data. What a terrible waste of resources.

Fortunately, both the mainframe and micro database companies have begun to change this. With products like SyBASE, 4th Dimension Server, and Focus, database companies are finally get-ting the word out to IS managers that true enterprise-wide com-puting tools exist.

During 1992, you must resolve to take advantage of these tools. You must also resolve to get serious about developing the right applications at your Mac desktops to give your users the strategic access they deserve. Enterprise-wide computing demands no less.

Managing the Macintosh Strategic Resource

Whether you are an old hand at the Macintosh management game, or have recently come to the party, one thing is for certain: the times, they are a changing. The idea that an installation of Macintosh computers could be a strategic resource to any compa-ny (small, medium, or large) used to be laughable. Hell, weren't we just crawling out of the primordial slime of the Macintosh Office? After all, the Mac was just a personal computer, albeit an easy-to-use one.

Note that I said "used to be." 1991 was a watershed year in the emergence of the Mac as a critical computing platform for many companies. 1992 will see that computing criticality become an important strategic resource. Planning to manage that resource will be anything but simple.

Many corporate Mac users, their developers, and their users find themselves being pulled in many directions at once by the opera-tional demands of their companies. With this background pressure to make the everyday stuff work smoothly, how can any of us plan our strategic futures?

One answer might be the adoption of better development tools, a position I have argued elsewhere before. But you need more than just good development tools if you are going to manage the change that has been, and will be, forced on you. You've got to understand the strategic nature of your Macintosh installation, and the people who use it, while still managing to address emerging technologies like QuickTime, client-serving computing (including Quadra-based high performance servers), and better seamless connectivity.

Data and applications that used to be the sole province of larger computers are being "migrated" down to Macs, where they can be better controlled and exploited. 1992 will mark a considerable increase in this migration for a lot of companies, because the tools necessary for this migration have matured during 1991.

What do you need? Deciding what tools to buy and use in 1992 will be easy compared to deciding how to apply them. What problems do you currently have that can be solved with Macintosh solutions? Keep in mind that your mix of Macs probably changed during 1991, and will likely change again in 1992.

Many companies replaced their standard Mac SEs and IIcx's with Mac IIci's during 1991. Many more plan this same change during 1992, as the IIci becomes the basic corporate Mac. Yet our planning and decision-making processes often don't change with the change in hardware. If we don't remember to extend our computing expectations as our hardware improves, we are likely to forget that better computing platforms give us many more possible computing solutions.

As you plan for the strategic systems that your Macs can be incorporated into during 1992, don't forget to include the changes that you have made to the rest of your computing infrastructure (like your network). Likewise, if you have not made those infrastructure changes, consider what impact they will have on your plans.

Parallelling the increased daily operational pressures that corporate Mac users will feel during 1992, you will find that your bosses expect you to perform strategic computing miracles "with all those new Macs you just bought."

Part of your strategic plans during 1992 must include looking to Apple for some guidance. Apple has made much of their new in-house IS plan (the so-called Vital architecture) for how to manage information resources with Macs. Despite the promises, savvy corporate Mac users know that Apple has yet to release the details of this architecture. Even when they do, most of us won't hold our breaths, since Apple's own IS track record has been anything but stellar.

In fact, Apple doesn't always keep its own strategic computing plans in focus when it makes decisions — a fact brought home most recently by their purchase of an expensive and brand new IS computing building (called the "Glass House" by some at Apple) in Marin county (near no other Apple facilities) from a bank corporation that decided it couldn't afford to use it.

With your bosses yammering at you, and Apple giving you alternately good and specious advice, corporate Mac users will need to rely a lot more on their own experience, and that of their users, than they did during 1991.

After all, who is better able to assess your strategic computing needs?

⨏

— Copyright 1992 © Don Crabb

⨏

Don Crabb is the Director of Laboratories and a Senior Lecturer for Department of Computer Science at the University of Chicago. He is a contributing editor and columnist for the Higher Education Product Companion, Query, Syllabus, Syllabus CS, *and the consulting editorial director for* Content World. *He is also a Contributing Editor and/or Columnist for* PC, BYTE, MacWEEK, MacUSER, NeXTWorld, SunWorld, Consumer Guide, InfoWorld, The Chicago Sun-Times, The MacAuthority, MAC/Chicago, The Weigand Report, *and the* Sister's Syndicate. *His new book,* MacWEEK Guide to System 7 *(Ziff-Davis Press) is now available. He can be reached on America Online as DonJCrabb, and on AppleLink as A0199.*

THE COMING REVOLUTION

DOUG CLAPP

Your computer will soon dissolve.

But it'll be fun. Trust me.

First, consider life today. There you are, mousing away. The computer's in the box, happily chugging away at one or more applications. One person, one computer.

Unless, of course, you're connected to a network and the application you're running is on another machine, down the hall. Or unless you're in Fiji with your PowerBook and decide to run an application back at the home office. In Peoria, Illinois.

The application may be in your computer, or it may not. The data may be in your computer, or it may not. Or—and Mathematica does this brilliantly—the application's "front end" interface may be in your computer, but the actual guts of the program—the "kernel"—may live in a Cray supercomputer, half a world away.

Soon, it won't matter where the application is. Only that you get what you want. (This is all being done for you, remember. Be flattered.)

That's the network revolution. And it will happen—fully and completely—because of another revolution: The bandwidth revolution.

As you read these words, U.S. telephone companies are busy installing electronic "switches" in central offices. Once installed, the phone companies will offer business and home users something called "ISDN"—the Integrated Services Digital Network.

Conventional telephone is analog. And slow. ISDN is digital.

And fast.

One flavor of ISDN is called Basic-rate ISDN. It consists of two 64Kbits/sec data channels and one 16Kbits/sec control channel. The three digital channels co-exist on standard "twisted-pair" telephone wires: regular old two-strand telephone wire. (Three channels on two wires? It's tricky; you don't want to know.)

Basic-rate ISDN (and a few other types of digital service) are already available in some locations. By November 1992, Basic-rate ISDN service will be available in 20 of the largest U.S. cities. If you live in one of those cities—and pay the price for ISDN service—you'll have access to a guaranteed data path of 64Kbits/sec. to any other ISDN-served city. That's not exactly 64,000 baud, but it's close. Use both channels at once and it's...well, not exactly 128,000 baud, but close.

What will ISDN lines cost? That's still undecided in many states. Massachusetts and California, however, have already announced prices. In Massachusetts, you pay an installation fee of $15 and a $8 monthly fee—in addition to the cost of a standard telephone line. In California, the monthly cost is somewhat less than $30.

How fast will ISDN lines be—really? Well, if we don't consider how fast your computer can pump out or receive data—if we just talk about the speed of the ISDN lines themselves, it works out, roughly, to this:

File Size in Megabytes	*Transfer Time in Seconds*
26,000,000	240
13,000,000	120
6,500,000	60
3,250,000	30
1,625,000	15
1,000,000	9
812,500	8
406,250	4

The Macintosh Reader weighs in, as I type these words, at about 1.6 megabytes. An ISDN line could blast every word and pixel to my editor at Random House in seconds. The cost? Less than a dollar, less than a quarter.

Want more? Then move up to ISDN Primary-rate service. Now you're got 23 data channels for a combined speed of 1.5 megabytes a second.

How fast is 1.5 megabytes a second? Usually newly announced MPEG compression standards, it's fast enough to deliver a motion picture to your home in real-time. Just call up "Movie by Phone Video" and settle back to watch "Batman III." No problem.

But there's more. On the heels of the first standard ISDN protocol services will come fiber-optic phone lines and "eat all you want" digital service. It's called "bandwidth on demand" and it means this: the more bandwidth you use, the more you pay.

This immense information capacity means more than movies-by-phone; more than high-quality, big screen video telephones (though that's surely one result).

Television, telephones, and computers will soon melt and meld and dissolve into something wonderful. ISDN and fiber optics will bring us text, graphics, data, high-definition video and CD-quality sound—all at once: right now.

ISDN will revolutionize computing. Good news for you. Bad news for Federal Express.

⟡

— Doug Clapp

WHERE THE MAGIC WENT...

From The New York Times, November 30, 1991.

3 Companies Said to Invest in Venture

By Andrew Pollack

Special to The New York Times

SAN FRANCISCO, Nov. 29 — Sony and Motorola have joined Apple Computer in investing in a closely watched Silicon Valley start-up company that is developing a new type of portable computing device, industry executives said today.

The start-up, General Magic, Inc., was formed last year by three former Apple Computer, Inc. employees with a minority investment from Apple. It is developing what it calls a personal intelligent communicator, which is believed to be a pocket-sized device that will help people organize personal notes and appointments and will receive and transmit faxes and computer data by radio waves.

Jane Anderson, a spokeswoman for General Magic, declined to comment on reports of the investments. "We're hard at work trying to make it happen," she said, referring the product development efforts. "We'll let you know when there's something to talk about."

Almost an Open Secret

But other industry executives said the investment had become almost an open secret. "I know that for a fact," said Jean-Louis Gassée, the former head of product development for Apple who now heads his own company, Be Labs, in San Jose. Mr. Gassée said executives from Motorola Inc. and the Sony Corporation had told him of their involvement in General Magic without making a great secret of it. In Japan an executive close to Sony confirmed that the company had taken a small stake in General Magic.

Motorola's investment was first reported by a Japanese newspaper, *Hihon Keizai Shimbun,* on Thursday, while Sony's investment was reported by *Fortune* magazine several weeks ago. Sony U.S.A and Motorola were closed today and spokesmen could not immediately be reached for comment.

It is not known how much the companies have invested in General Magic, but industry executives and news reports indicate that it is several million dollars apiece, giving each company a stake of about 5 to 10 percent. Apple is believed to have a somewhat larger investment.

Apple, Sony, and Motorola have worked together in the past, and a partnership would be logical. Sony brings expertise in miniaturization. It already makes a notebook computer for Apple, and executives of the two companies have said they plan to cooperate in other areas as well. Motorola, a supplier of chips to Apple, is also a leader in radio communications.

Product a Year Away

General Magic, based in Mountain View, Calif., is said to be more than a year away from having a product ready. Some industry executives expect that General Magic itself will not sell hand-held communicators, but will license its technology to other companies, like Apple, which will. Executives say it is also talking to several other companies, particularly Japanese consumer electronics companies.

General Magic's three founders are Andy Hertzfeld, who developed key software for the original Apple Macintosh, Bill Atkinson, who was the lead developer of Apple's HyperCard information management software, and Marc Porat, a former manager of business development in Apple's advanced technology group.

⌘

— © 1991, The New York Times.

WHERE THE MAGIC *REALLY* WENT...

The original Macintosh team has, for the most part, scattered. Some are still at Apple. Susan Kare, after a productive stint at NeXT, is in business for herself. Andy Hertzfeld and Bill Atkinson, as noted in the last article, are shrouded in secrecy at General Magic. Steve's NeXT computer—designed by many of the same people who made Macintosh—is a marvel. NeXT corporate has more surprises to come; wait and see.

Bruce Horn was last sighted at Carnegie-Mellon University. Dan Kottke is remodeling a house in Palo Alto. Bruce Toganzinni left Apple shortly after submitting his article to *The Macintosh Reader.* He's now, along with other former Apple Human Interface gurus, with Sun Microsystems. Good for Sun.

Chris Crawford, as always, is hard at work on another marvelous game. Mary Jane Mara and her hub, Jerry Daniels, have gone from spunky, visionary writing to custom development of mainframe front-ends—and they're damn good at it. James Horswell continues to write about Macintosh and consult and—once in a great while—act. And he'll be out hunting morel mushrooms in a few weeks.

Dennis James, after a season as the hottest software marketing consultant of them all, is on the verge of creating a new, Mac-specific software company. Karen Thomas can still party with the best, and does. John C. Dvorak, Guy Kawasaki, Bob LeVitus, Stewart Alsop, Don Crabb, and the Bove & Rhodes duo get up every morning to do what they do best: inform, educate, entertain and try—sometimes with success, sometimes not—to keep the industry honest, if not modest.

Michael Frasse just bought a new car—a Saturn. He loves it; says he's put 5,000 miles on it already, with nary the smallest glitch. Good to know ...

The Blue Meanies, you can be sure, are hard at work on "unannounced products." They could tell us what the products are, of course, but then they'd have to kill us.

Randy Nelson continues to be an oft-praised teacher of NeXT programming to aspiring NeXT developers. He's also now teaching others the art of teaching NeXT programming. Randy's wife just spent a week teaching Shakespeare to elementary school kids. And the Nelsons are thinking long and hard about starting "at-home" schooling for their own children; 10, 7 and 5—all very cute.

Apple Corporate, we've been told, is now in bed with IBM, conceiving the future under the sheets.

Macintosh has gotten both bigger and smaller. More affordable and vastly more expensive. Today, you can buy a Mac for under $1,000 or over $9,000. MacPaint and MacWrite have given way to PageMaker, Canvas, PhotoShop, Premiere, Word 5.0, Swivel 3D, 1-2-3 (at last, and it's not bad), VideoSpigot and VirtusVision— for those times when you really need to make a 3-D, fly-through, model. Carl Philabaum, by the way, is designing his hideaway Wisconsin cabin with walk-though 3D software; I "walked" through it a while back. Looked great.

See the magic? It never went away. It's right here, with me. And you. And more than seven million other people, around the world.

It's not in the box. It's in us.

And now, dear reader, at the end, just fourteen more words:

Thank you for spending time with us.

Do good and be wise.

Surprise us.

᷏

May 20, 1991

Edina, Minnesota

Colophon

This book was created by DMC & Company in Acton, MA, using Quark XPress 3.1 on a Macintosh IIcx with a Microtech external hard disk. The text was written and formatted in Microsoft Word 5.0.

The fonts used for this book are Adobe Garamond, Adobe Garamond Alternate, Adobe Garamond Expert, Letter Gothic, and Futura Condensed, all from Adobe Systems Incorporated.

Screens for this book were captured and converted to PICT files using Deskpaint 3.0. Other illustrations were created using MacPaint or MacDraw.

INDEX